A WAR THAT CAN'T BE WON

A War That Can't Be Won

Binational Perspectives on the War on Drugs

Edited by

TONY PAYAN,

KATHLEEN STAUDT,

AND Z. ANTHONY KRUSZEWSKI

THE UNIVERSITY OF
ARIZONA PRESS
TUCSON

The University of Arizona Press
© 2013 The Arizona Board of Regents
All rights reserved.

www.uapress.arizona.edu

Library of Congress Cataloging-in-Publication Data
A war that can't be won : binational perspectives on the war on drugs / edited by Tony
Payan, Kathleen Staudt, and Z. Anthony Kruszewski.
      pages cm
   Includes bibliographical references and index.
   ISBN 978-0-8165-3033-5 (cloth : alk. paper) — ISBN 978-0-8165-3034-2 (pbk. : alk.
paper)
   1. Drug control—United States.   2. Drug control—Mexico.   3. Drug traffic—
Mexican-American Border Region.   I. Payan, Tony, 1967–   II. Staudt, Kathleen A.
III. Kruszewski, Z. Anthony.
   HV5825.W3812957 2013
   363.450972—dc23

2013011197

Publication of this book is made possible in part by funding from the Lineae Terrarum
International Borders Conference and the College of Liberal Arts of the University of
Texas at El Paso.

♻

Manufactured in the United States of America on acid-free, archival-quality paper
containing a minimum of 30% post-consumer waste and processed chlorine free.

1007368140

18   17   16   15   14   13   6   5   4   3   2   1

Contents

Preface and Acknowledgments

We three coeditors come from different parts of the world: Tony Payan from Mexico, Kathleen (Kathy) Staudt from the United States (specifically Wisconsin, which seems like a different world), and Tony Kruszewski from Poland. We have crossed many borders in our pathway to this book. In those crossings, we have many people to acknowledge and thank.

From Origins to Pathways in This Book: Through the Border Lens

In crossing borders, we converged here, in the Paso del Norte Metropolitan Region, El Paso and Ciudad Juárez, where we teach courses on borders that cover our Mexican–U.S. borderlands and hundreds of comparative international borders in the now-burgeoning field of border studies. We are active members of the Association of Borderlands Studies and of Border Regions in Transition, both of which organize annual conferences in different borders around the world.

In 2006 we worked together on the largest-ever international borders conference, Lineae Terrarum. The conference was the brainchild of Tony Kruszewski, and Tony Payan organized the entire event—one that crossed the borders of nations, states, and university institutions. Approximately six hundred people attended, and presenters came from around the globe to share their research work on borders with each other. We met over four days in the United States and Mexico, in the states of Texas, Chihuahua, and New Mexico, and at three universities: University of Texas at El Paso (UTEP), Universidad Autónoma de Ciudad Juárez, and New Mexico State University. With papers partly from Lineae Terrarum, we coedited the first volume entitled *Human Rights along the U.S.-Mexico Border: Gendered Violence and Insecurity*, also published by the University of Arizona Press.

We have since led major efforts to expand border studies, and Tony Payan became president of the Association of Borderlands Studies in the period 2009–2010. We have also participated in a worldwide network of border scholars, Border Regions in Transition, which meets in a different border around the world every eighteen months or so.

Over our years on the U.S.–Mexican border, we have seen the good and the bad of life on the border. We live in a region where people use the border according to the law and thrive because of it, but we have also seen a border in which we witness the everyday violence wreaked on Mexico from the ineffective drug wars that have been militarized and in so doing have increased the crime and destruction of the social fabric of our border and ripped apart all sense of a binational community. As former El Paso City Council Representative Beto O'Rourke has said, it is a region where border people see that the "Emperor has no clothes," or, shall we say, that the emperors of both the U.S. and Mexican governments will not confront the reality of unworkable, ineffective policies for fear of being viewed as "soft on crime" or "drug pushers."

In an effort to simply *debate* the drug war policies, El Paso City Council Representatives Beto O'Rourke and Steve Ortega introduced an outrageous resolution to the eight-person El Paso City Council in early 2009. In so doing, they not only took the advice of the Cross-Border Relations Committee, where Tony Payan served at that time, but also became the *only* city council to make such a resolution in the entire U.S. democracy. Council members passed the resolution, only to confront wrath and threats from other politicians wedded to the idea that sacrosanct policies cannot be questioned without funds drying up. That this wrath would occur in a country that prides itself on free speech, open debate, and critical thinking makes 2009 all the more striking.

In 2009, Mexico decriminalized the possession of small amounts of marijuana. And various countries in Europe and Latin America have explored alternative policy options to the costly forty-year-old policy to which the United States is dedicated: punitive criminalization which, in a land of class and racial inequalities, results in the overrepresentation of impoverished people of color in jails and prisons. Decriminalization offers opportunities to treat addiction and to avoid expensive incarceration strategies while focusing on the kingpins and profiteers of illegal marketing.

However attractive decriminalization might be in some countries and states, the regulation, taxation, and legalization strategy is one that may address supply-and-demand dynamics, particularly when warped by ruthless criminals who operate underground. Like alcohol and tobacco, many who advocate limited government are found among those aligned with market solutions, including media outlets such as the *Economist* and *Wall Street Journal* and even Libertarians. The availability of legally prescribed medical marijuana in almost one-third of U.S. states demonstrates a model in federal systems of government. Yet people worry and wonder about *which* drugs would be legalized and what message might be sent about drug use. While rich countries are a far cry from the futuristic *Brave New World* that Aldous Huxley so presciently wrote about nearly a century ago, we are moving in the direction of what appears to be the excessive overuse of prescription drugs that consumers are constantly bombarded with in magazine, television, and Internet advertisements.

We want to assure readers that writers in this volume are not of one mind on drug policies and drug wars. Our contributors include diverse, interdisciplinary academics who come from Mexico and the United States and who frame their analyses from different vantage points. In the conclusion, Tony Payan and Kathy Staudt deal with the complexity of policy alternatives and impose on readers no particular strategy.

To Those We Give Thanks

Tony Payan would like to thank Kathy Staudt and Tony Kruszewski, his co-editors, for their mentorship during these twelve years on the U.S.–Mexican border. He thanks them for their guidance and advice all these years through the perilous roads of academic life. He also acknowledges the enormously important insights of his brother, Gustavo, in understanding the intricacies of the drug war that has raged on in Mexico over the last six years. Few people have studied this from a nonacademic perspective as Gustavo has. Without his keen insights, provocative questions, and long hours of discussions on the subject, this topic would be much more superficially explored in Tony's contributions to understanding it and its impact on the day-to-day life of border towns and people. He would also like to thank the James A. Baker III Institute for Public Policy of Rice University, especially the Latin America Initiative, ably led by Erika de la Garza, for its generosity in making possible a visiting researcher position for him during the 2012–14 academic year to finish the edition of this volume. His time spent in Houston helped him finish the work on this book by opening space and time to finalize the editorial tasks. It was a most pleasant time in the halls of the Baker Institute and on the grounds of Rice University, surrounded by stimulating thinkers.

Kathy Staudt would like to thank the many colleagues who supported her in research and writing at the margins of a sometimes insular and plodding discipline, political science. Tony Kruszewski was the chair when she was hired at UTEP in 1977. While her research appeared in mainstream political science journals, especially on the route to tenure and promotion, she often published in area studies, international development, and women/gender studies journals and books. Along the way, friends such as Jane Jaquette, Irasema Coronado, and Sandra McGee Deutsch have sustained her, as have her now-grown children, Mosi and Asha. When the time came to ask UTEP's president, Diana Natalicio, to support the campus-community Global Public Policy Conference on the War on Drugs, the president agreed. While the topic was risky, in a country of risk-avoidant higher education institutions, Kathy appreciated that her president recognized the place of a university in fostering debate among diverse academics, policy makers, and advocates (http://warondrugsconference.utep.edu). In organizing the conference, Kathy thanks all the committee members from the campus and the community, especially Linda Corchado, Josiah Heyman, and Vanessa Romero and Nubia Legarda, both leaders of the campus chapter of the nationwide Students for Sensible Drug Policy. Most important also, Kathy is awed by the courageous and resilient civil society activists in Ciudad Juárez who are an inspiration to antifemicide/antimilitarization activists throughout Mexico (though not yet enough of an inspiration to people in the United States). She thanks Zulma Méndez with whom she is coauthoring a forthcoming book on that activism.

Tony Kruszewski crossed many a border before reaching the Southwest borderlands with their intricate cultural and social mosaic. For decades, he has been attracted and fascinated by the phenomenon of borders, spending much of his academic career studying them closely, including the inexorable interplay of the attitudes, challenges, and problems that borders create. He has seen how they are shaped and reshaped by seemingly endless conflicts, from armed wars to drug wars. Borders engage scholars in heated discussions and invite thought to provide solutions to the many problems they generate, especially when current policies do not appear adequate or sufficient to resolve the daily lives of those caught in the many abnormal situations that borders produce. Over the years, much has been said about borders, but change is slow, and the production of good border policies is elusive. And yet alternative solutions to the problems that borders generate today are urgently needed, and to that we must continue to dedicate much time.

Tony Kruszewski would like to thank Kathy Staudt and Tony Payan for their enormous contribution to this book project but also for their intellectually stimulating activism and their concern for the Southwest border-lands, expressed in the countless hours they dedicate to study them and to provide alternative visions of them. Likewise, Tony cherishes the leadership that UTEP president Diana Natalicio has provided in working toward the creation of a First Tier University on the Rio Grande and for her work in providing opportunities for our binational students.

Finally, we three thank all of the authors of this volume for their willingness to share their research and their reflections in this book and for their patience in waiting for the collection to come together, the peer review process to work itself out, and the time it took to get this to press. We also thank the external reviewers who took the time and patience to comb our initial (half Spanish) and revised volume. They provided us with substantive comments and performed a magnificent service that strengthens scholarly publications. We also thank Kristen Buckles and Scott de Herrera of the University of Arizona Press, who patiently worked with us through the process of getting this publication out to the public.

Tony Payan
Kathy Staudt
Tony Kruszewski

Abbreviations

English

ACLU	American Civil Liberties Union
AIM	accuracy in media
BSIC	border security industrial complex
CBP	(U.S.) Customs and Border Protection
CDC	Centers for Disease Control and Prevention
CNN	Cable News Network
CSI	*Crime Scene Investigation* (a U.S. television show)
D	Democrat
DAs	district attorneys
DARE	Drug Abuse Resistance Education
DEA	(U.S.) Drug Enforcement Administration
DHS	(U.S.) Department of Homeland Security
DHS/CBP	(see CBP)
DOJ	(U.S.) Department of Justice
DPA	Drug Policy Alliance
DTOs	drug trafficking organizations
DUI	driving under the influence
EOP	(U.S.) Executive Office of the President
FBI	(U.S.) Federal Bureau of Investigation
FDR	Franklin Delano Roosevelt
GAO	(U.S.) Government Accountability Office
HSBC	Hong Kong and Shanghai Banking Corporation (Only in Asia is the full name used. Elsewhere in the world, HSBC is used.)

IACHR	Inter-American Commission on Human Rights
IANSA	International Action Network on Small Arms
ICE	(U.S.) Immigration and Customs Enforcement
ICESI	Citizenry Institute on Insecurity Studies
IDPC	International Drug Policy Consortium
ISO	International Organization for Standardization
LACDD	Latin American Commission on Drugs and Democracy
LAPD	Los Angeles Police Department
LEAP	Law Enforcement Against Prohibition
LSD	lysergic acid diethylamide ("acid")
MA	Massachusetts
MEPI	Mexican Foundation of Investigative Journalism
NAFTA	North American Free Trade Agreement
NATO	North Atlantic Treaty Organization
NGO	nongovernmental organization
NIDA	National Institute on Drug Abuse
NM	New Mexico
NORML	National Organization for the Reform of Marijuana Laws
NPR	National Public Radio
ONDCP	(U.S. White House) Office of National Drug Control Policy
POE	port(s) of entry
R	Republican
S.B.	Senate Bill
SFBNDD	Subject Files of the Bureau of Narcotics and Dangerous Drugs
TCOs	transnational criminal organizations
TX	Texas
UN	United Nations
UNDCP	UN Office for Drug Control and Crime Prevention
USBP	U.S. Border Patrol
USD	U.S. dollars
UTEP	University of Texas at El Paso

Spanish

AFI	Agencia Federal de Investigaciones
AGN	Archivo General de la Nación
CANACO	Cámara Nacional de Comercio
CCSP	Consejo Ciudadano de Seguridad Pública
CIDAC	Centro de Investigación para el Desarrollo, A.C.
CIFA	Centro de Inspección Fiscal y Aduanera
CISALVA	Centro de Investigación y Desarrollo en Prevención de la Violencia y Promoción de la Convivencia Social
CISEN	Centro de Investigación y Seguridad Nacional
CNDH	Comisión Nacional de Derechos Humanos
CONASUPO	Compañía Nacional de Subsistencias Populares
COPARMEX	Confederación Patronal Mexicana
DFS	Dirección Federal de Inseguridad
ENSI	Encuestas Nacionales sobre Seguridad
EPR	Ejército Popular Revolucionario
FMLN	Frente Farabundo Martí para la Liberación Nacional
FP	Revista *Foreign Policy*
GAFE	Grupo Aeromóvil de Fuerzas Especiales
GANFE	Grupo Anfibio de Fuerzas Especiales
ICESI	Instituto Ciudadano de Estudios sobre la Seguridad
IFAI	Instituto Federal de Acceso a la Información
INEGI	Instituto Nacional de Estadística, Geografía e Informática
INM	Instituto Nacional de Migración
IPS	International Private Security of México
ITAM	Instituto Tecnológico Autónomo de México
LSN/NSL	Ley de Seguridad Nacional / National Security Law
PAN	Partido Acción Nacional
PEMEX	Petróleos Mexicanos
PFP	Policía Federal Preventiva
PGR	Procuraduría General de la República
PRD	Partido de la Revolución Democrática
PRI	Partido Revolucionario Institucional
SCJN	Suprema Corte de Justicia de la Nación

SEDENA	Secretaría de la Defensa Nacional
SEMAR	Secretaría de Marina
SIMO	Sistemas de Inteligencia en Mercados de Opinión, S.A.
SSP	Secretaría de Seguridad Pública
UNAM	Universidad Nacional Autónoma de México

A WAR THAT CAN'T BE WON

partly prompted by the failures of the federal government in the drug war. The spillover of violence from Mexico into the United States has been foretold, so far, unsuccessfully by analysts, bureaucrats, and opportunistic politicians, but it has been used by imperialistic bureaucracies to increase their resources and commit human rights and due process abuses. In Mexico, the administration of justice system has been brought into question for its incompetence and corruption—including law enforcement agencies, investigators, lawyers, and judges. The military strategy of the Mexican federal government against the cartels, which has produced, according to some sources, as many as one hundred thousand deaths,[1] has been subjected to an increasingly heated national debate because it has let loose on the civilian population the military and, increasingly, a militarized federal police. The costs of the war on drugs itself, in terms of blood and treasure, have become the subject of much discussion. The role that American weapons play in the Mexican killing fields has also received renewed attention. The role that dirty money plays in corrupting the system, greasing the wheels of trafficking, and even in regional economic development, has received some attention too. Most agree that the war on drugs in Mexico also is a failure.

In view of this, and after four decades of a war on drugs that is increasingly considered a failure, hundreds of billions of dollars spent to stop illegal drugs without success, hundreds of thousands of people serving stiff penalties in both prison systems, and tens of thousands of bodies left scattered in streets and lots both in Mexico and in the United States, it is time to ask the following questions: How did we get into this? Where are we? How do we get out of it? Unfortunately, the criticisms of the war on drugs, and its trails of crime, corruption, wasted public resources, and death, are easier to come by than concrete solutions, public policy recommendations, and proposals that can advance the debate on the war on drugs and how to get out of it. The experience of Prohibition in the 1920s and 1930s barely provides a guide for this complex issue. In part, this has to do with the fact that most studies of the war on drugs are done from one angle or another: the American perspective and its labyrinthine paths, the Mexican viewpoint and its complex historical baggage, or the binational border and its conflicted and often brutal history. To this day, no study has yet brought together scholars and thinkers from Mexico and the United States, as well as from the border, to carry out a comprehensive, binational study of this problem. This book is, in that sense, the first analysis that brings together researchers from both Mexico and the United States, as well as from the border, to provide a geographically and thematically representative analysis of the war on drugs and to move the debate on illegal drugs a little further along toward a conclusion, before it becomes too late and another generation is lost to illegal drug-related crime, another half trillion dollars are wasted, and many more tens of thousands of deaths occur, let alone the permanent scars that it may leave in the binational relationship. If we do not now put our heads together, from both sides of the border, to understand the whole chain of illegal drugs and what these drugs have done to our societies, to our border, and to our communities, we will never transcend current failed policies and look for smarter ways to deal with illegal drugs.

Thus this book deals with several of the larger issues of the war on drugs, and many of its reflections have been prompted by the public safety and security crisis that Mexico has confronted in the last decade. Although by no means a comprehensive study of all the paths in the world-wide maze that is illegal drugs, this book addresses the issue in light of the many different layers and complexities that the issue presents for the United States, for Mexico itself, and for the border between the two countries. By bringing together perspectives from both sides, in Mexico and the United States, and from various disciplines and understandings of the problem, we have a much clearer understanding of the problem and a much greater appreciation that solutions are not easy—something that must not deter us from seeking them. Moreover, we arrive at the conclusion that whether it is dealing with corruption or institution building in Mexico, with public policy options in the United States, or with the disruptions caused to cross-border networks by illegal drug flows, the whole issue is much more complicated than we can imagine. In that sense, this book offers a broad view, with nuanced perspectives, on the genealogy and on how to end the public safety and security crisis that plagues Mexico and worries many Americans on a daily basis.

How We Got Here: A Century of Muddling Through

Before engaging the issues that afflict us today, it is pertinent to take a quick glance at the history of how we got here. Without this brief historical recount of the problem, it is nearly impossible to understand what is happening to us in our day. And to look down the kaleidoscope of time to make sense of all this, we have to go back to the early twentieth century, nearly one hundred years ago, to the prohibitionist impetus that gained momentum with the passage of the 1914 Harrison Narcotics Act in the

The American Dimension: From Inside Out

The premises that underlie the war on drugs are drawing increasing criticism, even if the criticism is slow in mounting, confined to a few corners, and somewhat void of solid alternatives to current policy. Dissenting voices are evident in the United States, where seventeen states and the District of Columbia have already passed laws legalizing marijuana under the justification that it has some medical value,[6] specifically in managing pain. Similarly, congressional representatives Barney Frank (D-MA) and Ron Paul (R-TX) presented in 2011 legislation to defederalize marijuana laws and to leave it up to the states to forbid it, allow it, or regulate it.[7] Mexico's public security crisis has not only forced many analysts within the United States to dig deeper into the philosophy behind prohibition (Franklin 2010) but has also cast doubts on the prohibitionist drug policy championed around the world, principally by the United States (Nadelmann 1990, 2007; Andreas and Nadelmann 2006), and the consequences that it has produced.[8] Authoritative voices now consider current drug policy largely a failed policy (Baum 1996; Gray 2001; also see large advocacy organizations such as the Drug Policy Alliance and Law Enforcement Against Prohibition and sustained opinion editorials by influential media such as the *Economist* and the *Wall Street Journal*). More voices in the United States and in Mexico are joining in to ask for a stop to what is now largely considered a failed and failing drug policy (see, for example, the commentary from former president Jimmy Carter in the *New York Times* on June 16, 2011). Former Mexican President Vicente Fox (2000–2006) has also come out with a statement in favor of the legalization of illegal drugs. The presidents of Mexico, Guatemala, and Colombia also presented a rough plan to move away from prohibition in the 2012 United Nations meetings of heads of state. They did so, conscious that all three nations are paying too high a price for current antidrug policies supported by the United States.

Others consider that the cost of the war on drugs is simply too high because it undermines development by fueling conflict, damages human rights regimes, promotes stigma and discrimination, threatens public health, creates crimes, enriches criminals, causes deforestation, pollutes, and wastes billions of dollars in a futile effort at law enforcement, according to a report by the Transform Drug Policy Foundation titled *The War on Drugs: Are We Paying Too High a Price?*[9] Paradoxically, all these side effects go against American stated goals in foreign policy. But government bureaucracies have a large stake in maintaining or expanding their juris-dictions, budgets, and staff, in the name of national or border security, or what has been called the Border Security Industrial Complex (Staudt, Payan, and Dunn 2009), referring to the collaboration among politicians, bureaucracies, and private-industry contractors who donate large sums to politicians' reelection campaigns. But the war on drugs is finally drawing alternative voices, not all of whom agree on the approach to psychotropic substances but all of whom agree that current drug policy is failing.

The problem of drugs, however, is not easy to resolve. Although there is broad consensus that illegal drugs are harmful, there is growing disagree-ment about how to deal with them (Goldstein 2010; Berent, Evans, Downs, and Pauling 1999). This ambivalence stems from a growing perception that the U.S. government is losing the battle against illegal drugs through mostly prohibitionist strategies (Boyum and Reuter 2005), but a serious alternative is hardly in sight. Although the federal government, according to the Office of National Drug Control Policy spends over $26 billion on its antidrug strategy, with steady increases nearly every year, and employs an army of agents, mobile X-ray machines, sniffing dogs, cameras, and many other methods to detect drugs (Office of National Drug Control Policy 2012), according to the Drug Enforcement Administration itself, as well as the United Nations *2011 World Drug Report*, drugs are cheaper and more abundant than ever before, and their potency and variety have only increased. State and local governments themselves spend billions in fighting illegal drugs. An estimated 32 million Americans smoke mari-juana; some 12 to 13 million people in North America use opioids and opiates; and some 5.5 million use cocaine, 3.4 million use amphetamines, and 3.2 million use Ecstasy. These numbers have only grown steadily over the forty-year-old war on drugs, even as scientific medical research con-cludes the far greater health dangers posed by regulated, though nonpro-hibited, drugs such as alcohol and tobacco compared to marijuana (Global Commission on Drug Policy 2011; United Nations Office on Drugs and Crime 2011). The ingenuity and the variety of drug producing, smuggling, and marketing methods are overwhelming. Government efforts to stop the flow of drugs are always running behind. Drug producers, traffickers, and dealers use cars, trucks, persons, light planes, underground tunnels, sub-marines, and hundreds of routes.

Dissenting voices are gaining traction in the form of state-led initiatives that have legalized "medical" marijuana—law enforcement use of dis-cretionary powers to end most prosecution of small-time possession of drugs—effectively decriminalizing drugs at the consumer level, and, more recently, as also noted earlier, an initiative by congressional members Barney Frank (D-MA) and Ron Paul (R-TX) to leave it to the states to regulate marijuana. This bill is important because for the first time we see the emergence of a congressional initiative in the direction opposite of prohibition. If the bill ever becomes law, it would be up to the states to figure out what restrictions to place on the production, commercialization, and consumption of marijuana. Marijuana, however, is easier. This ambivalence does not extend to cocaine, heroin, and chemical drugs, which further displays deep disagreements among those who are thinking about alternatives to current drug policy. In fact, hardly anyone takes a stand for the legalization of these drugs. This reinforces the idea that marijuana has a different place in the debate.[10] The arguments in favor of legalization come from various disciplines, from ethics (Husak 2002) to economics (Szasz 1992) to criminal justice (Gray 2001) to political science (Mares 2006) to sociology (Martin 2007) to history (Zimring and Hawkins 1992; Courtwright 2002). Most of this literature, now backed by the *2011 Report of the Global Commission on Drug Policy* (Global Commission on Drug Policy 2011), points to the failure of prohibition and the public policies that it has spawned to reduce the production, trafficking, and consumption of drugs. "The global war on drugs has failed," it states, "with devastating consequences for individuals and societies around the world. Fifty years after the initiation of the UN Single Convention on Narcotics Drugs, and 40 years after President Nixon launched the US Government's war on drugs, fundamental reforms in national and global drug control policies are urgently needed" (Global Commission on Drug Policy 2011, 2).

But there are also arguments in favor of continuing a prohibitionist approach to drugs. The major arguments are moral and health-based ones. Among the first are those who argue that illegal drugs are a problem of public morality and that the government has to maintain certain standards of public morality even if the war itself cannot be won. In the second group are those who argue that it is a matter of public health and that the government should continue to fight against illegal drugs because they damage human health and the authorities have a responsibility to protect it.[11] These arguments include the idea that the war on drugs should not simply be judged on the basis of its results—that there are today more drugs, cheaper drugs, and a wider variety of them—but should be judged on the attrition argument as well, that is, if we did not fight against drugs, they would be consumed by more citizens and would become a much more serious public morality and public health problem. The war on drugs should be measured, they say, not by what it has done or not done but by what it has prevented. The convenience of this argument, however, is that it cannot be proven or disproven. Deterrence is notoriously difficult to measure. And there is hardly any evidence that the government has deterred any of the problems associated with illegal drugs and has perhaps caused new problems instead. Nonetheless, these scholars argue that if the government stopped fighting drugs, the "problem" of drugs would only worsen.

What is true is that the prohibition regime, maintained by the United States at an increasing cost for itself and for other countries, has had dramatic effects worldwide. The violence in Colombia, the thousands of deaths within the United States, both violent and in emergency rooms or by the epidemics fueled by the clandestine nature of drug use (such as HIV infections), the brutality of the cartels, and other consequences of the drug regime make it clear that policy has real effects and often creates serious unintended problems without necessarily solving the problem it was meant to solve.

The Mexican Dimension: From the Water's Edge

The crisis of public safety and security that Mexico has lived during the Calderón administration cannot be understood outside the context of the drug prohibition regime and the illicit drug market, which has produced an enormously profitable industry that flourishes between Latin America and the United States and for which Mexico is a strategic passage. In fact, it is Mexico's location as an important route to the largest market for illegal drugs that fundamentally drives this crisis, framed by a failure to reduce drug addiction in the United States and since 2006 by an increase in the flow of powerful weapons to Mexico after the Assault Weapons Ban was left to expire by the Bush administration. This crisis of security is now of such depth that it brings into question the very approach to the war on drugs of the last forty years. And it is of such dimensions that it has now become a veritable North American security crisis, since Mexico's stability is of deep concern to both the United States and Canada. Moreover, this security crisis is central to North America because the roots of its inception reside in U.S. policy toward drugs, a policy later internationalized by U.S. pressure on other nations, including Mexico. But the crisis has now gone well beyond drug trafficking and has extended into various forms of organized crime, including kidnappings, extortions, generalized property crime, political corruption, public ambivalence toward illegal drugs, gruesome and cruel murders, a war of narco-messages unfurled over freeways and bridges, and even political and institutional instability, particularly within the police and justice forces (Monárrez Fragoso 2010). In the end, the crisis of violence has grown so deep that it now reaches well into all other aspects of Mexican life—social, political, economic, and cultural.[12]

The wave of violence Mexico experienced during President Calderón's administration (2006–2012), which revolves largely around the issue of illegal drugs and spun off a nationwide public safety crisis and exposed the inadequacies of the Mexican administration of justice system, has resulted in nearly one hundred thousand violent deaths by some accounts (Ríos and Shirk 2011; also see the Trans-Border Institute's monthly updates at http://justiceinmexico.org/). Since 2007, this wave of violence in Mexico has produced tens of thousands of bloody scenes, engulfing more and more states and cities throughout the country. Many of these scenes involve a display of gruesomeness seldom seen in a conflict—beheadings, dismemberments, mutilations, torture, and cruel symbolisms such as pig masks, severed genitalia, mass graves, car bombings, and terrorist-like attacks on buildings and civilians (Monárrez Fragoso 2010). The war among the Mexican drug cartels and their allied gangs has also become a psychological one. It has involved messages of intimidation and threats in the form of banners, graffiti, and videos uploaded on YouTube, from one organized criminal group to another and against the government. It has also uncovered the deep corruption of the Mexican police forces (Bailey and Chabat 2002; Bailey and Dammert 2005; Azaola 2009) as well as the ineffectiveness of Mexico's judicial system (Cornelius and Shirk 2007; Fondevila 2009). The number of bodies keeps mounting, bringing Mexicans to question whether it was worth confronting the drug criminal organizations (Langner 2010). Worse, the carnage may even put at risk Mexico's prolonged transition to democracy (Aguayo Quezada 2010) and bring about a renewed tension between Mexico and the United States over weapons smuggling, money laundering, and responsibilities for the bloodshed (Olson, Shirk, and Selee 2010; Benítez Manaut 2010). Although this public security crisis is not exclusive to Mexico but extends to much of Latin America (Chalk 2011), Mexico is at the center of the drug trade analysis and the crises it spins off because of its proximity to the largest illegal drug market in the world, the United States (United Nations Office on Drugs and Crime 2011).

This "war" on drugs—which at first President Calderón called a *war on drugs* and later argued that it was not a war—has dragged the Mexican armed forces (both the army and the marines) and hundreds of the 2,600 law enforcement agencies throughout the country into a messy, low-intensity conflict, where one cannot always distinguish who is the good guy and who is the bad guy, given the high levels of police corruption in Mexico. In many areas of Mexico, the violence and the government's response to it produced a de facto state of exception, with numerous violations of constitutional rights and thousands of violations of human rights (Meyer, Brewer, and Cepeda 2010). It drove many towns to take the law into their own hands, through lynching and extra-judicial executions. It has devastated entire towns through planned and random violence, from Praxedis Guerrero in the state of Chihuahua to Los Ramones in the state of Nuevo León, and emptied entire sectors in larger cities such as Ciudad Juárez, Chihuahua, and Camargo, Tamaulipas, from where thousands of families have had to flee to the United States and other less violent states within Mexico. Because the brutal war between cartels and their armed branches and allied gangs has also turned against the general citizenry by committing acts of extortion, kidnapping for ransom and robberies, burglaries and vehicle theft, many citizens have simply fled on account of the upsurge in these other kinds of criminal activity. The high level of impunity, the incompetence of the police, its complicity with criminal gangs, and the general crisis of the Mexican administration of justice system have scared many middle-class Mexicans who have sought to migrate to less dangerous zones or to the United States and even Europe. Violence levels have also exposed the deep connections between politicians and Mafia groups, revealing the deep levels of corruption of the Mexican political system as well.[13] At times, scholars and critics have spoken of the "Colombianization" of the Mexican drug war, as it has also escalated into car bombings, like the one that occurred in Ciudad Juárez on July 15, 2010, the attack on the Casino Royale in Monterrey on August 25, 2011, and the assassination of dozens of mayors and journalists. The Mexican war on drugs has also awakened international concern all over the world, particularly in regard to human rights, as the military has participated actively in it (Meyer, Brewer, and Cepeda 2010).

The role that the United States plays in the Mexican war on drugs has not gone unnoticed within Mexico either. There are among some critics of President Calderón those who believe that it has given the United States an unprecedented ability to intervene in Mexican domestic affairs, not only by having Mexico internalize a quintessentially American policy but by creating a channel for U.S. activities within Mexico, something that would have been inconceivable just a few years ago in the face of a deep-seated Mexican nationalism, largely shaped by its historic conflicts with the United States. It has, for example, put U.S. border law enforcement agencies on the edge, as they fear a spillover of violence, mostly without the country is governed by three main political parties, which at times operate to gridlock the system rather than to make it flow; they take advantage of each other's failures to profit electorally.

But this understanding of Mexican politics does not take away from the fact that the situation is dire on the ground. The war on drugs along the border has provoked a mass exodus of citizens, some to the United States and some to safer ground within Mexico, although the estimates vary from 30,000 to 300,000.[17] This exodus has been documented by a project within the University of Texas at El Paso known as "Mexodus."[18] The consequences have not stopped at an exodus of citizens from towns such as Ciudad Juárez, Ciudad Mier, Nuevo Laredo, Matamoros, and others but have also included the weakening of social life, the abandonment of public space, an increase in distrust among neighbors, and a generalized sense of uncertainty about the future. In addition, the cartels have given rise to various groups that are no longer or exclusively dedicated to the illegal drug business but have expanded their operations to all kinds of organized crime: extortion, kidnapping for ransom, robberies, burglaries, car theft, and other such activities. All types of crimes, according to the Instituto Nacional de Estadística, Geografía e Informática statistics, are up in Mexico.[19] The year 2012 was yet the worst.

Appropriately assessing the relationship between the border and the war on drugs requires analysts to consider the fact that the border is the passageway for all contraband and therefore is the target of most policies, even if the contraband originates away from the border and its destination is away from the border. In fact, often antidrug policies overemphasize the border in a punishing way. It is not clear if this is because public policy officials prefer to focus on a specific point along the crime chain, or because the resources are limited and reinforcing the border is easier. But one thing is clear; they have little success, as illegal drugs continue to cross the border without a problem. Moreover, a consequence of the excessive attention on the cross-border stage of the drug smuggling chain is that the border suffers from a democratic deficit. Thus it is fair to say that the border suffers from an excessive and somewhat undue attention of policy and centralization of power. It is in some ways a choke point and thus a convenient place to fight a war, even if borderlanders' lives are severely disrupted. Thus it can be accurately said that most decisions, from prohibition to the actual decision to engage in a "war on drugs," are made away from the border, but much of the war's front lines lie along the border. The funds, the strategies, the levels of agents, the responses, and nearly everything else come in the form of a directive from the capitals

(Mexico City and Washington, D.C.), and the border must adjust to them. Rarely are borderlanders consulted when formulating public policy (Payan 2006).

The Multidimensionality of the War on Drugs Crisis

The drug war-induced crisis in North America has become multidimensional and it merits a deep analysis in view of the fact that Mexico is important not only as a leading country within Latin America but as the only other neighbor of the United States. It also deserves a critical analysis given that it is a historical experience from which Mexico must come out with greater institutional strength or must risk a serious collapse of its institutional life and a crisis that would very well end up in U.S. hands in the form of a wave of refugees and exiles at a time when the country is in a bad mood in regard to immigration. In the end, the crisis shows two important things, one about the past and one about the future. Regarding the past, this security crisis tells us that drug policy needs a revision in Mexico and in the United States, whether one agrees with it or not. The current forty-year-plus prohibition regime has simply not worked. Evidence of its failure is all over the place: overcrowded prisons, increasing gang violence, money laundering, a brisk weapons black market, deepened suspicion between the Mexican and American peoples in spite of increasing intergovernmental cooperation, and foregone economic opportunities due to a larger insecurity climate. In addition, illegal drugs appear to obey their own logic, independent of how more or how less punitive public policies may be toward illegal drug producers, drug traffickers, pushers, and consumers. There is barely a relationship between heavy public investment in sustaining a prohibitionist policy and illegal drug consumption. Moreover, a whole security and law enforcement industrial complex has been built around reinforcing drug laws in the United States, at a time when many other services, from education to health care to social security, are being cut back. But revising drug policy has its complications, and it is not a simple or even a short-term affair. It will require smart work and numerous, lengthy public debates that are now beginning. American public opinion, as Mexican public opinion, is divided in its attitudes toward illegal drugs, and the resulting policies are likely to be somewhat of a mixed bag for the time being. What has become even clearer is that the current policies are unsustainable in the long run, even if where to go from here is not as evident. The discussions in this book delve into some potential ways

In chapter 3 Correa-Cabrera and Nava explore the relationship between the media and the drug war. Because many of our perceptions of the war on drugs, its successes and its failures, are mediated by the media, it is important that reliable and accurate information come to us. Correa-Cabrera and Nava, however, argue that in northeastern Mexico there is a "black hole" when it comes to news because the cartels have been able to intimidate journalists and media outlets into a silence that increases their impunity. This intimidation of the media, they suggest, is not limited to the war on drugs, however, but constitutes an important threat to the new Mexican democracy, particularly because no one knows exactly what the extent of the violence is once the media's reports are cut back due to intimidation or self-censorship.

In chapter 4 Flores Pérez explores the intricate and subtle relationship between the government and the cartels, which by omission or commission allowed the business of drugs to flourish and led to a weakening of national institutions. Flores Pérez uncovers some of the reasons the problem of governability has become worse in Mexico and attributes it partly to the fact that it is often difficult to distinguish the "good guys" from the "bad guys," as law enforcement and politicians in Mexico entered into a cozy relationship with drug cartels. This is a major contributor to Mexico's inability to fight the drug cartels, as corruption constitutes the grease that turns the wheels of organized crime in the country. Does the government protect the cartels? Whether the answer is yes or no, part of the problem is that in Mexico law enforcement and politics are not about public service. There is no culture among bureaucrats or politicians that they owe their loyalty to the public and not to organized crime or that they cannot ignore a growing public safety problem without paying a price themselves. Flores Pérez concludes that the Mexican system produces its own weaknesses. This is made even worse by the fact that the Mexican political landscape has become more complex. What kept it together in the past, a single-party system, has fallen away, and to the public safety crisis we now have to add the nasty democratic politics that is run-of-the-mill in the United States every day. With the end of the single-party system, the capacity of the system to "negotiate" implicitly or explicitly with the cartels has also been diminished. In sum, Flores Pérez raises important questions that elevate the problem of illegal drug trafficking and organized crime to a problem of survivability of the Mexican state and its ability to consolidate its own democracy in the future.

In chapter 5 Benítez Manaut asks a vital question: Is the government in Mexico winning or losing the war on drugs? Benítez Manaut's deep expertise on the problems of national security in Mexico enables him to answer this question by pointing out that the crisis of public safety cannot be understood without a deep understanding of the political processes within Mexico itself. Even so, he makes the argument that Mexico has made some progress, but the issue will not be resolved until the public policy itself—the approach to drugs—is reviewed and changed. The variables that make Mexico the ideal place for drug trafficking are unchanged, and thus the problem itself is simply impossible to resolve without thinking about geography, the consumer market, and the weaknesses of Mexican national institutions. Reform, he argues, has to consider all these different problems that surround and deepen the problem of illegalized drugs. Finally, he concludes, this "war" is not a war per se but a low-intensity conflict, and in low-intensity conflicts or asymmetric wars, states are hardly ever big winners without paying a very high price.

In chapter 6 Villalobos turns to the United States to further explore the way in which successive administrations have dealt with illegal drugs as a matter of public policy. Utilizing federalism as an overarching framework, Villalobos plays with the issue of drugs along the spectrum of American ideology, conservative versus liberal, and the political calculations and choices that presidents have made along those lines to deal with what has become a complex public policy environment. Presidential preferences in the war on drugs, Villalobos argues, depend on a variety of variables, making change quite difficult. Thus the war on drugs in Mexico is hardly a separate issue from the American consumer market or the American ideological approach to drugs—and even American politics, as Villalobos shows.

In chapter 7 Slack and Whiteford deal with yet another layer in this very complex debate on the security crisis in Mexico, the issue of undocumented workers and whether there are connections between illegal drug-based organized crime and human smuggling on the border. This is an important chapter because plenty of media pieces often try to relate these two phenomena, often with incendiary purposes in mind. Slack and Whiteford find that it is possible that organized crime attempts to use undocumented border crossers to carry drugs. They find few of these connections, but those that exist are disturbing. The two "businesses" have different logics and obey different incentives, but what connects these two problems is their illegality and a general geography of violence associated with the groups that perpetrate both types of crimes. Anecdotal examples of undocumented workers carrying a small bag with drugs may be found, even if it may not be terribly efficient for the kind of business that large-scale drug the entire chain, that is, source, distribution, or destination, reveal something about potential solutions to the problem of drugs? We have seen, they argue, that incarceration in the United States has hardly helped the problem within the country, and it has certainly done very little for Mexico. The problem, the authors suggest, is that we have treated this issue as a purely domestic one instead of a transnational one. We know that the problem is bilateral, but both countries insist in dealing with it as a national problem. That is a grave mistake, they say. We have to deal with how the different parts of the whole chain interact with each other, and we have to take a look at the macro as well as the micro level. When one zooms into the problem, the authors argue, it is easy to see that even the profit numbers are often misread. Much of the profit, for example, stays in the United States, given that most of the drug traffickers do not sell directly to the consumer but sell to the much finer, smaller distribution networks that exist in U.S. cities. This does not mean that their profit is small, of course, but it means that we have exaggerated the amount of money that actually makes its way across the border. We have to look at the market size and the market dynamics and treat this like an economic problem, along a whole chain, if we are to make progress in dealing with the issue overall, as the authors suggest, particularly if we are talking about actions that may be taken in the United States that are presumably designed to help Mexico, or vice versa. If we are to ask what kind of regime should replace the prohibitionist regime that we have today, we have to be careful that we do not adopt public policies that might turn out to be worse or might end up worsening the situation because we forget that this is a binational problem, not a national one. Decriminalizing drugs in the destination country, for example, might provide the incentive for many to enter drug production and trafficking in the source or even in the transit country. Thus without moving in tandem, individual or national decisions might actually worsen the problem of security. In the end, we must experiment with different scenarios to figure out which one is best. In addition, the authors suggest that demand control does not seem to work at all. Price, for example, may matter more, and thus our options may be either more limited or more greatly expanded than we think by considerations such as this one. Another example of the complexity of the situation is that even if we were to invest more heavily in demand reduction, the reduction itself may turn out to be long term, given that those who are consuming today will likely continue to consume for quite a few years and the problem may take time to deflate. It is a little bit like a boa that swallowed a rabbit. It will take time before it makes its way through the system and disappears or diminishes. These considerations are seldom taken into account when talking about potential public policy options. Of course, enforcement strategies, as the authors argue, have only resulted in raising the price, something which, in the end, might entice more people to enter the business of drugs and make the problem worse. Experimenting with economic and game models, therefore, is fundamental in dealing with public policy options. Otherwise, we risk making things worse than they are.

In the concluding chapter Payan and Staudt draw the major lessons that forty years of the war on drugs have to teach us. They contemplate the way in which the authors of the volume have framed the issues, the strategies that have both failed and succeeded, and the casualties of America's longest war—the drug war; finally, they summarize some of the most important points made in terms of the alternatives available to both the U.S. and Mexican governments to bring this war to an end.

Notes

1. The issue of the number of deaths that the Mexican war on drugs has produced will be discussed later in the chapter.

2. A clarification is pertinent here. The term "psychotropic substances" refers to all mind-altering drugs, legal and illegal. However, its use here is deliberate, as it is becoming clear that legal drugs, that is, those obtained by prescription, are in fact abused more than those that have been made illegal by the U.S. government, such as marijuana, cocaine, heroin, and other confection drugs. Today, part of the confusion emerges from the fact that our attention has gone to illegal drugs, but legal drugs are contributing to the problem of drug abuse as much if not more than "illegal" ones.

3. It was on June 17, 1971, that Richard M. Nixon stated at a press conference that drugs were "public enemy number one" in the United States and thus "declared" a war on drugs.

4. June 2011 *Report of the Global Commission on Drug Policy* by The Global Commission on Drug Policy. The commissioners that issued this report are Asma Jahangir, Carlos Fuentes, César Gaviria, Ernesto Zedillo, Fernando Henrique Cardoso, George Papandreou, George P. Shultz, Javier Solana, John Whitehead, Kofi Annan, Louise Arbour, Maria Cattaui, Mario Vargas Llosa, Marion Caspers-Merk, Michel Kazatchkine, Paul Volcker, Richard Branson, Ruth Dreifuss, and Thorvald Stoltenberg. These are some of the highest voices around the world raised against the current approach to illegal drugs and perhaps some of the most influential academic and political minds of different ideological persuasions and multiple approaches capable of bringing about a reconsideration of the way we deal with illegal drugs.

5. In 1971 the federal antidrug budget was $100 million. Today it is nearly $16 billion, about 160 times larger than in 1971 and 17 times larger when adjusted for inflation. Although there are many sites, several report slightly different numbers. See Transactional Records Access Clearinghouse at http://trac.syr.edu/tracdea/findings

Boyum, David, and Peter Reuter. 2005. *An Analytic Assessment of the U.S. Drug Policy.* Washington, DC: American Enterprise Institute Press.

Bunker, Robert J. 2011. *Narcos over the Border: Gangs, Cartels and Mercenaries.* New York: Routledge.

Campbell, Howard. 2010. *Drug War Zone: Frontline Dispatches from the Streets of El Paso and Ciudad Juárez.* Austin: University of Texas Press.

Chalk, Peter. 2011. *The Latin American Drug Trade: Scope, Dimensions, Impact and Response.* Santa Monica, CA: Rand-Project Air Force.

Cornelius, Wayne A., and David A. Shirk. 2007. *Reforming the Administration of Justice in Mexico.* Notre Dame, IN: University of Notre Dame Press.

Courtwright, David. 2002. *Forces of Habit: Drugs and the Making of the Modern World.* Cambridge, MA: Harvard University Press.

Fondevila, Gustavo. 2009. "Sociología y Cultura de la Policía." In *Atlas de la Seguridad y la Defensa de México,* edited by Raúl Benítez Manaut, Abelardo Rodríguez Sumano, and Armando Rodríguez Luna, 87–9. Mexico City: CASEDE.

Franklin, Fabian. 2010. *What Prohibition Has Done to America.* New York: Harcourt, Brace & Co.

Friman, H. Richard. 1996. *Narcodiplomacy: Exporting the War on Drugs.* Ithaca, NY: Cornell University Press.

Gahlinger, Paul M. 2004. *Illegal Drugs: A Complete Guide to Their History, Chemistry, Use and Abuse.* New York: Penguin Group.

Global Commission on Drug Policy. 2011. *War on Drugs: Report of the Global Commission on Drug Policy.* June. http://www.globalcommissionondrugs.org/wp-content/themes/gcdp_v1/pdf/Global_Commission_Report_English.pdf. Accessed October 22, 2012.

Goldstein, Margaret J. 2010. *Legalizing Drugs: Crime Stopper or Social Risk?* Minneapolis, MN: Twenty-First Century Books.

Gray, James P. 2001. *Why Our Drug Laws Have Failed and What We Can Do about It: A Judicial Indictment of the War on Drugs.* Philadelphia, PA: Temple University Press.

Husak, Douglas. 2002. *Legalize This! The Case for Decriminalizing Drugs.* London: Verso.

Langner, Ana. 2010. "Narcos ganan la batalla al gobierno, revela encuesta." *El Economista,* May 19. http://eleconomista.com.mx/sociedad/2010/05/19/narcos-ganan-batalla-gobierno. Accessed October 22, 2012.

Latin American Commission on Drugs and Democracy. 2009. "Drugs and Democracy: A Paradigm Shift." http://www.drogasedemocracia.org/english/. Accessed October 22, 2012.

Lynch, Timothy. 2000. *After Prohibition: An Adult Approach to Drug Policies in the 21st Century.* Washington, DC: Cato Institute.

Mares, David. 2006. *Drugs Wars and Coffeehouses: The Political Economy of the International Drug Trade.* Washington, DC: CQ Press.

Martin, William C. 2007. "The Damage Done." *Texas Monthly* (April): 104–11.

Meyer, Mareen, with contributions by Stephen Brewer and Carlos Cepeda. 2010. *Abuso y miedo en Ciudad Juárez: Un análisis de violaciones a los derechos humanos cometidas por militares en México.* Washington, DC, and Ciudad Juárez, Chihuahua: Washington Office for Latin America and Miguel Agustín Pro Juárez, A.C.

Miron, Jeffrey A. 2004. *Drug War Crimes: The Consequences of Prohibition.* Oakland, CA: Independent Institute.

Monárrez Fragoso, Julia. 2010. "Death in a Transnational Metropolitan Region." In *Cities and Citizenship at the U.S.-Mexico Border*, edited by Kathleen Staudt, César Fuentes, and Julia Monárrez Fragoso, 23–42. New York: Palgrave Macmillan.

Nadelmann, Ethan A. 1990. "Global Prohibition Regimes: The Evolution of Norms in International Society." *International Organization* 44, no. 4: 504–11.

———. 2007. "Think Again: Drugs." In *Foreign Policy* (September–October). http://www.foreignpolicy.com/articles/2007/08/15/think_again_drugs. Accessed October 22, 2012.

Naím, Moisés. 2005. *Illicit: How Smugglers, Traffickers, and Copycats Are Hijacking the Global Economy*. New York: Doubleday.

Office of National Drug Control Policy. 2012. *National Drug Control Budget FY2012 Funding Highlights*. Executive Office of the President. http://www.whitehouse.gov/sites/default/files/ondcp/policy-and-research/fy12highlight_exec_sum.pdf. Accessed October 22, 2012.

Olson, Eric L., David A. Shirk, and Andrew Selee, eds. 2010. *Shared Responsibility: U.S.-Mexico Policy Options for Confronting Organized Crime*. Washington, DC, and San Diego, CA: Woodrow Wilson International Center for Scholars and University of San Diego.

Payan, Tony. 2006. *The Three U.S.-Mexico Border Wars: Drugs, Immigration and Homeland Security*. Westport, CT: Praeger Security International.

———. 2010. "Crossborder Governance in a Tristate, Binational Region." In *Cities and Citizenship at the U.S.-Mexico Border*, edited by Kathleen Staudt, César Fuentes, and Julia Monárrez Fragoso, 217–44. New York: Palgrave Macmillan.

Ríos, Viridiana, and David A. Shirk. 2011. *Drug Violence in Mexico: Data and Analysis through 2010*. San Diego, CA: Transborder Institute.

Staudt, Kathleen, César Fuentes, and Julia Monárrez Fragoso, eds. 2010. *Cities and Citizenship at the U.S.-Mexico Border: The Paso del Norte Metropolitan Region*. New York: Palgrave.

Staudt, Kathleen, Tony Payan, and Timothy Dunn. 2009. "Closing Reflections: Bordering Human Rights, Social Democratic Feminism, and Broad-Based Security." In *Human Rights Along the U.S.-Mexico Border: Gendered Violence and Insecurity*, edited by Kathleen Staudt, Tony Payan, and Z. Anthony Kruszewski, 185–202. Tucson: University of Arizona Press.

Szasz, Thomas Stephen. 1992. *Our Right to Drugs: The Case for a Free Market*. Westport, CT: Praeger.

Transform Drug Policy Foundation. *The War on Drugs: Are We Paying Too High a Price?* http://www.countthecosts.org/seven-costs-summary-briefing#crime. Accessed October 22, 2012.

United Nations Office on Drugs and Crime. 2011. *World Drug Report 2011*. http://www.unodc.org/documents/data-and-analysis/WDR2011/World_Drug_Report_2011_ebook.pdf. Accessed October 22, 2012.

United States Congress. 2011. *The Department of Justice's Operation Fast and Furious: Accounts of ATF Agents*. Joint Staff Report. 112th Congress. June 14. http://www.whatthefolly.com/wp-content/uploads/2011/06/ATF_Report1.pdf. Accessed October 22, 2012.

Venkatesh, Sudhir. 2008. *Gang Leader for a Day: A Rogue Sociologist Takes to the Streets*. New York: Penguin Books.

Wall Street Journal. 2011. "Joint Effort? Barney Frank, Ron Paul Team Up on Mari-juana Bill." June 22. http://blogs.wsj.com/washwire/2011/06/22/joint-effort-barney-frank-ron-paul-team-up-on-marijuana-bill/. Accessed October 22, 2012.

White House. 2012. *National Drug Control Strategy, FY2012 Budget Summary.* http://www.whitehousedrugpolicy.gov/publications/policy/12budget/exec_summary.pdf. Accessed October 22, 2012.

Youngers, Coletta A., and Eileen Rosin, eds. 2005. *Drugs and Democracy in Latin America: The Impact of U.S. Policy.* Boulder, CO: Lynne Rienner.

Zimring, Franklin M., and Gordon Hawkins. 1992. *The Search for Rational Drug Control Policy.* Boston: Cambridge University Press.

PART ONE

Framing the Issues

CHAPTER ONE

Cartels, Corruption, Carnage, and Cooperation

William C. Martin

Introduction[1]

Few problems regarding the U.S.–Mexican border offer more challenge than those pertaining to illicit drugs. Trafficking in marijuana, cocaine, heroin, methamphetamines, and other psychoactive substances involves tens of billions of dollars, intricate networks of criminals in both countries, and cooperative arrangements with government agents, from local law enforcement to high levels of both the U.S. and Mexican governments. On the U.S. side, a key factor is an ineradicable demand for drugs, combined with a long-standing legal policy of prohibiting their use. This combination drives the retail prices of the drugs to levels far beyond the cost of production, generating enormous profits for criminals and those who abet their activities on both sides of the border. For decades, a symbiotic relationship between the political establishment and criminal organizations in Mexico served as a check on violence and threats to insecurity. In recent years, that balance has been upset, as criminal factions have raised the level of violence against each other as they struggle over control of the drug trade and against government forces attempting to stem that violence and establish a more legitimate democratic order. The United States has ramped up its antidrug forces along the border and has sent hundreds of millions of dollars to Mexico to help bolster efforts to control and perhaps defeat the increasingly violent drug cartels. In addition, the two countries are working, with mutual apprehensions, to increase collaboration among their several antidrug agencies. The outcome remains in doubt, and no panaceas are in sight.

The Growth of the Drug Cartels

In 1914 the U.S. Congress passed the Harrison Narcotics Tax Act, the country's first major effort to regulate the production, importation, and distribution of opiate drugs such as heroin, opium, and laudanum. Federal, state, and local laws against marijuana, cocaine, and other drugs soon followed, often accompanied by harsh penalties for their violation. Mexico, a major producer of marijuana and a significant source of opium, enacted similar laws, thus criminalizing what had long been legal behavior. The passage of such laws did little to affect the desire for the drugs in question, so Mexican farmers and entrepreneurs, now operating as outlaws, developed ways of smuggling their contraband products across the border to the United States. Although that task was fairly easy in the early years, the risks incurred in getting an illegal product from field to customer drove prices upward and produced substantial profits for those along the supply and delivery chain. The lure of lucre attracted a variety of criminal gangs to their enterprise. Eventually, consolidation occurred and a powerful Guadalajara-based crime figure, Miguel Ángel Félix Gallardo, managed to gain control over most of the cross-border drug business.

In September 1969 President Richard Nixon formally declared a war on drugs, aimed at marijuana, heroin (from Asia as well as Mexico), cocaine (from South America), and newly popular drugs such as LSD. The key components of that war, now waged for more than forty years, have been eradication, interdiction, and incarceration. Despite the eradication of millions of marijuana, coca, and opium plants, the seizure of hundreds of tons of contraband, and the incarceration of hundreds of thousands of offenders, accomplished at a cost of hundreds of billions of dollars, the successes of the war on drugs have been few and impermanent. Demand varies over time (though remains surprisingly stable over decades), but the supply is always sufficient to meet it. Difficulties in bringing a drug to market may raise the price, but that can also increase profits, assuring a ready supply of volunteers willing to take the risks.

Apparent success in one arena produces devastation in another. In the early 1980s, for example, U.S. operations aimed at thwarting the smuggling of cocaine from Colombia via Florida and the Caribbean via airplanes and "go-fast" boats proved sufficiently effective so that the Colombians turned to Félix Gallardo and the extensive organization under his control.

Mexico soon became the primary transshipment route for an estimated 90 percent of the cocaine that reached the United States, and the riches that accrued to that partnership grew to unimagined levels. Under Félix Gallardo's oversight, the Colombian–Mexican coalition operated rather smoothly, in spite of stepped-up efforts by U.S. agents at major transit spots along the border and U.S. pressure on the Mexican government to increase its own antidrug efforts. In 1989, prodded by the U.S. Drug Enforcement Administration (DEA), which furnished the Mexican government with intelligence about his activities and whereabouts, Mexican Federal Judicial Police arrested Félix Gallardo in his home. For a time he was able to oversee his operation by mobile phone from prison, but as key men in his organization began to jockey for the top position, he brokered an arrangement by which the emerging rivals divided up the major trade routes and associated territories, known as the "plazas," among themselves, thus giving birth to the four major cartels—Gulf, Sinaloa, Juárez, and Tijuana—that dominated the Mexican drug trade for more than two decades. In recent years, intergang rivalry, internal division, and the rise of new organizations have contributed to violence that has reached dramatic proportions.[2]

The Gulf Cartel, directed from Matamoros, across from Brownsville, Texas, and operating in the states along the Gulf of Mexico and under South Texas, including the valuable entry port at Nuevo Laredo, was first headed by Juan Nepomuceno Guerra, who had risen to wealth and power by smuggling whiskey into Texas during Prohibition. He was succeeded by several men, the most notorious of whom was Osiel Cárdenas Guillén. In the late 1990s Cárdenas persuaded a group of elite Mexican army commandos (many of whom had received training that included counternarcotics tactics from American Special Forces instructors at Fort Bragg, North Carolina) to desert in search of a more rewarding life of crime. Known as Los Zetas and later enlarged by new recruits, they became notorious for their extreme brutality and brazen ways but also for operations that reflect strategic planning, technological sophistication, and long-term aspirations.

The Sinaloa Cartel, ensconced in the western region that still produces most of the marijuana and opium grown in Mexico and the most powerful of the cartels, is headed by Joaquín "El Chapo" ("Shorty") Guzmán, one of the world's richest and most wanted criminals. For decades, the gang included a subset led by four Beltrán Leyva brothers so powerful that it was often considered a separate organization and eventually broke away in bitter conflict.

The Juárez Cartel, headquartered in El Paso's sister city, was originally led by another powerful Sinaloan, Amado Carrillo Fuentes. After he died in 1997 during plastic surgery intended to alter his appearance to foil authorities, the leadership fell to his brother, Vicente Carrillo Fuentes. Most of the murderous violence that wracked Ciudad Juárez in recent years stemmed from the efforts of the Juárez group to repel the Sinaloan Cartel's attempts to gain control of valuable cross-border smuggling routes and, more recently, the drug traffic in Juárez itself.

Félix Gallardo ceded control of northwest Mexico to his seven nephews and four nieces of the Arellano-Félix family, based in Tijuana, with direct access to the rich California market. Once enormously powerful and violent, the Tijuana Cartel was featured in the 2000 movie *Traffic*.

The Role of Corruption

It is crucial to recognize that these illegal operations, including a share of the violence, occurred with the knowledge, permission, blessing, and even encouragement of the Mexican political establishment, from local police and mayors to the highest levels of the ruling party, which for seventy years after its birth in 1929 was the Partido Revolucionario Institucional (PRI). Like other institutions in Mexican society, the gangs operated in a patron–client or "elite–exploitative" relationship (Pimentel 2000). In return for being allowed to carry on their business without significant interference (or with overt assistance) from law enforcement personnel, the gang leaders were expected to pay what amounted to a franchise fee or tax on their earnings. The officials in question might simply accept a reasonable offer or, particularly at higher levels, make their expectations explicit. Precise arrangements and levels of officials involved have varied, and accounts of these actions by historians, social scientists, and law enforcement agents differ on details, but there is little dispute regarding the overall pattern of thoroughgoing, institutionalized corruption. Luis Astorga, a sociologist at the Institute of Social Research of the National Autonomous University of Mexico and a premier authority on Mexican drug trafficking, summarized the situation well: "The state was the referee, and it imposed the rules of the game on the traffickers. The world of the politicians and the world of the traffickers contained and protected each other simultaneously" (Wilkinson 2008).

Criminal Enterprise

Smugglers have proven to be resourceful, adaptable, practical, and persistent, choosing and inventing means to suit opportunity and thwart resistance. They have used standard and ultralight aircraft, high-speed boats, container ships, fishing vessels, small pleasure boats, motorized rafts, and submarines and sent people across the border with drugs stuffed into backpacks and luggage, strapped to their limbs and torsos, secreted in body cavities, and swallowed in balloons to be eliminated on reaching their destination. "El Chapo" Guzmán even opened a cannery that shipped jalapeños stuffed with cocaine to Mexican-owned grocery stores in California (Keefe 2012, 40). In recent years huge quantities have slipped into the United States via under-border tunnels, some crude, some stretching more than 150 yards and equipped with lights, ventilation, flooring, and other signs of skilled engineering (Winter 2012). But by far the most common method of transshipment is by motor vehicle—cars, vans, buses, trains, and, predominantly, trucks specially outfitted for the task with ingenious secret panels and other measures to disguise the nature of their cargo. U.S. and Mexican antidrug forces develop new methods of detection and increase the number of inspectors at the border, but the North American Free Trade Agreement effectively guaranteed that such measures would have limited impact. According to U.S. Bureau of Transportation Statistics, nearly 4.9 million trucks and 61 million personal vehicles crossed the U.S.–Mexican border in 2011 (U.S. Department of Transportation 2011). Smugglers are caught from time to time, but the sheer volume of traffic makes it impossible for inspectors to check more than a small sample of vehicles. The news media periodically issue dramatic reports of record seizures of drugs, but supply on the street seldom seems affected for long, and antidrug agencies acknowledge that they have no reliable way of estimating the ratio of drugs seized to drugs available on the market. Few place the figure at higher than 10 percent; some think it is as low as 1 to 4 percent.[3]

Because marijuana is bulkier and smellier than other drugs in the trade, it is easier to detect. This, coupled with the fact that it is by far the most widely used of all illegal drugs and produces a substantial percent of drug-related profits—estimates range from 70 percent to a much lower but probably more realistic 20 percent—has led the cartels to produce more of it in the United States, closer to its markets. DEA and local law enforcement agents have discovered cartel-operated "grows" in more than a dozen states and deep in national forests in California and the Pacific Northwest, where the overgrowth shields their plants from DEA surveillance planes. Whether grown locally or smuggled across the border, it is transferred to storage facilities in cities and then distributed to regional wholesalers and retailers.

Although far more people use marijuana than any other illicit drug, most observers agree that cocaine accounts for a larger share of drug traffickers' profits, followed by heroin and methamphetamines. But like other successful large enterprises, the cartels have branched into other fields of action such as kidnapping, extortion, prostitution, importing guns and other weapons, smuggling migrants, pirating CDs and DVDs, and investing in real estate and various businesses, some for the purpose of laundering proceeds from crime, some just to make money in a legitimate business (U.S. Treasury 2012). One of the most profitable ventures in recent years has been siphoning gasoline and natural gas from the pipelines of the state-owned Pemex oil company and smuggling it into the United States, draining tens of millions of dollars from Mexico's coffers.

"Narcos" also spend money to win over their local communities and the wider populace. Snakeskin boots, gaudy jewelry, high-powered trucks and SUVs, and beautiful women create an image that young men with few hopes for meaningful legal employment want to emulate. Generous funding of roads, schools, medical centers, communication systems, and even churches and chapels helps soften disapproval and fear of their violent ways, turning them into folk heroes in the eyes of many and generating a music genre called *narcocorridos* that glamorizes their exploits. Gift shops sell trinkets that reference the drug trade, and people throughout Mexico who are involved in that trade pay homage to Jesús Malverde, a folklore figure they regard as their patron saint, asking him to deliver them from evil in the form of their rivals in crime and their enemies in law enforcement. And when the young narcos die in battle, as thousands have, their friends and relatives bury many of them in elaborate tombs that celebrate their brief careers. Before he turned forty but perhaps not expecting to die of natural causes—correctly, as it turned out, since he was killed in a shootout with the Mexican navy in October 2012—Zeta leader Heriberto Lazcano Lazcano had already built a large mausoleum, fronted by a shiny three-story metal cross, to house his remains (Borderland Beat 2012a).

Cooperation

Widespread discontent with the corruption and antidemocratic ethos of the PRI led to the rise and growing strength of the conservative National Action Party (PAN) and a leftist Party of the Democratic Revolution and also to pressures for reform within the PRI itself. Ernesto Zedillo, president of Mexico from 1994 until 2000, attempted some reforms, and a few crime figures went to prison during his six years in office, but the cozy arrangement between the gangs and the government persisted. The election of PAN member Vicente Fox in 2000 ended seven decades of PRI domination of the presidency. It also coincided with new levels of conflict among the cartels as they attempted to muscle in on valuable trafficking routes controlled by other gangs. Fox declared war on the cartels and sent federal police after them, resulting in the taking down of several high-profile drug trafficking figures, the most notable of which were Tijuana gang leaders Ramón and Benjamín Arellano-Félix, in 2002 and the 2003 arrest of Gulf boss Osiel Cárdenas. It also led to a sharp increase in violence as the gangs fought back and tried to take advantage of perceived weaknesses among their rivals. In 2004, with Cárdenas out of the way, "El Chapo" Guzmán and the Sinaloans thought it was time to annex some valuable Gulf Cartel territory, particularly the major Nuevo Laredo plaza, but they were beaten back by the better-equipped and trained Zetas, who were already strengthening their position within the Gulf Cartel to the point that analysts were beginning to refer to the gang as the Gulf-Zetas. As Ioan Grillo observes in his 2011 book, *El Narco*, this was the real beginning of the modern Mexican drug war (Grillo 2011). Los Zetas would later break away from the Gulf Cartel and cause a wave of bloodshed of their own, as other chapters in this book explain further.

On December 1, 2006, his first day in office after a hotly contested election, President Felipe Calderón, also a member of the PAN, declared his determination to oppose the cartels with the full force of his government (*Los Angeles Times* 2010). In keeping with its long-standing confidence in the efficacy of force, the United States endorsed and supported President Calderón's strategy. The United States has had antidrug agents in Mexico since the 1920s, not always with Mexico's approval and usually limiting their activities to intelligence gathering. Since the 1970s, however, the DEA has been an active partner in Mexico's antidrug programs. Its agents have shared intelligence with Mexican agencies and helped develop and carry out programs of eradication of marijuana and opium, seizure of contraband bound for the United States, arrest and conviction of drug traffickers by Mexican authorities, and disruption of money-laundering operations. The United States has also provided financial assistance to Mexico's antidrug efforts through the State Department's International Narcotics Control and Law Enforcement account (Cook 2007). These cooperative efforts had some successes, but the production and transshipment of drugs obviously did not cease.

In November 2006, after meeting with President-elect Calderón, who had already announced he intended to launch a major offensive against the cartels, President George W. Bush pledged to support those efforts with a significant increase in U.S. assistance. Originally called the Joint Strategy to Combat Organized Crime, the package became known as the Mérida Initiative and authorized $1.6 billion, to be disbursed over three years, to pay for military and law enforcement equipment, technical and tactical training, upgrading of intelligence capability, hardware such as helicopters and surveillance aircraft, and special equipment to detect drugs at border crossings. President Barack Obama signed on to the Mérida Initiative, viewing the widespread continuation of drug-related violence as a threat to both nations. In April 2009 new Homeland Security Secretary Janet Napolitano announced she would be sending hundreds more federal agents and other personnel to border areas, with a dual goal of helping President Calderón crack down on the cartels and preventing the violence from spilling across the border into the United States (Napolitano 2009).

Calderón moved quickly to implement his plan, sending thousands of army troops—the number eventually rose to nearly fifty thousand—to areas known to be centers of cartel activity, reorganizing and upgrading the federal police, and setting out professional standards for state and local police. He could and did claim impressive results: arrests of thousands of suspects, most of whom were released without being prosecuted (Longmire 2011; Wilkinson 2011), seizures of tons of drugs with an estimated street value in the tens of billions of dollars (*Los Angeles Times* 2008), and the extradition to the United States of several high-level drug traffickers, including Osiel Cárdenas, who was sentenced in 2010 to twenty-five years in federal prison and the forfeiture of $50 million. Early accounts described his sentence as "without parole," but the Federal Bureau of Prisons website indicates that he is serving his time in a Supermax prison in Colorado, with a projected release date of May 19, 2025. To receive such a relatively lenient sentence, given the enormity of his crimes, Cárdenas must have offered significant valuable information about cartel operations (U.S. Department of Justice 2010).

Carnage

Such gains, however, were offset by the horrendous conflagration of violence that accompanied Calderón's war on the cartels, disillusioning many Mexicans and sparking talk of the possibility of Mexico's becoming a "failed state." The country does not meet most accepted criteria for that status and is weak on several fundamental characteristics: the ability to control its territory, a monopoly on the legitimate use of violence, and modest levels of corruption and crime. In June 2010 the major newspaper, *El Universal*, observed that the chaos spreading through the country "requires us to change our view of the problem, that it is no longer a matter of organized crime but rather of the loss of the state." A few weeks later, Calderón himself acknowledged, "This criminal behavior . . . has become a challenge to the state, an attempt to replace the state" (Wilkinson and Ellingwood 2012). Indeed, narco gangs have superseded or seriously weakened legitimate government in a growing number of Mexican states and in previously safe cities such as tourist favorites Acapulco and Cuernevaca and industrial centers Monterrey and Guadalajara (The Fund for Peace 2012).

The worst violence occurred in Ciudad Juárez as the Juárez group fought to repel "El Chapo's" attempts to gain control of valuable cross-border smuggling routes. Between 2006 and 2012, the official death toll in the city topped ten thousand, most of those between 2008 and 2011, when the Sinaloans triumphed decisively, earning Juárez a deserved reputation as the most dangerous city in the world. Other major centers of carnage were Tijuana, where "El Chapo" moved in on the Arellano Félix gang, and the Sinaloan capital of Culiacán, where his troops were in a civil war with his former allies of the Beltrán Leyva organization. Early in 2010, long-festering tensions led to a split between the Gulf and Zeta factions and to vicious, spectacular battles that ultimately left the Zetas in control of Nuevo Laredo and Veracruz and weakened the Gulf hold on Tamaulipas. Emboldened further, Los Zetas launched an aggressive effort to recruit new members and expand their reach, establishing a strong presence in other parts of Mexico. Grillo notes that Los Zetas "were not thinking like gangsters, but like a paramilitary group controlling territory" (Grillo 2011, 106). Mike Vigil, retired head of international operations for the DEA and consultant for the Mexican government, agreed: "The Zetas have created a new model of organized crime and unleashed new levels of violence to try and unseat the older cartels. This has destabilized many areas of

and VCF, as I described above, the Mexican government would not be opposed at all" (Conroy 2012b). After violence in Juárez dropped by 45 percent over the next year, President Calderón credited job programs and other government investments for playing a key role. Analysts from Stratfor and other organizations contended that Sinaloa's victory over the Juárez cartel likely played a greater role (*BBC News* 2012).

Despite Calderón's assertions that his plan was working, the body count continued to grow, with six times as many deaths recorded in 2010, 2011, and 2012 as in 2007, the first year of his offensive. In January 2012 the government acknowledged that at least 47,515 people had been killed in "drug-war-related" incidents between December 2006 and September 2011, but it announced it would no longer update and release official figures (Pachico 2012). Using data from the Mexican National Institute of Statistics and Geography, the National System for Public Security, and her own tracing of deaths reported in the Mexican media but not included in these figures, such as bodies found in mass graves, Molly Molloy, New Mexico State University librarian, has estimated that the final total for Calderón's administration will exceed 110,000, not including an unknown but large number of people who are "missing" or "disappeared" and were likely killed. *Zeta*, a weekly magazine published in Tijuana, places the count at 109,000, noting that it does not include the missing (Borderland Beat 2012b). Other observers regard these estimates as too conservative. Few appear to believe the frequently reported figures of fifty thousand and sixty thousand (Molloy 2012).

Throughout his six years in office, President Calderón repeatedly asserted that over 90 percent of those killed in the violence were criminals, implying that the gangs may be weeding themselves out. U.S. officials, agents, and mainstream media have generally accepted this assertion. No doubt, much of the violence has been internecine, between cartels, factions therein, or opportunistic small gangs seeking to carve out a piece of the lucrative pie. The gangs have used violence as a way to taunt and terrorize, beheading their victims, hanging their obviously tortured bodies in public places, dissolving them in vats of lye or acid, and posting videos of their grisly deeds on YouTube. They have assassinated a candidate almost certain to become governor of Tamaulipas, slain mayors, police chiefs, legislators, and journalists. They have repeatedly committed mass murder, burying their victims in shallow graves or simply leaving them stacked in the backs of trucks. In some cases, authorities know who has been killed; in others, the dead may be rival gang members, kidnap victims, migrants who had paid the gangs to help them cross the border, innocents caught in the crossfire, or others deemed disposable.

More troubling, but difficult to prove, are repeated allegations, some based on eyewitness accounts, that uniformed military troops often acted as "death squads," storming into areas, executing victims in precision fashion, and racing out as swiftly as they came. In other versions, such troops stood by a block away from prolonged attacks by unknown assailants, as if protecting them from interruption or making sure the job was finished according to plan (Molloy 2008). According to e-mails obtained by WikiLeaks and shared with Stratfor, at least some of these troops are Mexican Special Forces "making use of intelligence, surveillance and paramilitary-like tactics to take out their victims." In this account, the victims may be drug trafficking cells or simply people the troops want out of the way, for whatever reason. A human rights worker in Juárez was quoted in London's *Guardian* newspaper as saying, "There are execution squads [in Juárez], forensically killing *malandros* ["down-and-outs, urchins, petty criminals and addicts"], planned assassinations of the unwanted. And if we look at exactly how they are done, they are experts in killing characteristic of training by the army or police. . . . I kept a map and watched how these [death] squads move across the army checkpoints without hindrance. Until I was told to stop" (Conroy 2012a).

Even apart from such allegations, the army, which has been one of the most respected institutions in Mexican society, came under increased scrutiny and criticism. Business owners have claimed that the presence of armed soldiers on the streets, sometimes storming into bars and restaurants to search everyone in the building, discourages tourism, a major component of the Mexican economy. Others have reported abuses that include illegal searches, arresting and detaining people without cause, beatings, theft, rape, and torture (*Los Angeles Times* 2009). Thousands of complaints against the army have been filed with Mexico's National Human Rights Commission (O'Neil 2012; Daly, Heinle, and Shirk 2012). A woman protesting such abuses said, in 2008, "Now you see all these big billboards, 'We [the army] have come to help you'—but it isn't true. They have come to pillage us, to ransack our homes. They take the food in the refrigerator, jewelry, anything . . . and they destroy property. It is not a secret who they are" (Bowden and Molloy 2012). Observers also fear that sizable numbers of the troops will follow the example of Los Zetas and desert to the cartels (Koughan 2009). That fear is not groundless; in some cities, Los Zetas have hung banners openly inviting the soldiers to join their ranks: "The Zetas operations group wants you, soldier or ex-soldier. We offer you a good salary, food, and attention for your family . . . benefits, life insurance, a house for your family and children. Stop living in the slums and riding the bus. A new car or truck, your choice" (Grillo 2011). The *Economist* magazine quotes Guillermo Zepeda of CIDAC, a think tank in Mexico City, expressing the fear that "We may end up without trustworthy police and without a trustworthy army" (*Economist* 2009a). Some Mexican reports charge that "the army has pulled off a coup d'état, morphing into its own terrorist, drug-money collecting, gun-wielding cartel—morphing into an enemy in uniformed disguise to terrorize physically and spiritually the Mexican citizenry" (*Seminal* 2009).

Paradoxically, the arrival of military and federal troops in a city has typically resulted in initial lower levels of violence, followed by a notable and prolonged increase. Professor Denise Dresser of the Instituto Tecnológico Autónomo de México notes that when the military have entered troubled cities, they usually removed local police forces, regarding them as under control of the cartels. Without denying high levels of corruption among local police, Dresser contends that they know their cities and are better equipped to deal with violence. The military lack both this knowledge and experience with police work. The result is a climate of lawlessness in which not just drug traffickers but all sorts of criminals and people whose violence had been kept in check are able to operate with impunity. Nathan Jones, a cartel expert at Rice University's Baker Institute, agrees, noting that an improved Tijuana police force, which was not disbanded when federal forces arrived, was able to manage "ordinary" violence more successfully than in some other large cities (Jones 2012c).

Corruption remains a pervasive problem. Most observers agree that the law enforcement agencies operating at the border are compromised. Throughout the country, local police, underpaid, undertrained, and underequipped, are clearly still on the take. Honest cops run the risk of contempt from their coworkers or of being killed because of fear they will expose the crooked ones. Hundreds of police have been killed since the Calderón initiative began. Some no doubt conscientiously opposed the drug gangs; others, reportedly a majority, simply worked for the wrong gang. Even those thoroughly vetted for trustworthiness may succumb to temptation or give in when a gang confronts them with the choice "*plata o plomo*"—silver or lead, bribe or bullet. The corruption extends far up the line. In 2008 at least thirty-five agents from an elite organized crime unit within the attorney general's office, including top officials ostensibly leading the crackdown against the cartels, were fired or arrested. According to news accounts, they had for several years been receiving monthly payments ranging from $150,000 to $450,000 each, in return for keeping the cartels informed about government operations (*Economist* 2009b). Payoffs of such size are apparently not unique; wiretaps used to bring indictments against members of the Gulf Cartel caught discussions of bribes of $2 million (Marosi 2009). In May 2009, guards at a Zacatecas prison offered no resistance as fifty-three inmates walked out and drove away in a seventeen-car convoy (Ellingwood and Wilkinson 2009). Later that same month, federal agents accused ten mayors from the state of Michoacán of abetting local drug traffickers (*Los Angeles Times* 2009). In July 2010, prison officials in Durango were found to be sending prisoners, using official vehicles and armed with prison weapons, on designated assassination assignments (Stevenson 2010). At about the same time, fifty-six members of Tijuana law enforcement agencies were arrested for corruption, adding to more than four hundred similar arrests or firings since January 2008. In May 2010, the mayor of Cancún was arrested on charges of aiding Los Zetas and the Beltrán-Leyva gang (Ellingwood 2010b). In July 2010, at least 140 inmates escaped from a prison in Nuevo Laredo, apparently with the aid of corrupt guards and the director (Ellingwood 2010a). In May 2011, Mexico's National Institute of Migration fired and detained seven regional directors suspected of turning over Central American migrants to kidnappers who could rob them, hold them for ransom, force them to work for the gangs, or, in the case of women, sell them into the sex trade (Ellingwood 2011). Observers assume that many such victims wind up in the mass graves that continue to be discovered.

The sordid stories continued to come to light in 2012. In January, the attorney general of Mexico informed the past three governors of Tamaulipas that they were being investigated for possible collaboration with Mexican drug cartels. In May, the Mexican government arrested three high-ranking army generals and a retired lieutenant colonel on suspicion of aiding the Beltrán Leyva gang (Archibold 2012a, 2012b). A month later, three federal policeman thought to be involved with drug traffic through Mexico City's International Airport killed three of their fellow officers. In August, all 348 federal policemen assigned to the airport were replaced. In September, 131 inmates escaped from a prison in Piedras Negras, across from the South Texas town of Eagle Pass, through a tunnel that had obviously been under construction for some time. Authorities speculated it had been arranged by Los Zetas, probably with the knowledge of prison officials (Villalba et al. 2012). A June 15, 2012, *New York Times Magazine* article reported that a former police official from Ciudad Juárez, the city hardest hit by the violence between the Sinaloa and Juárez Cartels, claimed that the entire police department, including the former police official, had been on the Sinaloan payroll. Mexico's secretary of public security speculated that, in addition to officials further up the line, "the cartels spend more than a billion dollars each year just to bribe the municipal police." Civilians such as cabdrivers are also on the payroll, alerting traffickers to such things as stepped-up inspections or increased police presence at the border (Keefe 2012, 42). Not surprisingly, competing gangs complain, sometimes in full-page newspapers ads, that the police are colluding with their rivals (Arsenault 2010).

Those who criticize the gangs publicly, or attempt to expose the corruption that enables them, do so at their own peril. In April 2009 a Roman Catholic archbishop in Durango wondered publicly why the authorities seemed unable to locate "El Chapo," since he was widely known to be living nearby. According to the *Los Angeles Times*, most local media did not report the explosive comments, and copies of national papers that ran the story appeared on few newsstands. A day or two later, the archbishop backpedaled, claiming that he was simply repeating things of the sort people say to their pastor (*Los Angeles Times* 2009). As a further safety measure, he began traveling with bodyguards and ordered an armored car (*ABC News* 2012). The timidity of the media in this case is understandable. Gangs have attacked newspaper offices and TV stations after they have published or aired stories attacking the cartels or exposing their ties to public officials. In 2012, the Knight Center for Journalism in the Americas reported that at least eighty journalists had been killed and seventeen were missing in Mexico since 2000 (*ABC News* 2012). The International Press Institute Death Watch called Mexico "the deadliest country in the world for journalists in 2011" (International Press Institute 2012). Arrests and prosecutions of those responsible for the journalist killings are essentially nonexistent. Many journalists exercise self-censorship, ignoring stories on drug trafficking and confining their reporting to "weddings, *quinceañeras*, and baptisms" (*Los Angeles Times* 2008). In a stunning admission of helplessness, *El Diario*, in Ciudad Juárez, ran a front-page editorial in September 2010 after two staffers had been murdered by drug gangs, asking cartel "Lords" to "explain to us what you want from us. What are we supposed to publish or not publish, so we know what to abide by. You are at this time the de facto authorities in this city because the legal authorities have not been able to stop our colleagues from falling" (Archibold 2010). In July 2012, after its offices were attacked with grenades and rifle fire, *El Mañana*, the major regional newspaper, based in Nuevo Laredo, announced it would stop reporting on "violent disputes," citing the "lack of adequate conditions for freely exercising professional journalism" (Wilkinson 2012).

Corruption is not the special province of Mexicans. As the U.S. Customs and Border Protection agency has stepped up hiring, it has had problems not only with agents who go bad while on the job but with some who are already in the employ of the cartels when they come to work (Archibold 2009). And it would be naive to imagine that the dispersal of drugs across the United States does not receive assistance from law enforcement agents, lawyers, judges, bankers, and business owners willing to profit from their positions. Since June 2006, the website stopthedrugwar.org has published a regular feature, "This Week's Corrupt Cop Stories," describing illegal behavior by U.S. drug-law enforcement agents from small towns to major cities, from local police to federal agents, and from prison guards to district attorneys and judges. Each issue describes several instances of malfeasance. The September 12, 2012, issue was number 750 in the series (Stop the Drug War n.d.).

Reading through these items is depressing, but their significance pales in comparison to the activities of banks that abet cartel efforts to launder the stains from their drug money and turn it into easily usable funds in Mexico or wherever the drug bosses want or need it. In addition to banks in Mexico and offshore tax havens, banks north of the border often look the other way when large sums of money start churning through accounts belonging to customers they have not thoroughly vetted. Some of the world's largest banks have been party to such schemes. In 2010, Wachovia, now owned by Wells Fargo, acknowledged that it had turned funds from Mexican *casas de cambio* (money-exchange houses) into $378 billion deposited in Wachovia accounts, despite the fact that the transactions violated a number of antimoney-laundering warning signs. To avoid prosecution, Wachovia settled out of court for $160 million in penalties, less than .001 percent of the amount laundered. No one responsible for allowing these transactions was prosecuted. The whistle-blower whose task was to spot and report such abuses lost his job (Vulliamy 2011; Smith 2010).

Another large international bank, the London-based HSBC, with operations in more than eighty countries, has been accused of failing to monitor billions of dollars in wire transfers from its Mexican affiliates and trillions from other countries, including Russia, Iran, and Bangladesh. A congressional Committee on Homeland Security and Governmental Affairs investigating the HSBC case chastised not only the bank for its flouting antimoney-laundering regulations but also the U.S. watchdog Office of the Comptroller of the Currency for laxity in oversight (U.S. Senate 2012). More recently, the FBI has alleged that Los Zetas have laundered modest amounts—one million dollars a month—through the Bank of America but blames laxity rather than deliberate oversight by the bank (*Huffington Post* 2012).

Whether laundered or still bloodstained, much of the drug money gets back to Mexico in the same ways the drugs get out—smuggled by some of the same people using some of the same means, even some of the same vehicles making return trips. U.S. and Mexican authorities agree that they are able to intercept no more than 1 percent of the billions that flow across the border each year (Booth and Miroff 2010). Less straightforward ways of sterilizing blood money include using dollars to buy goods such as silk or toys or electronics products from a third country such as China and then having those items shipped to Mexico where they can be sold through legal businesses. Los Zetas laundered millions through a horse breeding operation in Ruidoso, New Mexico (Thompson 2012). Reflecting on the difficulty of damning the river of dirty money on its way back to the gangs, Calderón said in October 2011 during a meeting with drug-war victims, "Without question, we have been at fault. The truth is that the existing structures for detecting money-laundering were simply overwhelmed by reality" (Ellingwood and Wilkinson 2011).

These problems, coupled with concern over the financial cost of Calderón's war on drugs at a time when the Mexican economy is already weak, led to doubts that the campaign will succeed. A March 2010 poll, published in the daily newspaper, *Milenio*, indicated that only 21 percent of the Mexican public thought the government was winning its fight with the cartels (Camp 2009; Ellingwood 2009). Surveys by the Pew Global Attitudes Project were considerably more positive, with 45 percent in 2011 and 47 percent in 2012 saying they thought the campaign against drug traffickers was making progress. More than 80 percent in both surveys approved of using the Mexican army in the effort, but 74 percent in the 2012 poll called human rights violations by the military and police a serious problem (Pew Research Center 2012).

However they received their information—from the Sinaloans, DEA agents working with Mexican counterparts, or Mexican intelligence personnel working on their own—Mexican military and federal police were able to score some notable victories. Some cartels have lost key players, with an undoubted negative effect, temporarily for some, more significantly for others. The killing of Arturo Beltrán Leyva in December 2009 and the subsequent arrest of his two brothers and another key leader, Edgar "La Barbie" Valdez Villarreal, left the Beltrán Leyva organization severely weakened. The whereabouts of a remaining brother were unknown in late 2012, and Mexican authorities regarded the organization as defunct, though remnants were still working with Los Zetas.

A smaller but formidable gang, La Familia Michoacana, specialized in meth trafficking and gained notoriety for horrendous attention-grabbing violence—for example, rolling heads of victims onto a dance floor in 2006—and its incongruous profession of a form of fundamentalist Christianity espoused by its leader, Nazario Moreno González, aka "El Más Loco" ("The Craziest One"). After federal troops killed Moreno in a firefight in December 2010 and federal police captured another key leader in June 2011, La Familia faded, but leading members of the gang formed another organization known as Knights Templar, which professed an interest in social justice and retained traces of respect for religion—when Pope Bendict XVI visited Mexico in March 2012, they hung banners on bridges in seven cities proclaiming "The Knights Templar Cartel will not partake in any warlike acts, we are not killers, welcome Pope" (*Milenio* 2012).

In January 2010 federal police arrested Teodoro "El Teo" García Simental, who had risen to the top in Tijuana after the fall of the Arellano Félix clan and was regarded as the most vicious trafficker in the country. That reputation was underscored ten days later with the arrest of Santiago Meza López, known as "El Pozolero" (The Stew Maker) for his practice of disposing of El Teo's victims by dissolving their bodies in vats of acid (Miller Llana 2010). In November 2010 Mexican marines, believed to be acting on information provided by the DEA, killed Osiel Cárdenas's brother, Antonio, a top commander in the Gulf Cartel known as "Tony Tormenta," in an hours-long gun battle in Matamoros (Wilkinson 2010). The cartel, weakened by the split with Los Zetas and continuing to lose territory and power, suffered what appeared to be a crippling loss in September 2012 when marines arrested Mario Cárdenas, who had taken Tony's place, and Jorge Eduardo Costilla Sánchez, believed to be the actual top man in the cartel. Seven more alleged key members of the Gulf gang were arrested a week later (Rodríguez 2012). Of thirty-seven gangsters on Mexico's most-wanted list, twenty-four had been killed or captured (Wikipedia 2012).

Such losses take their toll, whether in the form of internal strife as remaining members seek to take over or through the efforts of rival gangs to take advantage of presumed disruption. But Nathan Jones cautions against prematurely announcing a cartel's demise. The Gulf Cartel has been in business for decades, has deep roots in northeastern Mexico, knows the trafficking game, and has extensive wholesale networks in the United States. These make it unlikely that it will simply fade away. Similarly, he notes that although the once powerful Tijuana Cartel has clearly been weakened by the death or imprisonment of all the key Arellano-Félix brothers and other important figures, and may have lost its dominance over Baja California, it appears to have worked out a satisfactory arrangement with the Sinoloa Cartel to share the Tijuana "plaza," including the right to a "piso" (toll) on drugs sent through its territory (Jones 2012a).

Internal rivalries within the larger organizations and with and between the smaller ones, as well as aggressive efforts by military and law enforcement agencies, make it difficult to sketch the situation with any confidence about long-range accuracy. But in 2012 the Mexican drug cartels had evolved into recognizable coalitions, with a Sinaloan aggregate controlling most of the western part of the country, including Baja California, and Los Zetas holding sway in the northeast and Gulf regions, although torn internally by a split between two original leaders, Heriberto Lazcano Lazcano and Miguel Ángel Treviño Morales. Smaller organizations formed alliances of convenience with each other and the major cartels. Peaceful acceptance of the situation, as in the old days of Félix Gallardo, did not appear to be on the horizon. In March, "El Chapo" gave notice that he was ready to make another run at Nuevo Laredo when his gunmen killed fourteen Zetas, dumped their bodies, and plastered the area with *narcomantas* (banners) announcing his intention to free the city from Zeta control. Deriding Los Zetas as "a bunch of drunks and car-washers," the banners declared, "We are narcotics traffickers and we don't mess with honest working or business people. . . . I'm going to teach these scum to work Sinaloa style, without kidnapping, without payoffs, without extortion." They also warned that anyone giving in to extortion demands from Los Zetas would be considered a traitor. "Don't forget," the banner warned, "I am your true father." Addressing Miguel Treviño, the notoriously violent Zeta leader in control of the city, by his code name Z-40, "El Chapo" added a taunt, "As for you, 40, I tell you that you don't scare me." Former DEA chief Mike Vigil said "El Chapo" hoped to gain popular support by portraying himself as "the protector of the poor people against Los Zetas. Obviously it is a vested interest because it behooves him and the other cartels to get rid of Los Zetas that are causing a lot of problems for them" (Althaus and Schiller 2012).

Poor people may not have been "El Chapo's" only intended audience. He was no doubt aware that in 2011 the White House had issued an executive order naming four groups around the world as "transnational criminal threats." The list included a Japanese syndicate, a Mafia-style Italian outfit, a multiethnic international organization led from Russia—and Los Zetas. It did not include the Sinaloa Cartel. A White House spokesman explained that the groups on the list were engaged in a "wide variety" of crimes, whereas the Sinaloans engaged mostly in drug trafficking and were already a major target under a separate initiative (Johnson 2011). That did not amount to a free pass, but it seemed to offer "El Chapo" an advantage, and he intended to keep it. According to a *New York Times* report, a captured cartel member said that "El Chapo" "specifically instructed his subordinates not to dabble in protection rackets and insisted that Sinaloa territory remain 'calm' and 'controlled.'" He considered extortion, kidnapping, and the like too risky. "They want the big business," the captive explained, "and the big business is in the United States" (Keefe 2012, 43).

The ability of Mexico's top drug trafficker to remain alive and free and continue to run and expand his far-flung operation was such an obvious embarrassment to President Calderón that some speculated his government might be planning a "June surprise" in advance of the July 2012 presidential elections, giving Calderón a coveted victory and boosting the chances of the PAN candidate against the popular (and ultimate winner) Enrique Peña Nieto, who sought to lead the PRI back to power. In an article titled "Mexico's Presidential Contest: Calderón's 'Hail Mary' Pass?" George Grayson, a cartel expert at the College of William and Mary, ventured that "bringing down "El Chapo" would alter Calderón's place in his nation's books from a chief executive who waged a bloody, unfocused drug war to a leader who eliminated a criminal compared favorably with Osama bin Laden, Butch Cassidy, and Al Capone" (Grayson 2012).[4] Similar thoughts were apparently afoot in Washington, where the Pentagon is reported to have prepared a detailed plan for a surgical strike on "El Chapo," similar in nature to the mission that killed Osama bin Laden in Pakistan in 2011 and to be carried out by the Navy Seals of the Northern Command as part of their mission to capture and kill targets they consider terrorists and a threat to national security. According to the report, Calderón liked the idea but could not sell it to the leaders of his armed forces, primarily because they regarded it as an unconstitutional affront to Mexican sovereignty. Pentagon officials who were involved indicated that they would raise the matter again with Calderón's successor (Carrasco and Esquivel 2012; *Daily Mail* 2012).

"El Chapo" Guzmán is a brutal criminal. He is also a brilliant executive overseeing a sprawling transnational enterprise dealing in global commodities. He is amazingly well protected, but he is not superhuman. If rivals from other gangs or from within his own circles do not kill him, it is quite believable that Mexican or U.S. forces will succeed in bringing him down. That would be a triumph for whoever accomplished it and would likely be heralded as yet another sign that the war on drugs is being won. But in the short term, it would almost certainly raise the level of violence as various interested parties moved either to ascend to the top spot or to wrest territory away from an organization weakened by the loss of its leader. As Luis Astorga has aptly observed, "The capture of capos doesn't necessarily mean defeat for the cartels. It just means new criminal coalitions, new alignments, and that process can lead to more expansive waves of violence, not less" (Padgett 2011).

In his successful campaign for the presidency, Peña Nieto insisted that "there will be no truce or deals with either organized crime or drug trafficking," but he contended that use of the military had exacerbated the violence in Mexico. "We can't continue that way," he told *TIME* reporters. "So we're going to follow a strategy focused on three central crimes: murder, kidnapping and extortion. But make no mistake: it's our duty to finish off organized crime gangs, including drug traffickers" (Padgett 2012). Bruce Bagley of the University of Miami told a *Forbes* reporter, "He said he's going to place less emphasis on the military and more on social and social-economic things—but what exactly that means is unclear. Me and my colleagues in Mexico are saying that means basically that he's going to lighten up—in the hopes that there would be far less bloodshed and fewer bodies." Veteran Mexican journalist Dolia Estévez agreed. "The Mexican people are asking for a change on that kind of war," she said. "It's clear. "Mexico has been insistent . . . that the problem is the demand in the U.S., and the flow of guns to Mexico. They [ask], 'Why are we going to be fighting this war that has no possibility of being won?'" (Carlyla 2012).

Clearly a key factor in this discouraging process is the truly enormous amount of money that can be made by dealing drugs, especially by those in charge of the dealing. The money enables the cartels to recruit whatever personnel they need, whether they be drivers and pilots, accountants and lawyers, computer and communications experts, or assassins and bodyguards, and to equip them with whatever they need to ply their trade. It also funds the corruption of law enforcement, political, and financial systems on both sides of the border, more extensive in Mexico but also significant in the United States. And some observers assert that this influx of money, much of which is pumped into the legal economy, has caused many Mexicans, especially those living far away from the border states, where most of the violence has occurred, to view the cartels as less threatening to their lives than the government's efforts to eradicate them.

It has long been obvious that the great bulk of that money comes from buyers in the United States, but only recently have Mexicans and other Latin Americans begun to insist that the United States acknowledge this fact and take sweeping steps to deal with its implications. In the process they have begun to urge the United States to reconsider its adamant insistence on prohibition of the drugs in question. President Calderón challenged the United States to take stock of its own failings, especially with regard to drug consumption and laws that facilitate the trafficking in guns and other weapons that have strengthened the cartels in their struggle with the federal police and the army (*Los Angeles Times* 2009). Even more significantly, the former presidents of Mexico (Ernesto Zedillo), Colombia (César Gaviria), and Brazil (Fernando Henrique Cardoso) cochaired a blue-ribbon Latin American commission whose 2009 report *Drugs and Democracy: Toward a Paradigm Shift* explicitly called on the United States to acknowledge that its decades-long war on drugs had failed and to give serious consideration to "diverse alternatives to the prohibitionist strategy that are being tested in different countries, focusing on the reduction of individual and social harm" (Latin American Commission on Drugs and Democracy of the Open Society Institute 2009). This call was repeated in a 2011 report by what is now billed as the Global Commission on Drug Policy, adding such luminaries as former UN secretary General Kofi Annan, former NATO secretary General Javier Solana, former U.S. secretary of state George Shultz, former U.S. Federal Reserve chairman Paul Volcker, former prime minister of Greece George Papandreou, former president of Switzerland Ruth Dreifuss, Mexican writer Carlos Fuentes, and British entrepreneur Richard Branson (Global Commission on Drug Policy 2011).

This message has been received. In her first visit to Mexico as secretary of state, in 2009, Hillary Clinton acknowledged that the "insatiable demand for illegal drugs [in the United States] fuels the drug trade" (Landler 2009). The director of the U.S. Office of National Drug Control Policy,

Gil Kerlikowske, has announced that his office will place greater emphasis on prevention and treatment. In addition, authorities at the local, state, and national levels are calling for a comprehensive and open-minded examination of alternatives to drug policies notable for repeated failure. That said, no sweeping change in U.S. policy is in sight, and Mexico cannot plan around one.

Because at least the major cartels have developed into full-scale criminal organizations, the Mexican government has little choice but to attempt to check their power and the damage they cause. Aggressive action by the Mexican government, advisable or not, has exacerbated the violence far beyond Calderón's imagining. Although actions against criminals should be waged by the police rather than the army insofar as possible, Calderón's use of the army and navy was understandable, given their numbers, advanced weaponry, and reputation as less corrupted institutions, but the costs of that decision have been steep. The Mexican government should work to shift from a mind-set of war to one of crime fighting and to reduce the role of the military, while strengthening that of the police. It must continue to build and reinforce professional civil service, law enforcement, and judicial systems, from the local to federal levels, with effective measures to prevent, identify, check, prosecute, and punish corruption and violation of the rights of citizens. This will involve improvement in pay, higher educational requirements, vigilant screening, and continuing reinforcement of appropriate values and attitudes. Obviously this is a mammoth and daunting task. The United States can offer assistance, but most of this work will have to be done by Mexicans.

During his campaign, Peña Nieto announced that he intended to form a "national gendarmerie," a deployable police force comprising ex-soldiers who had already proved to be able and reliable while fighting in Calderón's war. Such a force could serve as a backup to local police, with power to make arrests, but could also act as a commando-style elite strike force against cartel cells. Response to the idea has been unenthusiastic. Tony Payan noted that many mayors and governors had created such forces, "only to see them become corrupt, ineffectual, and eventually dismantled. The record shows that many of the specially trained officers end up dead, spend much of their time protecting each other from cartels, or desert and join the criminals" (Payan 2012).

No one seriously suggests that the Mexican government should acknowledge that Calderón's war on the cartels was a mistake, then simply pull back in admission of defeat, but Jorge Castañeda, Mexico's foreign minister under President Vicente Fox, has called for an informal accommodation in which the government relaxes its opposition to the cartels in return for a significant reduction in violence (Castañeda 2010). Castañeda's critics argue that giving cartels tacit permission to operate would undermine public confidence in the rule of law (Bonner 2010). In a variation of the idea, however, Eric Olson, a senior associate at the Mexico Institute of the Woodrow Wilson International Center in Washington, has suggested that a viable approach might be for the Mexican government to designate one group as "most violent," using transparent and openly announced criteria, then go after them aggressively with the support of the United States. This, he contends, should create incentives among criminal organizations to avoid the "most violent" label for themselves and to cut ties with the group so labeled, lest they be targeted as well. Ideally, this would produce "commercial leprosy" that would further weaken the organization (Olson 2012).

Even the most optimistic of observers may believe that eventual success lies years in the future and will come only with great effort and cost. Toward that end, both countries must work to improve educational and employment opportunities so that young people in particular do not turn to drugs and crime because they have abandoned hope of achieving a meaningful life by legal means. And finally, both countries, in dialogue with other nations in the hemisphere, in Europe, and elsewhere, should examine the drug policies and programs of other countries to consider viable alternatives to a policy of strict prohibition. A growing number of countries have adopted such policies, either officially or de facto. Usage rates have generally remained stable, without an increase in problems popularly associated with the drugs in question. Equally notable, the quite high usage rates in the United States persist, despite some of the harshest penalties in the world. Looking with an open mind at alternative systems should help dispel the fear that any change to current policies will lead to catastrophe.

The hope that the governments of the United States and Mexico will act on these recommendations is profound. The expectation that they will do so is modest. An observer with deep ties and personal experience in both the United States and Mexico compared the conflict among the cartels and between the cartels and the government to a sporting event. Spectators in both the government and the public may keep score as individual contests are won or lost and as teams move up or down in the standings, but regardless of the treasure expended and the damage done, drugs will still be desired, provided, and sold. And as long as societies and their governments treat drug use as a crime rather than as a matter of public health, the deadly game will continue, season after season.

Notes

1. In addition to cited sources, along with many other published books and articles, I have benefited from continuing dialogue with Tony Payan, Baker Institute Scholar for Immigration and Border Studies; Nathan Jones, Alfred C. Glassell III Postdoctoral Fellow in Drug Policy; and retired U.S. Drug Enforcement Administration intelligence chief Gary J. Hale, now head of the Grupo Savant think tank and a nonresident Fellow for Drug Policy at Rice University's Baker Institute; and from interviews, mostly on condition of anonymity, with present and former agents of the DEA, the National Drug Intelligence Center, the Federal Bureau of Investigation (FBI), and the U.S. Border Patrol (USBP). These people are referred to in this chapter as "observers" or "sources." I have recordings of all these interviews. I also freely acknowledge an obvious debt to Ken Ellingwood and Tracy Wilkinson and their colleagues at the *Los Angeles Times* for their long-running series "Mexico under Siege," which provides an excellent chronological account and analysis of the ongoing conflict.

2. I use the term "cartel" in the familiar sense, meaning large, recognizably distinct drug-trafficking organizations, which may themselves constitute a network of organizations that cooperate in criminal activity. Though the term may have been somewhat apt in Félix Gallardo's day, it no longer describes the situation. The Mexican drug-trafficking organizations do not collude to set prices, rig bids, allocate market share, regulate total industry output, or otherwise reduce competition. When they coexist in relative peace, it may well be because one has triumphed over the other or both have grown exhausted from the battle for supremacy. That said, "cartel" has gained such currency in the popular parlance as to render the fight for linguistic precision rather pointless. It also works well in titles.

3. 1 to 4 percent estimate, DEA speaker at Rice University's Baker Institute program, July 8, 2011.

4. I was led to this research note and the speculation regarding a *June surprise* by Ken Ellingwood, "Mexico Drug Lord's Fate Is Focus of Election Year Speculation," *Los Angeles Times*, March 12, 2012. http://articles.latimes.com/2012/mar/12/world/la-fg-mexico-politics-chapo-20120313. Accessed September 24, 2012.

Bibliography

ABC News. 2012. "U.S. Journalist Disappears in Mexico Drug Cartel Stronghold." June 26. http://abcnews.go.com/Blotter/us-journalist-disappears-mexico-drug-cartel-stronghold/story?id=16645695#.UE6b-6Se7Co. Accessed September 24, 2012.

Althaus, Dudley, and Dane Schiller. 2012. "Is 'El Chapo' Back in Border City of Nuevo Laredo?" *Houston Chronicle: Narco Confidential Blog*, April 18. http://blog.chron.com/narcoconfidential/2012/04/with-butchery-and-a-warning-is-mexicos-el-chapo-back-in-border-city-of-nuevo-laredo/. Accessed September 24, 2012.

Archibold, Randal C. 2009. "Hired By Customs, but Working for Mexican Cartels." *New York Times*, December 17.

———. 2010. "Mexico Paper, a Drug War Victim, Calls for a Voice." *New York Times,* September 20. http://www.nytimes.com/2010/09/21/world/americas/21mexico.html ?_r=2&scp=1&sq=juarez&st=cse. Accessed September 24, 2012.

———. 2012a. "Mexico: Former Defense Officials Are Accused of Aiding Traffickers." *New York Times,* August 1. http://www.nytimes.com/2012/08/02/world/americas /mexico-former-defense-officials-are-accused-of-aiding-traffickers.html. Accessed September 24, 2012.

———. 2012b. "Mexico Holds 4 High-Ranking Army Officers." *New York Times,* May 18. http://www.nytimes.com/2012/05/19/world/americas/mexico-detains-3-gener als-tied-to-drug-cartel.html?_r=1&pagewanted=all. Accessed September 24, 2012.

Arsenault, Chris. 2010. "U.S.-Trained Cartel Terrorises Mexico." *Al-Jazeera,* November 2. http://www.aljazeera.com/indepth/features/2010/10/20101019212440609775 .html. Accessed September 24, 2012.

BBC News. 2012. "Mexico Drug Wars: Murders Down in Ciudad Juárez, Latin America & Caribbean." February 17. http://www.bbc.co.uk/news/world-latin-america -17082002. Accessed October 24, 2012.

Bonner, Robert C. 2010. "The New Cocaine Cowboys." *Foreign Affairs* (July–August): 35–47.

Booth, William, and Nick Miroff. 2010. "Stepped-Up Efforts by U.S., Mexico Fail to Stem Flow of Drug Money South." *Washington Post,* August 25. http://www.wash ingtonpost.com/wp-dyn/content/article/2010/08/25/AR2010082506161.html ?sid=ST2010083004208. Accessed September 24, 2012.

Borderland Beat. 2012a. "Heriberto Lazcano, R.I.P." http://www.borderlandbeat.com /2012/02/heriberto-lazcano-lazcano-rip.html. Accessed September 24, 2012.

———. 2012b. "Zeta Magazine Says True Drug War Death Toll is 100K Plus." http:// www.borderlandbeat.com/2012/06/zeta-magazine-says-true-drugwar-death.html. Accessed September 24, 2012.

Bowden, Charles, and Molly Molloy. 2012. "Mexicans Pay in Blood for America's War on Drugs." *Phoenix New Times,* July 26. http://www.phoenixnewtimes.com/2012 -07-26/news/mexicans-pay-in-blood-for-america-s-war-on-drugs/6/. Accessed September 24, 2012.

Camp, Roderic Ai. 2009. "Drugs, Guns and Money: A Violent Struggle across the Border." *San Diego Union-Tribune,* March 15.

Carlyla, Erin. 2012. "Attention, Billionaire Druglords: Mexico's People Want to End Calderón's War on Drugs." *Forbes,* July 2. http://www.forbes.com/sites/erincarlyle /2012/07/02/attention-billionaire-druglords-mexicos-people-want-to-end-the -bloody-war-on-drugs/. Accessed September 24, 2012.

Carrasco, J., and J. Esquivel. 2012. "Tiene EU plan para terminar con El Chapo como lo hizo con Obama." *Proceso* 1867, August 11. http://www.proceso.com.mx /?p=316815. Accessed September 24, 2012.

Castañeda, Jorge. 2010. "What's Spanish for Quagmire: Five Myths That Caused the Failed War Next Door." *Foreign Policy* (January–February).

Conroy, Bill. 2011. "Zambada Niebla Case Exposes U.S. Drug War Quid Pro Quo." *Narcosphere,* December 10. http://narcosphere.narconews.com/notebook/bill -conroy/2011/12/zambada-niebla-case-exposes-us-drug-war-quid-pro-quo. Accessed September 24, 2012.

———. 2012a. "Specially Trained Troops Conducted 'Surgical' Strikes on Narco-Trafficking Cells, Gangs and Addicts." *Narco News*, September 17. http://narcosphere .narconews.com/notebook/bill-conroy/2012/09/mexican-special-forces-employed -death-squads-drug-war-email-records-rel. Accessed September 24, 2012.

———. 2012b. "U.S., Mexican Officials Brokering Deals with Drug 'Cartels,' WikiLeaks Documents Show." *Narco News Bulletin*, August 20. http://www .narconews.com/Issue67/article4621.html. Accessed September 24, 2012.

Cook, Colleen W. 2007. "Mexico's Drug Cartels." *Congressional Research Service Report for Congress*. October 16. http://www.fas.org/sgp/crs/row/RL34215.pdf. Accessed October 22, 2012.

Daily Mail. 2012. "Is the U.S. Sending Seal Team Six to Capture Top Drug Cartel Kingpin?" August 14. www.dailymail.co.uk—Is-U-S-sending-Seal-Team-Six-cap ture-drug-cartel-kingpin-American-military-plotting-military-operation-similar -bin-Laden-mission.html. Accessed September 24, 2012.

Daly, Catherine, Kimberly Heinle, and David A. Shirk. 2012. "Armed with Impunity: Curbing Military Human Rights Abuses." Trans-Border Institute. http://justicein mexico.files.wordpress.com/2012/07/12_07_31_armed-with-impunity.pdf. Accessed September 24, 2012.

Economist. 2009a. "A Toker's Guide." *Economist*, March 5. http://www.economist .com/node/13234134. Accessed October 22, 2012.

———. 2009b. "Levels of Prohibition: A Toker's Guide." *Economist*, March 15. http:// www.economist.com/displaystory.cfm?STORY_ID=13234134. Accessed September 24, 2012.

Ellingwood, Ken. 2009. "12 Slain in Mexico Were Federal Police Officers." *Los Angeles Times*, July 15.

———. 2010a. "At Least 140 Escape Prison in Nuevo Laredo." *Los Angeles Times*, December 17.

———. 2010b. "Cancun Mayor's Arrest Adds to Mexico Worries." *Los Angeles Times*, May 27. http://articles.latimes.com/2010/may/27/world/la-fg-mexico-cancun-20100527. Accessed September 24, 2012.

———. 2011. "Mexico Immigration Agency Fires Top Officials after Reports of Collusion with Kidnappers." *Los Angeles Times*, May 12. http://articles.latimes.com /2011/may/12/world/la-fg-mexico-migrants-20110513. Accessed September 24, 2012.

Ellingwood, Ken and Tracy Wilkinson. 2009. "Drug offensive stirs 'wasps nest.'" *Los Angeles Times*. July 13. http://www.latimes.com/news/nationworld/world/la-fg -mexico-drugwar13-2009jul13,0,1796109.story. Accessed September 24, 2012.

———. 2011. "Mexico Seeks to Fill Drug War Gap with Focus on Dirty Money." *Los Angeles Times*, November 27. http://articles.latimes.com/2011/nov/27/world/la-fg -mexico-money-laundering-20111127. Accessed September 24, 2012.

The Fund for Peace. 2012. "Failed States Index." http://library.fundforpeace.org/fsi12. Accessed October 22, 2012.

Global Commission on Drug Policy. 2011. "War on Drugs: Report of the Global Commission on Drug Policy." http://www.globalcommissionondrugs.org/wp -content/themes/gcdp_vl/pdf/Global_Commission_Report_English.pdf. Accessed September 24, 2012.

Grayson, George. 2012. "Foreign Policy Research Institute E-Notes, March." http://www.fpri.org/enotes/2012/201203.grayson.calderonshailmary.html. Accessed September 24, 2012.

Grillo, Ioan. 2011. *El Narco*. New York: Bloomsbury Press.

———. 2012. "Special Report: Mexico's Zetas Rewrite Drug War in Blood." Reuters, May 13. http://www.reuters.com/article/2012/05/23/us-mexico-drugs-zetas-idU.S.BRE84M0LT20120523. Accessed October 23, 2012.

Huffington Post. 2012. "Mexican Drug Cartel Laundered Money through BofA, FBI Alleges." September 7. http://www.huffingtonpost.com/2012/07/09/los-zetas-laundered-money-bank-america_n_1658943.html. Accessed September 24, 2012.

International Press Institute. 2012. "Deadly Trends for Journalists in 2011, 103 killed." IPI, January 4. http://www.freemedia.at/regions/americas-caribbean/singleview/article/new-deadly-trends-for-journalists-in-2011-103-killed.html. Accessed September 24, 2012.

Johnson, Tim. 2011. "Do U.S., Mexican Officials Favor One Cartel over Another?" *Miami Herald*, August 8. http://www.miamiherald.com/2011/08/23/v-fullstory/2371828/do-us-mexican-officials-favor.html#ixzz1VxRhVlOl. Accessed September 24, 2012.

Jones, Nathan. 2012a. "Gulf Cartel Will Likely Survive Arrest of High-Level Leaders." *Houston Chronicle Baker Blog*, September 14. http://blog.chron.com/bakerblog/2012/09/gulf-cartel-will-likely-survive-arrest-of-high-level-leaders/. Accessed September 24, 2012.

———. 2012b. "Tijuana Cartel Survives, Despite Decade-Long Onslaught." *InSight Crime*, June 19. http://www.insightcrime.org/investigations/tijuana-cartel-survives-despite-decade-long-onslaught. Accessed September 24, 2012.

———. 2012c. "Tijuana's New Calm Shows Benefits of Local Policing in Mexico." *InSight Crime*, May 24. http://www.insightcrime.org/news-analysis/tijuanas-new-calm-shows-benefits-of-local-policing-in-mexico. Accessed September 24, 2012.

Keefe, Patrick Radden. 2012. "Cocaine Incorporated." *New York Times*, June 15, 40, 42, 43.

Koughan, Frank. 2009. "U.S. Trained Death Squads?" *Mother Jones* 34, no. 4 (2009): 31.

Landler, Mark. 2009. "Clinton Says U.S. Feeds Mexico Drug Trade." *New York Times*, March 25. http://www.nytimes.com/2009/03/26/world/americas/26mexico.html?_r=0. Accessed September 24, 2012.

Latin American Commission on Drugs and Democracy of the Open Society Institute. 2009. *Drugs and Democracy: Toward a Paradigm Shift*. Statement by the Latin American Commission on Drugs and Democracy, Open Society Institute, February 2009.

Longmire, Sylvia. 2011. *Cartel: The Coming Invasion of Mexico's Drug Wars*. New York: Palgrave.

Los Angeles Times. 2008. "Mexico under Siege." June 3, 11; July 13.

———. 2009. "Mexico under Siege." March 26; April 4; May 29.

———. 2010. "Mexico under Siege." July 1.

Marosi, Richard. 2009. "U.S. indictments target Mexico's Gulf cartels." *Los Angeles Times*. July 21. http://www.latimes.com/news/nationworld/nation/la-na-mexico-drug-war21-2009jul21,0,1531532.story. Accessed September 24, 2012.

Milenio. 2012. "Caballeros Templarios ofrece tregua por visita del Papa." September 24. http://www.milenio.com/cdb/doc/impreso/9131321. Accessed September 24, 2012.

Miller Llana, Sara. 2010. "Mexico Captures 'El Teo,' Top Drug Trafficker in Tijuana." *Christian Science Monitor,* January 12. http://www.csmonitor.com/World/2010/0112/Mexico-captures-El-Teo-top-drug-trafficker-in-Tijuana. Accessed September 24, 2012.

Molloy, Molly. 2008. "Massacre at CIAD #8 in Juarez. Masked Gunmen Unleash AK-47s on Drug-Rehab Center; Mexican Soldiers Parked 50 Yards Away Do Nothing." *Narco News Bulletin,* August 18. http://www.narconews.com/Issue54/article3181.html. Accessed September 24, 2012.

———. 2012. "Mexican Death Toll in Drug War Likely Higher Than Reported." *Phoenix New Times,* July 26. http://www.phoenixnewtimes.com/2012-07-26/news/mexico-s-unknown-drug-war-death-toll/P. Accessed September 24, 2012.

Napolitano, Janet. 2009. "Napolitano Promises More Agents at San Diego Check Points." In "Mexico under Siege." *Los Angeles Times,* April 2.

Olson, Eric. 2012. "Considering New Strategies for Confronting Organized Crime in Mexico." March 8. Mexico Institute of the Woodrow Wilson International Center for Scholars. http://wilsoncenter.org/sites/default/files/Newpercent20Strategies_1.pdf. Accessed September 24, 2012.

O'Neil, Shannon. 2012. "Human Rights and the Mexican Military." CNN *Global Public Square Blogs,* August 22. http://globalpublicsquare.blogs.cnn.com/2012/08/22/human-rights-and-the-mexican-military/. Accessed September 24, 2012.

Pachico, Elyssa. 2012. "Mexican Govt Stops Publishing Data on Crime-Related Deaths." *InSight Crime,* August 16. http://www.insightcrime.org/news-analysis/mexican-govt-stops-publishing-data-on-crime-related-deaths. Accessed September 24, 2012.

Padgett, Tim. 2011. "Mexico's Fearsom La Familia: Eerily Quiet." *TIMEWorld,* January 31. http://www.time.com/time/world/article/0,8599,2044696,00.html. Accessed September 24, 2012.

———. 2012. "Peña Nieto Tells TIME: I Want to Make Mexico an Emerging Power Again." *TIMEWorld,* July 9. http://world.time.com/2012/07/09/pena-nieto-tells-time-i-want-to-make-mexico-an-emerging-power-again/?xid=rss-topstories. Accessed September 24, 2012.

Payan, Tony. 2012. "Recycling a Failed Idea in Mexico." *Baker Institute Blog. Houston Chronicle,* July 27. http://blog.chron.com/bakerblog/2012/07/recycling-a-failed-idea-in-mexico/. Accessed September 24, 2012.

Pew Research Center. 2012. "Mexicans Back Military Campaigns against Cartels." *Pew Global Attitudes Project,* June 20. http://www.pewglobal.org/2012/06/20/mexicans-back-military-campaign-against-cartels/. Accessed September 24, 2012.

Pimentel, Stanley A. 2000. "The Nexus of Organized Crime and Politics in Mexico." In *Organized Crime and Democratic Governability: Mexico and the U.S.–Mexican Borderlands,* edited by John J. Bailey and Roy Godson. Pittsburgh, PA: University of Pittsburgh Press.

Rodríguez, Olga R. 2012. "Mexico: Purported Gulf Drug Cartel Leader Caught." *USA Today,* September 13. http://www.usatoday.com/news/world/story/2012/09/13/mexico-purported-gulf-drug-cartel-leader-caught/57772160/1. Accessed September 24, 2012.

Roston, Aram. 2012. "Tinker Tailor Soldier Kingpin." *Daily Beast/Newsweek*, January 30. http://www.thedailybeast.com/newsweek/2012/01/29/el-chapo-guzm-n-mexico -s-most-powerful-drug-lord.html. Accessed September 24, 2012.

Seminal. 2009. "Is the Mexican Army the Biggest Cartel of All?" *Seminal*, August 10.

Smith, Michael. 2010. "Banks Financing Mexico Gangs Admitted in Wells Fargo Deal." *Bloomberg*, June 28. http://www.bloomberg.com/news/2010-06-29/banks-financing -mexico-s-drug-cartels-admitted-in-wells-fargo-s-u-s-deal.html. Accessed September 24, 2012.

Stevenson, Mark. 2010. "Mexican Drug Cartel Inmates Let Out of Prison." *Globe and Mail*, July 26. http://www.theglobeandmail.com/news/world/americas/mexicandrug cartelinmatesletoutofprisontocarryoutassassinationmissions/article1651693/. Accessed September 24, 2012.

Stop the Drug War. n.d. "This Week's Corrupt Cop Stories." Electronic document series. http://stopthedrugwar.org. Accessed September 24, 2012.

Thompson, Ginger. 2012. "A Drug Family in the Winner's Circle." *New York Times*, June 12. http://www.nytimes.com/2012/06/13/us/drug-money-from-mexico-makes -its-way-to-the-racetrack.html?_r=1&hp. Accessed September 24, 2012.

U.S. Department of Justice. 2010. "Cardenas-Guillén Sentenced to 25 Years' Imprisonment." News release, February 24. http://www.bop.gov/iloc2/LocateInmate.jsp. Accessed September 24, 2012.

U.S. Department of Transportation. "Border Crossing/Entry Data Border Crossing/ Entry Data." http://www.bts.gov/programs/international/transborder/TBDR_BC/ TBDR_BCQ.html. Accessed September 24, 2012.

U.S. Senate. 2012. "U.S. Vulnerabilities to Money Laundering, Drugs, and Terrorist Financing: HSBC Case History." Homeland Security & Governmental Affairs Permanent Subcommittee Investigations, July 17. http://www.gpo.gov/fd sys/pkg/CHRG-112shrg76061/html/CHRG-112shrg76061.htm. Accessed April 11, 2013.

U.S. Treasury. 2012. "U.S. Treasury Maintains a List of More Than 200 Mexican Businesses It Believes Engage in Money Laundering for the Drug Traffickers." http://www.treasury.gov/ofac/downloads/ctrylst.txt. Accessed September 24, 2012.

Villalba, Oscar, et al. 2012. "Mexico Suspects Zetas Cartel behind Prison Break." *AP, Houston Chronicle*, September 18. http://www.chron.com/news/article/Mexico -suspects-Zetas-cartel-behind-prison-break-3875543.php. Accessed September 24, 2012.

Vulliamy, Ed. 2011. "How a Big US Bank Laundered Billions from Mexico's Murderous Drug Gangs." *Guardian*, April 2. http://www.guardian.co.uk/world/2011/apr /03/us-bank-mexico-drug-gangs. Accessed April 11, 2013.

Wikipedia. 2012. "List of Mexico's 37 Most Wanted Drug Lords." http://en.wikipedia .org/wiki/List_of_Mexico<#213>s_37_most-wanted_drug_lords. Accessed September 24, 2012.

Wilkinson, Tracy. 2008. "In Sinaloa, the Drug Trade Has Infiltrated 'Every Corner of Life.'" In "Mexico under Siege." *Los Angeles Times*, December 28. http://www .latimes.com/news/nationworld/world/la-fg-mexico-drugwar28-2008dec28,0 ,6322674.story. Accessed October 22, 2012.

———. 2010. "Mexico Drug Kingpin Slain in Fierce Gun Battle with Military." *Los Angeles Times*, November 6. http://articles.latimes.com/2010/nov/06/world/la-fg-mexico-druglord-20101106. Accessed September 24, 2012.

———. 2011. "Calderón Replaces Mexico Attorney General." *Los Angeles Times*, April 1. http://articles.latimes.com/2011/mar/31/world/la-fg-mexico-attorney-general-20110401. Accessed September 24, 2012.

———. 2012. "Mexico Cartel Attacks on Press Take Toll on Drug War Coverage." *Los Angeles Times*, July 22. http://www.latimes.com/news/nationworld/world/la-fg-mexico-press-20120724,0,990064.story. Accessed September 24, 2012.

Wilkinson, Tracy, and Ken Ellingwood. 2012. "Mexico Drug Cartels Thrive Despite Calderón's Offensive." *Los Angeles Times*, August 8. http://articles.latimes.com/2010/aug/08/world/la-fg-mexico-cartels-20100808. Accessed September 24, 2012.

Winter, Michael. 2012. "2 Well-Built Drug Tunnels from Mexico Uncovered." *USA Today*, July 12. http://content.usatoday.com/communities/ondeadline/post/2012/07/2-well-built-cross-border-drug-tunnels-uncovered/1#.UEpbO2ie7Co. Accessed September 24, 2013.

CHAPTER TWO

President Felipe Calderón's Strategy to Combat Organized Crime[1]

Marcos Pablo Moloeznik

Organized Crime: Highest Threat to Mexico's National Security

To understand criminal patterns in Mexico, it is crucial to acknowledge the importance of its geographic position as a neighbor of the United States. Mexico shares a land border of two thousand miles with the United States, an ideal geographical position for criminal groups to operate powerful transnational networks. At the same time, Mexico is a bi-oceanic country, a geopolitical position that is also important in understanding criminal activity, since these vast maritime borders with the United States are an increasingly favored area of operations for criminal organizations. The Mexican Navy Sector Program acknowledges that security at sea is threatened by illicit activities perpetrated mainly by organized crime, such as drug, human and firearms trafficking, piracy, and even sabotage activities committed by subversive groups (Department of the Navy 2008). If geography is destiny, these observations are relevant because the United States is not only the world's foremost economic and military power but also the largest consumer market of illegal narcotics and psychotropic substances and a major destination of many undocumented migrants. Add to this the fact that Mexico borders Central America, a cluster of developing nations with similar, and perhaps worse, social and economic problems as Mexico, including migration, poverty, unemployment, and illegal human trafficking, as well as narcotrafficking and other forms of organized crime. Thus Mexico's geographic location between the

United States and Central America makes more evident the reasons the country requires heightened attention when it comes to security issues, particularly when it comes to transnational organized crime. In sum, these geopolitical considerations and socioeconomic development conditions in and around Mexico, which make the country a natural corridor for transnational organized crime, particularly drug trafficking, have to be considered carefully in analyzing and fighting trends in organized crime.

Another important variable when analyzing criminal patterns in Mexico is the reliability of the data. Mexican official data show that approximately 1.5 million crimes are committed every year. However, according to the National Survey on Insecurity (*Encuestas Nacionales sobre Inseguridad*—ENSI), the figure is closer to 4.5 million crimes annually, which means that most crimes (3 million per year) are not reported to the authorities at all. This figure is often referred to as "the black number" Citizenry Institute on Insecurity Studies. Although the Calderón administration has presided over an increase in the number of reported crimes, we still do not know exactly how many crimes go unreported. On the upside, greater reporting brings about greater transparency and accountability. On the downside, the increase in reported crime has made an impact on Mexican society because it creates a sense of panic, as has been the case with crime related to drug trafficking, which falls under the federal government's responsibility and which has had broad coverage by the media (Calderón 2006). But what has risen faster, the number of crimes being committed or the percentage of crimes being reported? We know that during the Calderón administration, executions rose dramatically. In Mexico there were an estimated sixty thousand executions between December 1, 2006, and December 31, 2011—although some put the number at closer to one hundred thousand murders if the year 2012 is included. Still, while the number of deaths is increasingly being debated, there is a broader consensus that these murders are generally related to the settlement of accounts among criminals, a phenomenon known as "narco-violence," which was quite visible in the Calderón administration. Table 2.1 illustrates the dramatic rise in the level of violence in Mexico during the Calderón administration.

It is important to point out that there are no reliable procedures to determine the exact number of casualties in the war on drugs. In fact, nongovernmental organizations present different figures, from sixty thousand to eighty thousand and beyond, depending on the source. Most of these numbers are, in any event, produced by media outlets or by academics re-

Table 2.1. Deaths from organized crime

Fox Administration	2001	2002	2003	2004	2005	2006
	1,080	1,230	1,290	1,304	1,776	2,221
Calderón Administration	2007	2008	2009	2010	2011	2012
	2,826	6,838	9,614	15,273	12,903	Not available

Source: Adapted from information from the Mexican Attorney General's Office (Procuraduría General de la República) and the Report on the Anti-Crime Battle, March 2010: http://www.pgr .gob.mx; http://www.eluniversal.com.mx/nacion/192833.html; http://www.eluniversal.com.mx /notas/822078.html.

lying on information presented by the media. The "most reliable" source is the one produced by forensic services throughout the country. However, even these numbers are not accurate, as they only indicate the cause of death but not the possible link with organized crime activities. For these reasons, our table relies on data produced by the government, even if they must also be taken with a grain of salt.

While the dust settles and we consider the key variables influencing crime trends in Mexico, one thing is certain: During the two PAN-led administrations in Mexico (2000–2012), transnational organized crime became a serious threat to Mexican national security, reaching levels that threatened the Mexican state's own stability and even its integrity. Non-governmental actors, specifically organized criminal groups, are challenging the state for territorial control and have attained control of certain public spaces that are now beyond the control of the Mexican government. How did Mexico get to that point?

Explaining Mexico's Levels of Violence: The Past as Prologue

Just as there are key variables to consider in analyzing Mexico's trends in organized crime, there are also four main factors that explain the increase in the levels of violence in Mexico (Moloeznik 2006). One is the failure of Mexico's security policies during the Vicente Fox administration (2000–2006). A second factor is the conscious choice to militarize the government's response to organized crime. A third factor is the clashes among the different organized criminal groups as they fight for territorial control. And, finally, there are the actions of a specific criminal group, Los Zetas, which will be analyzed separately later in this chapter. Among these factors, a major cause of the increase in violence has been the conflict between criminal groups, particularly those based on drug trafficking. In fact, even President Calderón recognizes this:

> Narcotrafficking bands are fighting over control of territories and cities, which has provoked an increase in the number of executions. For example, during the first years of this decade, there was a battle between the Sinaloa Cartel and the Gulf-Zetas Cartel for control of the country's northeast. Thus, more than a "war of the government against narcotrafficking," the most lethal war is the one being fought by the criminal gangs among themselves. In general, the government can reasonably obtain leads on the causes of the homicides committed in 70 percent of the cases. Approximately 90 percent of these homicide cases have some clue of their cause, which corresponds to persons very probably linked to criminal organizations, showing that these individuals are killed during shootouts or executions between rival criminal bands. In the clash for control of territory, violent homicides occur, such as decapitations, collective executions or torture; and vendettas are generated that, again, produce another slew of executions and an even greater level of violence. (Calderón 2006)

It is noteworthy that many of these criminals were military personnel recruited from the army by organized criminal groups. The number of deserters during the Vicente Fox administration (2000–2006) was considerable. The personnel turnover in the Department of National Defense (Secretaría de la Defensa Nacional–SEDENA) is shown in table 2.2. To understand the dimensions of this problem, it should be noted that SEDENA has 191,143 military personnel.

Moreover, according to Calderón's last State of the Union address, delivered on September 1, 2012, from December 2006 until June 2012 there were 43,827 desertion cases within SEDENA, while in the Department of the Navy (Secretaría de la Marina–SEMAR), from January 2007 until June 2012, 4,660 members had been fired because they were absent from their posts for three days without justification (Presidencia de la República 2012). Even if during the Calderón administration the number of deserters from the armed forces was reduced in relation to the previous administration, the fact that there are still more than 44,000 cases is an unacceptable situation and clearly reflects a structural problem within the armed forces to keep their personnel.

Table 2.2. Army desertions during the Vicente Fox administration, 2000–2006

Rank	Number of deserters
Colonels	1
Lieutenant Colonels	9
Majors	38
Captains (First Grade)	50
Captains (Second Grade)	49
Lieutenants	459
Sublieutenants	782
Sergeants (First Grade)	354
Sergeants (Second Grade)	2,239
Corporals	9,919
Soldiers	109,318
Total	123,218

Source: Response to a request filed on February 19, 2007, before the Federal Institute for the Access to Public Information (Instituto Federal de Acceso a la Información Pública–IFAI), Request Number 0000700030907, received on March 4, 2007.

This represents a fairly high degree of institutional disintegration, which necessarily implies a risk of corruption. Many of the so-called Zetas were deserters from the Mexican Army's Special Forces' Air-mobile and Amphibious Groups (abbreviated as GAFE and GANFE, respectively) and the Paratrooper Brigade, both components of elite forces, trained in antidrug and antiterrorist operations (many of them trained in the United States). Thus many Zetas can handle sophisticated communications equipment, weapons systems, and intelligence techniques. Some of the unusual levels of violence in various regions of Mexico since the first few months of 2007 were perpetrated by these former military, something not often acknowledged by public officials. Thus

the structural disintegration that this phenomenon implies and its consequences for the integrity of the overall [antidrug] strategy . . . were the object of institutional silence . . . [but] the official handling of this sobering fact has been rather erratic. The authorities have admitted to the problem because of internal pressure from non-governmental human rights organizations, the media, etc., and external pressure from U.S. human rights organizations and the U.S. government . . . [but] the Mexican government's response has been rather scant and inadequate. (Tirado 2006)

Table 2.3. Drug traffickers arrested between December 2000 and July 2006

Categories	Arellano Félix	Carrillo Fuentes	Amezcua Contreras	Palma Guzmán	Osiel Cárdenas	Díaz Parada	Luis Valencia	Total
Leaders	2	7	1	1	3	0	1	15
Financiers	5	26	1	7	10	1	3	53
Territorial Leaders	12	26	1	8	19	1	5	73
Hit Men	96	66	2	84	120	6	15	389
Government Officials Involved	37	53	2	30	57	2	9	190
Collaborators and Retail Distributors	16,794	17,955	6,886	14,717	10,410	3,469	3,764	73,995
Total	16,946	18,133	6,894	14,847	10,619	3,479	3,797	74,715

Source: Mexican Attorney General's Office (Procuraduría General de la República), http://www.pgr.gob.mx/.

Given this, it is appropriate to consider the legacy of the Vicente Fox administration on security as a failure. Nevertheless, in his last address to the National Congress, the former president praised his administration's results in combating drug trafficking, particularly in regard to the arrests of members of the seven drug cartels targeted by the Mexican attorney general's office. Table 2.3 shows these numbers.

In spite of former President Fox's claims, table 2.3 shows that the Mexican federal government failed, since it arrested only fifteen leaders, out of dozens or even hundreds of them, managing an estimated total of 74,715 drug traffickers. Perhaps the worst mistake of the Vicente Fox administration was to disband the National Investigation and Security Center (Centro de Investigación y Seguridad Nacional—CISEN). During Calderón's First State of the Union address, Francisco Javier Ramírez Acuña, secretary of the interior, asserted that during the Vicente Fox administration, one thousand positions were eliminated from CISEN; that there was no investment in technology to detect groups such as the Popular Revolutionary Army (EPR); and that the budget for CISEN was cut back. He stated that he had received a crumbling CISEN, with "unclear" conditions to carry out its intelligence work. Rightfully, some Calderón officials blame the previous administration for the prevailing security situation in Mexico, arguing that this is something they inherited. In light of this, and from almost any perspective, the Vicente Fox administration's strategy failed to alter the landscape of organized crime in Mexico.

In contrast, official sources state that between December 2006 and March 2010, 121,199 individuals linked to organized crime were arrested. Of these, 27 percent were members of the Gulf and Zetas Cartels, and 24 percent were from the Pacific and Sinaloa Cartels. Next on the list were members of the Juárez Cartel, with 17 percent; the Beltrán Leyva Cartel, with 14 percent; and the Arellano Félix/Tijuana Cartel, with 13 percent. The Calderón administration claims that in 2009 alone, seventy leaders of all the cartels were captured, that is, during that year more regional capos were arrested than the total number of drug traffickers captured during the six years of the Vicente Fox administration. It is worth pointing out that the intelligence agenda for Mexico's national security (Centro de Investigación y Seguridad Nacional [CISEN] 2011) lists, among others, the following threats: (1) armed groups; (2) organized criminal groups; (3) terrorism; (4) transition and state reform; (5) social movements; (6) environmental threats; and (7) public safety. In light of the complexity of the Mexican intelligence agenda and the challenge to the country's security, the Calderón administration acknowledges that

> it is necessary to articulate a system of information for the exchange, in real time, of audio, video and text data on crime, criminal statistics and public safety personnel registration. Unfortunately, Mexico does not yet possess such systems at the national level and among the different levels of government. (National Development Plan 2007–2012 2007)

Thus Calderón inherits an intelligence system, conceived to protect democracy and the rule of law, in shambles. Unfortunately, this is not new. The history of intelligence agencies and services in Mexico is one of failure, although this happens everywhere. Thus a key question is whether Mexico's intelligence services, specifically the CISEN, constitute an obstacle to success rather than an asset toward it. The Vicente Fox administration weakened it and rendered it unable to even detect any risks and, consequently, incapable of intervening opportunely when threats to national security were detected (García Luna 2007). The CISEN was dismantled and neutralized, according to Francisco Ramírez Acuña, and its remains were used to create the Preventive Federal Police (PFP) and the Federal Investigations Agency (AFI). But, in any event, it is not clear that it was very effective prior to President Fox dismantling it. Still, security, particularly vis-à-vis organized criminal groups, as a matter of public policy, under the responsibility of President Fox, can be characterized as a failure (Peón 2007).

Mexico's Public Safety Failure: Power Fragmentation and Underdevelopment

The democratization process in Mexico has left intergovernmental coordination in shambles as well. The Calderón government acknowledges the following:

> Coordination among the three levels of government, in the framework of the National Public Security System, has not reached the expected results because respect for local government autonomy has . . . [become an obstacle] . . . to joint . . . action among the different layers of policing responsibility. The lack of . . . coordinating mechanisms among the

1,661 police departments that operate in Mexico has not allowed the channeling of available resources to fight crime as a single, coherent police force. This lack of coordination is also manifest in the absence of shared public safety policies and in the unequal development of policing abilities. . . . This situation has allowed crime, particularly organized crime, to invade . . . public spaces in certain regions of the country, creating a climate of violence and insecurity that on occasion has overtaken the local authorities and made evident the need for strengthening the coordination mechanisms among the three levels of government in order to reestablish basic security conditions. (Secretaría de Seguridad Pública 2007, 15)

President Calderón's remarks point to a general institutional underdevelopment in Mexico's police forces, a trait that opens them up to charges of incompetence, which in turn is perceived by the public as impunity. This ultimately results in the loss of trust in the institutions responsible to watch over the citizenry's public safety. Add to the prevailing, uneven economic and social development in the country and you have an explosive combination. As the president stated:

Criminal activity is not an isolated incident. It occurs in a social context characterized by a lack of opportunities and jobs due to social inequality, distrust in the authorities, the loss of public spaces, family and community disintegration, and family violence. In Mexico there is a serious crisis in terms of respect for the law. . . . [This] can be understood from two perspectives: First, there are cultural factors that hold back the people from seeing the Rule of Law as something socially useful and desirable; secondly, the country's institutions do not distribute benefits among the people in an equitable manner, which is why often it seems more profitable to act outside the law than to adhere to it. (Secretaría de Seguridad Pública 2007, 15)

Paradoxically, in a context of democratic transition, both Fox and Calderón opted for a *manu militari* kind of response to the lack of public safety and, thereby, may have contributed to human rights violations and may have fed a spiral of violence that took the country even further from the rule of law. If you add to this the clashes among organized criminal groups, Mexico turned into a war zone.

President Felipe Calderón's Strategy to Fight Organized Crime

Facing the growing influence of organized crime and rising levels of violence, both of which created a generalized perception of defenselessness among Mexicans, President Calderón stated:

> In facing organized crime's growth, we made the decision to confront it to stop the disintegration of the country's social and institutional life. The activities of these criminal organizations were spreading to all spheres of the nation's life and to all corners of the country. The options were very clear: To ignore the problem and simply manage it to try to avoid the costs of resolving it for good, which would have implied abandoning society to the hands of criminals, or to face it head on with the State's force and resolve it once and for all. (Calderón 2006)

In light of this, Mexico's president opted for the second choice and used the armed forces to do so. For the president, the main challenge consisted in taking back territories "conquered" by crime, especially drug cartels. He said the following in his first State of the Union address:

> Narcotrafficking is an illicit activity with very high profits, which generates high levels of violence and social fragmentation. Drug trafficking cartels constitute, without a doubt, the most powerful kind of organized crime, which, besides using Mexico as a drug corridor, seeks to transform it into a consumer country. That is why this government, as never before, is applying all of the State's force to recover the spaces that have been seized by narcotrafficking gangs and other criminal organizations and to prevent the possibility that the Mexican Republic turn into its hostage. (Presidencia de la República)

Thus Calderón's team designed two strategies for the recovery of public spaces. One was "Policing Operations," within the Integral Strategy for Preventing and Combating Crime, which prioritizes "the territorial recovery of public spaces for the community and the reestablishment of the minimal conditions for safety." Another was "Crime Prevention and Citizen Participation," acknowledged the importance of "recovering public spaces to promote the rehabilitation of these spaces for social interaction with freedom and safety." Calderón's intentions led to the establishment of a program titled "Let's Clean Mexico: Area in Recovery," which was launched in Guadalajara (García Luna 2007). This plan consisted of

> recovering public spaces . . . and giving them to those that are their legitimate owners: the citizens; and thereby contribute to preventing crime . . . to recover spaces . . . such as parks, city squares, gardens, sports fields, public streets, because the battle for public spaces is the battle for the right to live safely and peacefully. (Periódico Ocho Columnas 2007, B-1)

Similarly, Calderón bet on the rule of law:

> The progress of a nation is founded on effective justice sustained in the rule of law. Human development requires unrestricted respect for the law, because it is through the law's application that people can access better opportunities, participate freely and responsibly in democracy, and enjoy a safe life. No democratic State can become whole without the total vigilance of the rule of law. (Plan Nacional de Desarrollo)

From very early on, the Calderón administration declared war on drug cartels and determined that the use of the armed forces was the quickest route to defeat them (Moloeznik 2006). In the framework of the Integral Strategy for Crime Prevention and Combating Drug Trafficking, the Department of Public Safety, in coordination with the Ministry of Defense (SEDENA), the navy, and the attorney general's office, carried out six joint operations in nine states. During these operations, SEDENA engaged some 45,723 of its military personnel each month (Calderón 2006). Calderón committed the military to recovering the public spaces that the states had abandoned to organized crime. This, however, exposed the weaknesses of state and municipal authorities who had virtually abandoned certain territories to criminal groups. Surrendering public spaces to organized crime had already become a serious threat to national security and had overtaken the capabilities of local governments to do anything about it. These factors and the shortcomings of the policies on national security under Fox obliged the new administration in late 2006 to engage in a war without time limits against narcotrafficking, further adding that this fight could easily extend indefinitely. Even though exceptional problems require exceptional measures, deliberate planning should take into account all potential consequences. In hindsight, the Calderón administration may have acknowledged at some point that it was not possible to engage the military apparatus indefinitely in policing activities and that it was not prepared for all the risks involved, specifically the consequences of using the military to carry out policing duties. In fact, Calderón was right: doing so may have further eroded the rule of law. By 2009, the army was being called back from the streets.

Additionally, public resources are scarce, a situation that favors organized criminal groups. All criminal groups have to do is wait for the government's budget to run out, something that happens more quickly when the armed forces have been committed. In short, the participation of the armed forces in the drug war should probably have been more selective in time and space and, once specific objectives were accomplished, the soldiers should have returned to their military quarters. Add to this the stress on the armed forces. Any observer can see that the multiplicity of missions and functions entrusted to the Mexican armed forces, from the physical security of the president to undertaking policing activities to lending assistance during natural disasters and aiding social organizations, have strained the personnel. A corollary to this is the dispersion of its focus and a degree of inattention to its main missions, such as providing security to vital installations, fighting counterinsurgency, or fighting armed movements. Perhaps because of this, the army failed to prevent acts of sabotage on July 7 and September 10, 2007, against PEMEX installations and pipelines. Incidents occurred at distribution centers in Cadereyta (Nuevo León), Salamanca, Celaya, and Valle de Santiago (Guanajuato), Coroneo (Querétaro), La Antigua, Omealca, Minatitlán, La Balastrera and Actopan (Veracruz), and Delicias, in the municipality of Cuapiaxtla (Tlaxcala). The EPR claimed responsibility (García Luna 2007). The EPR made a qualitative leap, given that before these actions it had limited itself to sporadic attacks against police stations in the states of Guerrero and Oaxaca. SEDENA was unable to anticipate the EPR and thus was unable to prevent these attacks.

In view of the experience obtained and the lessons learned up to this point, President Calderón presented what is called the National Security Strategy, with five components:

To favor joint operations in support of the local authorities and citizens

To modernize the operational and technological capacity of the country's armed forces

To carry out legal and institutional reforms

To create a framework for a more proactive policy in crime prevention

To strengthen international and Inter-American cooperation

This was a strategic shift. President Calderón's initial strategy was based on the ubiquitous presence of the armed forces to increasingly challenge criminal groups on a frontal battle. That strategy was designed in fact to crush these groups with superior force. In other words, the initial strategy resorted to a central element of power: brute public force. This new strategy shifted to launching joint operations, in which the Federal Police (FP) and the armed forces are deployed to several regions of Mexico but with the objective of strengthening the hand of the local public authority and reestablishing minimal conditions of security and local stability. According to President Calderón:

> We had to deploy the federal forces in order to support local authorities . . . as I have repeatedly said, precisely in those places where the authorities were being threatened by the actions of criminal groups. It is at the request of the local governments that we have launched joint operations in several areas of the country, with the participation of the Federal Police, the armed forces and the attorney general's office, to support the local authorities and the people. (Calderón 2010)

The second component of the new National Security Strategy was cleaning out the FP and the general attorney's office and adopting new technology to carry out intelligence activities against organized crime. From this a new police model emerged, with the explicit acknowledgment that the work of combating organized crime was primordially a job for the police.

The Mexican Armed Forces: Redefining Their Role

Some ten years ago the United Nations carried out an analysis of Mexico's public safety, criminal justice, and human rights conditions. The organization presented several recommendations. Among them was "[t]o promote a progressive and reliable substitute of the military forces in public safety functions." This point, found in a chapter titled "Civil Rights," interprets the relationship between justice and the military as follows,

> The separation between the military and justice is a requirement in any democratic society. The risk of undue interference by the military in the justice system appears . . . in the prosecution of crimes related to drug trafficking. . . . This has been observed by the UN Special

Rapporteur on Extrajudicial Executions, which has recommended the Mexican government to avoid delegating to the military the fight against crime. (Office of the High Commissioner for Human Rights in Mexico 2003)

Similarly, the Inter-American Commission on Human Rights stated that it is fundamental to make a clear separation between the functions of the police and national defense as a function of the armed forces, as these institutions are substantially different in terms of the purposes for which they were created and as to their training and preparation.

Thus the active participation of the armed forces in public safety in Mexico has come under scrutiny before, and the claim that they are needed based on a presumed state of emergency has come to dominate the national political debate. In any event, there are many doubts surrounding the principles and the legal grounding for using the armed forces for policing duties. This is evidenced by the aftermath of their involvement. Between 2006 and 2009, there was a 1,000 percent increase in complaints against SEDENA for alleged violations of human rights (Department of National Defense [SEDENA] 2011). Whereas these complaints represented 3 percent of all citizen complaints filed with the National Ombudsman for Human Rights during the administration headed by Vicente Fox Quesada (2000–2006), they increased to represent 6 percent in 2007, 16 percent in 2008, and 33 percent in 2010. That means that of every three complaints received by the National Commission on Human Rights in 2010, one was filed against SEDENA. And while it is true that a complaint does not necessarily mean an actual violation of a human or due process right, there is some concern regarding these increases even within SEDENA, as well as in the navy (SEMAR). This is particularly worrisome, given that these complaints are often complaints of last resort and indicate gross violations of basic rights. Thus SEDENA received the most recommendations (twenty-two) by the Mexican human rights ombudsmen, with other government entities falling well below that number, according to a National Human Rights Commission Report in 2010: (1) SEDENA, 22; (2) Federal Department of Public Safety, 8; (3) Institute of Security and Social Services for State Employees, 8; (4) Oaxaca State Congress, 7; (5) Department of the Navy, 6; (6) Guerrero State Congress, 5; (7) Chihuahua State Government, 3; (8) Ministry of Health, 2; (9) Attorney General's Office, 2; (10) National Institute of Migration, 2.

But the military's role in public safety and security is never easy to resolve. Just as complaints against the armed forces were mounting, the Mexican

Supreme Court issued an opinion on Article 129 of the Constitution, which allowed for the inclusion of both SEDENA and the navy in the national Public Safety Council. According to the then chief justice of the Supreme Court, Mariano Azuela Güitrón, the participation of SEMAR and SEDENA on the council in 1995 is not unconstitutional. Hence, the Mexican military was ratified as an active participant in missions and functions that are often understood to be the sole jurisdiction of the police. The armed forces were effectively allowed to police, even when there was no state of emergency. But the Supreme Court established two conditions for the armed forces' participation in policing activities: (1) the involvement of the military must respond to a legitimate request by a political authority, for example, a governor or mayor, and (2) the armed forces, during policing activities, are always subordinate to political authority. In view of this, it should be noted that, in regard to (1), the military has intervened in policing activities always at the request of the state and local political authorities, and in regard to (2), the armed forces have not been held accountable for their actions to any political authority beyond the president himself. On the contrary, experience has shown that the military has been characterized by a high degree of autonomy. Thus, de facto, the direct involvement of the military in police missions and functions has severely affected the rule of law in Mexico.

A New Federal Police (FP)

President Calderón sought to rebuild the FP. Under his watch, there was an increase in the technical and operational capabilities of the FP, the number of officers grew considerably, and more advanced technology and better weaponry were introduced. The new FP also implemented a more rigorous personnel recruitment and selection process, part of which is the application of trustworthiness tests. In addition, the Mexican attorney general's office underwent a thorough reform. Mexican federal prosecutors were professionalized, and those who did not pass the trustworthiness tests were fired. The office launched Operation Cleanliness, and many officials were arrested for their links to organized crime. These changes have had a positive impact on the effective combat against crime.

Platform Mexico

A powerful high-tech tool is the Unified System of Criminal Information, a formidable criminal information database shared by federal, state, and municipal authorities. The Mexican government claims that the generation of actionable intelligence information has allowed it to dismantle many operational, logistical, and financial networks of criminal groups. Therefore, it is possible to conclude that an important component of fighting organized crime is having the information technologies that generate the intelligence needed to efficiently combat crime. This tool came to be known as Platform Mexico (*Plataforma México*), a complex, high-tech information system shared by the authorities of the thirty-one states of Mexico, the Federal District, and the 150 municipalities with the highest crime rates.

Strengthening the Armed Forces

The Calderón administration constantly sought to increase the budget for the armed forces with the objective of improving its operational conditions and equipment. At the same time, the salaries and benefits of its personnel have been increased as well, particularly at the lowest-paid levels. Other benefits also have been increased, such as larger mortgage credit lines for military personnel and a full scholarship grant system so that the children of soldiers can study at the public or private high school or university of their choice. At the same time, the administration implemented the Strategy for Strengthening, Training, and Updating the Capacities of the Armed Forces and for the Modernization of Its Equipment. The number of troops also increased by 6.3 percent from the beginning of the Calderón administration (2006–2012).

The contrast between the Vicente Fox and the Calderón administrations reaches into the navy as well. The personnel of the Mexican navy at the beginning of the Vicente Fox administration in 2000 totaled 55,223. At the end of his administration (2006), there were only 47,471 marines. In contrast, Calderón increased the number of marines within SEMAR by mid-2011 to 53,617, a figure similar to the navy's 2000 personnel level. In addition, the marines also faced a new challenge, which consisted in reorganizing their units to increase their presence in the coast guard in order to fight drug trafficking at sea. In a recent report, the Mexican govern-

Table 2.4. Mexican Armed forces resources

Year	Total	SEDENA	SEMAR
2000	237,552	182,329	55,228
2001	234,308	185,143	49,165
2002	238,169	188,143	50,026
2003	238,447	191,143	47,304
2004	238,459	191,143	47,316
2005	238,787	191,143	47,644
2006	244,238	196,767	47,471
2007	246,742	196,710	50,032
2008	254,035	202,355	51,680
2009	258,992	206,013	52,979
2010	259,237	206,013	53,224
2011	259,630	206,013	53,617

Source: SEDENA and SEMAR; Federal Government's Statistical Annex of the Fifth Report on Government, II. National Statistics, State Law and Security, page 81, at http://quinto.informe.gob.mx/informe-de-gobierno/anexo-statistic.

ment indicated that 78 percent of the equipment of the navy has been modernized. The reorganization helped generate synergy in the efforts of the federal government to combat organized crime and to support local authorities when required. The Mexican marines have in fact participated actively in pinprick operations against drug cartels, with a high degree of effectiveness (see table 2.4).

Overall, there has been a considerable increase in the active personnel of the Mexican military, something the Calderón administration considered essential to its security policy. Betting on the military in the drug war brings with it the need to give them cover, which is why an initiative was sent to the Mexican Congress in order to modify the National Security Law (NSL). The NSL had already been approved by the Senate, but it was still under discussion in the House of Representatives. The NSL sought to give the authorities, as well as the military, greater certainty and clarity on their responsibilities and functions in preserving the domestic security.

Proposal for a New Policing Model

The federal government is seeking to lay the foundations for a smooth transition process from the current decentralized policing model, in which federal, state, and municipal police corporations coexist, to a centralized one, based on a single command and control center. This proposal has the endorsement of the overwhelming majority of the governors and mayors, as President Calderón acknowledged:

> I welcome the fact that during this session of the National Public Security Council we will discuss the proposal to move toward a new policing model, made up of 32 state police corporations with a single and reliable command center in each state and with the support of the Federal Police, a model which has also been discussed and proposed by the National Conference of Governors. (Calderón 2010)

Presumably, the new policing model will allow more coordinated actions among federal and state police corporations, given the new single command center. It will also facilitate testing the trustworthiness of the police personnel, the training of better and more reliable police leadership, and making better use of state and local resources in the fight against organized crime. Thus the Calderón administration is betting on fundamental reforms. As the president stated:

> And that is why, in the setting of the National Council on Public Security discussions, I hereby commit myself to present in the next session of the Congress an initiative of constitutional and legal reform that will promote the new policing model, based on 32 state police departments with a single and reliable command center in each of those police departments, which will allow us to move forward with greater command, clarity and unity in coordination among the different levels of government. This reform effectively means the elimination of the municipal preventive police departments, whose officers will later join the ranks of their colleagues in the state police departments. (Presidencia de la República 2010)

Betting on the Coercive Instruments of the State: Quantity over Quality

The Calderón National Security Strategy placed major emphasis on quantifiable factors, relatively easy to measure. President Calderón has made it clear that it was necessary to increase the force of the state and to work to clean, modernize, and professionalize the security and justice institutions in the country. He added:

We have tripled the number of officers in the Federal Police. Moreover, to guarantee the honesty of law enforcement agents, we have institutionalized the mechanisms of trustworthiness control in the security agencies of the Federal Government, and also, increasingly, in the local governments. Today, we have 40 Trustworthiness Evaluation Centers. At least one located in each state of Mexico. (Presidencia de la República 2010)

Meanwhile, in little more than a year, the total number of police officers in Mexico went from 332,874 to 386,043, an increase of more than 53,000 officers. This meant that the government had placed quantity over quality. This priority extends to SEDENA, since the number of active personnel also increased considerably to a total of 196,767 troops for fiscal year 2007, or 5,624 additional soldiers in comparison to the total number of soldiers authorized during each of the previous four years. Quality-driven efforts are not absent, however. The Department of Public Security sought to merge various federal police departments into a single body. This proposal came to be known as the Federal Unified Police, or Federal Police Department, seeking to integrate into a single agency all federal law enforcement agencies to create a Federal Police Department that would merge the AFI and the PFP, bringing together the AFI's tactical analysis and investigative mission with the PFP's territorial deployment capability and power to react (García Luna 2007). Genaro García Luna, the secretary of public safety, managed to delineate this merger in his Strategic Axis 1 in the following way:

To bring together the capabilities of the Mexican State against crime, contemplating as the main point "The integration of the efforts of the different federal police corporations, with a single command center for the PFP, AFI, the National Migration Institute (INM), and the Fiscal and Customs Inspection Agency (CIFA)." (Secretaría de Seguridad Pública)

This objective was also expressed in Sectorial Objective 1: To align the Mexican state's capabilities to combat organized crime in order to reestablish the security conditions necessary for society in all of the national territory.

The new model was based on the principles of effectiveness and efficiency. The unification of the federal police into a single command, the strengthening of the intra-institutional coordination, and the cooperation among the police forces of the three levels of government represent the pivots of law enforcement evolution in Mexico from a reactive model to a model based on prevention and on the adoption of uniform methods of action to ensure the presence of the state apparatus in cities and towns with high crime indices. The goal of the new model was to protect national strategic installations and to reestablish public safety. The following strategies and action points delineate this:

Strategy 1: To implement the processes of the new law enforcement model and establish systematic operating procedures, consistent with and certified by international standards in the 32 states.

Strategy 2: To carry out joint operations to reestablish public safety and peaceful conditions in regions most affected by organized crime.

Action 1: To strengthen coordination among the Departments of National Defense, the Department of the Navy, and the attorney general's office, as well as with the state and municipal governments in order to recover public spaces occupied by criminal gangs. (Secretaría de Seguridad Pública 2007)

On April 25, 2007, the Department of Public Security published Act 05/2007 in the Official Journal of the Federation, by which it created the Coordinating Office of the Federal Police.

These were important structural reforms, but increasing the number of officers and soldiers was still privileged over improving their quality. This became even more evident when the Department of Public Administration decided to cut the basic training courses for the PFP's Academy in San Luis Potosí, reducing the training period from one year to three months, with the argument that Mexico needed the new law enforcement officers in the streets as soon as possible. In fact, statistics show that in 2006 the PFP had 6,489 members and in 2012 the number increased to 36,940, which means that in this period the institution grew five times (Presidencia de la República 2012). I visited the PFP's Academy and I received information about the course characteristics.

The third component of the Strategy under analysis rests with the justice system, which clearly does not abide by the constitutional principle of guaranteeing prompt and speedy trials. The need to reform the justice administration system is readily acknowledged in the strategic documents.

We proposed, and it was finally approved, a Constitutional Reform to the Criminal Justice System, with which Mexico will adopt a system of oral trials, simplified, with more transparent processes, as well as a system for the protection of the rights of victims. Now the judge must hear, in person, the allegations of the parties involved and must be personally present during the presentation of the evidence.

In this setting, Article 20 of the Mexican Constitution establishes that the penal process should be adversarial and oral and that all evidence should be presented and weighed in a public hearing and before a judge. This reform grants the authorities more tools to fight crime because it gives the police new investigation tools as well. Judges can also request evidence more quickly. With this, it is expected that victims will also be better protected. However, this reform will be in vain unless the judiciary branch is also purged of all corruption and strengthened, given that chronic levels of impunity in Mexico are linked to the high ease with which prosecutors and judges can be bought. If the citizens, the judiciary, and state and local authorities cannot guarantee honesty in the conduct of prosecutors and judges, the problem of impunity and its noxious effects on public security will continue. Thus Mexico has to continue to reform its legal system to make it more effective and transparent.

Another axis of the government strategy is the so-called New Active Policy for Crime Prevention, which starts with the acknowledgment that:

> Criminal groups have taken control of public spaces essential for social life. Schools, parks, town squares, and public gardens have ceased to being secure spaces and the problem of [drug] addiction had worsened. That is why it is impossible to postpone the recovery of these public spaces from the hands of criminals and give them back to the citizens. . . . For that purpose, we have launched a preventive strategy with three components: the Safe School Program, that is now in place in approximately 25,000 elementary education campuses; the Rescuing Public Spaces Program, that has refurbished 2,700 parks, squares and sports facilities all over the country; and the Addiction Prevention Program, "New Life," in place in more than 300 centers that treat drug addiction. (Presidencia de la República 2010)

This was a turnabout that acknowledged that there was another leg missing from the overall anti-crime strategy. According to President Calderón:

> We found at the beginning of my administration a need to mend the social fabric damaged by crime and to offer opportunities for the

development, education, health, recreation and well-being of families, but particularly of the young. For that purpose, we took actions to strengthen the citizenry's trust and to promote a culture of crime prevention, legality and crime reporting. We launched the Safe School Program to lower violence and drug consumption in education facilities. . . . This program operates in approximately 25,000 school campuses. . . . Likewise, we have implemented the Recovery of Public Spaces Program to return to the citizenry spaces that had been taken over by criminal gangs. It is not only a matter of rebuilding sports facilities, parks and playgrounds, as is in fact being done, but also of organizing the neighborhoods so that space can be rescued and used by that community's families. To date, we have recovered 2,700 public spaces all over the country. We have also built more than 300 "New Life" Centers, for the prevention and treatment of addictions. (Presidencia de la República 2010)

Ciudad Juárez was one of the major beneficiaries. "We Are All Juárez: Rebuilding the City" is a typical example of this type of program.

The fifth and last component of the strategy launched by Calderón's office was international cooperation. It was premised on the idea of shared responsibility by the United States. It was cemented by Mexico–U.S. bilateral relations, specifically the Mérida Initiative, based on the acknowledgment that organized crime is a common problem and that it is important to tackle it together, since crime is a public enemy that for whom the border is not an obstacle. An official at the Department of Foreign Affairs states that, all in all, the balance is a positive one, considering the fact that for the first time in the history of relations between the two countries

the United States acknowledges and assumes its co-responsibility in the complex problem of the drug trade within the framework of the bilateral agenda . . . with an added . . . commitment to undertake efforts to reduce the consumption and demand for drugs in the United States and the flow of weapons to Mexico. (Padilla 2007)

This also explains why by the end of Calderón's first year in office he had extradited fifty-six Mexican citizens to other countries, most of them to the United States. For instance, Osiel Cárdenas Guillén, the brothers Gilberto and Ismael Higuera Guerrero, Jesús Héctor Palma Salazar, Gilberto Salinas Doria, José Alberto Márquez Esqueda, and Gracielo Gardea

Carrasco were prominent cases among these extraditions (Calderón 2006). Six extraditions from the United States to Mexico also took place. Binational training and cooperation programs were established as well. This is a major historical reversal, which places Mexico among the fifteen countries in the world that receive the most military and police aid from the United States. Mexico came to occupy the fourth place in the Americas, behind Colombia, Peru, and Bolivia. It is fair to say that police reform in Mexico, particularly the creation of the AFI, cannot be understood without this support from abroad (García Luna 2011).

> We negotiated and obtained technical support and training from police agencies in Spain, France, Germany, Colombia and the United States. Most important was the support of the Federal Bureau of Investigation (FBI) . . . which granted a vote of confidence to the model on which the AFI was structured. As part of its contribution, the FBI opened its training facilities to our police commanders in Quantico, Virginia, in order to strengthen AFI's command structure. (García Luna 2011)

Conclusion

The Vicente Fox administration (2000–2006) neglected the issue of public safety and security, something that was very damaging and resulted in the loss of public spaces to crime and in the growing power of organized crime in Mexico, especially drug trafficking, in addition to the high levels of violence that this produced. As a result, Calderón appeared to have no other choice but to resort to the military to confront the scourge of organized crime and to recover control over vast swaths of territory lost to criminal gangs. Unfortunately, President Calderón opted for an initial response that neglected the use of other components of public safety and security, opting to hammer drug trafficking organizations by brute force. But toward the end of his administration, an evaluation of the national security strategy in Mexico shows that this paradigm did not remain intact. In other words, there is a need to evaluate the federal government's efforts in security, including mistakes, but also in light of the slew of changes and legislative reform initiatives that transformed the policing model. Some noteworthy points of the Calderón strategy follow:

1. It privileged national security over public safety, under the logic of the so-called war on drugs.

2. It favored direct confrontation against organized crime under a state-centric concept, arguing that drug trafficking groups threatened the integrity, stability, and permanence of the Mexican state.

3. It relied on a militarized strategy, directly engaging the armed forces against organized crime.

4. It favored the military as a tool of national power and initially neglected other tools at the disposal of the Mexican state, especially social policy.

5. After more than three years, it finally looked for a national consensus, arguing that the Mexican society's will and national unity were required. It did so through the so-called public safety roundtables.

6. The overall strategy did not decrease either quantitatively or qualitatively the levels of violence across the country or recover public spaces to the extent desired, although there were some optimistic signs at the end of the administration.

7. By choosing the *ultima ratio* (force) as a first tool, it may have generated even more violence.

8. The strategy was criticized by many because the use of the armed forces in matters of public safety is not well regulated in Mexico. The legal framework under which they police was questioned and, as an added consequence, it may have caused the armed forces to neglect other tasks.

9. It left out citizen-centric public security models and other possible mechanisms to create social synergy against crime, such as proactive citizen participation in the design, monitoring, and evaluation of the Mexican criminal justice policies and crime prevention.

10. Finally, it ignored critical issues such as domestic and family violence, gender and self-inflicted violence, and violent deaths associated with alcohol and other social ills.

In addition to these important flaws, the Calderón administration may have engaged in a conflict without an (easy) exit strategy. Although everyone acknowledges that exceptional situations often call for exceptional measures, the historical experience of democracies shows that all programs and plans should be carefully organized in time and space, with clear exit strategies. It is possible that Calderón even failed to demonstrate that the country was facing an emergency situation. In the end, the federal government did and should in the future bet on intangible elements, especially justice system reform, the professionalization of the police, public involvement, crime prevention, human rights, and tackling the sources of antisocial behavior. Coordination among the three levels of government to confront structural violence is also key. Additionally, if the military is to be committed to missions and functions of a police nature, it should be done so to carry out discreet duties, with clear goals and exit strategies and clear rules of engagement within the framework of the rule of law. It should be recognized that there are no magical or short-term solutions to the problem of public safety and human security, and organized communities may be better able to look after their own public safety. Finally, public safety and national security should be conceived of as long-term state policies, and the qualitative components of public life should be prioritized.

Note

1. Translated by Rafael Núñez and Tony Payan.

Bibliography

Astorga, Luis. 2007. *Seguridad, traficantes y militares. El poder y la sombra*. Mexico City: Tusquets, Editores.

Calderón, Felipe. 2006. *Remarks by the President in the State of the Union Address* and 2012 *Remarks by the President in the State of the Union Address*. Mexico City: Mexican Presidency, 3, 89. http://www.informe.gob.mx/pdf/INFORME_ESCRITO/01_CAPITULO_ESTADO_DE_DERECHO_Y_SEGURIDAD/1_01_Certeza_Juridica.pdf; http://www.informe.gob.mx/pdf/INFORME_ESCRITO/01_CAPITULO_ESTADO_DE_DERECHO_Y_SEGURIDAD/1_08_Defensa_de_la_Soberania_y_de_la_Integ_del_Ter.pdf. Accessed October 1, 2012.

———. 2010. *Discurso del Presidente Calderón en la inauguración en la XXVIII Sesión del Consejo Nacional de Seguridad Pública*. Mexico City: Mexican Presidency, June 3. http://www.presidencia.gob.mx/index.php?DNA=109&page=1&Contenido=57326. Accessed September 24, 2012.

Centro de Investigación y Seguridad Nacional (CISEN). 2011. http://www.cisen.gob.mx/. Accessed September 26, 2012.

Centros Nueva Vida. 2010. http://es.scribd.com/doc/28536914/Direcciones-de-Centros-Nueva-Vida-Mexico. Accessed October 1, 2012.

Department of National Defense (SEDENA). 2011. *Secretaría de la Defensa Nacional*. http://www.sedena.gob.mx/. Accessed September 26, 2012.

Department of the Navy. 2008. "Decree Approving the Sectorial Program of the Navy 2007–2012." *Official Journal of the Federation Mexico*, 4th section: 3.

Gómez Rodríguez, César A. 2007. "The Public Security Policy of Felipe Calderón's Government." *Centro de Estudios Sociales y de Opinión Pública* (CESOP) 4, 21.

García Luna, Genaro. 2007. "Against Crime. Why 1,661 Police Forces Are Not Enough (Past, Present and Future of the Police Forces in Mexico)." *Official Journal of the Federation.* Mexico City: Department of Public Security. http://www.ssp .gob.mx/CEVAVI/ShowBinary?nodeId=/BEA%20Repository/386198//archivo. Accessed September 24, 2012.

———. 2011. *Para entender el nuevo modelo de seguridad para México.* Mexico City: Nostra Ediciones.

Instituto Ciudadano de Estudios sobre la Inseguridad, A.C. (ICESI). 2011. http://www .icesi.org.mx. Accessed September 26, 2012.

Inter-American Commission on Human Rights (IACHR). 2011. *Organization of American States.* http://www.oas.org.end/iachr. Accessed September 26, 2012.

Moloeznik, Marcos Pablo. 1990. "Doctrinas esenciales del pensamiento estratégico-militar contemporáneo." *Revista de Estudios Sociales* 8 (May–August): 81–94.

———. 2006. "Public Security and Police Reform in the Americas." In *Public Security and Police Reform in Mexico,* edited by J. Bailey and L. Dammert, 169–86. Pittsburgh, PA: University of Pittsburgh Press.

National Development Plan 2007–2012. 2007. *Información e inteligencia.* http://pnd .calderon.presidencia.gob.mx/index.php?page=informacion-e-inteligencia. Accessed September 26, 2012.

National Human Rights Commission. 2010. *Activity Report of the National Commission on Human Rights.* January 26. Mexico City: National Human Rights Commission.

Office of the High Commissioner for Human Rights in Mexico. 2003. *Diagnosis of the Situation of Human Rights in Mexico.* Mexico City: Office of the High Commissioner for Human Rights in Mexico, 44. December. http://www.hchr.org.mx /files/doctos/Libros/8diagnosticocompleto.pdf. Accessed September 24, 2012.

Padilla, Agustín Maciel. 2007. "Conference at the Auditorium Adalberto Navarro Sánchez of the University Center for Human and Social Sciences of the Universidad de Guadalajara." Guadalajara, Jal. November 9.

Peón, Jorge Tello. 2007. *Seminary of National Security and Public Security.* Mexico City: Colegio de México.

Periódico Ocho Columnas. 2007. "Más espacios, menos delincuencia." Guadalajara, July 6, B-1.

Plan Nacional de Desarrollo. "Eje 1. Estado de Derecho y Seguridad del Plan Nacional de Desarrollo, 2007–2012." http://pnd.calderon.presidencia.gob.mx/index.php ?page=eje1. Accessed September 24, 2012.

Presidencia de la República. *Primer Informe de Gobierno.* 1.1.3 Crimen Organizado. http://www.informe.gob.mx/1.1_ESTADO_DE_DERECHO/?contenido=145.

———. 2010. *La lucha por la seguridad pública.* Mexico City.

———. 2012. *Sexto Informe de Gobierno.* Mexico City: Seguridad Nacional: 89. October 1. http://www.informe.gob.mx/pdf/INFORME_ESCRITO/01_CAPITULO _ESTADO_DE_DERECHO_Y_SEGURIDAD/1_08_Defensa_de_la_Sobera-nia_y_de_la_Integ_del_Ter.pdf. Accessed October 1, 2012.

Secretaría de Seguridad Pública. *Estrategia Integral de Prevención del Delito y Combate a la Delincuencia.* http://www.oas.org/dsp/documentos/politicas_publicas/mexico _estrategia.pdf. Accessed September 24, 2012.

———. 2007. *Programa sectorial de Seguridad Pública 2007–2012*. Mexico. Diario Oficial de la Federación, November 28. 1st section, 15.

Tirado, Erubiel. 2006. "The Civilian-Military Relationship in Mexico and the Democratic Deficit of the Political Alternation, 2000–2006." Unpublished paper.

PART TWO

Current Strategies and Casualties

CHAPTER THREE

Drug Wars, Social Networks, and the Right to Information

Informal Media as Freedom of the Press in Northern Mexico

Guadalupe Correa-Cabrera and José Nava

Introduction

In the last few years, and in the context of the United States' and Mexico's wars on drugs, violence in the southern country has reached unprecedented levels, particularly since the launch of military operations against drug trafficking organizations—today known as transnational criminal organizations (TCOs)[1]—in December 2006 by the administration of President Felipe Calderón (2006–2012). To this day, Mexico's "war" has claimed over forty thousand lives.[2] This exponential increase in violence has reached several states of Mexico and is particularly significant in the country's border states, such as Tamaulipas, Nuevo León, Coahuila, and Chihuahua. The current wave of violence affecting Mexican border cities—particularly those located in the Tamaulipas border region—has also silenced the media, in a clear demonstration of the power that criminal enterprises exert over border society. This represents an additional cost of the so-called war on drugs battled at both sides of the U.S.–Mexican divide.

The state of Tamaulipas—and especially its border areas—represents a "black hole" with regards to news and information of the violence brought on by its local drug cartels. While military operations, executions, apprehensions, and actions alike are kept under wraps and unreported in the traditional Mexican mass media, informal sources such as blogs and Internet forums have taken on the role of informing the populace and the rest of the world of the actions that take place in the struggle between Mexican federal forces and their targeted organizations, becoming the most reliable sources of information for society in general.

The aim of this chapter is to point out the effects that more sophisticated and ruthless methodologies, as employed by Mexican TCOs' paramilitarized enforcers, have had on conventional communication means and how this has led to the surge of unconventional media through digital means as a free channel through which information on the region's status with regard to organized crime and violence can be published, leading to a wider dissemination across borders. This work illustrates how informal media—particularly online sources—are utilized as an alternative to continuous news reporting in conflict-ridden regions, such as the Tamaulipas border with Texas.

The first part of this chapter briefly describes the effects and costs of the war on drugs in Mexico, particularly the problem of drug-related violence in the Tamaulipas border region. The subsequent section examines the paramilitarization process that TCOs have undergone in the "new democratic era,"[3] as well as the subsequent silencing experienced by conventional media as a result of the increased threats posed by organized crime. The third section of the chapter analyzes the popularization and widespread utilization of social networks and blogs, among other digital outlets, as informational sources that can be considered free of the state and private subjugation. In other words, this part explains the rise of informal media as the freedom of press's lifeline in northeastern Mexico during drug war times. The final part of this chapter explains the notion of "structural violence" and its impact on the media's inability to conduct their duties in a context of negation of information and disinformation campaigns that permeate journalism in the U.S.–Mexican border region. It also exemplifies this phenomenon with an explanation of the imprecise number of deaths associated with the ongoing Mexican war on drugs reported by formal media and official sources.

Drug-Related Violence in Today's Mexico

The Mexican War on Drugs and the Escalation of Drug-Related Violence

Felipe Calderón assumed the Mexican presidency on December 1, 2006. The political panorama in Mexico has changed substantially since that time, particularly as a result of the so-called war on drugs declared by the Mexican government and the escalation of the drug trafficking problem in the country.[4] Among the symptoms that stem from the ongoing conflict between Mexican TCOs and governmental forces are the momentous increase in violent, drug-related deaths in the last few years (with particular emphasis from 2006 onward); the practice of savage, terror-inflicting methodologies such as dismemberment, decapitation, or the complete dissolution of human remains; corruption of government officials at all levels; the failure of the Mexican state to subdue criminal organizations and its subsequent loss of the "monopoly of violence"; extortion practices committed against businesses, entrepreneurs, and society in general; the emergence of a new drug market in Mexico that provides affordable doses of any type of drug(s) to domestic consumers; and the use of unconventional terror tactics, such as car bombs, mass kidnappings, grenade attacks, blockades, and executions of public officials.

Drug violence has spread across the country and has predominantly affected the northern/border states of the Mexican Republic. According to official statistics, 34,612 people were killed since December 2006 through December 2010 (see table 3.1).[5] The year 2010 only registered 15,273 drug-related murders. Violence tended to be concentrated in Mexico's northwestern border region, especially Chihuahua, as well as in Pacific states such as Sinaloa, Michoacán, and Guerrero. Ciudad Juárez registered the highest number of homicides; in 2010, approximately 3,100 people were killed in this border city. Now violence has spread to other regions of Mexico and has particularly increased in the states of Nuevo León and Tamaulipas. In 2010, half of the drug-related murders took place in Chihuahua, Sinaloa, and Tamaulipas.

The continual state of violence in Mexico—and more specifically in its northern border—can be attributed to a number of factors, such as an increased tempo in U.S. federal law enforcement activities, an increased military presence, and internal dissention in the drug trafficking organizations. What has been established beyond any doubt is that along with this

Table 3.1. Drug-related murders, 2006–2010

	2006	2007	2008	2009	2010	*Total*
Tamaulipas	0	80	96	90	1,209	1,475
Mexico (total)	62	2,826	6,837	9,614	15,273	34,612

Source: Federal Government, Office of the Presidency. The figures for 2006 are for the month of December only.

increase in violence, the brutality of tactics employed has increased as well. Gone are the days of traditional gangland executions. Present today are recorded beheadings; public displays of human bodies—at times completely dismembered, others hanging from overpasses; full-blown commando units disappearing persons involved in organized crime or against it; and car bombs aimed at the general public.

Violence in the Southern Part of the Texas–Tamaulipas Border

The Texas–Tamaulipas border is a strategic region in terms of trade, migration, and drug trafficking and has been overlooked by U.S. and Mexican scholars. In fact, the Mexican state of Tamaulipas is key as a point of distribution of drugs to the United States.[6] It is also a major route for arms trafficking from the United States to the south of the American continent

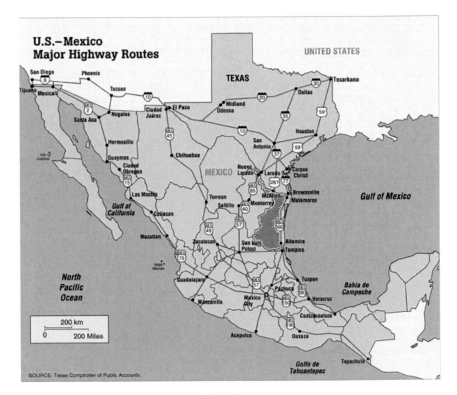

Figure 3.1a. The Texas–Tamaulipas border

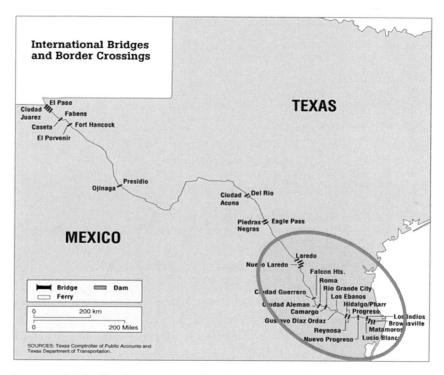

Figure 3.1b. The South Texas–Tamaulipas border with 15 bridge crossings circled

and for human trafficking from Central and South America to the United States. This is due to the fact that Tamaulipas shares a long border with the United States and has an extensive ocean coast; it is also the state with the largest number of international bridges (seventeen along the northern border, from Nuevo Laredo to Matamoros; see figures 3.1a and 3.1b).

Violence in Tamaulipas has increased exponentially in the last couple of years, particularly since January 25, 2010, with the definite rupture between the main TCOs operating in the state: the Gulf Cartel and its once-armed wing, the Zetas. In 2009 Mexico's federal government reported ninety drug-related murders in Tamaulipas, while the figure for 2010 was 1,209 (see table 3.1 and figure 3.2). In fact, violent drug-related incidents in the state have become public due to their notoriety and sociopolitical impact and have started to figure in both national and international media. The year 2010, in particular, was plagued with a high number of executions that involved gunmen and federal/military personnel, civilians, and even high-level political figures, such as Rodolfo Torre-Cantú, Tamaulipas governorship candidate—executed in the month of June by an unknown

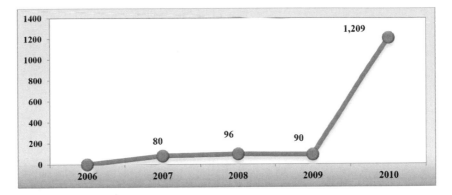

Figure 3.2. Drug-related murders in Tamaulipas, 2006–2010

armed commando. The assassination of seventy-two migrants in the municipality of San Fernando in August 2010 and the discovery of nearly two hundred bodies buried in the same area in April 2011 are also major examples of the increasing and unprecedented levels of violence in the state.

Violence in Tamaulipas can be attributed to a number of factors, such as the failure of the *maquiladora* industry to fulfill the promises of an adequate source of income for the state's population; the degradation of the various social control agents due to the degree of influence that drug cartels exercise over them; and divisions between the two main TCOs operating in the state. But the new wave of violence in Tamaulipas seems to be mainly driven by three factors: (1) the paramilitarization of TCOs in the state; (2) the definite rupture between the Gulf Cartel and the Zetas; and (3) endemic corruption in "new democratic" times. The new configuration of the Mexican political system—as a result of the democratization process—and high levels of corruption and weak political institutions (local and federal) seem to have had a major impact on the extreme levels of violence observed in this Mexican state.

The Paramilitarization of Organized Crime in Mexico's "New Democratic Era"

The "New" Mexican Democracy: Organized Crime Redux

The current state of social decomposition in Mexico can be traced back to the fall of the PRI (Institutional Revolutionary Party, or Partido Revolucionario

Institucional) regime, which lasted more than seventy years. During this period, the PRI exercised complete political control and assured the cooperation of all three levels of government and their corresponding police forces. The PRI was finally ousted from power in the 2000 presidential elections. This fact, combined with the lack of a majority in any of the two congressional chambers, governmental divisions in all thirty-two states, and the subsequent weakening of the rule of law, "led to the dismissal of any perceived limits by the drug cartels to wage war as we perceive it today" (Nava 2011, 16).

In fact, evidence shows that the evolution toward the current state of affairs in some localities affected by organized crime—such as those located in the Texas–Tamaulipas border region—can be traced back to the political changes that swept Mexico in 2000. The transition toward a "truly democratic state" shook the then traditional political power structure and did away with previously established controls that not only kept traditional segments of the population under state control but also organized crime groups. The state had held an important degree of influence over organized crime, even delineating TCOs' courses of action and establishing guidelines for them to follow. This was due to a system (of "narco-corruption") that enabled a sense of stability through bribery and arbitration that guided criminal organizations' behavior. The power transition that ensued after the 2000 presidential election in Mexico attempted to decentralize the established political apparatus without a complete understanding of the symbiotic nature that the political sphere had developed with many of the country's facets, including organized crime. This process also lacked an adequate framework to institutionalize such changes in an effective and expedited way.

Along with these failed changes, the press was also a sector that found itself adrift with the policies of the new regime. Traditionally, the press in Mexico had been influenced and coerced by the state through conventional methodologies, such as monetary bribes, as well as more succinct but more effective methods—for example, providing concessions and paper subsidies while engaging in a reciprocal exchange of partisan support toward the state. The advent of an entirely new and inexperienced political regime failed to ensure and provide effective safety measures for protecting and fostering a truly democratic and safe environment for media personnel. Such a situation evolved into unforeseen levels of control by not only the state apparatus but also by private criminal organizations, resulting in what can be called a form of "structural violence" against media representatives. This was particularly evident in the Tamaulipas border area.

While silencing practices are not an entirely new phenomenon, the ways in which such practices are enforced in the Tamaulipas region are unique. The precedent that set the tone for media silencing in the region can be traced back to the murders of reporters Ernesto Flores and Norma Moreno on July 17, 1986, in Matamoros, Tamaulipas, on behest of then Gulf Cartel leader Juan García-Ábrego (Cantú 2010, 60–62). The primary difference between the past practices and current ones is that media silencing has become institutionalized as a result of the professionalization and subsequent paramilitarization process that cartel enforcement wings have gone through in previous years, effectively handicapping regional media's ability to convey information in any way.

The Paramilitarization of Organized Crime in a "Failed" Mexican State

While the current state of violence and disarray can be attributed, to some extent, to the Mexican democratic transition and democratization process, the increase in violence and the change in killing methodologies and intimidation practices used by TCOs can be attributed to the subsequent paramilitarization process that organized crime has undergone in Mexico. This phenomenon currently plagues the whole country and even Central American nations with an unprecedented wave of violence and bloodshed.

The evolution in the organizational structure of Mexico's TCOs and their subsequent paramilitarization has also created an informational "black hole" with regard to the state of affairs in active drug zones in the country. This is true for the state of Tamaulipas, particularly its border region with Texas. Despite the commonplace occurrence of bloody incidents in this area—such as mass executions, gunfights between rival cartel members and government forces, abductions of large numbers of immigrants, rampant corruption of city officials and law enforcement personnel at all levels, and the disappearance of entire passenger buses traveling through the state's roads—misinformation and, at times, the complete lack of information to the civilian population are pandemic in the region.

The paramilitarization of organized crime in Mexico can be traced to the inception of the Zetas. The creation of this group composed of former soldiers of the Mexican "Special Forces," by former Gulf Cartel leader Osiel Cárdenas Guillén, set the precedent for the current degree of professionalization that has become "mainstream" in drug cartels' enforcer wings. The application of paramilitary practices into the organized crime industry raised the demand for more sophisticated enforcement practices. This phenomenon has contributed to raising the levels of violence in the drug industry and has allowed for the surge of a host of similar groups. The transformation of groups such as *Los Negros, La Línea, Los Pelones, Gente Nueva, MS-13, Artistas Asesinos,* the inclusion of foreign former military personnel such as Guatemalan *Kaibiles* in enforcer wings, and the creation of organizations such as *La Familia Michoacana* (which later bifurcated to the group denominated *Los Caballeros Templarios*) are examples of the trend set by the Zetas' paramilitary practices.

Along with the increase in drug-related violence came the erosion of the state's ability to uphold its monopoly of violence. According to Max Weber (1919, 2), the state

[c]laims the *monopoly of the legitimate use of physical force* within a given territory. . . . Specifically . . . the right to use physical force is as-cribed to other institutions or to individuals only to the extent to which the state permits it. The state is considered the sole source of the "right" to use violence.

Through evolved coercive practices and continuous press silencing, or-ganized crime groups, aided by their paramilitarized enforcer wings, have taken control over the monopoly of violence in some places of the Mexi-can Republic—such as the state of Tamaulipas, and particularly its border region with Texas. In these places, organized crime groups have effectively supplanted local as well as state governments, and at times even federal dependencies, as the sole purveyors of a legitimate means of violence. In such cases, TCOs have become de facto governing bodies, "supplanting governmental structures and imposing their rhetoric, rules, and organiza-tional methodologies on the population, effectively becoming a social control mechanism" (Nava 2011, 20).

Information Media: A Freedom of Press's Lifeline in Drug War Times

Gagging the Media in the Texas–Tamaulipas Border Region

The current wave of violence affecting Mexican border cities—particularly those located in the Texas–Tamaulipas border region—has silenced the media, in a clear demonstration of the power that criminal enterprises exert over border society in drug war times. While American journalists cover some reports of the various gunfights and drug-related murders that take place in the Mexican region, their counterparts seem to be recalcitrant to do so, turning a blind eye to the events that unfold in the region, negating their existence, the very occurrence of such events, and downgrading them to a state of collective psychosis.

The state of Tamaulipas—especially its border areas—represents a "black hole" with regard to news and information of the violence brought on by its local drug cartels. The recent upsurge in violence in Tamaulipas has enmeshed the state in an environment of uncertainty that has been magnified by the repression against news media representatives by both state and federal authorities, as well as by organized crime. In other words, there is a forced information gag upon the localized media brought on by both law enforcement and organized crime factions, sometimes even in collusion with each other.

As stated previously, regional media in the Tamaulipas border region—as well as in the rest of the state of Tamaulipas—have been subdued in an unprecedented manner by the extremely violent methodologies favored by organized crime. While the general populace experiences countless incidents regarding this violent upsurge, due to the constrictive nature of the secrecy veil imposed in the region, all those incidents are reduced to nothing more than rumors. Monica Campbell best reflects the aforementioned statement in the following words regarding self-censorship (2008, 43):

> [I]t has become a matter of self-preservation, and news outlets are avoiding publishing or broadcasting anything that could trigger a reprisal. For many that means no cartel names, no witness identities, no revealing photographs. Some newspapers have dropped bylines, and others have abandoned crime stories altogether. Intimidation is a factor for every journalist, from community radio reporters to top editors at the most influential outlets.

Aiding the enforcement of such silencing is the traditional complicity of the state itself. Journalist Víctor Ronquillo states that "for organized crime to rise as a factitious power, corruption and complicity is necessary. The most frequently identified journalist aggressors are public functionaries" (2010, 3–4). Due to the corruptive and coercive nature of organized crime—coupled with the weak and extremely corruptible state security and political institutions—one could infer that, regionally, media organizations are left with no room for bias-free decision-making processes regarding the reporting of any news/notes about organized crime or any of its derivative actions. A more descriptive statement on the current state of media relations in Mexico—particularly in the U.S.–Mexican border region—is provided in a report elaborated by MEPI Fundación (2010, 30):[7]

> In the northern . . . regions of this large nation, the drug organizations have created black news holes where little, or nothing, about incidents related to the brutal drug war makes it to the media. Editorial decisions about what appears on the front pages of newspapers or the first minutes of television news programs are today less dependent on basic news worthiness than on the whims of narcos who are not shy to express what they want printed or broadcast. The new bosses have crafted relations with media with the help of unwritten, and sometimes even unspoken, agreements between traffickers, reporters, and editors.

The Advent of Informal Media and Social Networks

In sum, little is known about the events that the ongoing battle on the Mexican side among federal forces and rival cartels generates on a daily basis in the form of verifiable news coverage. Formal media sources have been silenced by both government agencies, as well as by criminal organizations, in an effort to silence the real status quo of some regions of Mexico. The silencing/co-optation of local media outlets by both governmental and nongovernmental actors has led the populace to seek alternative methods to inform the society at large about the events that unfold in some regions of Mexico with regard to the ongoing war on drugs. Hence, society has started to utilize digital instruments such as social networks, as well as a host of blogs, in order to disseminate information related to the violence generated by the confrontation of government forces and cartel members, which is otherwise neglected coverage by traditional news forums.

It is worthwhile establishing a symptomatic link between media control in problematic areas of Mexico—such as the Tamaulipas border region— and the rise of what is called in this writing "informal media." This type of alternative tool has been working as the lifeline of not so much news channels, dailies, or radio shows but as the common folk trapped in this violent state of affairs in drug war times, while at the same time salvaging some sense of freedom of information in these areas. Online social networks such as MySpace, Facebook, Fotolog, Metrolog, Twitter, and YouTube, as well as a host of forums and blogs—some privately created, others controlled by news institutions—most notably the blog *El Blog del Narco*, have unofficially supplanted traditional news forums, such as television news programs, radio shows, and printed media as the outlets where the circumstances surrounding the ongoing conflict between the federal government and the various TCOs are presented.

Usually such outlets present the information to us in gory detail, accompanied by graphic pictures and videos of executions, gunfights, and torture sessions, as well as interrogations of individuals involved in drug trafficking activities that end up with the execution of the abducted person(s) and, lately, by forums through which TCOs convey messages to the authorities and the general public. As stated in the show *Noticias y Reportajes con Adela Micha*,[8] the most notorious of all these forums, *El Blog del Narco*, has stirred the controversy since its recent inception, to the point of initiating official investigations and even the arrest of public functionaries who colluded with criminal organizations as a result of the notes published on the site.

El Blog del Narco has taken the lead with regard to the dissemination of information that neither governmental nor private media institutions have been willing to present to the general public. The site is allegedly run by two individuals: one is, presumably, a journalist and the other is a university student specializing in computer systems. The few interviews that they have given to certain members of the press have been conducted with the utmost secrecy, employing encrypted communication measures to do so. They claim that their site's objective is to inform the public of the events and circumstances surrounding Mexico's war on drugs, and that it is neutral— does not have partisan interests, nor allegiances. They also allege that due to the site's very nature, it is a costly affair because of the constant security upgrades it has to undergo to protect their location and, consequently, the identities of those involved in it from governmental forces as well as organized crime groups. Robert Donnelly, an analyst of the Woodrow Wilson International Center for Scholars, stated that the importance of *El Blog del Narco* is its ability to "surpass media's self-imposed censorship."[9] Without a doubt, that is what makes informal media outlets special and vital, despite criticisms stating a lack of objectivity by them. The very notion of anonymity afforded by technology allows such forums to raise public awareness and forces authorities to take action on activities that have been publicly ventilated by such sites.

Another activity that has risen with the advent of informal media is the employment of the citizenry, officials, and even members of criminal organizations as informants of these sites. Once again, while these actions question their objectivity and raise questions as to what standards are employed to deem information publishable, they have taken news reporting to another level, free of any compunctions that traditional media might have. What is stated with this work is the notion that all things related to the struggle personified in the Mexican war on drugs have changed, including the nature of news reporting. With the spiraling of violence in certain regions of Mexico and the expansion of criminal organizations into other economically viable activities, the reporting community has been set aside, hog-tied, gagged, and blindfolded by various players in this bloody struggle. Informal media have set the tone in the struggle to maintain the notion of freedom of press, particularly in northern Mexico, where it has been severely limited.

While the objectivity and standards of some virtual sites and practices can be questioned—especially since they are also utilized as propaganda platforms by organized crime itself—informal media, as addressed here, have provided citizenry with the capacity of communicating a hidden truth to society at large, not only at a regional or national level but internationally as well. The aforementioned site, *El Blog del Narco*, provides a perfect example of the power that such venues possess in a gagged media region such as northern Mexico—particularly the state of Tamaulipas—since the anonymity afforded by such digital mediums allows them to raise public awareness and at times forces authorities to take action in activities that would otherwise go untreated while surpassing media's self-imposed censorship.

The Mexican Media and (Mis)Information in Times of "Structural Violence"

Structural Violence and the Media

According to Johan Galtung, structural violence is defined as "the cause of the difference between the potential and the actual, between what could have been and what is. Violence is that which increases the distance between the potential and the actual, and that which impedes the decrease of this distance" (1969, 168). Applying the previous statement to the situation encountered by media representatives in the Tamaulipas border region, the "potential" would be their ability to conduct their professional activities in a safe environment, as well as the unobstructed reporting of all events that are relevant to the well-being of the region's society. The "actual" would be the present situation exerted over the media by traditional and nontraditional elements, limiting the freedom of speech and information of a whole community. And violence, as it is presently employed, is the factor that keeps increasing the distance between these two dimensions.

According to Tord Høivik, in a situation of structural violence the loss of lives is caused by "social conditions," and the victims would be social groups instead of individuals. In other words, violence would only occur at the "collective level" (1977, 60). While some may argue that death rates of media personnel are far from numbers suggesting a systematic extermination campaign, the effects of structural violence are felt more in the form of an imposed collective consensus to comply with external mandates. Despite the high victimization numbers of journalists and media personnel in Mexico, the measuring standard used here to present the notion of structural violence is the media's inability to conduct their duties due to the negation of information and disinformation campaigns that, aided by either state or private parties, permeate journalism in the U.S.–Mexican border region. An example of this is the imprecise number of deaths associated with the ongoing Mexican war on drugs that have being reported by formal media and official sources.

Misinformation and the Fallacy of Numbers

Starting with more reputable sources, such as national newspapers, academic reports, and public governmental sources, there are some incongruences in the compilation of drug-related homicide statistics that offset any conclusive research on the subject. As already mentioned, Mexico's federal government website (Office of the Presidency; www.presidencia.gob .mx) reported a total of 1,475 drug-related homicides in the state of Tamaulipas and a national total of 34,612 deaths from December 2006 to December 2010 in its official drug-related homicides database (see table 3.1). Meanwhile, *Milenio*, one of Mexico's leading news agencies, reported an overall tally of 31,604 drug-related homicides for the period January 2006–December 2010. The University of San Diego Trans-Border Institute's "Justice in Mexico" project presented 1,052 homicides for the state of Tamaulipas and a nationwide total of 26,175 for the same period. As stated in the Trans-Border Institute report, *Drug Violence in Mexico: Data and Analysis from 2001–2009*, their methodology consisted of compiling the numbers handled by the Mexican newspaper *Reforma*.

In these three sources alone we see substantial differences, ranging from 8,437 reported drug-related homicides between the highest official count (Office of the Presidency) and the lowest one (the University of San Diego Trans-Border Institute). But death tolls are not the only indicator affected by the present situation in Mexico. Measuring instruments such as the census are also affected by a tightly regulated environment. According to the Mexican nongovernmental organization ICESI,[10] governmental dependencies such as INEGI[11] (Mexico's statistical organization) tend to report incomplete statistics due to the difficulties presented to their researchers in areas of conflict. The Seventh National Poll on Insecurity (ENSI-7), carried out by INEGI, selected 3,500 households in the state of Tamaulipas to conduct its research, of which 1,174 (33.5 percent) chose not to participate, or the household was abandoned (ICESI 2010, 10).

Structural violence against media representatives in the Tamaulipas border region, as well as in the entire state, is not only reflected in the publication of misleading and erroneous reports, incongruous homicide tallies, or the subjugation and terrorization of media representatives, but it is also present in the form of limited access to official figures. During this investigation we searched for official regional statistics related to organized crime in Tamaulipas and found that public access to such information through the state's website, the state attorney's office, and the public safety secretariat was blocked or limited and that, in most cases, electronic request for information was offline. This situation negates the most basic information to the populace at large. And this is again an additional cost that Mexican citizenry has to pay for the so-called war on drugs.

As an alternative to gather more reliable information on drug-related homicides, the present investigation undertook an examination of two local newspapers: (1) *El Bravo* from Matamoros, Tamaulipas, and (2) the *Brownsville Herald* from Brownsville, Texas, from January 1, 2010, to December 31, 2010, in search of any notes published on drug-related deaths in the region. The criteria employed to qualify notes as related to homicides with ties to organized crime took some key elements utilized by the three primary sources mentioned earlier in this chapter (Office of the Presidency, *Milenio*, and the Trans-Border Institute). Thus our selection of events considered the following elements:

The use of automatic weapons/high caliber weapons
Execution-style methodologies employed

Involvement of state, federal, and military forces

Direct mention of any criminal organization by name

Death of civilians due to military operations

The examination of *El Bravo* yielded 29 incidents reported with a homicide tally of 222 victims, while the *Brownsville Herald* reported 30 incidents with 160 victims (Nava 2011, 51, 56).[12] It is important to note that while the count derived from the analysis of a local newspaper presented over 200 drug-related homicides, Tamaulipas authorities reported an overall total of 725 homicides in all of its modalities. For the same period, the federal government's drug-related homicides database reported 1,209 events of that nature alone (see table 3.1; also see Ortega 2011).

These enormous divergences in reported data on drug-related homicides, as well as the negation of information at the local level, are detrimental to the very social development of the region. The present situation not only maintains the population in a state of unawareness as to drug trafficking organization's activities but also stumps key social development programs for the population that might be provided by state or federal authorities.

The 2010 Mexican census was "atypical" due to the degree of violence that had enveloped Mexico. Census workers themselves were victims of the wave of violence afflicting Mexico, with INEGI reporting that 3 of its census workers were murdered, 10 died in traffic accidents, and 276 were assaulted. This situation left 17,666 dwellings uncovered. While 17,666 dwellings may not be considered a significant number from a national perspective (0.06 percent), this number goes beyond dwellings; it represents a segment of the population that is virtually nonexistent, thus people who are distant from any governmental program. Tamaulipas was the state that presented more difficulties, with 534 problematic localities (Michel 2011).

It is also worthwhile to note the key differences regarding informational content between the two local newspapers—one Mexican and one American—mentioned earlier here. While *El Bravo* presented a general overview of the events in its notes, the *Brownsville Herald*—although lagging behind in the reporting of homicides with links to organized crime—did present a unique characteristic in the notes related to drug violence. The American newspaper tended to publish the names of individuals involved in particular incidents, their location, or the organization to which the suspects belonged—whether they may have been members of the Gulf Cartel, the Zetas, or any other organized crime group.

As to body counts following certain particularly intense gunfights, the difference between the notes published in Mexico and those published in the United States is that the American publication provided alongside the official statement with regard to the number of casualties in such incidents a more suitable number derived from unofficial sources that best suited the specific act in question. Consider, for example, the November 5, 2010, gunfight that ended with the killing of one of the heads of the Gulf Cartel (Antonio Ezequiel Cárdenas-Guillén, also known as "Tony Tormenta"). With regard to this event, many rumors and stories abound both on the Internet as well as in personal accounts as to the many killed in several points of the city on that fateful day, stories that if put together far surpass the official number reported in *El Bravo*.[13]

While it cannot be certain that the American press—at least the one established alongside the border region—is free of TCOs' influence, the mere fact that it publishes personal information on actors involved in drug-related events and mentions the TCOs by name hints at a freer press than that located south of the border. Even though the local Mexican press published a higher number of drug-related homicides than its American counterpart, this does not take into account the quality of reporting present in the publications, nor the lack of follow-through on such incidents, as well as the apparent willful neglect to report incidents that might be detrimental to a state agency's public perception. Hence, the present analysis that was conducted on the local press reveals several facts:

First, that the violence and self-imposed censorship on media representatives in the region has become ingrained to the point that it has become "structural," with the flow of information being controlled by both state and nonstate parties.

Second, that the subsequent paramilitarization of TCOs has led to changes in censorship practices that have broken previous boundaries and have transformed reporting practices to fit their needs.

Third, that so-called informal media outlets such as digital social networks and blogs specializing in the coverage of the violence issue in Mexico have contributed in an unprecedented manner to maintain the flow of information and to provide a space for the citizenry to expose their outcry and present evidence of the acts that the ongoing war on drugs has generated.

Conclusions

Time changes everything, from cultural fads, to political ideologies, to economic systems, and crime is no exception. Traditional methodologies utilized by TCOs have evolved to the point that they have become paramilitarized, transforming entire regions into criminal fiefdoms. So far, this writing has established the notion that at least regionally the monopoly of violence has shifted from the states to nongovernmental institutions that have infiltrated, corrupted, and dominated governmental bodies, becoming the controlling forces behind their respective regions. In this context, freedom of the press and its representatives have undergone a tremendous change for the worse, having been effectively gagged and subdued by the brutal practices exerted by organized crime. Consequently, violence against reporters and media representatives has become "structural," with criminal organizations taking over the role of the state as the oppressor and exerting violence over journalists as an effective regulating measure. These are some of the most visible costs of the so-called war on drugs.

The degree of informational coercion, co-optation, and intimidation against regional media outlets, such as newspapers, dailies, radio, and television, has evolved to the point that complete "informational black holes" have developed in some areas of Mexico—particularly in the Tamaulipas border region—prompting the utilization of digital channels to convey information concerning drug-related violence. Informal media sources such as Twitter and YouTube, blogs such as Borderland Beat and the premier Mexican site *El Blog del Narco*, as well as myriad online news channels, have taken advantage of the anonymity afforded by the web and, in some instances, have supplanted traditional publications as the purveyors of information in areas where communications and journalistic reports are under the complete scrutiny of criminal parties. The dynamics analyzed in this chapter show how new technologies allow for the dissemination of information in areas where oppression by both state and private actors controls people's everyday lives. The paramilitarization of organized crime has forced the evolution of the news media, in this case with the utilization of informal media venues to provide a respite from the repressive tactics encountered in the region during drug war times.

In sum, the events that have unfolded in the Mexican state of Tamaulipas from 2010 to the present day as a result of the ongoing conflict between opposing TCOs show us three unique dynamics that have made the aforementioned conflagration so complex and increasingly violent: (1) the paramilitarization process that TCOs have undergone in recent years, changing previous violence methodologies and escalating the levels of violence to unseen levels; (2) the subsequent silencing that conventional media have experienced as a result of the increased threats posed by organized crime, and (3) the popularization and widespread utilization of social networks as informational sources that can be considered free of state and private subjugation. Freedom of the press is an important aspect of any healthy society and, in this case, the lack of it is symptomatic of a cancerous element that thwarts any collective growth that the populace might reach by negating, controlling, coercing, and influencing its traditional media. The informal media seem to be the last bastion of hope for a future change in the current state of affairs of news media in northern Mexico.

Addendum

In the latter part of 2011, a troubling turn of events occurred in the world of online social media in the state of Tamaulipas with the murder of four bloggers (one of them a news editor for a local online newspaper) in the city of Nuevo Laredo. Not only has violence become a physical reality to individuals involved in online publications, but these individuals also have encountered governmental measures in the form of arrests under "state terrorism by-laws" and recent initiatives by several states to regulate the usage of social network sites. Violence against reporters of more traditional means has not subsided in any manner—consider, for example, the eight reporters killed in 2011, the burning of the newspaper *El Buen Tono* in Veracruz by an armed group in November 2011, and the most recent attacks on *El Norte*'s offices in Monterrey and *El Mañana*'s in Nuevo Laredo (2012). What is more, the recent inclusion of online media into the scope of action of criminal groups has endangered what could be considered the last bastion for effective freedom of speech in many regions of Mexico.

In September 2011, Reporters without Borders described Mexico as "the western hemisphere's most dangerous country for the media." According to this organization, as of that date, eighty journalists had been killed since 2000 and fourteen had been reported missing since 2003 (Reporters without Borders 2011).[14] Along with these numbers, the number of fatalities attributed to Mexico's ongoing war on drugs has augmented substantially. Tijuana's publication *Semanario Zeta* estimated a total of 60,420 drug-related murders during the first five years of President Calderón's administration (Mendoza 2011a, b).[15] This represented a significant increase from the 34,612 drug-related murders reported in 2010 by the federal government (see table 3.1).

As it pertains to northern Mexico, the discovery of nearly two hundred bodies in several mass graves in San Fernando, Tamaulipas, made public what up to April 2011 was only known to locals and authorities in that area: the disappearance of entire passenger buses (as well as private vehicles), and entire regions in the state of Tamaulipas that had effectively fallen into the hands of organized crime, completely displacing any local governmental institutions.

The practices that derived from the case mentioned earlier—if observed from a casual standpoint—would suggest nothing more than sadism and blood lust exerted by individuals in a power frenzy. But while this might be true to a degree, it also exposes us to an overhaul on methods and techniques employed by enforcer wings to control areas and disrupt operations through terrorizing practices, massive disappearances, the forced recruitment of young men into the rank and file of enforcer bodies, and continuous control over regional media.

The practices mentioned previously are the latest developments in the continuous paramilitarization process that drug trafficking organizations have undergone in their endless quest to attain supremacy over their foes. As an ever-evolving field of study, the paramilitarization of organized crime groups, the continuous "media blackouts" in regions such as the border, and the emergence of more digital forums through which the topic is exposed for the world to see paint an uncertain picture for the future of press relations and antidrug policies. While this writing does not have a definite answer to either the changes in enforcer practices or the plight of media personnel, the hope is that the exposure of such happenings in regions so close to the American soil—regions that happen to share cultures, economies, and bloodlines—might bring about more serious study that will ultimately lead us to develop effective controls and policies to realistically address major transnational concerns, such as drug-related violence and organized crime.

Online sources have demonstrated their value in public relations campaigns and social awareness many times over, even though some government officials minimize such effects. But the importance that they have can also mark them as a valuable tool for criminal organizations to further dominate a region and even expand their influence into new territories, providing them with another tool to control the population as well as wage a more effective media campaign against governmental forces and rival criminal organizations.

In Tamaulipas, if the silencing of online media sources continues, the informational blackout would effectively extend itself to every single communication outlet, allowing for the isolation of the region and effectively submerging it in a complete state of disinformation while permitting the continual control by criminal organizations of the entire region's population and of people's lives, providing a de facto death knell to the state's freedom of information. And, ultimately, this would be the consequence of a war on drugs that was supposedly designed for improving our lives.

Notes

1. The term "drug trafficking organizations" (DTOs) has recently fallen out of use in favor of the more updated term of "transnational criminal organizations" (TCOs). Hence, we will use this last term in the present work to describe the various drug cartels vying for hegemony in Mexico.

2. According to official estimates, at least 45,515 Mexicans have died from the beginning of the Calderón administration until September 2011 (Herrera 2012). This figure was released on January 12, 2012, by the Office of the Mexican Attorney General (*Procuraduría General de la República*).

3. Although organized crime groups in certain regions of Mexico (in Tamaulipas, for example) are not true paramilitary units, the term as it is utilized in this work alludes to the change in operational and institutional practices by criminal organizations in their bid to attain regional and national supremacy over other competing criminal organizations as well as state forces.

4. Mexico's warring cartels have killed thousands of people in the last few years, particularly since President Felipe Calderón took power in December 2006 and "sent some 45,000 army troops and federal police to a handful of states to take on drug gangs" (Luhnow and Casey 2010).

5. These statistics were released by the Office of the Presidency (*Oficina de la Presidencia de la República*) at http://www.presidencia.gob.mx/?DNA=119. Accessed May 10, 2011.

6. In comparison to other border and coastal states, Tamaulipas's border cities are the closest destinies (and, therefore, the safest ones) for organized crime groups that operate in the ports of Quintana Roo, Yucatán, and the Gulf of Mexico, as well as in the most important ports of the Mexican Pacific between Puerto Madero and San Blas (Guerrero 2010).

7. MEPI stands for Mexican Foundation of Investigative Journalism (*Fundación Mexicana de Periodismo de Investigación*).

8. *El Blog del Narco: La Entrevista*, December 7, 2010, http://www.youtube.com /watch?v=R3QF3P-gm4o. Accessed February 11, 2011.

9. In *Noticias y Reportajes con Adela Micha* 2010.

10. ICESI stands for *Instituto Ciudadano de Estudios sobre la Inseguridad* (Citizenry Institute on Insecurity Studies).

11. INEGI stands for *Instituto Nacional de Estadística, Geografía e Informática* (National Institute of Statistics and Geography).

12. There is a considerable gap in reported homicides between these two publications. The Mexican publication shows an advantage over its American counterpart by being at the very epicenter of the phenomena. Another factor that can explain the relatively low numbers of regional drug-related homicides, as reported in the *Brownsville Herald*, is that it did not cover the whole spectrum of events that unfolded in the state of Tamaulipas, concentrating instead in the immediate region of the Rio Grande Valley and its bordering neighbors to the south.

13. While this can be construed as nothing more than hearsay, one need only look at the numerous videos posted online to develop the perspective that more than six casualties resulted from the hours of intense fighting that took place in the city on November 5, 2010. These videos can be found either on YouTube or *El Blog del Narco*.

14. According to these data, Mexico and Iraq ranked jointly as the second most dangerous countries in the world for journalists, after Pakistan.

15. Other sources report higher numbers. For example, Molly Molloy, a researcher at New Mexico State University, who maintains the discussion site *Frontera List*, posits that the actual number of drug-related murders in this period "is much higher . . . by almost double" (O'Reilly 2012, para. 2). See *Frontera List* at http://groups.google.com /group/frontera-list?hl=en. Accessed April 19, 2013.

Bibliography

Blog del Narco 2010. "Noticias y Reportajes con Adela Micha." *El Blog del Narco: La Entrevista*, December 7. http://www.youtube.com/watch?v=R3QF3P-gm4o. Accessed February 11, 2011.

Campbell, Monica. 2008. "At Risk in Mexico: Drug Violence Is Silencing the Press." *Columbia Journalism Review* (November–December): 43–45.

Cantú, Jesús. 2010. "La Censura de los Cárteles." *Proceso* 1778 (November 30): 60–62.

Edmonds-Poli, Emily. 2006. "Decentralization under the Fox Administration: Progress or Stagnation?" *Mexican Studies* 22, no. 2: 387–416.

Flores Pérez, Carlos Antonio. 2008. *El Estado en Crisis: Crimen Organizado y Política: Desafíos para la Consolidación Democrática*. Mexico City: Centro de Investigaciones y Estudios Superiores en Antropología Social (CIESAS).

———. 2010. "Historias de Polvo y Sangre: Génesis y Evolución del Tráfico de Drogas en el Estado de Tamaulipas." http://ichantecolotl.blogspot.com/2008/07/editorial .html. Accessed October 2, 2012.

Galtung, Johan. 1969. "Violence, Peace, and Peace Research." *Journal of Peace Research* 6, no. 3: 167–91.

Guerrero, Eduardo Gutiérrez. 2010. "La Guerra por Tamaulipas." *Nexos en línea*, August 1. http://www.nexos.com.mx/?P=leerarticulo&Article=248541. Accessed September 12, 2012.

Herrera, Rolando. 2012. "Reportan 47,515 Narcoejecuciones." *Reforma*, January 12. http://reforma.vlex.com.mx/vid/reportan-narcoejecuciones-344529378. Accessed February 12, 2012.

Høivik, Tord. 1977. "The Demography of Structural Violence." *Journal of Peace Research* 14, no. 1: 59–73.

Instituto Ciudadano de Estudios sobre la Inseguridad (ICESI). 2010. *Consideraciones acerca de la Séptima Encuesta Nacional sobre Inseguridad.* http://www.icesi.org .mx/documentos/encuestas/encuestasNacionales/consideraciones_ENSI-7.pdf. Accessed May 4, 2011.

Instituto Nacional de Estadística, Geografíae Informatica (INEGI). 2010. *Séptima Encuesta Nacional sobre Inseguridad: ENSI 2010 (Síntesis Metodológica).* http:// www.inegi.gob.mx/est/contenidos/espanol/metodologias/encuestas/hogares/sm _ensi-07.pdf. Accessed May 4, 2012.

Luhnow, David, and Nicholas Casey. 2010. "Killing Escalates Mexico Drug War for a Few Dollars Less." *Wall Street Journal,* June 29. http://online.wsj.com/article/SB1 0001424052748703964104575334942693439322.html?mod=dist_smartbrief. Accessed March 11, 2012.

Mainwaring, Max G. 2010. *Gangs, Pseudo-Militaries, and Other Modern Mercenaries: New Dynamics in Uncomfortable Wars.* Norman: University of Oklahoma Press.

Medellín, Jorge. 2010. "De Orden Superior: Contrainteligencia en Tamaulipas . . . El Otro Estado de Sitio." *Eje Central,* March 16. http://columnas.ejecentral.com.mx /deordensuperior/2010/03/16. Accessed May 4, 2011.

Mendoza, Enrique. 2011a. "Cinco Años de Guerra, 60 Mil Muertos." *Proceso* 1832 (December 10). http://www.proceso.com.mx/?p=290774. Accessed December 22, 2011.

———. 2011b. "Quinto Año de Gobierno: 60 Mil 420 Ejecuciones." *Semanario Zeta* (December 12, 1967). http://www.zetatijuana.com/2011/12/12/quinto-ano-de-gobi erno-60-mil-420-ejecuciones/. Accessed December 22, 2011.

MEPI Fundación (Fundación Mexicana de Periodismo de Investigación). 2010. "México: La Nueva Espiral del Silencio." *Fundación MEPI* (November 17). http:// www.fundacionmepi.org/narco-violencia.html. Accessed May 4, 2011.

Michel, Víctor H. 2011. "Los Hoyos Negros del Censo." *Milenio,* March 6. http://www .milenio.com/cdb/doc/noticias2011/3caab1c4736e2260b6f80d90cf45b848. Accessed May 4, 2011.

Nava, José. 2011. "Gagging the Media: The Paramilitarization of Drug Trafficking Organizations and Its Consequences on the Freedom of Press in the Texas–Tamaulipas Border Region." MA thesis, Interdisciplinary Studies in Sociology, University of Texas at Brownsville.

O'Reilly, Andrew. 2012. "Mexico's Drug Death Toll Double What Reported, Expert Argues." *Fox News,* August 10. http://latino.foxnews.com/latino/news/2012/08/10/mexico -drug-death-toll-double-what-reported-expert-argues/. Accessed August 22, 2012.

Ortega, José A. 2011. "El Rasurado de las Cifras de la Violencia." *Milenio,* February 10. http://www.milenio.com/node/643279. Accessed May 4, 2012.

Ravelo, Ricardo. 2009. *Osiel: Vida y Tragedia de un Capo.* Mexico City: Grijalbo.

Reporters without Borders. 2011. *Mexico: Country Report 2011. Reporters without Borders,* September. http://en.rsf.org/report-mexico,184.html. Accessed November 29, 2011.

Ronquillo, Víctor. 2010. "La Geografía de la Narcocensura: Chihuahua, Tamaulipas, Michoacán, Oaxaca, Veracruz y Durango son Entidades donde el Ejercicio Periodístico puede Considerarse de Alto Riesgo." *Milenio Semanal,* August 15. http:// www.msemanal.com/node/2809. Accessed November 2, 2011.

Shirk, David. 2009. *Drug Violence in Mexico: Data and Analysis from 2001–2009*. San Diego: Trans-Border Institute, University of San Diego.

Sinova, Justino. 1987. "Poder Público y Medios de Comunicación: Síntomas de la Tentación Autoritaria." *Cuenta y Razón del Pensamiento Actual* 31: 53–58.

Weber, Max. 1919. "Politics as a Vocation." http://www.ne.jp/asahi/moriyuki/abukuma /weber/lecture/politics_vocation.html. Accessed November 2, 2011.

CHAPTER FOUR

Political Protection and the Origins of the Gulf Cartel[1]

Carlos Antonio Flores Pérez

Introduction

The official narrative of organized crime in Mexico attempts to convince the public that (1) the environment is generally hostile to criminal organizations; (2) government officials as a whole have no knowledge, except in unusual cases, of the illicit activities of the criminal groups they are in charge of prosecuting; (3) the documented cases of corrupt linkages between criminal organizations and public officials at various hierarchical levels are the result of individual transgressions but are not institutionalized practices, widespread within the government; and (4) the criminals are the ones who corrupt government officials. In this chapter the opposite is argued. The penetration of governmental structures by organized crime in Mexico is institutional and systemic, reaches all levels of government, and helps sustain the operations of organized crime. The existence of wide networks of crime–government links is vital for the operations of criminal groups, and the existence of corruption within the governmental and political arenas is crucial for their work and carefully cultivated.[2] This argument is not new. Although there is no consensus on a definition of organized crime, many academic studies point out the importance of the existence of corrupt networks within politics and government for a criminal group to operate and endure (Naylor 1997, 6; Albini 1971; Bailey and Godson 2000, 19; Geffray 2002, 47; Chambliss 1978; Block 1994, 10; McIllwain 1993, 304). In addition, the analysis of organized crime–government links is fundamental to understanding the depths of corruption in Mexico and its effect on the country's governability.

This chapter focuses on the most powerful kind of organized crime, drug trafficking, and its penetration of the Mexican government. A historical analysis of this issue indicates that among the actors that played a role in the growth of drug trafficking in Mexico were major political figures and bureaucrats, who used their positions of power and public influence to provide protection for the trafficking of illegal drugs. Moreover, the characteristics of the Mexican political regime made it easy for these politicians and bureaucrats to play a role in organized criminal activities and were decisive in sustaining them. In fact, sometimes, criminals were under the control of politicians and bureaucrats, not the other way around. In this chapter, historical evidence will be presented pointing to the existence of high-level political protection and the role it played in the emergence of one powerful drug trafficking organization in Mexico, the Gulf Cartel. Originally headquartered in the state of Tamaulipas, the Gulf Cartel was able to develop national and transnational logistics to traffic drugs using its networks of institutional protection. Protection for the Gulf Cartel was provided by high-ranking officials from the Federal Security Directorate (DFS), the General Attorney's Office, local police officers, and politicians from both the federal and the Tamaulipas state government. Research conducted in local and national media sources as well as in the archives of the DFS and the Directorate of Political and Social Investigations (IPS), mostly through direct requests to the Federal Institute for Access to Information, revealed the Gulf Cartel–government connections. The DFS and IPS were the intelligence arms of the Mexican federal government and were housed in the Interior Ministry, the most powerful cabinet-level position in Mexico. They reported to the Minister of the Interior and to the president directly. Both agencies were dismantled in 1985, after a scandal surrounding the DFS's involvement in protecting drug trafficking broke out as a consequence of the murder in that year of Enrique Camarena, a Drug Enforcement Administration (DEA) agent. The period analyzed here is the 1960s–1990s.

The conclusions in this chapter do not constitute proof of guilt, something only a court can establish. Instead, carefully examined here are the networks of individuals involved in order to show that organized crime in Mexico could not have flourished without carefully knitted criminal organization–government links. It should also be considered that the issue addressed in this chapter is clandestine by nature, and that there is a deliberate effort by participants to keep these links hidden. Thus research in this area requires quasi-forensic skills and even then some parts may be off, given the nature of the subject. Those who study organized crime and prosecute it know that any criminal group employs strategies designed to avoid being detected, and that this kind of research necessarily involves some guesswork. The level of impunity enjoyed by those in power was remarkable, and digging through historical evidence to uncover these links takes time and carefully crafted hypotheses. In addition, the opacity of the Mexican political regime made it even easier to hide these links and the incompetence of the judicial system made it even more difficult to know the truth. In mathematics, the theorems of Gödel and Tarski demonstrate that no system can be proven based on the foundations of its own premises (Morín 1991, 191–93). If we assume this when researching organized crime, we can see that necessarily some of its tracks will have been erased forever and that we have to fill in the gaps. Fortunately, there is enough historical evidence and some good memories to show that certain government officials protected drug traffickers. However, it could not be assumed that the people mentioned were doubtlessly implicated in crime, or that they were the only ones. Additional work will be required in the future to establish firmer conclusions on the links that we establish in this chapter.

Corruption, Public Officials, and Organized Crime

Collusion between government officials and criminals falls within the definition of corruption. In its simplest sense, it can be understood as the misuse of public power for private gains (Rose-Ackerman 1999, 91). Government officials engage in corruption when, in the administration of the resources under their custody, they exchange favors in the exercise of their public power for private gain. Among specialists who analyze organized crime, corruption is an indispensable factor in the existence of criminal groups (Lupsha 1988, 2).[3] Only with the cooperation of at least some public actors can an illegal activity of an organized nature—and the group of individuals who carry it out—flourish in a context in which the state has formally banned it and concentrates a considerable proportion of its efforts to combat it.

The previous observation holds true in any context in which organized crime operates. However, government–criminal organization links are specific and more concretely related to the history of each country. The breadth and depth of this complicity are determined by several factors, including the structural features of the political environment. In fact, the

Table 4.1. Proposed typology of relations between organized crime and politics

	Strong State–Authoritarian Regime	Strong State–Democratic Regime	Weak State–Authoritarian Regime	Weak State–Democratic Regime
Regime	Totalitarianism	Liberal democracy	Authoritarianism	Democracy with weak liberal content
Type of link with the endogenous criminal organizations	Monopolic-descendent-limited	Fragmented-multidirectioned-limited	Centralized-descendent-incremental	Atomized-multidirectioned-incremental
Characteristics	The state effectively monopolizes coercion and is capable of controlling all social subjects, so that it vertically plunders criminal groups. Criminal activities are limited to those that are allowed and sanctioned by public officials. The political corruption implied by the link between criminals and officials exists in specific areas of the public apparatus, but it	The state effectively monopolizes coercion; government officials have interiorized a sense of service to the public good. The link between criminals and officials exists, with variable fluctuations in those who control the relationship. The criminal-political link is limited by the fragmentation of power typical in a democracy, the existence of controls and effective	The state tends to monopolize coercion, with variable deficiencies, according to the historical case. It tends to centrally organize the social control mechanisms, allowing it to dominate, variably, the various social actors, including criminal groups. The discretional use of legality and the patrimonial and patronage concepts in public practice allow for the widespread	The state tends to monopolize coercion, with variable deficiencies, according to the historical case. Power is atomized. Political institutions operate with patrimonialist and/or patronage criteria, and interpret law at their convenience. Power's fragmentation allows multiple links between public officials and criminal organizations with variable fluctuation in those that have the leadership role

remains generally limited because a large part of the officials who make up the bureaucratic apparatus has internalized notions of service to the public good and loyalty to the state.

institutional counter-weights, and the professionalization of public service. The actors to be corrupted are too many and not all of them are corruptible.

proliferation of the link between criminals and politicians, and of political corruption in general. The central security institutions may compete among themselves for the extortion of criminals, but the activity of these, in general, requires the steady protection of the central power.

in the relationship. The dispersal of control leads to more widespread confrontations within the governmental apparatus, motivated by collusion with different criminal interests, because there are not lasting agreements to regulate illicit activities.

Source: Bureau of Justice Statistics, http://bjs.gov/index.cfm?ty=tp&tid=13.

transactional relationship between officials and criminals can be articulated under different conditions of equilibrium, depending on the state's strength or weakness, and can be magnified or attenuated by the conditions of the political regime. These factors constitute the ground on which the exchanges between public officials and criminals emerge and develop. These factors also determine the resources that one group or the other may rely on in order to maximize its profit.

Presented in this chapter is a theoretical framework that explains the influence that the state's structural strength or weakness exerts, jointly with the political regime's features, on the links between officials and criminals (Flores Pérez 2009, 105–36). It then offers a typology of government–criminal organization links. The typology is based on three criteria: (1) the concentration or dispersion of the actors that exercise dominant control in corruption links; (2) the direction of the influence, that is, the existence of a relatively clear hierarchical relationship between officials and criminals or a sense of who has the upper hand at any given point in time; and (3) the degree of negative impact these links have on the functions of the state.

In countries where the distinction between public and private interests is tenuous, public resources are often used to benefit the private interests of governmental actors. In them, the political regime does not usually require transparency, accountability, and compliance with the law in all areas and by all actors. As a result, the existence of opportunities for collusion between officials and criminals is considerably greater. In these conditions, corruption links are not limited to the lower rungs of authority within power structures but can become widespread.

As table 4.1 shows, collusion between public officials and criminals can be conceived as an unequal relationship. The former participate in the relationship to obtain profit in addition to their legitimate incomes, and the latter *must* share their profit with public officials as a way of avoiding law enforcement action and sometimes make use of an agency's resources to carry out their illegal activities. In this relationship, the resources that each actor has at its disposal are different. Public officials employ the resources of institutionalized violence entrusted to them by the state to extract concessions from the criminals or help them in their activities. Criminals depend on their own resources, that is, their accumulated fortunes and capacity to exercise violence alone. These conditions give the upper hand to government officials because they have at their disposal the entire force of the state (Flores Pérez 2009, 119–36). In cases of state weakness, the malfeasance of public officials reaches proportions where the line between them and the criminals becomes blurred, and the distinction between one group and the other may be relevant only in analytical terms.

Historical and Contextual Variables and Criminal Groups

From the 1930s to the 1990s, the capacity of the authoritarian regime to exercise political and social control over Mexican society extended to criminal organizations. The control of the state over society was consolidated in the 1940s. Since then and into the 1990s, the Mexican political regime was characterized by a considerable number of authoritarian features. They were articulated around a central institutional figure, the Mexican presidency (Cosío Villegas 1982, 28–29). This institution of the presidency constituted the axis of the system. It had powerful formal and informal prerogatives and, additionally, it relied on extralegal privileges that allowed it to subordinate the other branches of government and the state and local governments (Carpizo 1987, 191; Meyer 2000, 915; Camacho Solís 1977, 618). To be sure, state control over the country's territory was imperfect at best, even if it was comparatively stronger than that attained by other Latin American governments. In fact, statements from officials of the Mexican army point to the precariousness of the state's control over vast regions of the country, even during the period of greatest authoritarian centralization of power in the 1960s and 1970s (Flores Pérez 2009, 172–75). The centralization of political control in a single political party, the Institutional Revolutionary Party (PRI), after the Mexican Revolution and the characteristics of the authoritarian regime that emerged from that centralization of power supported the evolution of the relationship between the country's criminal underbelly and the political sphere (Morris 1991, 25–26).

The political preeminence of the federal executive over national, state, and local institutions was reinforced by the control the president exercised over the PRI, the ruling party, another crucial piece of the regime. Virtually all of the country's elected officials, and all of the public servants in the different government spheres, were members of the PRI. The pivot of all political decision making was the president, who took the final decision on candidacies and appointments and formal and informal privileges (González Casanova 1972, 45). The president was not only the head of state but also the head of government, head of the party, and the ruler of the entire political class. As a consequence, his immediate collaborators, his staff, his cabinet, and anyone he designated had preeminence in national politics. Finally, running through the formal structure of the national, state, and local political institutions was a well-articulated and complex set of social networks. They were cliques or political groups. In a context of limited competition, these cliques employed their political influence and their contacts with other social actors to deliberately manipulate governmental resources. This was done to advance their political aspirations and to protect their private interests and those of their clienteles and partners (Meyer 2002, 919; Camacho Solís 1977, 619). Under these networks and due to a lack of transparency and checks and balances, corruption in many areas of government increased. It was under the political geometry of an authoritarian and centralized scheme that drug trafficking, present in Mexico since the start of the twentieth century, grew and prospered (Astorga 2003, 14; Flores Pérez 2009, 137–228).

The links that existed between public officials and criminals during this period can be characterized as fitting a model of control labeled "centralized-descendant-incremental." It was highly desirable for organized criminal groups to have the protection of political and governmental actors. The centralization of power made negotiations relatively simple (Astorga 2003; Flores Pérez 2009). This in turn guaranteed a criminal organization's continuity. The state's institutions and the officials in charge of them determined which illicit activities would be tolerated and who could perform them. In other words, state actors determined the relevant formal and informal rules to which criminal groups would adhere. Under this scheme, criminals were replaceable parts in the dynamics of illegal activities, and they came and went. Criminals were in a relationship where state actors had the upper hand. Corrupt officials received enormous economic profits from the illicit activities of others (Flores Pérez 2009, 169–227).

Hence, between the 1940s and 1990s, organized crime prospered within the parameters imposed by state actors. Nevertheless, criminals had different roles and hierarchies. At the lower level were conventional criminals who developed their illicit activities but who were always subject to extortion by public officials. These criminals were the weakest link in the chain. Their durability in the criminal enterprise and even their physical survival were determined by the threshold of impunity dictated by their associates within government. At a mid-level were law enforcement agencies, which served as intermediaries between politicians and criminals. These agencies collaborated directly with criminal groups. Agents supported the operations and logistics of illicit businesses and even committed crimes. Although they had remarkable autonomy in their daily activities, agencies were subordinate to high-level policy makers who appointed or removed their leaders. This structure at the national level was replicated at the state and local levels. Naturally, local arrangements operated always following the rules imposed by the political regime, where the local officials were at once subordinated to the centralized institutions above them, all the way to the federal executive. At the higher level were high-ranking politicians and bureaucrats who often appointed their criminal subordinates to public safety, security, and even judicial posts down the ladder. They manipulated the decision-making process and institutional functions to guarantee cover for organized criminals. Laterally, there were economic actors at various levels with the ability to insert criminal profits in the formal economy. This subgroup has been much more difficult to examine because there is not enough available information in comparison to other actors.

Actors, Institutions, and Drug Trafficking in Tamaulipas

In the state of Tamaulipas, a major base for organized crime today and one of the most violent regions in the country during the Calderón administration, drug trafficking developed as an extension of other illicit activities already established in the area for many years, especially merchandise smuggling. Reports from the 1850s show the existence of important networks engaged in merchandise smuggling in cities that years later would become drug trafficking corridors. Ferdinand Von Seiffert, Prussian consul general, informed Berlin that year of the consequences of smuggling after the signing of the Guadalupe Hidalgo Peace Treaty of 1848. Referring to Matamoros, Tamaulipas, he pointed out that such cities "[a]re almost of no importance any longer in regard to legal commerce, nor for commerce coming from Europe" (Bernecker 1994, 126–27). In the then recently annexed Texas, there was one city on the border, Brownsville,

> whose almost sole activity is smuggling to Mexico. Brownsville is today the repository of all the prohibited merchandise destined to enter clandestinely the Mexican Republic. From there, they flow upriver to Camargo, where, as in all places, custody is so bad that the impudence of the Yankees does not have limits, and the goods, through Monterrey, travel to Coahuila, Zacatecas and San Luis. (Bernecker 1994, 126–27)

These remarks are relevant to the present:

Customs officials, upon seeing that with tariff revenues they couldn't even complete their own salaries, decided to ally themselves with the smugglers to keep more or less some commercial traffic in the city. For a fee, or for part of the profit of the contraband, they grant all kinds of certifications. The government is incapable of controlling this, and even if it had the means to do so, it wouldn't dare for fear that the border states would secede from the [Mexican] Federation, because what currently maintains commerce alive in those states is contraband.[4] (Bernecker 1994, 126–27)

The original founder of the Gulf Cartel, Juan Nepomuceno Guerra Cárdenas (Juan N. Guerra), was a smuggler who ventured into drug trafficking. His criminal career benefited from his relationship with many members of public safety agencies and political institutions. Evidence suggests that officials were protectors of his criminal enterprise. It was Juan N. Guerra, uncle of Juan García Ábrego, who set up the criminal organization's links with law enforcement and cultivated political support. Some sources indicate that the first political relationships Juan N. Guerra cultivated were with political groups from the state of Hidalgo, specifically with the Rojo Gómez family. His brother, Roberto Guerra Cárdenas, became a *compadre* to Jorge Rojo Lugo, who would become the head of the Mexican Department of Agricultural Reform and later governor of Hidalgo during the 1976–1982 José López Portillo administration (Figueroa 1996, 35, 146). Years later, Rojo Lugo became head of the PRI in Tamaulipas and, along with Governor Emilio Martínez Manautou, would choose Jesús Roberto Guerra Velasco, nephew of Juan N. Guerra, to be the mayoral candidate and eventually mayor of Matamoros, Tamaulipas (1984–1987). Martínez Manautou played a role in the Gulf Cartel's development (AGN, Public Version of Emilio Martínez Manautou's file, DFS, Docket 1: 27–28).[5] This also marks the beginning of the leadership of Juan García Ábrego in the Gulf Cartel. In addition, Roberto Guerra Cárdenas, Juan N. Guerra's younger brother, was head of the state district attorney's office in Tamaulipas during the administration of Governor Praxedis Balboa in 1963. Roberto would become one of the biggest political figures in that state. In a biography written by his widow, it was reported that he had a deep friendship with "the former President Mexico Emilio Portes Gil and with former Tamaulipas governors Norberto Treviño Zapata and Enrique Cárdenas" (Solorio Martinez n.d., 360). This is intriguing, because one of the brothers of the region's main trafficker was in charge of the state agency responsible for tax collection.

Equally puzzling is the fact that Enrique Cárdenas González had been appointed Undersecretary of Investigations at the Mexican Treasury Department (Secretaría de Hacienda y Crédito Público) in 1972 by President Luis Echeverría (Martínez 1999). One of his duties was combating border smuggling. He resigned from that position to accept the PRI candidacy for governor of Tamaulipas. He was governor from 1976 to 1981 (Camp 1992, 95). Since the beginning of the 1970s, there had been references in the media to the participation of the Guerra family in drug trafficking. Early in that decade, a truck transporting a half ton of marijuana and destined for Tamaulipas was caught in Nuevo León. But drug trafficking would become even more conspicuous in the period 1981–1987 with the arrival of Emilio Martínez Manautou as governor of Tamaulipas.

Although he became governor toward the end of his political career, Martínez Manautou was not a secondary figure in national politics. He had been senator from 1958 to 1964, chief of staff for President Gustavo Díaz Ordaz between 1964 and 1970, and was mentioned as a potential candidate to succeed Díaz Ordaz as president of Mexico, finally losing the designation to Luis Echeverría. His personal relationship to President Gustavo Díaz Ordaz allowed him to maintain a strong influence in his home state of Tamaulipas. The testimony of Manuel A. Ravizé, governor of Tamaulipas from 1969 to 1975, is revealing:

> I became governor because of Emilio Martínez Manautou, when he was Chief of Staff during the administration of Gustavo Díaz Ordaz. It was with Emilio that President Díaz Ordaz discussed any issue related to Tamaulipas. That is why, when they revealed that Luis Echeverría was the PRI candidate to succeed Díaz Ordaz, my first impulse was to turn in my resignation to President Díaz Ordaz. . . . [Martínez Manautou] named the state government's secretary general, senior officers, the chief of police, and almost all the mayors of the important municipalities. (*Diario de Nuevo Laredo* 1986, 1, 6C)

The defeat of Martínez Manautou by Echeverría for the presidential succession kept the former ostracized during Echeverría's administration. However, Martínez Manautou returned to public life as the secretary of Health and Public Welfare during the José López Portillo administration. López Portillo had been Martínez Manautou's subordinate when the latter was chief of staff. It was López Portillo who invited Martínez Manautou to become governor of Tamaulipas at the end of the 1970s. He was officially named candidate for governor of Tamaulipas on June 15, 1980 (*El Bravo de Matamoros* 1980b, 1, first section). His first campaign act in the state took place in Matamoros. Martínez Manautou had begun his political career in that city as a city councilman (*El Mañana de Nuevo Laredo* 1980b, 4, second section). He had aspired to become governor in 1962, but Adolfo López Mateos, then Mexico's president, had blocked him. The nomination went to Praxedis Balboa Gojon instead. His luck would change when President López Mateos named Gustavo Díaz Ordaz his successor, because he was a close friend of Martínez Manautou. However, a document from the Dirección Federal de Seguridad (DFS) shows that a careful analysis of the candidates had been conducted and it had pointed out the close ties of his brother-in-law, Augusto Cárdenas, ex-mayor of Matamoros, to drug trafficking. The report indicated that he was "an accomplice of Juan N. Guerra, well known smuggler of all types of merchandise and even drugs" (AGN, Public Version of Emilio Martínez Manautou's file, DFS, Docket 1: 46). It was becoming known that several members of the political clique to which Martínez Manautou belonged had a lot to do with the growth of influence of the Guerra family. Thus who the allies of Martínez Manautou were is worth looking into.

A memorandum of the DFS, dated August 1962 and signed by the then head of the DFS, Manuel Rangel Escamilla, refers to a meeting among former presidents Emilio Portes Gil, Lázaro Cárdenas del Río, and Aldolfo Ruiz Cortines, where Portes Gil stated that the former secretary of Industry and Commerce, Raúl Salinas Lozano, was backing Emilio Martínez Manautou as candidate for governor of Tamaulipas (AGN, Public Version of Emilio Martínez Manautou's file, DFS, Docket 1: 60–62). Years later, according to statements made by his son, former president Carlos Salinas de Gortari, Raúl Salinas Lozano had also backed him in his search for the Mexican presidency (Castañeda 1999, 233).

Toward the end of the Díaz Ordaz administration, among the figures close to Martínez Manautou and who supported his presidential aspirations for the succession was Carlos Hank González. Hank González had been head of the Food Supply National Agency (*Compañía Nacional de Subsistencias Populares* or CONASUPO), governor of the state of Mexico, mayor of Mexico City, and fellow congressman with Martínez Manautou in the late 1950s and early 1960s. Hank González had a close relationship with Raúl Salinas Lozano, according to DFS documents, with whom he had investments in several businesses that, according to the same source, were practically property of General Bonifacio Salinas Leal, former governor of Nuevo León and, according to the document, a close relative of Salinas Lozano. Bonifacio Salinas's representative in those businesses was Roberto González Barrera, father-in-law of Hank González's son (AGN, Public Version of Hank González's file, IPS, Docket 2: 21–23).

Years later a secret document of the Center for Antidrug Intelligence of the Mexican Army, whose extracts circulated in the media in 1997, and to which the author of this chapter had access, pointed out alleged links among Hank González Salinas Lozano, and González Barrera with the Gulf Cartel. It even implicated Carlos and Raúl Salinas de Gortari (Boyer 2001, 115–43). Of the brothers, the former (Carlos) became president and the latter (Raúl) was prosecuted and convicted of money laundering. According to this information, Raúl was linked to, among others, the group led by Juan García Ábrego, who would become leader of the Gulf Cartel. Raúl Salinas was also imprisoned for ten years for being the intellectual author of the assassination of José Francisco Ruiz Massieu, a PRI leader, who was in fact his brother-in-law. In 2005, Mexican courts threw out his conviction.

Apparently the relationship between Hank González and Martínez Manautou included other businesses. A brother of Emilio Martínez Manautou, Federico, was secretary general of the state of Baja California, from 1965 to 1971 (Blancornelas 1997), and mayor of Mexicali, Baja California, between 1960 and 1962. According to DFS reports, during his time as secretary general, Federico had a conflict with the state's governor, Raúl Sánchez Díaz, at least that is what was said in the local press at the time. The DFS report stated that the newspapers attributed the dispute to the governor's attempt to regulate various clandestine activities, such as gambling and prostitution, which generated resistance by Federico, who, according to media reports, gave them protection. His brother, Emilio, was the chief of staff of the Mexican presidency, and Federico felt that he did not have to pay heed to his hierarchical superior (the governor). The report ended with a denial, signed by the head of the DFS, Fernando Gutiérrez Barrio, eulogistically exonerating the brother of the powerful potential presidential candidate, Emilio Martínez Manautou (AGN, Public Version of Emilio Martínez Manautou's file, DFS, Docket 1: 109–11).

In any case, years later, a letter published in *Proceso*, by a reader named Roberto Soto, affirmed that in the state of Baja California there were rumors that Federico Martínez Manautou had received as a gift a mansion located in Playas de Rosarito. The mansion had in the past been a casino. The gift allegedly came from a businessman named Johnny Alessio. Since 1963, Alessio had been given the license to operate the Agua Caliente racetrack. Alessio was apparently linked to the Italian American Mafia.

The racetrack and various gambling shops related to it have for years been linked to the Hank family (Martínez 1999, 161–73). Jesús Garduño, Agua Caliente's manager, had been a Hank González subordinate in different public posts (*Proceso*, 1984a). Alessio had also invested in several casinos and racetracks along the Mexican northern border. Businessman José María Guardia, former owner of Ciudad Juárez's racetrack, said in an interview that this establishment had belonged, until 1990, to Johnny Alessio. Permission to operate this business had been offered to Guardia by Fernando Gutiérrez Barrios, the interior secretary (Secretario de Gobernación) in the 1990s (*Revista Fortuna* 2005). In 1983 a racetrack in Nuevo Laredo opened its doors, inaugurated by Emilio Martínez Manautou, political associate of Hank González (*Proceso*, 1984a).

Another member of the political clique that had backed the presidential candidacy of Martínez Manautou was Leopoldo Sánchez Celis, former member of Congress and Hank González's colleague. He had been governor of Sinaloa (1963–1968) and has been identified by multiple sources as a personal friend of Miguel Ángel Félix Gallardo, a major capo from the state of Sinaloa and main figure of the drug trafficking world in Mexico during the 1970s and 1980s. Miguel Ángel Félix was a pioneer of massive cocaine trafficking from South America through Mexico and then into the United States (*Proceso* 1989).[6] At the end of his administration, Sánchez Celis was welcomed by Carlos Hank González, then governor of Mexico State, who gave him various responsibilities in the state government. Hank González and Sánchez Celis became close friends. In fact, during his last State of the Union address as governor, Hank González expressed his gratitude to Sánchez Celis. DFS reports detail that "a great number of Congressmen received financing for their campaigns from Professor Hank González through Leopoldo Sánchez Celis" (AGN, Public Version of Carlos Hank González's file, DFS, Docket 2: 274). Apparently Sánchez Celis's ability to obtain campaign resources was legendary. Already in 1962, having been a potential candidate for governor of Sinaloa, sources cited by the renowned historian of drug trafficking in Mexico, Luis Astorga, identified Sánchez Celis as the candidate of the opium poppy or "sleepy plant" producers, who provided financing for him (Astorga 2003, 144–45).[7]

The relationship between Sánchez Celis and Martínez Manautou was also close. The Political and Social Investigations Directorate reported trips made together by Sánchez Celis and a brother of Martínez Manautou, with whom he toured several Sinaloa municipalities during a week in April 1972 (AGN, Public Version of Leopoldo Sánchez Celis's file, IPS,

Docket 1: 7). Sánchez Celis had backed Martínez Manautou's maneuvers to oust the president of the National Autonomous University of Mexico (Universidad Nacional Autónoma de México, or UNAM), Ignacio Chávez. A DFS report states the operations of a "Sinaloa Group" made up of students from the National Polytechnic Institute (Instituto Politécnico Nacional) and the UNAM were involved. The report explicitly points out that

> the activities of the so-called Sinaloa Group have Leopoldo Sánchez Duarte as their common denominator. Sánchez Duarte is the son of the former governor of Sinaloa, and we considered that, through him, the money for these activities was supplied. (AGN, Public Version of Leopoldo Sánchez Celis's file, DFS, Docket 2: 201)

In 1966 the mobilization of Sánchez Duarte's student group received lenient treatment from the head of the Special Services Section of the Mexico City Police, Raúl Mendiolea Cerecero. Mendiolea Cerecero was directly linked with another ally of Martínez Manautou's in the bid to succeed Díaz Ordaz, Óscar Flores Sánchez. Flores Sánchez had been governor of Chihuahua during the 1960s and would be Mexican attorney general from 1976 to 1978. According to a DFS document, classified as "secret" and dated August 1978, Flores Sánchez was a supporter of Martínez Manautou in his bid to succeed Díaz Ordaz and the political protector of Raúl Mendiolea Cerecero. When Flores Sánchez became attorney general, Mendiolea Cerecero was appointed chief of the Federal Judicial Police. Flores Sánchez also promoted Carlos Aguilar Garza, coordinator of the Mexican Federal Attorney's Office in Sinaloa, Chihuahua, and Durango during Operation Condor. The document explains:

> We do not have any evidence that demonstrates that Mr. Flores Sánchez has been part of, or directly involved in this commerce in any way. However, we have ample evidence that some of his closest collaborators were in fact involved, and continue to be involved at this time, directly or indirectly, in the business of drug trafficking. And we also think that it is impossible for Flores not to have any knowledge of these past and present activities. (AGN, Public Version of Raúl Mendiolea Cerecero's file, DFS, Docket 1: 155–69)

Among the individuals mentioned in the report are Mendiolea Cerecero and Aguilar Garza, calling them protectors of narcotrafficking (AGN, Public Version of Raúl Mendiolea Cerecero's file, DFS, Docket 1:

155–69). One of the main operational contacts for Félix Gallardo during the 1970s was, precisely, Carlos Aguilar Garza, who years later would be transferred to Tamaulipas with the same functions, practically simultaneously with the designation of Martínez Manautou as candidate for governor of Tamaulipas in 1980. Óscar Flores Sánchez, attorney general, and Raúl Mendiolea, his chief of the Judicial Federal Police, announced the designation of Carlos Aguilar Garza as coordinator of the Mexican Attorney General's Office in Tamaulipas on June 17, 1980, two days after the designation of Martínez Manautou as candidate for governor (*El Mañana de Reynosa* 1980b). Years later, in 1985, still during the governorship of Martínez Manautou, Aguilar Garza crashed in Nuevo León in a light aircraft coming from Chetumal, Quintana Roo, and headed for Nuevo Laredo, Tamaulipas. The pilot was the commander of Civil Aeronautics of the Airport of Nuevo Laredo, Manuel Amozorrutia, who stated to the authorities that the plane was loaded with cocaine and that Aguilar Garza participated in cocaine trafficking with Juan N. Guerra (Federal Judicial Police Act 1989).[8]

On June 16, 1980, a day after Emilio Martínez Manautou was named the PRI candidate for governor of Tamaulipas, Emilio López Parra was officially named the new commander of the Federal Judicial Police (PJF) in Matamoros, as per instructions from the head of the PJF, Raúl Mendiolea Cerecero. During the year prior to his designation, he had held the same position in Tijuana, Baja California. At the time, the federal attorney in charge of the Regional Coordination of the Mexican Federal Attorney Office for that area was Carlos Aguilar Garza (*El Bravo de Matamoros* 1980a). In May 1989, López Parra was arrested and charged with money laundering. On November 18, 1990, he was freed because of lack of evidence. In 1993, witnesses protected by U.S. authorities offered testimony about the institutional protection that Emilio López Parra gave to García Ábrego's organization (Figueroa 1996, 231–33).

Again on June 14, 1980, one day before the designation of Martínez Manautou as candidate for governor, another figure in security was sent to Tamaulipas. It was Brigadier General Manuel Díaz Escobar, appointed commander of the 8th Military Zone, headquartered in Tancol, Tamaulipas. A few years prior, Díaz Escobar had been in charge of Operation Condor in Badiraguato, Sinaloa, one of the emblematic towns in the history of drug trafficking in Mexico (*El Mañana de Reynosa* 1980a, 1, third section). Manuel Díaz Escobar had been the officer in charge of training a paramilitary group known as *Los Halcones* (The Falcons) that participated in the repression against student protests in 1968 and in the massacre of students on Corpus Christi Day (June 10, 1971), known in Mexico as *La Masacre del Jueves de Corpus* (*El Universal* 2008). In 1971, Díaz Escobar operated under the institutional mandate of the then regent of Mexico City, Alfonso Martínez Domínguez. *Los Halcones* were paid through the government office under his charge. Martínez Domínguez was another old ally of Martínez Manautou, and, in 1980, when the latter was named candidate for governor of Tamaulipas, the former was serving as governor of Nuevo León.

On Sunday, November 30, 1980, the closing of Martínez Manautou's campaign would be held in Matamoros. A similar act was programmed for that afternoon, for the closing of the campaign of the opposition candidate for the mayor of Matamoros, Jorge Cárdenas González, brother of ex-governor Enrique Cárdenas González. The local paper reported that the Mexican army had patrolled the street the day before in vehicles that had machine guns mounted on them. The operation was headed by the commander of the military zone, Manuel Díaz Escobar (*El Mañana de Nuevo Laredo* 1980b, 1, second section).

Additionally, that same paper pointed out that the day before partisan assault groups had arrived in Matamoros, sent by the governor of Nuevo León, Alfonso Martínez Domínguez. Their orders were to support Martínez Manautou and prevent, or squash, protests in favor of Jorge Cárdenas González (*El Mañana de Nuevo Laredo* 1980b, 1, second section). Jorge Cárdenas González would win in Matamoros, despite opposition by the government. The relationship between Jorge Cárdenas and Martínez Manautou was tense. To succeed Jorge Cárdenas in 1984, the governor, Emilio Martínez Manautou, would support, for the PRI candidacy, an individual named Jesús Roberto Guerra Velasco. He was the son of Roberto Guerra Cárdenas, the nephew of Juan N. Guerra, and the cousin of Juan García Ábrego.

The relationship of Martínez Manautou with the new mayor was close. The Interior Department detailed in its reports multiple meetings and tours that the governor and Guerra Velasco took together, to inaugurate public works financed with state and municipal funds. Some of these public works were valued in MX$1,500 million (AGN, Public Version of Emilio Martínez Manautou's file, IPS, Docket 1: 45–47, 50–51), an amount that contrasts with the ebb of public resources that the predecessor major suffered from Martínez Manautou's government (AGN, Public Version of Emilio Martínez Manautou's file, IPS, Docket 1: 296). Guerra Velasco and Martínez Manautou even carried out joint acts with the then secretary of national defense, Juan Arévalo Gardoqui, who in an official visit to the state would make a stop in Matamoros, where he would be received by

Mayor Guerra Velasco and Governor Martínez Manautou (AGN, Public Version of Emilio Martínez Manautou's file, IPS, Docket 1: 72). This was a peculiar meeting, taking into account the existence of several versions of the participation of General Arévalo Gardoqui in drug trafficking during that era (Astorga 2005, 143–44; Cabildo 1992).

Concerning the DFS, in 1980, Commander Rafael Chao López was the regional commander in the northeastern part of the country. He was the main decision maker in the offices of the Federal Police in Tamaulipas. Chao López held that position until the beginning of 1984 (*Diario de Nuevo Laredo* 1984a, 3C). In 1973, he was chief of state security—it doesn't say which agency or institution he belonged to—in Sinaloa, according to the director of the DFS, Cap. Luis de la Barreda Solórzano (AGN, Public Version of Rafael Chao López's file, DFS, Docket 1: 1). The DFS public version of Chao López's personal file states that, in this period, he was charged with antidrug tasks and arrested various drug traffickers in the region (AGN, Public Version of Rafael Chao López's file, DFS, Docket 1: 1).

In the late 1970s, Miguel Nazar Haro, then head of the DFS, sent Chao López to the northwestern region (AGN, Public Version of Emilio Martínez Manautou's file, DFS, Docket 2: 88–91). Chao López had the support of a political group different from that of Martínez Manautou, one that backed Nazar Haro, originally aligned under the orders of Fernando Gutiérrez Barrios. Toward the end of the 1970s, Nazar Haro had changed his political loyalty to another ex-director of the DFS and political figure, Javier García Paniagua (Aguayo Quezada 2001, 234). Because of this, the activities of Chao López in Tamaulipas, between the end of the 1970s and the beginning of the 1980s, show more direct extortion of drug traffickers, various criminals, and even people without any apparent criminal background (AGN, Public Version of Rafael Chao López's file, DFS, Docket 1: 6). In 1979 the DFS reported the arrest of individuals who served as "aids" of commander Chao López, engaged in extortion (AGN, Public Version of Rafael Chao López's file, DFS, Docket 1: 6). Chao López was detained five years later in Manzanillo, Colima. His own nephew accused him, after being himself detained in possession of a load of cocaine hidden in a truck carrying apples (*El Norte* 1989b).

Years later, Chao López was also identified as a protector of narcotrafficking groups from Sinaloa. He was accused of protecting in 1985 the escape to Sinaloa of Rafael Caro Quintero's relatives, after they had killed an agent of the Federal Highway Police in Nuevo León. After his arrest, Rafael Caro Quintero himself stated that he had paid bribes to Chao López. According to a newspaper story, in mid-1985, federal authorities had detected properties belonging to Chao López valued at 2 billion pesos (*El Norte* 1989a).

In Tamaulipas, research of DFS agents headed by Chao López shows a treatment toward local criminals based on traditional extortion schemes. That even led to occasional tensions and disputes between traffickers, local police corporations, and their political backers, on the one hand, and DFS agents, on the other. This is evident, for example, in the political pressures applied by the associates of Martínez Manautou against the commanders of the DFS. Most of this pressure was aimed at removing them. Such a situation could also be gleaned from the information contained in a DFS document, dated May 28, 1981, signed by Miguel Nazar Haro, head of the DFS, and sent to the subsecretary of the interior, Fernando Gutiérrez Barrios. In the document, Nazar Haro answered Emilio Martínez Manautou's complaints in regard to Chao López and his agents (AGN, Public Version of Emilio Martínez Manautou's file, DFS, Docket 2: 88–91).[9] In another case, DFS agents made a special display of their investigative capabilities to pressure Governor Martínez Manautou, as they investigated the alleged smuggling of eighteen-wheelers loaded with PVC pipes, presumably belonging to him. The DFS commander followed this case with persistence (AGN, Public Version of Emilio Martínez Manautou's file, IPS, Docket 2: 20–21).

Considering the background of those involved, a dispute for the booty from drug trafficking and other types of smuggling between two different political groups should not be discarded. In the end, the economic interests over drug trafficking would dilute these differences. After his arrest, in his first statements to the authorities, Chao López accepted being involved in drug trafficking and indicated the participation of Carlos Aguilar Garza. He confirmed that the plane in which the latter had crashed was transporting 600 kilograms of cocaine, and that Chao López himself had been in charge of guaranteeing that the drugs would be unloaded from the plane and then hidden. He provided immediate protection for Aguilar Garza, as well as the lawyer and his associate, Miguel Ángel del Bosque Cardona, and the pilot, Manuel Amozorrutia Silva, the commander of the DFS, Manuel García García, and the copilot, Fernando de la Jara Martínez, all of whom were in the plane crash (*El Norte* 1989b).

It was during this period that cocaine trafficking began through the northeastern region of the country, especially through Tamaulipas. In April 1977, the head of the Attorney General's Office in this zone stated that between April 1977 and June 1980 the Federal Judicial Police had only confiscated 10.4 kilograms of this drug (*El Mañana de Nuevo Laredo* 1980c). In October 1984, the local newspapers reported on the biggest cocaine seizure until then, 300 kilograms, in Nuevo Laredo (*Diario de Nuevo Laredo* 1984b). The cocaine was transported from Medellín to Guadalajara (*Diario de Nuevo Laredo* 1984c). Miguel Ángel Félix Gallardo, linked to Carlos Aguilar Garza, commanded drug trafficking in Guadalajara. The cocaine boom in Tamaulipas occurred after Aguilar Garza was transferred to that state.

It was also during this period that the violence associated with drug trafficking started getting worse in Tamaulipas, as a result of the building of the criminal organization headed by Juan N. Guerra and his nephew, Juan García Ábrego. The support of key political and security authorities was a determining factor in this. Manuel Amozorrutia, Carlos Aguilar Garza's pilot, who confessed to transporting the cocaine in the plane in which both crashed, explained the drug trafficking links between Aguilar Garza and Juan N. Guerra (Federal Judicial Police Act 1989).

According to Amozorrutia, Aguilar Garza and Juan N. Guerra authorized the execution of an old associate in narcotrafficking, Casimiro Espinoza Campos, in Matamoros. The attack occurred under the supervision of Juan García Ábrego. The original attack, carried out by Óscar López Olivares, a subordinate of the latter, had failed. Óscar López Aguilar later became a protected witness of the U.S. authorities. He stated that his failure had led to an additional attack, to be carried out while Espinoza Campos was wounded and convalescing in a hospital in Matamoros. Seven patients at that hospital died in that attack, which could be considered the first public violent attack by the organization that in the following years would be known as the Gulf Cartel. Paradoxically, Espinoza Campos survived that attack and died several days later because of his wounds.

The municipal police under Mayor Jesús Roberto Guerra Velasco, the State Public Security Agency under the orders of Major Abdón Trejo Nava, an old collaborator of Martínez Manautou's in the Office of the Presidency, the State Judicial Police, under Ricardo Zolezzi Cavazos, appointed by the governor, Emilio Martínez Manautou, the DFS, and the PJF all seemed incapable of finding the individuals responsible for that hospital attack.

Conclusion

It is possible that all of these individuals were only coincidentally involved in the circumstances referred to here. A more logical conclusion is that all of these facts add up to more direct and indirect participation, cover-up, concealment, and abetting of narcotrafficking by several of the most important political and security institutions and figures in the country and in the state of Tamaulipas. A DFS document dated 1970 and sent to the agency's head, Captain Luis de la Barreda Moreno, clearly describes a similar situation, narrating meetings carried out in the state of Nuevo León, neighboring Tamaulipas, to "organize smuggling in accordance with the Headquarters of . . . Customs . . . based in Monterrey." There, Captain Alfonso Domene—brother of José Juan Domene, the senior administration officer of the Office of the Mexican Presidency, only a few months earlier headed by Emilio Martínez Manautou—had meetings with politicians that stood out "as supporters" of Martínez Manautou in his presidential aspirations. According to the report, among those present at the meetings was "Juan N. Guerra, a famous smuggler, pimp and trafficker from Matamoros, a generous contributor to the campaign of his friend, Doctor Martínez Manautou" (AGN, Public Version of Emilio Martínez Manautou's file, DFS, Docket 1: 182–83).

According to several sources, everything worsened by 1988. At least until 1994, most of the traffickers arrested in Tamaulipas would be rival members of organizations of Juan N. Guerra and Juan García Ábrego. Juan N. Guerra was arrested in 1991, but he was promptly freed. He died a free man in Matamoros in July 2001 (*El Universal* 2001). Juan García Ábrego was not arrested until 1996. In 1989, answering a direct question about his career as a "politician," given that there were rumors that he had financed political campaigns in Tamaulipas, Juan N. Guerra himself indicated: "I am not a politician . . . but I am their friend. One thing's for sure, I am a *priísta*. I've always been one and I vote for its candidates." According to the reporter, he then showed him his PRI membership card (*Proceso* 1991). Those statements were made a short while after the celebration of a rally in which a country roadway was reinaugurated, a road that led directly to land owned by Juan N. Guerra. According to the media, the work was paid for with resources from the National Solidarity Program (Programa Nacional de Solidaridad), whose goal was to reduce poverty. According to the newspaper, among those present were Senator Manuel Cavazos Lerma and federal congressman Tomás Yarrington (*Proceso* 1991). Some years afterward, both became governors of the state of Tamaulipas. Yarrington is currently being investigated by the federal government for corruption, drug trafficking, and money laundering, along with two other recent Tamaulipas governors.

This analysis suggests that the drug trafficking–government links are well at work in Mexico and that they grease the whole industry. Political actors played a vital role in the formation and growth of criminal organizations because criminals were sheltered and disciplined by the intermediaries of the security institutions. Tamaulipas is an egregious case, but there are other regions of the country where a similar case could be made. The PRI's loss of the presidency in 2000 upset this equilibrium, resulting in a profoundly altered relationship between crime in and with the government. This political seismic shift implied the rupture of the old mechanisms of collusion and extortion and control over criminal groups, without ending the endemic corruption that had proliferated during the preceding regimes. These new conditions can be described as belonging to the model labeled "atomized-multidirectioned-incremental" in our typology.

In Tamaulipas, the persistence of corruption and the power vacuum left after the arrest of Juan García Ábrego would further give way to the emergence of a new organization, headed by Osiel Cárdenas Guillén. This new trafficker did not come from a privileged position within the networks of the Juan N. Guerra–Juan García Ábrego criminal group. Notwithstanding, he consolidated his power in the northeast region of Mexico, even against the onslaught of the Fox and the Calderón administrations. But his would be and would have to be a new, much more violent organization, which laid the foundation for recruiting a highly capable enforcer group, *Los Zetas*. The core of *Los Zetas* was made up of deserters from the special forces of the Mexican army, a fact that would strengthen their operational capability and their ability to fight and spread in several states of the country, no doubt partly fueled by the new fractured political class. However, this is a topic that needs to be tackled in another analysis. A final cautionary note is that although association does not equal guilt, network analysis is often a good beginning to determine motives and means in organized crime. And given the cultural and political context in Mexico, and the association between those whose guilt has been demonstrated and those whose guilt is not yet demonstrated, we can safely assume that any investigation should follow these connections as a lead to research the extent of collusion between politicians and bureaucrats and organized crime.

Appendix A

Names mentioned in this chapter and short biographies

This list is not intended as an attribution of guilt but simply as an informational section for the reader to understand who the individuals mentioned in this chapter are and the relationships among them.

Aguilar Garza, Carlos. Coordinator of the Mexican Federal Attorney's Office in Sinaloa, Chihuahua, and Durango during Operation Condor in the late 1970s and responsible for the same task in northeast México (Nuevo León, Tamaulipas, and Coahuila) in the early 1980s.

Alessio, John. Former operator of the Agua Caliente and Ciudad Juárez racetracks.

Amozorrutia, Manuel. Chief of Nuevo Laredo's airport and associate of Carlos Aguilar Garza.

Arévalo Gardoqui, Juan. Secretary of Defense, 1982–1988.

Balboa Gojon, Praxedis. Governor of Tamaulipas, 1963–1969. Roberto Guerra Cárdenas was a member of his cabinet.

Cárdenas, Augusto. Mayor of Matamoros, 1955–1957, and brother-in-law of Emilio Martínez Manautou. DFS files link him to Juan N. Guerra.

Cárdenas González, Enrique. Investigations Undersecretary at the Mexican Treasury Department charged with combating smuggling. Member of President Luis Echeverría's cabinet, 1970–1975; governor of Tamaulipas, 1975–1980; senator, 1991–1997.

Cárdenas González, Jorge. Mayor of Matamoros, 1981–1983, and brother of ex-governor Enrique Cárdenas González.

Cárdenas Guillén, Osiel. Main drug lord in Tamaulipas during the late 1990s and early 2000s.

Caro Quintero, Rafael. Drug lord from Sinaloa who ordered the murder of DEA agent Enrique Camarena.

Cavazos Lerma, Manuel. Former congressman and senator from Tamaulipas; governor of the state, 1993–1999.

Chao López, Rafael. Commander of the DFS, in charge of operations in Tamaulipas and Nuevo León; associated with Carlos Aguilar Garza and Juan N. Guerra; protégé of Miguel Nazaro Haro, head of the DFS.

De la Barreda Solórzano, Luis. Former head of the DFS.

Díaz Escobar, Manuel. Brigadier general appointed commander of the 8th Military Zone, headquartered in Tancol, Tamaulipas, in 1981. Díaz Escobar formerly had been in charge of Operation Condor in Badiraguato, Sinaloa. He also was in charge of training a paramilitary group known as *Los Halcones* (The Falcons).

Domene, Alfonso (Captain). Deputy chief of customs in Monterrey, Nuevo León, in 1970; brother of José Juan Domene, senior administration officer of the Office of the Mexican Presidency, when it was headed by Emilio Martínez Manautou.

Espinoza Campos, Casimiro. Drug trafficker and Gulf Cartel's victim.

Félix Gallardo, Miguel Ángel. Main drug lord in Mexico during the 1970s and 1980s.

Flores Sánchez, Óscar. Former Undersecretary of Agriculture in the cabinet of Miguel Alemán Valdés, 1946–1952; governor of Chihuahua in the 1960s; Mexican attorney general from 1976 to 1978; and supporter of Emilio Martínez Manautou in the 1970s presidential succession.

García Ábrego, Juan. Drug trafficker; head of operations of the Gulf Cartel from the late 1980s through the mid-1990s; nephew of Juan N. Guerra.

García Paniagua, Javier. Former head of the DFS in the 1970s and Secretary of Agrarian Reform in the López Portillo administration; aspiring presidential candidate in 1982.

Garduño, Jesús. Manager of the Agua Caliente racetrack in the 1980s and former subordinate of Carlos Hank González in different public posts.

González Barrera, Roberto. Business owner of *Maseca* and *Banorte*; father-in-law of Carlos Hank González's son; personal friend of Carlos Hank González. A DFS document considered him surrogate of General Bonifacio Salinas Leal.

Guardia, José María. Owner of Ciudad Juárez racetrack in the 1990s.

Guerra Cárdenas, Juan Nepomuceno. Also known as Juan N. Guerra. Drug trafficker and smuggler; founder and head of the criminal organization that became the Gulf Cartel; brother of Roberto Guerra Cárdenas; uncle of Juan García Ábrego; uncle of Jesús Roberto Guerra Velasco.

Guerra Cárdenas, Roberto. Brother of Juan N. Guerra; father of Jesús Roberto Guerra Velasco; head of the Tamaulipas State Treasure Office during the administration of Praxedis Balboa Gojon.

Guerra Velasco, Jesús Roberto. Nephew of Juan N. Guerra and cousin of Juan García Ábrego; mayor of Matamoros, Tamaulipas, 1984–1987.

Gutiérrez Barrios, Fernando. Interior Minister in the Salinas administration; former governor of Veracruz; undersecretary of government, 1970–1982; and head of the DFS.

Hank González, Carlos. Former head of the Food Supply National Agency (Compañía Nacional de Subsistencias Populares, or CONASUPO); ex-governor of the state of Mexico, 1969–1975; mayor of Mexico City, 1976–1982; Secretary of Tourism and Secretary of Agriculture in the cabinet of President Carlos Salinas de Gortari.

López Olivares, Óscar. Former subordinate of Juan N. Guerra and Juan García Ábrego. He was a collaborating witness of U.S. authorities.

López Parra, Emilio. Commander of the PJF in Matamoros; protector of Juan García Ábrego's organization.

Martínez Domínguez, Alfonso. Former national president of the PRI and mayor of Mexico City. He resigned from this position because of the student massacre in June 1971. He was a supporter of Emilio Martínez Manautou's candidacy in 1970 and governor of Nuevo León from 1979 to 1985.

Martínez Manautou, Emilio. Congressman and senator during the late 1950s and mid-1960s; secretary of the presidency during the administration of Gustavo Díaz Ordaz, 1964–1970; PRI's strong presidential precandidate in 1969, defeated by Interior Minister Luis Echeverría; Secretary of Public Health in the cabinet of José López Portillo, 1976–1980; governor of Tamaulipas, 1981–1987.

Martínez Manautou, Federico. Secretary of government of the state of Baja California, 1965–1971; brother of Emilio Martínez Manautou; secretary of the presidency (until 1970).

Mendiolea Cerecero, Raúl (General). Former deputy chief of Mexico City's Police Department during the 1968 student protests; head of the Federal Judicial Police, 1976–1978; subordinate and supporter of Óscar Flores Sánchez.

Nazar Haro, Miguel. Head of the DFS in the early 1980s.

Portes Gil, Emilio. Governor of Tamaulipas and president of Mexico. Roberto Guerra Cárdenas claimed that Portes Gil was his personal friend.

Rangel Escamilla, Manuel (Colonel). Head of the DFS in 1962.

Ravizé, Manuel A. Governor of Tamaulipas, 1969–1975; personal friend of Emilio Martínez Manautou, who supported him to become governor, while the latter was secretary of the presidency.

Rojo Lugo, Jorge. Head of the Mexican Agrarian Reform Ministry and governor of Hidalgo during the administration of José López Portillo, 1976–1982; head of the PRI's state office in Tamaulipas in the mid-1980s.

Ruiz Massieu, José Francisco. Governor of Guerrero and secretary general of the PRI; murdered in Mexico City in September 1994; former brother-in-law of Carlos and Raúl Salinas de Gortari.

Salinas de Gortari, Carlos. President of Mexico, 1988–1994; former secretary of budget during the administration of President Miguel de la

Madrid, 1982–1988; son of Raúl Salinas Lozano and brother of Raúl Salinas de Gortari.

Salinas de Gortari, Raúl. Brother of President Carlos Salinas de Gortari and son of Raúl Salinas Lozano.

Salinas Leal, Bonifacio (General). Former governor of Nuevo León; commander of the military zone in Tamaulipas during the 1940s; governor of Baja California Sur, 1959–1965; business associate of Roberto González Barrera.

Salinas Lozano, Raúl. Secretary of industry and commerce in Adolfo López Mateos's cabinet, 1958–1964; father of President Carlos Salinas de Gortari and Raúl Salinas de Gortari; political associate of Emilio Martínez Manautou.

Sánchez Celis, Leopoldo. Former member of Congress and friend of Emilio Martínez Manautou and Carlos Hank González; governor of Sinaloa, 1963–1968; personal friend of Miguel Ángel Félix Gallardo, a capo from Sinaloa State. Sánchez Celis worked for Carlos Hank González when Hank González was governor of the state of Mexico.

Sánchez Duarte, Leopoldo. Son of Leopoldo Sánchez Celis.

Trejo Nava, Abdón (Major). Head of the State Public Security Agency during the Martínez Manautou administration in Tamaulipas; former underling of Emilio Martínez Manautou in the secretary of the presidency.

Treviño Zapata, Norberto. Former governor of Tamaulipas, 1957–1963. Emilio Martínez Manautou was his assistant.

Yarrington, Tomás. Former congressman; mayor of Matamoros, 1993–1995; governor of Tamaulipas, 1999–2004.

Zolezzi Cavazos, Ricardo. Chief of the State Judicial Police during the Martínez Manautou administration in Tamaulipas.

Notes

1. Translated by Rafael Núñez and Tony Payan.

2. In 2000, in the characterization of work that was to be understood internationally as an "organized criminal group" within the framework of the United Nations Convention against Transnational Organized Crime, held in Palermo, Italy, a large number of assistants strongly pleaded to include several characteristics that incorporated the systematic use of violence and government corruption (United Nations Office on Drugs and Crime 2002, 4–5).

3. For example, Peter Lupsha, one of the most renowned specialists in the analysis of the political links of organized crime, said: "The key macro variable to both the

propagation and the persistence of organized crime is politics: political culture, and the operation of political systems. Organized crime cannot prosper without governments creating black markets, regulatory, economic and social bottlenecks, and exacerbating conditions of strain and discontinuity" (Lupsha 1988).

4. The same report by Von Seiffert also said that in other areas of the country, contraband also flourished significantly, such as in Sinaloa and Chihuahua, geographical points of prime importance for drug trafficking.

5. These documents are publicly available at the National General Archive (AGN) in Mexico City, Mexico, in the files of the former Federal Security Directorate (DFS) and the files of the Directorate of Political and Social Investigations (IPS).

6. In the late 1990s, Roberto Sánchez Duarte, son of Sánchez Celis, who was baptized by Félix Gallardo, was executed using an AK-47 assault rifle and a .9 mm pistol in Ecatepec. His brother, Leopoldo, then adviser of Hank González in the Department of Agriculture and Water Resources, told reporters that it was not the press's business but a family affair to be handled privately (*Proceso* 1990).

7. Astorga refers a letter from John Reese, an American based in Mazatlán, Sinaloa, to Captain James Hamilton, of the intelligence division of the LAPD. The documents are dated August 20 and 29, 1962, U.S. National Archives, DEA, SFBNDD, 1916–1970, RG, 170, NACP.

8. The Federal Judicial Police Act, which contains Amozorrutia's deposition, dated July 11, 1989, can be viewed on national journalism award winner Óscar Treviño's site, http://careldematamoros.blogspot.com/2007_02_01_archive.html.

9. DFS abuses were published in the Tamaulipas press. Some can be read in *El Mañana de Nuevo Laredo* (1981), 1, second section; *El Bravo de Matamoros* (1981), 5–6; and *El Bravo de Matamoros* (1984), 1, second section.

Bibliography

Aguayo Quezada, Sergio. 2001. *La Charola. Una Historia de los Servicios de Inteligencia en México.* Mexico City: Grijalbo.

Albini, Joseph. 1971. *The American Mafia: Genesis of a Legend.* New York: Appleton Century Crofts.

Astorga, Luis. 2003. *Drogas sin Fronteras. Los Expedientes de una Guerra Permanente.* Mexico City: Grijalbo.

———. 2005. *El Siglo de las Drogas. El Narcotráfico, del Porfiriato al Nuevo Milenio.* Mexico City: Plaza y Janés.

Bailey, John, and Roy Godson. 2000. "Introducción: El Crimen Organizado y la Gobernabilidad Democrática: México y Estados Unidos. Las Zonas Fronterizas Mexicanas." In *Crimen Organizado y Gobernabilidad Democrática. México y la Zona Fronteriza,* edited by John Bailey and Roy Godson, 11–49. Mexico City: Grijalbo.

Bernecker, Walther L. 1994. *Contrabando. Ilegalidad y Corrupción en el México del S. XIX.* Mexico City: Universidad Iberoamericana, Department of History.

Blancornelas, Jesús. 1997. "Querer y no Poder." In *Pasaste a mi lado.* Tijuana, México: Centro Cultural Tijuana.

Block, Alan. 1994. *East Side–West Side: Organizing Crime in New York City, 1930–1950.* New Brunswick, NJ: Transaction.

Boyer, Jean Francois. 2001. *La Guerra Perdida Contra las Drogas. Narcodependencia del Mundo Actual*. Mexico City: Grijalbo.

Cabildo, Miguel. 1992. "Caracterizado Como Represor, a Bartlett se le Acusa de Ligar a Gobernación con el Narco." *Proceso*, June 8. http://www.proceso.com.mx/. Accessed October 3, 2012.

Camacho Solís, Manuel. 1977. "Los Nudos Históricos del Sistema Político Mexicano." *Foro Internacional* 17, no. 4 (April–June): 587–651.

Camp, Roderic Ai. 1992. *Biografías de políticos Mexicanos 1935–1985*. Mexico City: FCE.

Carpizo, Jorge. 1987. *El Presidencialismo Mexicano*. Mexico City: Siglo XXI.

Castañeda, Jorge G. 1999. *La Herencia. Arqueología de la Sucesión Presidencial en México*. Mexico City: Extra-Alfaguara.

Chambliss, William. 1978. *On the Take: From Petty Crooks to Presidents*. Bloomington: Indiana University Press.

Cosío Villegas, Daniel. 1982. *El Sistema Político Mexicano: Las Posibilidades de Cambio*. Mexico City: Cuadernos de Joaquín Moritz.

Diario de Nuevo Laredo. 1984a. "Carlos Aguilar Garza podría suceder a Chao López." January 23.

———. 1984b. "Confirman captura de contrabando de cocaína más grande de la historia." November 16.

———. 1984c. "Habrá más detenciones aquí." November 16.

———. 1984d. "Herido en una gangsteril emboscada." May 18.

———. 1986. "Tamaulipas es un botín de caciques." March 23.

El Bravo de Matamoros. 1980a. "Nuevo Comandante de la Policía Judicial Federal en Matamoros." June 17.

———. 1980b. "Servir y Honrar a Tamaulipas; Único Poder al que Aspira MM." June 16.

———. 1981. "Aprehenderán a Federales por Extorsionadores." July 1.

———. 1984. "Se Generaliza la Protesta Contra la DFS." March 12.

El Mañana de Nuevo Laredo. 1980a. "En todo lugar hice honor a mi tierra y a mi gente: EMM." June 9.

———. 1980b. "Patrulla el ejército en Matamoros; MM cierra su campaña." November 30.

———. 1980c. "Transfieren a Sonora al Lic. Juárez Jiménez." June 17.

———. 1981. "Denuncian ante Gobernación y la PGR, abusos de la Federal de Seguridad." May 20.

———. 1982. "Asumió Solezzi la dirección de la polijudicial." April 16.

El Mañana de Reynosa. 1980a. "Asumirá el Mando Militar." June 14.

———. 1980b. "Nuevo Coordinador de la Campaña Antidrogas." June 18.

El Norte. 1989a. "Chao protege a primos de Caro Quintero." July 5. http://www.elnorte.com/. Accessed October 3, 2012.

———. 1989b. "Delata Chao a otros quince implicados." July 13. http://www.elnorte.com/. Accessed October 3, 2012.

El Universal. 2001. "Falleció el fundador del Cártel del Golfo." July 12. http://www.el-universal.com/. Accessed October 3, 2012.

———. 2008. "Fallece el general Manuel Díaz Escobar, presunto creador de Los Halcones." September 11. http://www.eluniversal.com/. Accessed October 3, 2012.

El Universal Gráfico. 1971. "Capturan Cocaína Pura Valuada en un Millón de Pesos, en Culiacán." August 6.

Federal Judicial Police Act. 1989. "Deposition of Manuel Amozorrutia. Mexico, DF." July 11. http://careldematamoros.blogspot.com/. Accessed October 3, 2012.

Figueroa, Yolanda. 1996. *El capo del Golfo. Vida y captura de Juan García Ábrego.* Mexico City: Grijalbo.

Flores Pérez, Carlos Antonio. 2009. *El Estado en Crisis: Crimen Organizado y Política. Desafíos Para la Consolidación Democrática.* Mexico City: CIESAS.

Geffray, Christian. 2002. "Drug Trafficking and the State." *Globalisation, Drugs and Criminalisation.* Final Research Report on Brazil, China, India and Mexico. 253: Management of Social Transformations, UNESCO. Neuilly-Sur-Seine, France. http://www.unesco.org/most/globalisation/drugs_vol2.pdf. Accessed October 3, 2012.

González Casanova, Pablo. 1972. *La Democracia en México.* Mexico City: Era.

INEGI (National Institute of Statistics and Geography). 1990. *XI Censo General de Población y Vivienda.* http://www.inegi.org.mx/. Accessed October 3, 2012.

Lupsha, Peter. 1988. "Organized Crime: Rational Choice, Not Ethnic Group Behavior: A Macro Perspective." *Law Enforcement Intelligence Analysis Digest* (Winter): 1–8.

Martínez, José. 1999. *Las enseñanzas del profesor: Indagación de Carlos Hank González. Lecciones de poder, impunidad y corrupción.* Mexico City: Océano.

McIllwain, Jeffrey Scott. 1993. "Organized Crime: A Social Network Approach." *Crime, Law, & Social Change* 32: 301–23.

Meyer, Lorenzo. 2002. *"La Institucionalización del Nuevo Régimen."* In *Historia General de México, Versión 2000,* edited by Centro de Estudios Históricos, 825–79. Mexico City: El Colegio de México.

Morín, Edgar. 1991. *El Método. IV. Las ideas. Su hábitat, su vida, sus costumbres, su organización.* Madrid, España: Cátedra.

Morris, Stephen D. 1991. *Corruption and Politics in Contemporary Mexico.* Tuscaloosa: University of Alabama Press.

Naylor, R. T. 1997. "Mafias, Myths, and Markets: On the Theory and Practice of Enterprise Crime." *Transnational Organized Crime* 3, no. 3: 1–45.

Proceso. 1984a. "Alemán, Hank, Balsa, Larrea, Moreno Valle Jr., entre los dueños. El gobierno bendice y subsidia el juego en cuatro hipódromos." May 28. http://www.proceso.com.mx/. Accessed October 3, 2012.

———. 1984b. "Datos sobre Federico Martínez Manautou (Carta de lector)." June 18. http://www.proceso.com.mx/. Accessed October 3, 2012.

———. 1989. "Alternaba públicamente con políticos y funcionarios Félix Gallardo 'el hombre más buscado del mundo' durante 18 años, nunca se ocultó." April 17. http://www.proceso.com.mx/. Accessed October 3, 2012.

———. 1990. "Asunto de familia, dijo su hermano. Rodolfo Sánchez Duarte y dos amigos, ametrallados." November 26. http://www.proceso.com.mx/. Accessed October 3, 2012.

———. 1991. "A los 77 años y en silla de ruedas 'New York Times' censuró la impunidad en México y en seguida la Judicial capturó a Juan N. Guerra." October 28. http://www.proceso.com.mx/. Accessed October 3, 2012.

Revista Fortuna. 2005. "José María Guardia ¡Me pueden llamar el Zar de los casinos!" September. http://fortunaweb.com.ar/. Accessed October 3, 2012.

Rose-Ackerman, Susan. 1999. *Corruption and Government: Causes, Consequences, and Reform*. Cambridge: Cambridge University Press.

Ruiz-Cabañas, Miguel. 1993. "*La Campaña Permanente de México: Costos, Beneficios y Consecuencias*." In *El Combate a las Drogas en América*, edited by P. H. Smith, 206–220. Mexico City: FCE.

Solorio Martínez, José Ángel. n.d. *Grupos de gobierno. Tamaulipas 1929–1992*. http://www.viraje.com/, p. 360. Accessed October 3, 2012.

Trujillo Bautista, Jorge. 2006. "Marginación y Pobreza en Tamaulipas, Retrospectiva y Planteamientos futures." Paper presented at the Autonomous University of Tamaulipas, Tamaulipas, Mexico.

United Nations Office on Drugs and Crime. 2002. *Results of a Pilot Survey of Forty Selected Organized Criminal Groups in Sixteen Countries*. Global Program against Transnational Organized Crime. September. UNODC: Vienna. http://www.unodc.org/pdf/crime/publications/Pilot_survey.pdf.

Zorrilla, Juan Fidel and Manuel Ignacio Salinas Domínguez. 1987. "El Noreste: Tamaulipas." In *Visión histórica de la frontera norte. Tomo VI La frontera en nuestros días*, edited by David Piñera Ramírez, 67–86. Mexicali, Baja California: Universidad Autónoma de Baja California, Editorial Kino/El Mexicano.

CHAPTER FIVE

Organized Crime as the Highest Threat to Mexican National Security and Democracy[1]

Raúl Benítez Manaut

Introduction

During the authoritarian governments of the Institutional Revolutionary Party (PRI), from the 1930s to the 1990s, the security agenda and the security decision-making process in Mexico hardly changed. The effects of illegal activities, particularly those of drug trafficking, went largely unnoticed by Mexican society. By the end of the twentieth century, however, organized crime was becoming a serious concern, but not yet a priority in the national political agenda. The first opposition government in seventy years, the Vicente Fox administration (2000–2006), did not fundamentally alter the basic Mexican security framework either, nor did it modify the organizational structure of the two military departments, the Department of National Defense (SEDENA) and the navy (SEMAR).[2] Inevitably, however, some changes were afoot. The Fox administration did seek to broaden the concept of national security by adding to it a set of social issues, including immigration. The security agenda during this administration also grew to include the problem of public safety, due to the citizenry's demand for greater safety in streets and neighborhoods.[3] At the same time, the September 11 terrorist attacks parachuted international terrorism onto the Mexican security agenda, a factor that would be the foundation for a new era of unprecedented security cooperation with the United States.

Before taking office, in December 2006, Felipe Calderón visited Washington, D.C., and outlined Mexico's new security "challenge," the power of organized crime syndicates. He also stated that this threat could not be confronted with the country's institutional capabilities alone. He called on help from the United States, a call that marked the beginning of a new era of binational cooperation on security issues, particularly against organized crime. What came out of that visit came to be known as the Mérida Initiative, a $1.4 billion pledge from the United States to fight organized crime in both Mexico and Central America.[4] The implications were clear; during the Calderón administration, the number-one security priority came to be combating drug cartels. "It will be an all-out war, because the possibility of co-existing with drug trafficking organizations is no longer viable," Calderón stated. "There is no turning back. It's us or them."[5] At the end of the Calderón administration, in 2012, much public discussion in Mexico involved controversies such as whether the government was winning or losing this "war," as former president Calderón himself had called it; whether the cartels had evolved from drug trafficking organizations into more versatile and sophisticated criminal groups, which could endanger the country's stability and its democratic consolidation; and whether the new Peña administration should continue this war on drugs. Today, in 2013, these key issues are not yet resolved.

The Ascent and Consolidation of Drug Trafficking in Mexico

The Mexican cartels originated with the advent of a market for marijuana and heroin in the United States soon after World War II. In Sinaloa state, the main illegal drug producer, drug trafficking, trade, and politics became closely intertwined. In response, from the 1950s to the 1990s, the government's policy toward the drug business went from tolerance to control. Along that line, since the 1970s, growing but modest binational cooperation with the United States on the issue of drug control began to take place.[6] This cooperation had some lows, including the murder of the Drug Enforcement Administration (DEA) agent Enrique Camarena in Guadalajara in 1985[7] and the 1997 arrest of the Mexican general José de Jesús Gutiérrez Rebollo on corruption charges. In 2001 an army court convicted General Gutiérrez of illicit enrichment.[8] These incidents confirmed the links between law enforcement agencies and the armed forces and criminal organizations—something that fueled American suspicion throughout this cooperation. Mexico, in response, maintained that General Gutiérrez's corruption case was an isolated incident and did not signify systemic corruption in Mexican institutions.

Through the 1990s, however, Mexican drug trafficking groups increased their power and influence and came to replace the Colombian Medellín and Calí Cartels in the supply of illegal drugs to the U.S. market, after these were wiped out by U.S.–Colombian efforts through Plan Colombia, an aid and advising agreement between the U.S. and Colombia to curb drug smuggling and fight the leftist insurgency in the 1990s. The results of Plan Colombia and American success in closing the Caribbean as a cocaine shipment route and the defeat of the Colombian cartels only led Mexican drug trafficking organizations to grow and gain control of the cocaine trade through Central America, Mexico, and now the Pacific Ocean.

Perhaps the most disturbing consequence of the aggressive attacks on Colombian drug traffickers is that the Mexican trafficking organizations became the beneficiaries. . . . Mexican traffickers benefited from the disruption of the cocaine trade in the Caribbean as the Colombians sought an alternate route to the United States via the Southwest border. Successes in the early 1990s associated with the results of the "king-pin" strategy in Colombia created new opportunities for Mexican narco-traffickers to get into the cocaine wholesale and distribution business in the United States.[9]

An added consequence of this "success" was that drug trafficking became even more globalized by the transborder relationship among production (Andean countries), commerce (Mexico and Central America), and consumption (U.S. market).

During the latter half of the 1980s, the role of traffickers based in Mexico and the use of Mexican territory increased dramatically. Mexico's strategic location, midway between source and consumer nations, and an increasingly powerful international drug mafia headquartered in Mexico made it an ideal transit point for South American-produced cocaine. Mexico's topography offered several seaports along its Pacific and Gulf coasts, and countless airstrips scattered across its interior allowed vessel and aircraft refueling to be quickly and easily accomplished. Equally significant was Mexico's 2,000-mile land border with the United States, over 95 percent of which had no fences or barricades. Moreover, the remoteness of many border areas made patrolling and surveillance exceedingly difficult. Cocaine traffickers from Colombia expanded their trafficking routes to include Mexico and increasingly used Mexico as a shipping point.[10]

By the beginning of the twenty-first century, the major Mexican cartels became consolidated: (1) the Sinaloa Cartel, led by "El Chapo" Guzmán, considered by *Forbes* magazine as one of the world's richest and most powerful men;[11] (2) the Tijuana Cartel, headed by the Arellano–Félix family, considered in 2000 as Latin America's most important criminal organization; (3) the Gulf Cartel, with Los Zetas as their armed force, controlling the route that goes from the Guatemala–Mexico border to Tamaulipas and Texas; (4) the Los Zetas group, which split from the Gulf Cartel in 2007 and is responsible for the gruesome violence in the northeastern part of Mexico; (5) the Beltrán Leyva Brothers Cartel, whose leader, Arturo, was killed in Cuernavaca in December 2009, and its splinter, the South Pacific Cartel; (6) the Juárez Cartel, founded by Amado Carrillo Fuentes and led today by his brother, Vicente; and (7) a recently created criminal organization, *La Familia Michoacana*.[12]

In the beginning, the power of the cartels was exercised quietly. When they became stronger, however, they started a war among themselves for the control of shipments, transit routes, warehouses, and points of entry into the United States. A level of violence never seen before in Mexico was unleashed and transformed some Mexican cities bordering the United States into some of the most dangerous places in the world, with high numbers of violent homicides. Cities such as Ciudad Juárez, Tijuana, Reynosa, Matamoros, and Nuevo Laredo were occupied by the cartels. In these places, municipal police corporations became institutions at the service of organized crime. The federal government was incapable of stopping it. Between 2003 and 2004, the sole option was the deployment of the army. The incorporation of the armed forces proceeded apace, and in 2007 the navy entered the drug war too. This led to the *militarization*

Table 5.1. Number of members of Mexico's police forces, 2009–2010

Police corporations	Number of agents
Public Security Secretariat (2010)	35,386
Attorney General's Office of Mexico (2010)	10,533
State Preventive Police (2009)	198,897
State Ministerial Police (2009)	26,495
Municipal Preventive Police (2009)	160,967

Source: Department of Public Safety (SSP) and Attorney General's Office (PGR) 2010. See also *Enfoque Reforma* (2011, 7). For state, ministerial and municipal corporations, see *Reforma* (2010, 6).

Table 5.2. Mexico's military members involved in the war on drugs, 2006–2010

Period	Engaged in combat and totals	
December 2006–August 2007	45,723	196,710 (total)
September 2007–August 2008	45,000	202,355 (total)
September 2008–August 2009	48,750	206,013 (total)
September 2009–August 2010	70,864	206,013 (total)

Source: Calderón 2011, 36–45.

of the fight against drugs. This strategy was the last resort by Calderón's government. This decision was made because state police forces did not have the wherewithal to face the cartels' power.[13] It should be noted also that the armed forces became an option because law enforcement in Mexico is highly decentralized, making it largely incoherent and fragmented into small, easily corruptible, and vulnerable agencies. In early 2009 the total number of police elements in the country was 432,278 individuals (see table 5.1), most of them in small state and local departments.

The temptation to use the highly centralized 200,000 members of the army and the 50,000 members of the navy was high.[14] Table 5.2 shows the number of military personnel involved in the drug war.

The "War on Drugs": A Key Element of the Government's Strategy

The security relationship between Mexico and the United States is a chain that begins with the demand for drugs in the United States, even if the last link is the spiral of violence in Mexico. The bloodshed in Mexico cannot be understood without considering the enormous drug market that is the United States. Table 5.3 shows a small consumption comparative among some countries in the Americas.

Faced with an insatiable market and the determination of many criminal groups to supply it, many analysts hold that the Mexican government's strategy is a *failed* strategy. Two high-level officials of the Fox administration assert this and suggest the need for a radical change in the strategy and invite a debate on the legalization of drugs as an option. Others maintain that the government can win the war and that the results are barely starting to show. They point to the crushing of a number of criminal

Table 5.3. Consumption: Drug abuse (in relation to total population)

Central America	Cocaine	Marijuana	Methamphetamines	Ecstasy
Panama	1.2 (2003)	4.0 (2003)	0.6 (2003)	0.4 (2003)
Guatemala	1.2 (2003)	9.1 (2003)	0.7 (2003)	0.2 (2003)
Belize	0.7 (2002)	6.7 (2003)	—	0.2 (2003)
Honduras	0.9 (2005)	1.6 (2002)	0.6 (2003)	0.2 (2003)
Nicaragua	1.0 (2003)	2.2 (2002)	0.8 (2003)	0.1 (2003)
El Salvador	2.5 (2004)	5.0 (2004)	0.6 (2003)	0.1 (2003)
Costa Rica	0.4 (2000)	1.3 (2001)	1.0 (2000)	—
North America				
United States	2.8 (2004)	12.6 (2004)	1.5 (2004)	1.0 (2004)
Canada	2.3 (2004)	16.8 (2004)	0.8 (2004)	1.1 (2004)
Mexico	0.4 (2002)	1.3 (2002)	0.1 (2002)	0.01 (2002)

Source: Adapted from the UNDCCP (2007, 385–90).

cartels and the arrests of their most important leaders. The debates are fierce. Some argue that "legalization" as an option does not take into account the differences between different types of drugs and whether this policy would in fact resolve the outbreak of violence among the criminal groups. Others argue that consumption does not necessarily imply violence per se, because in consumer countries the levels of violence are lower, and so forth. In this, the U.S. position is clear. Former U.S. secretary of state Hillary Clinton had even pointed out that Mexico faces a "narcoterrorist" offensive: "These drug cartels are showing many of the attributes of terrorist groups and insurgents in the world. For the first time, they are using car bombs. You see them organized as paramilitary."[15] Others talk about a "criminal insurgency." Following this line of reasoning, a counterinsurgency strategy should be designed, they argue, in particular one that adapts to the nature of the enemy and is led by the intelligence services and the armed forces.[16] President Calderón has internalized this rhetoric and has implemented a military strategy that has more to do with fighting a war than with law enforcement.

> The strategy has two horizons: one in the very short term, which consists of repositioning the authority and jurisdiction of the State through the mobilization of public force and the Army. We cannot lose territories, states in which the rule of law has broken down. The second is a long-term strategy, which implies the reconstruction of our institutions, not only the police but also the rest of the governmental structures. This means purging and strengthening police corporations, generating

new systems of information and intelligence and creating a new legal framework, such as the one we have presented to Congress. First there is a constitutional reform and then a legal reform. And also, of course, a new orientation focused on prevention that we haven't had yet in this country, something worth noting.[17]

Nonetheless, the onslaught of violence that has followed the war on drugs is seen as the weakening of the Mexican state and has led some analysts to say that Mexico is on the brink of becoming a "failed state."

Discounting Mexican public concerns and tacit admissions to that end, many indicators point to the beginning of what could be considered failing state and local governments in northern Mexico, particularly in the State of Tamaulipas. The criteria that define the "tipping point" . . . or in this case, the point at which credible authority is lost and a fall toward anarchy . . . can occur, are an abstract jumble of social factors, security considerations, political outcomes, and political will at all levels of government.[18]

Moreover, military analysts in the United States suggest that the Mexican government cannot stop the ascent of the criminal organizations' power, which is why the United States must act more forcefully.

Now is the time during the opening months of a new U.S. administration to jointly commit to a fully funded, major partnership as political equals of the Mexican government. We must jointly and respectfully cooperate to address the broad challenges our two nations face. Specifically, we must support the government of Mexico's efforts to confront the ultra-violent drug cartels. We must do so in ways that are acceptable to the Mexican polity and that take into account Mexican sensitivities to sovereignty. The U.S. government cannot impose a solution. There is political will in Mexico to make the tough decisions that are required to confront a severe menace to the rule of law and the authority of the Mexican state. Where our assistance can be helpful, we must provide it. The challenge is so complex that it will require sustained commitment and attention at the highest levels of our two governments. We cannot afford to fail.[19]

The diagnosis on Mexico's security crisis necessarily involves its capacity to fight organized crime at different levels. Mexico's political organization is complex. There are federal, state, and municipal governments, and

The Geopolitical Links Colombia–Central America–Mexico–United States

According to UN sources, in 2007, 88 percent of the cocaine coming from Colombia and Venezuela to the United States transited through the Central America and Mexico corridor—50 percent through the Pacific Ocean, and 38 percent through the Atlantic coastal regions of Central America and the Gulf of Mexico.[26] The supply of drugs now exceeds the demand. Because of this, drug trafficking organizations are trying to create new consumer markets in Mexico and Central America. Demand is also a crucial motivator, but supply plays a role. While demand is still basically located in the United States and, on a smaller scale, in Canada, it is growing in Latin America. Add to this the drug cycles. The latest fad, methamphetamine, pushed new organizations to enter the fray, some dedicated to import precursor chemicals from China which arrive in Mexican Pacific ports (Manzanillo). This is one of the main businesses of *La Familia Michoacana*. Similarly, in Central America, criminal groups have appeared in every country. The homicide rates are the highest in the continent. For example, during 2010 in Honduras the rate was 80 per 100,000; in El Salvador, 68; and in Guatemala, 40.[27] Besides organized criminal gangs such as the *Maras*, cartels linked to the Colombian and Mexican groups have also appeared. The South American supply routes make Central America an ideal corridor to Mexico, to the United States, and to Canada. In 2010 nearly 60 percent of the cocaine that arrived in the United States came from Central America. Honduras was the main transit country, sending drugs to the Guatemala–Mexico border. Cocaine was often carried by speedboats.[28] This activity is mainly dominated by Mexican cartels, but local Central American cartels increasingly participate.

Weapons Flowing South

Arms trafficking to Mexico, as a threat to national security, was not included in any of the government's documents. Since the 1980s, arms trafficking had been detected on the southern border of Mexico, due to the Central American armed conflicts and to the growing Mexican criminal organizations. After that, small-time weapons trafficking (*tráfico hormiga*) developed on the U.S.–Mexican border. The Mexican 1972 Federal Law on Firearms and Explosives regulates the sale and use of firearms. SEDENA is the agency in charge of enforcing it. However, this law has not been able to stem the flow of illegal firearms through Mexico's northern and southern borders. The enforcement of the law is simply too lax in the areas of gun transportation and possession. Drug trafficking organizations take advantage of this and are the main users of illegal firearms in Mexico. Furthermore, during the past ten years, the cartels have been adding to their weapons arsenals semiautomatic machine guns such as the AK-47 and the Barrett .50 and even missiles. According to SIMO, a polling consultancy, 15 percent of the people interviewed in a survey in Mexico said they have a gun in their home.[29] This means that some four to five million households have firearms. SEDENA's Firearm Destruction Program confiscated and destroyed 79,074 firearms captured in military roadblocks during the last ten years (2000–2009). Of those, 44,000 were confiscated during the last three years.[30] For all of these reasons, arms trafficking has become a serious problem, one that feeds the Mexican national security crisis.

In Central America, 70 percent of violent deaths are perpetrated with firearms. As in Mexico, there is a growing appeal to self-defense because people do not trust the government. According to the International Action Network on Small Arms (IANSA), "There are an estimated 1.6 million handguns in Central America, of which approximately 500,000 are legally registered. Many of these guns are remnants of military conflicts that took place in the region during the 1980s, especially in El Salvador, Guatemala and Nicaragua. After these conflicts were over, thousands of military firearms were sold in the black market. From there, they began to flow to other Central American countries with less of a history of generalized armed violence, such as Costa Rica, Nicaragua, and Panama."[31] figure 5.1 shows these numbers.

In 2000 there were 509,826 registered firearms in Central America, most of which were in El Salvador (170,000) and Guatemala (147,581).

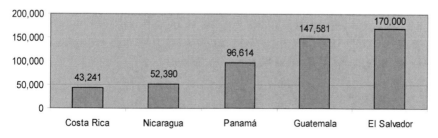

Figure 5.1. Number of registered firearms in Central America

During the last seven years, this amount, difficult to quantify accurately, has at the very least doubled. According to the Arias Foundation of Costa Rica, this country went from 43,241 to 100,000 firearms, and El Salvador increased its legal firearms to 300,000.[32] If the increase in legal arms is any indicator of potential sources of violence, it is even more serious that illegal firearms apparently exceed registered guns. In El Salvador there are possibly 224,000 illegal weapons, while in Guatemala the figure could be more than one million. In Nicaragua, illegal firearms were double the amount of registered ones by 2006. Estimates show that illegal firearms in Central America increased to 2,300,000.[33] These figures show that the threat to Mexico's security by the problem of illegal firearms in Central America is considerable. If the Cold War fed the conflict in Central America by a steady flow of weapons, these can now generate a new type of social conflict just as violent, or even more violent, than the armed confrontations experienced by those countries in the 1980s.

This concern became part of the Mérida Initiative as Mexico insisted, and the United States finally agreed, on the creation of a special task force on firearms trafficking and the implementation of nonintrusive inspections on the border. Numerous agreements of judicial coordination have been signed in order to strengthen the "intelligent borders" agreements signed in 2002,[34] and some were added in the 2005 Security and Prosperity Partnership of North America (SPP).

Public Insecurity in Mexico

The most comprehensive measure of drug violence, homicides per 100,000 inhabitants, shows that in Mexico there was a considerable downtrend between 1990 and 2007. The national average decreased from 3,451 homicides in 1990 to 1,218 in 2007. Among the states that had a significant decrease was Chiapas (from 274 in 1990 to 101 in 2007) and Mexico City (from 1,273 in 1990 to 838 in 2007) but also others such as Michoacán, Oaxaca, Veracruz, and Zacatecas. This was due to various factors, including the reduction of political violence in rural areas. These figures clash with the public's perceptions, as violent deaths have increased significantly in the last ten years and have become the main concern of the general population.[35] Interestingly, Mexico had seen a downward trend in violent crime up until 2007, when the number of crimes jumped dramatically as a result of the actions perpetrated by the criminal groups beginning in 2008. That year alone, the number of victims of violent crime increased by 50 percent and by another 50 percent in 2009.[36] The statistics for 2010 show a very important concentration of criminal violence in the state of Chihuahua, primarily in Ciudad Juárez. We have to understand the issue of federalism in Mexico as well. Ninety-three percent of crimes reported fell within state and local jurisdictions and were mostly thefts or robberies. Seven percent of reported crimes fell within federal jurisdiction and included drug trafficking (see figure 5.2).

In this analysis one has to take into account the so-called black data (*cifra negra*),[37] which would be the number of nonreported crimes, whether because of fear or negligence. This number is large, since the general population does not trust the justice system and considers it a "waste of time" to report a crime. See table 5.4 for this important number.

In those states where violence has increased among drug trafficking groups, homicides have increased markedly. Mexico's northern states that have a border with the United States, where the "war" between cartels has been concentrated in order to centralize the drug trade into the United States, register the highest homicide rates in the country, something that has also led to an increase in other types of crimes. In Ciudad Juárez, particularly, in addition to violent homicides there are also serial murders of women, which have caused panic among the general population.[38] The number of homicides increased from 2,013 in 1990 to 2,365 in 2007

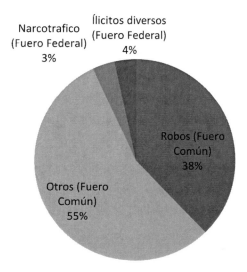

Figure 5.2. Reported crimes by state and federal jurisdiction

Table 5.4. Reported crimes and "black data," 2000–2008

Year	Reported crimes Federal, State, and Local	Black data Federal, State, and Local
2000	1,420,251	3,319,919
2001	1,512,450	3,529,050
2002	1,516,027	3,537,396
2003	1,517,925	3,541,825
2004	1,505,844	3,513,636
2005	1,505,223	3,512,187
2006	1,580,742	3,688,398
2007	1,715,974	4,003,939
2008	1,540,789	3,594,941

Source: Adapted from the Second Special Report by the National Human Rights Commission (2011) on the actual exercise of the fundamental right to public security in Mexico. Figures through November 31, 2008.

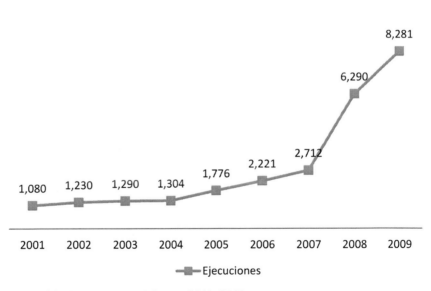

Figure 5.3. Executions in Mexico, 2001–2009

(17.49 percent). Among them, the murders of government personnel dedicated to security tasks, military servicemen, and policemen went from 68 in 1990 to 149 in 2007, registering a rise of 119.12 percent, due to the so-called war on drugs. Figure 5.3 shows how the number of executions increased significantly from 2001 to 2009 and rose again in 2010.

Table 5.5. Number of homicides in the northwestern region, 1990–2007

Year	Civilians (Criminals and Innocents)	Security and Defense Personnel	Total Deaths	Percentage of Deaths of Security and Defense Personnel over the Total Number of Homicides[1]	Percentage of Deaths of Civilians
1990	1,945	68	2,013	3	97
1991	2,399	90	2,489	4	96
1992	2,918	101	3,019	3	97
1993	2,485	110	2,595	4	96
1994	2,743	107	2,850	4	96
1995	2,926	120	3,046	4	96
1996	2,732	119	2,851	4	96
1997	2,591	105	2,696	4	96
1998	2,845	107	2,952	4	96
1999	2,682	118	2,800	4	96
2000	2,296	93	2,389	4	96
2001	2,337	80	2,417	3	97
2002	2,301	91	2,392	4	96
2003	2,256	103	2,359	4	96
2004	2,141	67	2,208	3	97
2005	2,429	101	2,530	4	96
2006	2,528	103	2,631	4	96
2007	2,216	149	2,365	6	94
1990–2007[2]	13.93%	119.12%	17.49%		

[1] The percentage of deaths is proportional to the total population.

[2] Percentage variation of deaths calculated for 1990, compared to 2007.

Source: Polanska 2009.

Table 5.6. Drug-related murders, 2006–2009

Month	2006	2007	2008	2009
January	181	204	247	480
February	164	198	251	633
March	155	275	378	508
April	113	255	270	546
May	184	279	493	510
June	216	244	505	769
July	144	217	509	854
August	220	284	555	748
September	253	236	448	826
October	179	202	669	840
November	252	183	701	682
December	170	196	635	859
Total	**2,231**	**2,773**	**5,661**	**8,255**

Source: Milenio. January 1, 2010.

From this data, it is possible to draw a hypothesis. There is a perception among the general population, even in the international community, and transmitted through the press, that Mexico "is at war."[39] This assertion is not sustainable if one analyzes the crime figures, which have in fact decreased. Nevertheless, in some Mexican states where drug trafficking activities are concentrated, there has been an exponential rise in violence, homicides, and state jurisdiction crimes.[40] As table 5.5 shows, from 1990 to 2007, homicides rose approximately 17 percent in the northwestern region.

Nonetheless, the great crisis in drug trafficking homicides and executions begins precisely in early 2007 (coincident with President Calderón's militarized strategy), as shown in table 5.6.

Ciudad Juárez: War Zone

To argue that Mexico is a failed state or that it is heading that way is a fallacy. However, there are Mexican cities and states where that argument could be made. That is the case of Chihuahua state and particularly Ciudad Juárez. In November 2009 the president of the Twin Plant Association (*Asociación de Maquiladoras*) and the leader of the local chamber of commerce called on the United Nations to send in the Blue Helmets (UN peacekeeping troops) due to the seriousness of the situation. They claimed that because of the high levels of violence, approximately six thousand businesses had already closed and moved to areas outside of Ciudad Juárez and the rest of Chihuahua (many of them to El Paso, Texas).

> We are asking that a group be formed to request the Inter-American Human Rights Commission to intervene, as well as that a group of UN Peacekeeping troops be sent to put a stop to this uncontrollable situation of violence. Juárez has not received any kind of attention from the authorities, which is why it is thought of as the most violent city in the world, with [the] world's highest death rate. With a rate of more than 10 deaths per day, it is considered a war zone.

This statement demonstrates the distrust that the citizens of Ciudad Juárez have toward the government authorities (municipal, state, and federal), which for years had not been able to reduce, much less stop, the level of impunity and the confrontations between rival criminal groups. The Mexican government replied that the request was absurd and out of place. For his part, the president of the Citizens' Council for Public Security and Penal Justice of Juárez compared his city to the most dangerous ones in Latin America:

> In Juárez, the number of homicides increased dramatically in a very short period of time, more rapidly than in any region of Mexico and even any part of the world. Between 2007 and 2009, homicides increased more than 800 percent. During 2009, in Juárez, there were 191 homicides per 100,000 inhabitants. In second place is the Honduran city of San Pedro Sula, with 119 homicides, and then San Salvador, with 95.[41]

When Felipe Calderón took office, violence between cartels had not yet arrived in Chihuahua. In December 2006 there was only one person executed; in December 2007, 11; in December 2008, 173; and in December 2009, 231. The level of violence in the entire state during 2007 resulted in 148 executions. In 2008 there were 1,652. In 2009 there were 2,082. These figures become disturbing if we consider that in the 1990s, the most violent years of the drug war in Colombia, the homicide rate was never higher than 100 murders per 100,000 inhabitants in the cities of Medellín and Cali. The most recent national statistics of drug-related homicides reveal that January 9, 2010, was the most violent day of Calderón's administration, with 52 murders.

In the case of Ciudad Juárez, the Calderón administration's strategy to control crime was not very successful and barely showed positive results. Since 2007 the Mexican federal government deployed 5,500 army personnel to Ciudad Juárez. By mid-2009, that number had grown to 6,000. In January 2010, 2,000 federal police were deployed in the city. All operations were to be directed by the Federal Police. The militarized strategy proved unable to diminish the violence, which is why it can be stated that the increase in the use of the military forces has not produced any positive results. Tony Payan defined this phenomenon as the "perfect storm."[42] This is a city where it has been frequently reported that the federal forces have been violating human rights in a significant way. The government of Ciudad Juárez was compelled to open an office where the citizenry could file complaints and report violations of human rights by the armed forces and the Federal Police. In general, the use of the armed forces has led various institutions, both national and foreign, to point out that the immunity that the military enjoys, derived from military law or tradition, allowed them to take actions in conditions of impunity, particularly because the justice system favors the military when in conflict with the civilian population.

> Military authorities routinely assert jurisdiction to investigate and prosecute Army abuses. As a result, the vast majority of Army abuse cases are never successfully prosecuted. The military justice system lacks the independence necessary to carry out reliable investigations and its operations suffer from a general absence of transparency. The ability of military prosecutors to investigate Army abuses is further undermined by a fear . . . which inhibits civilian victims and witnesses from providing information to military authorities.[43]

Final Reflections: Is the Mexican Government Winning or Losing the War?

The current debate on national security in Mexico centers on this question: Is the government winning or losing the war on drugs? The Rand Corporation asserts that Mexico simply lacks a strategy to protect national security.

> The lack of a cohesive security strategy in Mexico has led to shifting responsibilities, the duplication of services in a number of agencies, and general instability in Mexico's security structure. In addition, this has

created a situation in which the military is more involved in internal security than is the case in most countries. The Mexican military is generally viewed to be less corrupt than the police and is seen as the institution of last resort when all others have failed. These ambiguous, shifting, and overlapping responsibilities have also led to uncoordinated efforts (and often animosity) across federal, state, and local security forces (particularly among police forces).[44]

These weaknesses in the functioning of Mexican institutions of national security are utilized by criminal organizations. One of the most notable elements in favor of drug trafficking organizations is the lack of cooperation among police bodies, the military, and the justice administration system. The Mexican government's critics point out that the federal political structure is the major vulnerability of the Mexican state. To respond, Mexico has begun to implement two strategies to transform the capabilities of the federal government. First are the deep reforms to the national security, defense, intelligence, justice, and police systems at all three levels of government. Second is the acceptance of U.S. aid. This aid is utilized to support these structural reforms and equip the Mexican security and justice agencies with technologies generally not available in the marketplace. These strategies are designed to tackle the fragmented security infrastructure, the lack of interagency and intergovernmental coordination, the low levels of professionalization in the bureaucracy, and the high levels of corruption that favor drug cartels. This strategic turnaround was also a response to the fact that in spite of the successes, which included capturing, killing, or extraditing the highest leaders of the main cartels, weakening many criminal organizations, the violence did not abate. Even the Mérida Initiative had to be retooled to include more comprehensive tools to address social issues.

In spite of the violence, President Calderón had strong support from the general population because it felt unprotected, and therefore, the use of the army was not seriously questioned by public opinion. With the implementation of the Mérida Initiative, Mexico temporarily surpassed Colombia as the principal recipient of U.S. aid in the hemisphere.[45] Notwithstanding the fact that some of its cooperation programs are important to strengthen the institutional capacities of intelligence and justice services, as well as to improve the technology employed by the armed forces and the Federal Police, this aid has not been very effective to enhance the capacities of the Mexican government in its fight against organized crime syndicates. It is worthwhile mentioning that the 1.4 billion U.S. dollars of assistance between 2008 and 2010 were insufficient in relationship to the size of the security, justice, intelligence, and defense agencies.

One of two assertions could be made, depending on one's stand vis-à-vis the war on drugs. First, the declaration of war against drug cartels made by former president Calderón; the increase in executions; the exponential increase in U.S. aid; the increased presence of the armed forces in the combat against narcotrafficking and in the public security strategies of the high-risk cities; the conversion of Juárez into the most dangerous city in the world; the increased consumption of cocaine; and the perceptions that Mexico could become a failed state would allow one to assert, on the one hand, that the Mexican state is losing the war on drugs and that, consequently, the strategy should be radically revised. The change in strategy, according to some of the most important critics of the war on drugs, should include decriminalization and even drug legalization. On the other side of this divide are those who argue that the government's strategy of direct confrontation with organized crime and hammering away at drug trafficking organizations is correct, and they advocate staying the course all the way to victory. They assert that the strategy will be victorious in the end because the built-in advantages that it contains are barely beginning to become active in the overall scenario. This group asserts that in the end staying the course will produce results favorable to the government, even if only in the medium and long run. For this group, the price in violence and death is worth paying for the sake of establishing a more peaceful, law-abiding society.

The so-called war on drugs in Mexico can be assigned to the category of the so-called asymmetrical conflicts, low-intensity wars, irregular wars, and borderless wars. It is clear that it is a transnational conflict, because Mexico is a country of cocaine transit, geographically situated between the American consumers, where the profits are made (the U.S. government confiscates very little of the money that is generated by this criminal activity), and the countries where cocaine is produced. This leads one to posit that the confrontation is not only Mexican and that the coherence of the strategies should be multinational. It is also a prolonged war or conflict. Its origins go back to the 1950s, with the production of marijuana and heroin to satisfy American consumers, and later, to the 1980s, with the entrance of cocaine into the production-trafficking-consumption cycle, adding Colombia, which built very powerful criminal networks.

Many asymmetric, irregular, or low-intensity conflicts were classified and analyzed as part of a situation of "strategic draw or tie," in which one cannot assert that the war is won or lost. This was the case of the civil war of El Salvador (1980–1992), where the draw or tie was resolved through nonmilitary means, since both military strategies, that of the Farabundo Martí Front for National Liberation (Frente Farabundo Martí para la Liberación Nacional—FMLN) and that of the government backed by the United States, had become bogged down, had been at an impasse, and had been provoking severe geopolitical tensions.

In the confrontation between the Mexican governmental forces and the cartels, the social impact of violence damages the government, because it gives off an image of the loss of the so-called legitimate monopoly of force and the requisite territorial control that all states should exercise. The perception that Mexico is a state headed for failure is based on the wrong assumption that what is happening in the city of Juárez is a reflection of what is happening in the whole country.

Overall, it is difficult to categorically state that the government is winning the war but also to assert that the government strategy has failed. Because of this, the current situation could be defined as a "strategic morass" that will prove to be right or wrong according to the degree of success (or failure) of the government's military campaigns. At the same time, the final result will be determined by the degree of progress in the implementation of the reforms within the rest of the national security agencies. With regard to the cartels, their power will depend on the outcome of the confrontations among them and their capacities to survive the offensive of the government.

Notes

1. Translated by Rafael Núñez and Tony Payan.

2. In Mexico, there is no civilian defense ministry. The decision-making process begins with the president, and, under his command, there are two military departments: (1) SEDENA, which includes the army and the air force, and (2) SEMAR, the navy (see Guevara 2011, viii).

3. Manaut 2010, 181.

4. Silke and Finklea 2010.

5. Calderón 2009, 17.

6. Astorga 2005, 87.

7. According to the DEA, "On May 3, 1985, a new DEA investigative team was established to coordinate and investigate the abduction of Camarena and Captain Zavala. This investigation was given the name Operation Leyenda (the Spanish word meaning legend). Through evidence gained from cooperating individuals and relentless investigative pursuit, this team was able to ascertain that five individuals abducted Special Agent Camarena and took him to a house at 881 Lope de Vega Street in Guadalajara on February 7, 1985. Ultimately, the agents were successful in securing the

indictments of several individuals connected to the abduction and murder. . . . In retrospect, Operation Leyenda was a long and complex investigation, made more difficult by the fact that the crime was committed on foreign soil and involved major drug traffickers and government officials from Mexico. It took several years to develop the facts, to apprehend the perpetrators, and to finally bring them to justice." See United States Drug Enforcement Administration 1985–1990.

8. Camp 2005, 263.

9. Flynn 2001.

10. United States Drug Enforcement Administration 1985–1990.

11. Forbesonline.2011.http://www.forbes.com/profile/joaguin-guzmen-loera/. Accessed June 17, 2013.

12. Stratfor 2009, 157.

13. Bailey 2010, 332.

14. It is important to note also that there are some 150,000 private security agents in Mexico, raising the national total to 800,000, or 0.7 percent of the country's population.

15. Clinton 2011.

16. Sullivan and Elkus 2008.

17. Calderón 2009, 18.

18. Hale 2011.

19. McCaffrey 2008.

20. Peón 2009, 22.

21. Governor Villanueva was indicted in 1999 but not captured until May 24, 2001. He is the first high-ranking Mexican politician who was requested for extradition to the United States. In 2008 he was convicted and sentenced to thirty-six years in prison for drug trafficking. See *El Universal* 2008.

22. García Luna 2011, 91.

23. *Enfoque Reforma* 2011, 6.

24. The numbers are controversial all around, and there are many different counts. In this book, other numbers are also mentioned.

25. *Excelsior* 2010a, 1 and 8–9.

26. UNDCCP 2007, 14.

27. UNDCCP 2011, 23.

28. *Latin American News* 2010.

29. Mexican National Poll 2009.

30. *Excelsior* 2010b.

31. IANSA 2007.

32. Fundación Arias Para la Paz y el Progreso Humano 2007.

33. Ibid.

34. U.S. Government, Mexican Government, "Alianza para la Frontera México-Estados Unidos. Declaración a favor del fortalecimiento tecnológico y la cooperación para promover un flujo seguro y eficiente de personas y bienes a lo largo de la frontera," Monterrey, Mexico, March 22, 2002.

35. Gonzalbo 2009.

36. See table 7 in Gonzalbo 2009. "Evolution of drug-related murders, 1990–2009." Escalante, Fernando. op. cit., 41.

37. The so-called black data (*cifra negra*) refer to those crimes that are not registered in the official records and include crimes that were not reported to the relevant

authorities; those that are not subject to preliminary investigation after being re-ported; several crimes committed in a single event against one or several victims that are registered in a single preliminary investigation; and crimes that are not registered due to problems with the official statistical system.

38. Monarréz Fragoso 2011, 43; also see Monárrez Fragoso 2009.

39. Several government officials consider national media "irresponsible" due to the fact that they contribute to an increased perception of insecurity and fear among the population. At the same time, they consider international media respon-sible for transmitting the impression that Mexico is a "failed" and corrupt state; this has led credit rating agencies to assign the country very low "rankings" due to the conditions of insecurity prevailing in several areas of the Mexican territory. Never-theless, due to the lack of systematization, opacity, and partiality in the reporting of official information, national and international media become the main sources of information.

40. This perception is also transmitted by credit rating agencies that place Mexico at the same level as Colombia, Perú, El Salvador, and Guatemala. See Control Risks, Risk Map 2008, http://www.controlrisks.com/RiskMap/Pages/Security.aspx.

41. "Juárez, la más violenta del mundo," Reforma, January 11, 2010.

42. Payan 2011, 127.

43. Human Rights Watch, *World Report 2010*, 238.

44. Shaefer, Bahney, and Riley 2009, 15.

45. In 2008 U.S. aid to Mexico was approximately $440 million, while Colombia received $395 million; in 2009 Mexico got $672 million, and Colombia received $400 million.

Bibliography

Astorga, Luis. 2005. *El Siglo de las Drogas. El narcotráfico del Porfiriato al Nuevo Mi-lenio*. Mexico City: Plaza y Janés.

Bailey, John J. 2010. "Combating Organized Crime and Drug Trafficking in Mexico: What Are Mexican and U.S. Strategies?" In *Shared Responsibility: U.S.–Mexico Policy Options for Confronting Organized Crime*, edited by Eric Olson, David A. Shirk, and Andrew Selee, 327–250. Washington, DC, and San Diego, CA: Univer-sity of San Diego.

Benítez Manaut, Raúl. 2010. "Reforming Civil-Military Relations during Demo-cratization." In *Mexico's Democratic Challenges, Politics, Government and Society*, edited by A. Selee and J. Peshard, 162–86. Washington, DC: Woodrow Wilson Center Press; Stanford, CA: Stanford University Press.

Calderón, Felipe. 2009. "La guerra al crimen organizado." In *Atlas de la Seguridad y la Defensa de México 2009*, edited by Raúl Benítez Manaut, Abelardo Rodríguez Sumano, and Armando Rodríguez, 17–21. Mexico City: CASEDE.

———. 2011. *Quinto Informe de Gobierno*. Gobierno de México. September 1. Mexico City: Gobierno Federal; 36–45. http://quinto.informe.gob.mx/archivos/informe_de _gobierno/pdf/1_4.pdf. Accessed September 1, 2011.

Camp, Roderic A. 2005. *Mexico's Military on the Democratic Stage*. Westport, CT and Washington, DC: CSIS-Praeger Security.

Clinton, Hillary. 2011. "Mexican Narco: Terrorists and Insurgents, Says Hillary Clinton." January 22. http://www.uyxnotices.com/mexican-narco-terrorists-and-insurgents-says-hillary-clin/. Accessed October 4, 2012.

Comisión Nacional de Derechos Humanos. 2008. "Segundo Informe Especial de la CNDH Sobre el Ejercicio del Derecho Fundamental a la Seguridad en Nuestro País." Mexico City: CNDH. http://www.cndh.org.mx/sites/all/fuentes/documentos/informes/especiales/2008_segpublica1.pdf. Accessed October 4, 2012.

Control Risks. "Control Risks Map." http://www.controlrisks.com/RiskMap/Pages/Security.aspx. Accessed April 22, 2013.

El Universal. 2008. "Sentencian a Mario Villanueva a 36 años de prisión." June 4. http://www.eluniversal.com.mx/notas/512316.html. Accessed April 22, 2013.

———. 2010. "Récord de muerte: Diario matan a 28." August 7. www.eluniversal.com.mx. Accessed October 4, 2012.

Enfoque Reforma. 2011. "Combate al narcotráfico." June 23. http://www.reforma.com/. Accessed October 4, 2012.

Escalante Gonzalbo, Fernando. 2009. "Homicidios 1990–2007." *Nexos.* September 1. http://www.nexos.com.mx/?p=leerarticulo&Article=776. Accessed June 17, 2013.

Excelsior. 2010a. "Análisis Confidencial del Ejército. Se agrupan narcos en 2 megacárteles." January 24. http://www.excelsior.com.mx/. Accessed October 4, 2012.

———. 2010b. "Destruyen armas incautadas en los últimos 10 años." January 19. http://www.excelsior.com.mx/. Accessed October 4, 2012.

Forbes. 2009. "Drug Lord 'El Chapo' Guzmán on Forbes' Most Powerful List." March 11. http://www.forbes.com/lists/2009/10/billionaires-2009-richest-people_Joaquin-Guzman-Loera_FS0Y.html. Accessed May 3, 2013.

Flynn, Stephen E. 2001. *U.S. Support of Plan Colombia: Rethinking the Ends and Means. Strategic Studies Institute.* Carlisle, PA: U.S. Army War College. www.dtic.mil/cgi-in/GetTRDoc?Location=U2&doc=GetTRDoc.pdf&AD=ADA390538. Accessed October 4, 2012.

Fundación Arias Para la Paz y el Progreso Humano. 2007. "Reunión heptanacional sobre transferencia y control del tráfico de armas." *Panamá* (December 6–7).

García Luna, Genaro. 2011. "El nuevo modelo de seguridad para México." Mexico City: Nostra Ediciones; 91. http://www.cies.gob.mx/pdf/Nuevo%20Modelo %20de %20Seguridad%20para%20Mexico.pdf. Accessed October 4, 2012.

Gonzalbo, Fernando Escalante. 2009. "Homicidios 1990–2007." *Nexos,* September. http://www.nexos.com.mx/?P=leerarticulov2print&Article=776. Accessed October 4, 2012.

Guevara, Íñigo. 2011. "Adapting, Transforming, and Modernizing under Fire: The Mexican Military 2006–11." *The Letort Papers.* Strategic Studies Institute. Carlisle, PA: U.S. Army War College.

Hale, Gary J. 2011. "A 'Failed State' in Mexico: Tamaulipas Declares Itself Ungovernable." James A. Baker II Institute for Public Policy, Rice University. July 26. http://bakerinstitute.org/publications/DRUG-pub-HaleTamaulipasFailedState-072611.pdf. Accessed October 4, 2012.

Human Rights Watch. 2010. *World Report 2010. Events of 2009.* http://www.hrw.org/sites/default/files/reports/wr2010.pdf. Accessed October 4, 2012.

IANSA. 2007. "International Action Network on Small Arms." http://www.iansa.org/regions/camerica/camerica.htm. Accessed October 4, 2012.

Latin American News. 2010. "Cocaine Smugglers Using High-Tech Boats." www
.lamnews.com/cocaine_smugglers_using_high-tech_boats.htm. Accessed October 4, 2012.

McCaffrey, Barry R. 2008. "Memorandum of 29 December." West Point, N.Y. (March) http://www.mccaffreyassociates.com/pdfs/Mexico_AAR_-_December_2008.pdf. Accessed October 4, 2012.

Mexican National Poll. 2009. *Encuesta Nacional en Vivienda.* SimoMexico. http://www.seguridadcondemocracia.org/biblioteca.seguridadnacional3.pdf. Accessed October 4, 2012.

Monarréz Fragoso, Julia E. 2009. *Trama de una injusticia. Feminicidio sexual sistemático en Ciudad Juárez.* Mexico City: El Colegio de la Frontera Norte.

———. 2011. *Feminicidios en México. Aproximación, tendencias y cambios, 1985–2009.* Mexico City: ONU-Mujeres.

Payan, Tony. 2011. "Ciudad Juárez: La tormenta perfecta." In *Migración y Seguridad: Nuevo Desafío en México,* edited by Natalia Armijo, 127–43. Mexico City: CASEDE.

Peón, Jorge Tello. 2009. "La seguridad pública en México. Síntesis social." In *Atlas de la Seguridad y la Defensa de México 2009,* edited by Raúl Benítez Manaut, A. Rodríguez Sumano, and A. Rodríguez, 21–4. Mexico City: CASEDE.

Polanska, Malgorzata. 2009. "Homicides by State and Regions, 1990–2007." In *Atlas of the Security and Defense of México 2009,* edited by Raúl Benítez Manaut, Abelardo Rodríguez Sumano, and Armando Rodríguez. Mexico City: CASEDE. 354.

Reforma. 2010. *Juárez, la más violenta del mundo.* January 11. http://www.reforma.com. Accessed April 22, 2013.

———. 2011. *Las otras policías.* June 23. http://www.reforma.com. Accessed October 4, 2012.

Shaefer, Agnes Geriben, Benjamín Bahney, and K. Jack Riley. 2009. *Security in Mexico. Implications for U.S. Policy Options.* Santa Monica, CA: Rand Corporation.

Silke, Clare Ribando, and Kristin M. Finklea. 2010. *U.S.–Mexican Security Cooperation: The Mérida Initiative and Beyond.* Washington, DC: Congressional Research Service.

Stratfor. 2009. "Mexico in Crisis: (Addendum) 2008 Cartel Report." In *Mexico in Crisis: Lost Borders and the Struggle for Regional Status,* edited by Michael Mc-Cullar, 265–271. Austin, TX: Stratfor.

Sullivan, John P., and Adam Elkus. 2008. "State of Siege: Mexico's Criminal Insurgency." *Small Wars Journal.* http://www.smallwarsjournal.com/blog/journal/docs-temp/84-sullivan.pdf. Accessed October 4, 2012.

UNDCCP. 2007. *World Drug Report 2007.* United Nations Office for Drug Control and Crime Prevention. New York: United Nations Publications.

———. 2011. *Global Study in Homicide 2011.* United Nations Office for Drug Control and Crime Prevention. New York: United Nations Publications.

United States Drug Enforcement Administration. *DEA History Book.* 1985–1990. http://archive.is/1wF5. Accessed October 4, 2012.

CHAPTER SIX

A Federalist George W. Bush and an Anti-Federalist Barack Obama?

The Irony and Paradoxes behind Republican and Democratic Administration Drug Policies

José D. Villalobos

Introduction

Policy debates concerning the war on drugs often revolve around topics such as combating organized crime, militarizing the U.S.–Mexican border, and employing punitive approaches to substance abuse. Alternatively, scholars, pundits, and the public have also debated the pros and cons of drug legalization—primarily as it pertains to the decriminalization of medicinal marijuana (see, for instance, Cohen 1976; Inciardi 1999; Trebach and Inciardi 1993; Stimmel 1996; Schaler 1998; Boyum and Reuter 2005; Ferraiolo 2007). Therein, policy discussions on drug legalization have focused mainly on sociopolitical, emotional, ethical, and health concerns while largely ignoring questions concerning philosophical views over Federalism,[1] particularly over whether drug policy should be executed at the national versus state level. However, a deeper look at the issue and how politicians have attempted to address it reveals a major irony in the positions taken by liberal and conservative political leaders. Namely, Republicans have clamored to have more federal power given to the Drug Enforcement Administration (DEA) and other federal entities to uphold a nationwide ban on marijuana and other drugs, while Democrats have gradually moved toward a position that favors states' rights to help jump-start the decriminalization movement, especially in states such as California, Oregon, and Colorado, which have relaxed laws concerning the sale and consumption of medicinal marijuana (Greenwald 2009; Khan 2009). Although it is no surprise that Democrats have taken a more liberal position on drug enforcement and Republicans a more conservative one, what is somewhat unusual is the extent to which Democrats have adopted a states' rights approach, while Republicans have shunned states' rights in the process.[2]

During President Bill Clinton's two terms, eight states successfully pushed toward decriminalizing medicinal marijuana (see table 6.1). These changes in drug laws sparked debates not only over the policies themselves but also over whether and how the federal government should react to such state-level changes. In the midst of such debates, then-governor of Texas George W. Bush told the *Dallas Morning News* in October 1999 that he believed the federal government should let each state "choose that decision as they so choose" (Drug Policy Alliance 2006). However, upon leaving the governor's mansion for the presidency, Bush subsequently flip-flopped on his state-centered philosophy, focusing instead on his role as head of the executive branch in enforcing federal drug laws. Almost immediately, Bush fell in line with his Republican predecessors in continuing the war on drugs by using federal laws to push back against state-level efforts to legalize marijuana use. In doing so, Bush demonstrated a high level of responsiveness to his base of social conservative supporters, as well as to his own social policy preferences, though at the expense of his states' rights values.

Bush's successor, President Barack Obama, initially took quite the opposite route by calling on the DEA and other federal forces to pull back and allow states to continue the process of decriminalizing the sale and consumption of medicinal marijuana (Greenwald 2009; Schor 2010; see also Khan 2009). Although Obama's move to allow for more state-level control over medicinal marijuana highlighted his willingness to delegate

Table 6.1. Statewide votes for medical marijuana, 1996–2000

State	Year	Number	Yes	No
California	1996	Proposition 215	56%	44%
Arizona	1996	Proposition 200	65%	35%
Alaska	1998	Question 8	58%	42%

federal power, he nevertheless remained publicly opposed to the full legalization of marijuana or other drugs for recreational use and has charged the DEA to lead in enforcing that policy realm (see O'Brien 2010; Hecht 2011; Saunders 2011). To clarify its position and goals, the Obama administration released its initial *National Drug Control Strategy* in May 2010 (recently updated for 2012), which outlined the president's comprehensive approach to dealing with the various public health and safety consequences caused by drug use (Office of National Drug Control Policy 2010, 2011, 2012). In essence, Obama presented himself as being supportive of state-level drug decriminalization efforts but also concerned about the health and safety issues related to drug use and determined to uphold federal law when it comes to perceived abuse by medicinal marijuana providers. Needless to say, there is more than meets the eye when it comes to presidential preferences on drug policy enforcement. To better understand how and why presidents have taken certain positions on federal and state drug policies requires a more nuanced exploration of the manner in which presidents perform a juggling act between their personal policy preferences and their Federalist philosophies in dealing with the issue.

Placing Obama, Federalism, and the Drug Policy Debate in Today's Context

Taking the current political atmosphere into consideration, Barack Obama's actions in allowing states to decriminalize marijuana seem particularly out of place considering the broader, widely scrutinized debate over his true philosophical leanings. Since his inauguration as the nation's forty-fourth president, Obama's strongest critics on the Far Right fringes of the ideological spectrum—namely, Ann Coulter, Rush Limbaugh, Sean Hannity, and Glenn Beck—have sought to label him as a big government "socialist," bent on suppressing states' rights and usurping federal power in an attempt to subvert influence over public policy in a manner they claim threatens the very fabric of U.S. democracy (e.g., see Beck 2009; Limbaugh 2009; see also Paul 2011, chap. 8). However, Obama's measured deference to state-level control over drug policy largely contradicts these untamed allegations. Nevertheless, conservatives and liberals alike have had surprisingly little to say about Obama's stance on states' rights regarding decisions concerning drug policy reforms, instead placing the focus more on the basic liberal versus conservative debate over social values concerning the issue. As for former president George W. Bush, his change in positions on whether federal or state governments should lead and control drug policy reforms went largely unnoticed.

Such lack of attention to questions of Federalism with respect to U.S. drug policy lies in stark contrast to incidents concerning other policy realms, such as the uproar directed toward George W. Bush and Barack Obama when it came to the bank bailouts. In that case, not only did the public clearly express anger at the use of tax dollars to bail out the banks, but conservatives in particular were outraged at what they viewed as excessive overreach by the federal government (Rasmussen 2009). In fact, despite his appeals that such an act was necessary to preserve the free market, Bush was branded by some on the Far Right as having committed an act of "socialism" in orchestrating the initial bailout efforts (e.g., see Kincaid 2008). Obama's subsequent efforts to further supplement the banks with additional bailout funds helped lay the groundwork for many of the charges that he is a "socialist," charges frequently churned out by Tea Party activists and other right-wing conservatives (see Street and DiMaggio 2011). It is interesting that such strong sentiments over the federal state of government have been levied to such extremes when it comes to a topic like bank bailouts but have so easily been set aside when it comes to the drug policy debate.

In contrast, it is far easier to assess views on Federalism in observing the recent controversy over immigration policy in Arizona concerning Senate Bill (S.B.) 1070 (Archibold 2009).[3] Although a large amount of media coverage over the bill centered on racial profiling and liberal versus conservative views on undocumented immigrants, much of the focus also lay on federal versus state-level enforcement of immigration policies. On behalf of the Obama administration, Attorney General Eric Holder argued that federal jurisdiction over immigration policy trumped the intention of S.B. 1070, which aimed to, as conservatives argued, uphold the laws that the national government had failed to enforce. U.S. District Court Judge Susan Bolton thereafter struck down key portions of the law in a clear ruling against Arizona's bid for expanded state-level control over immigration policy, instead reinforcing the interpretation of the Constitution's Supremacy Clause that confers federal government dominance over the states (Curtis 2010). In the midst of further debate and judicial appeals, liberals have continued calling for more federal efforts to stop other conservative state-level policy changes on immigration policy, including Alabama's more recent immigration law reforms (see Reeves 2011; Mears 2011). From the side of conservatives, their opportunity to strengthen border security and enforcement remains under attack by a liberal administration they perceive as far too fond of big government control over public policy.

Given the presence of such highly polarized and inflamed rhetoric over government involvement in people's lives in cases such as the federal bank bailouts and the recent immigration law reform efforts seen in Arizona and Alabama, it is interesting that such strong sentiments over issues related to Federalism have so easily been set aside when it comes to the drug policy debate. On the surface, it is understandable why the policy debate over medicinal marijuana has focused more on personal preferences linked to social values than on the inconsistencies concerning the tug-of-war over national versus state control of drug policy. After all, neither Republicans nor Democrats wish to draw attention to their strategic dismissal of Federalist values. Nor do members of either party wish to risk placing their Federalist philosophies above their partisan policy preferences when so much of what is at stake is being driven by public sentiment in connection to social values and health issues. At the same time, the way in which the debate over drug reform policies is currently playing out is also in large part a product of how George W. Bush's and Barack Obama's predecessors tackled it. Oddly enough, it was Richard Nixon who pushed for greater enforcement of federal drug prohibition policies and oversaw the creation and institutionalization of the DEA while also promoting what he referred to as his "New Federalism" philosophy, which favored decreasing the size of national government and delegating more power and funding to the states. So what explains these various approaches to U.S. drug policies and Federalist philosophies across political parties and presidential administrations?

To better understand the dynamics at play regarding presidential stances on drug policy, it is important to review the historical development of our Federalist system and connect it to the evolution of U.S. drug policy from Nixon's time in office to the present day. To do so, I first briefly review some of the more important historical developments that have influenced how Republicans and Democrats today express their views and preferences regarding our federal government. I then outline the evolution of drug policy as related to Federalism and how presidents have dealt with the issue from Nixon's launch of the war on drugs to more current affairs. From there, I look specifically at the cases of former president George W. Bush and President Barack Obama to further assess whether and to what extent Federalist philosophies have evolved, how they have affected policy decisions on drug issues, and what the political and institutional implications may be going forward.

Overview of Federalism and Historical Developments as Related to Drug Policy

Since 1787, when the Federalists outmaneuvered the Anti-Federalists in adopting the measures of the Virginia plan and hammering out the Connecticut Compromise for the creation and ratification of the U.S. Constitution, the United States has radically evolved as a federal system of government. Over time, two main forms of Federalism have emerged in the debate over how much government power should be concentrated at the state versus the national level: dual Federalism and cooperative Federalism (see, for instance, Zimmerman 1992; Walker 1999; Morgan and Davies 2008). Dual Federalism defines the relationship between the national government and the states on a coequal basis and does so through a narrow interpretation of the Constitution's Commerce Clause, Supremacy Clause, Necessary and Proper Clause, and Tenth Amendment. Cooperative Federalism, on the other hand, designates the national government as clearly superseding the states through a wide interpretation of the Constitution. Cooperative Federalism dominated the 1930s under Franklin Delano Roosevelt's administration, leading to an unprecedented growth in federal government size and influence for much of the twentieth century. Nevertheless, an enduring demand for scaling back the national government by delegating more influence and responsibility to the states has persisted over time in the post–FDR era, particularly among small government conservatives and libertarians over the last several decades.

Evolution of Federalism and Drug Policy from FDR to Clinton

Scholars recognize Franklin Delano Roosevelt as the father of the modern presidency. Presiding over the federal government during the Great Depression and World War II, FDR was faced with tremendous social and economic challenges. Across the country, states found themselves strapped for cash and under pressure from their constituents to be more responsive to their needs. Given the circumstances, the nation turned to the federal government for help, and FDR responded by assigning the Brownlow Committee to consider ways to further grow and institutionalize the executive branch (Dickinson 1996, chap. 3).[4] The result was a growth of the president's staff through the creation of the Executive

Office of the President, as well as a subsequent ballooning of the size and scope of the outer executive branch that rapidly expanded the government's involvement in addressing social issues and stabilizing the economy in cooperation with state governments (see, for example, Burke 2000; Hart 1995).

In keeping with FDR's efforts, succeeding presidents largely continued to further expand and institutionalize bureaucratic entities in the federal government until Richard Nixon's term in office. Arguing that the national government had become cumbersome in its growth and amount of spending on social programs, Nixon embarked on a mission to reintroduce a form of dual Federalism he termed a "New Federalism" that would seek to shift influence away from the national level and instead delegate more responsibility, funding, and decision-making power over policy to the states. Thereafter, Republican presidents have tended to favor Nixon's limited Federalist approach, while Democrats have largely preferred FDR's more expansionist approach.

Although Nixon generally favored greater state-level influence wherever possible, he made an exception in dealing with drug policy. On July 14, 1969, he delivered a special message to Congress in which he singled out drug abuse as "a serious national threat" and signaled the need for national antidrug policies and abuse treatment programs to be pushed at the federal level and extended to the states (NPR 2007). Two years later, in June 1971, Nixon officially declared the war on drugs in an effort to expunge illicit drugs from society and lower drug-related crimes. By July 1973, the DEA was created under Nixon's leadership to lead other agencies in conducting a federal effort to fight the drug war. Despite Nixon's move in further expanding the federal government's size and role in addressing the issue, the potential for criticism among conservatives was largely suppressed by the popularity of his stance against drug abuse and his efforts to simultaneously extend federal enforcement of drug prohibition policies in concert with the states. It was also during this time that the controversial Rockefeller Drug Laws went into effect (Gray 2009).

After Nixon's resignation from office, former governor Jimmy Carter emerged as the Democratic candidate for president, beating out Gerald Ford in the 1976 election. During the election campaign, Carter openly proposed to end federal criminal penalties for possession of up to one ounce of marijuana (NPR 2007). Carter's support for decriminalizing marijuana helped set the current terms of debate between conservatives and liberals on the issue. Although such liberal preferences for decriminalization were stymied by a majority of public opposition at the time, others on the left have since followed Carter's lead in developing the liberal–progressive decriminalization movement we see today.

When President Ronald Reagan entered the White House, he pushed for smaller government across all areas of the executive branch in a renewed effort to transfer power and responsibility back to the states. However, there were two major exceptions to his smaller government stance. One was Reagan's much-talked-about military buildup in the arms race against the Soviet Union and the other was his administration's tough federal approach to drug prohibition. Picking up where Nixon left off, Reagan reinvigorated the war on drugs by instituting a zero tolerance policy and enacting stricter minimum sentencing laws that many viewed as biased against minorities and those in the lower-income brackets (Lusane and Desmond 1991; Nunn 2002). More popular, perhaps, was First Lady Nancy Reagan's symbolic "Just Say No" campaign directed at the nation's youth. George H. W. Bush continued Reagan's policies by placing additional pressure on Mexico to crack down on drug lords. Both presidents shared a strong affinity for states' rights but depended heavily on federal jurisdiction in the realm of drug policy.

Shortly after his 1992 election victory, Bill Clinton embarked on his campaign for a national health care initiative but fell short in his efforts amid formidable political and public opposition against greater federal control in the public health arena.[5] While Clinton's efforts at expanding federal control over health policy failed, his drug policies remained largely in the construct of his two predecessors and saw some additional federal expansion. Perhaps most notably, Clinton raised the position of director for the Office of National Drug Control Policy to cabinet-level status in 1993 (see Schaler 1998, chap. 2).

Drug Policy Paradoxes of Presidents George W. Bush and Barack Obama

This brings us to more recent history concerning the presidencies of George W. Bush and Barack Obama. As mentioned at the outset, George W. Bush was not always in favor of full federal enforcement of drug policies concerning marijuana. Bush once pushed a states' right approach to drug enforcement as governor of Texas, supporting the idea of letting states make their own choices on the matter (Drug Policy Alliance 2006). For Bush, endorsing a states' rights approach worked well as governor of the "red" state of Texas, where efforts toward decriminalizing marijuana have been largely outweighed by conservative opposition. As a small government conservative, Governor Bush could have his cake and eat it too. Once he became president, however, Bush soon changed his tune, calling on the DEA to take charge in raiding locations in places such as California, where state-level enforcement efforts had been relaxed. Bush found himself in new territory, in charge of the entire nation with over a dozen states willing to have medicinal marijuana come into the open. No doubt feeling the pressure from his conservative base, and with the federal forces of the DEA at his fingertips, Bush became a strong proponent and instigator of federal enforcement efforts. In proving himself to his base of social conservative supporters while also satisfying his own personal policy preferences, Bush's states' rights values were simultaneously and necessarily thrown under the bus, so to speak.

The behavioral changes exhibited by Bush illustrate a paradox among Republican presidents that mirrors the general paradox faced by conservatives concerning classic liberalism and social values. In essence, Bush's priorities changed in accordance with the level of executive position (federal versus state) he held at a certain point. As governor of Texas, classic liberalist values seemed to have won out as Bush promoted a states' rights approach. Bush did so knowing full well that a majority of Texans were against legalized medicinal marijuana. However, Bush lost his openness to states' rights once he became president and inherited a greater amount of authority, which he wielded in fighting against state-level drug legalization efforts against numerous states open to reform efforts. Once the dust settled, it became clear that President Bush's Anti-Federalist philosophy hung lower on the totem pole than his social values. As for his Republican predecessors, certainly Nixon, Reagan, and George H. W. Bush's strong moral opposition to all forms of legalization and decriminalization dominated over their affinity for limiting federal authority over states' rights, particularly given their institutional position and power atop the executive branch.

Toward the end of Bush's second term in November 2007, Barack Obama was in full swing campaigning for the presidential nomination. Asked about his views on legalizing drugs, he expressed conditional support for legalized medicinal marijuana (Anburajan 2007):

> My attitude is if the science and the doctors suggest that the best palliative care and the way to relieve pain and suffering is medical marijuana then that's something I'm open to because there's no difference between that and morphine when it comes to just giving people

relief from pain. But I want to do it under strict guidelines. I want it prescribed in the same way that other painkillers or palliative drugs are prescribed.

After a long campaign, the newly elected Obama wasted no time in shifting policy during his first year in office. Very quickly, he directed his then newly appointed attorney general, Eric Holder, to have federal agents "relax their enforcement of marijuana laws and go after only those distributors who violate both state and federal law" (Schor 2010; Khan 2009). Asa Hutchinson, George W. Bush's former DEA head, acknowledged that the changes Obama made were "a significant and dramatic change in drug policy" (Schor 2010).

As it stands now, fourteen states have largely decriminalized the use and sale of medicinal marijuana, while seventeen states and the District of Columbia have adopted some type of state medical marijuana program (see table 6.2). In addition, states such as California have recently started moving toward the approval of "industrial" sized marijuana farms (Mick 2010). Early in Obama's first couple of years in office, it appeared that such changes at the state level were relatively safe from federal interference. However, just because Obama was supportive in allowing states to gradually decriminalize medicinal marijuana did not mean he was equally as enthusiastic about broader legalization efforts for marijuana and other substances that could potentially increase recreational use of "soft" drugs.

Halfway through his second year in May 2010, the Obama administration announced the release of its *National Drug Control Strategy* for addressing drug use as more of "a public health issue than a criminal justice problem" (Hananel 2010). One of the key goals of Obama's plan was to reduce the rate of youth and adult drug use by 15 and 10 percent. Each year since, the administration has released an updated version of its strategy (see Office of National Drug Control Policy 2011, 2012). Among its core principles, the strategy has focused on intervention, the integration of substance treatment and recovery, and improving information systems as a means to better analyze and understand drug use trends and their consequences (Office of National Drug Control Policy 2010). In releasing its plan, the administration pointed to the significant annual expenditures that drug use has imposed on our health care and criminal justice systems. In addition, Obama took the rare step of openly stating that U.S. demand for drugs—directly bankrolling the continual supply of illegal drugs from South America and Mexico—is what has largely kept the war

Table 6.2. States that have decriminalized marijuana

State	Decriminalized	Active State Medicinal Programs
Alaska	X	X
Arizona		X
California	X	X
Colorado	X	X
Connecticut	X	
Delaware		X
District of Columbia		X
Hawaii		X
Maine	X	X
Maryland		X
Massachusetts	X	
Michigan		X
Minnesota	X	
Mississippi	X	
Montana		X
Nebraska	X	
Nevada	X	X
New Jersey		X
New Mexico		X
New York	X	
North Carolina	X	
Ohio	X	
Oregon	X	X
Rhode Island		X
Vermont		X
Washington		X

Sources: NORML 2011a, 2011b, 2011c.

on drugs from succeeding (Hananel 2010). Echoing the president, drug czar Gil Kerlikowske declared that "we [Americans] have a responsibility to reduce our own drug use in this country" (Hananel 2010; see also Boaz 2010; Schor 2010).

As California prepared a "Proposition 19" ballot initiative for the 2010 midterm elections that would have allowed for the regulation and taxing of marijuana as a fully legal substance (available for medical as well as recreational use), the Obama administration took the position as "firmly" opposing the move well before it failed to pass on Election Day (O'Brien 2010; Sánchez 2010). Previously, during a March 2009 town hall meeting, Obama tackled the following question: "With over 1 out of 30 Americans controlled by the penal system, why not legalize, control, and tax marijuana to change the failed war on drugs into a money making, money saving boost to the economy?" (Stein 2009). In response, Obama noted his opposition to full legalization for economic purposes, saying "No, I don't think that's a good strategy to grow our economy" (Stein 2009). That comment, coupled with his previous remarks in 2007 noting his preference for adopting strict guidelines for any decriminalization measures, sent a clear signal of caution about the Obama administration's opposition to full-blown drug legalization efforts across states.

Most recently, President Obama has upped the ante in making sure that his administration's deference to states in decriminalizing medicinal marijuana does not result in the sale of the substance for recreational use. Specifically, the Obama administration has been intent to follow up on "charges against dispensaries and speculators allegedly raking in cash from purportedly nonprofit marijuana stores" (Hecht 2011). For instance, in October 2011, four U.S. prosecutors in California announced that the state's medicinal marijuana laws had been "hijacked by profiteers" and abused to the point that prosecutions and property seizures against certain targeted dispensaries, their landlords, and property owners were in order (Saunders 2011; Hecht 2011). Given these charges of abuse amid an otherwise burgeoning medical marijuana industry, one might argue that the Obama administration has become as stringent—if not more stringent—than its predecessors, at least in terms of oversight in this realm.

Considering these historical developments, one cannot help but wonder how drug policy might be different if presidential (and public) Federalist values had historically trumped social values rather than the other way around. Republican presidents might continue to decry drug use but limit their federal action to respectful disagreement with states moving toward legalization. For Democrats, if their preferences for federal involvement in the policy-making process were placed above all else, then their openness toward decriminalization would more likely be sought through policy changes at the national level. Given the political vitriol we often witness today when it comes to Federalism issues where politicians often employ harsh rhetoric against their opponents (such as the charges of big government—or even socialism—that have been levied against Barack Obama as of late), it would be very interesting to see how politicians would react if a larger portion of the public (e.g., beyond the libertarian voting block) began placing its Federalist preferences above its personal social values with respect to the drug policy debate.

The Role of Institutional Fragmentation
amid the Federalist Debate

One final factor to consider is the extent to which institutional fragmentation has impacted administrative behavior and performance in instituting U.S. drug policies and reforms. Specifically, institutional fragmentation between the White House, the Department of Justice (DOJ), and the DEA has led to an increasing number of DEA raids of state-compliant marijuana dispensaries despite stipulations by President Obama and Attorney General Eric Holder that no raids would occur as long as the dispensaries were operating in accordance with state laws. For instance, in 2010, DEA federal agents raided the home of Chris Bartkowicz, a Colorado resident, who was running a medical marijuana dispensary out of his basement, after he had volunteered to be interviewed by a local news channel on how one could grow marijuana legally according to Colorado state law (*Talk Left* 2010; *Huffington Post* 2011). Reportedly, once the head of the DEA in Denver, Jeffrey Sweetin, had caught wind of the news interview, he instructed agents to conduct the raid. Afterward, when asked for comment by the local news station, Sweetin noted that regardless of whether Bartkowicz was operating legally under Colorado law, his actions were nevertheless illegal under federal law and thus justified the raid.

Although Eric Holder had issued an official memorandum on behalf of the DOJ and with President Obama's approval stating that the administration would pull back and not prosecute medical marijuana cases where state laws had decriminalized the practice, the Denver DEA exhibited its own intentions to continue fully enforcing federal laws. In fact, Denver DEA head Sweetin further asserted to the local news channel that "Nothing in federal law has changed. Wanting federal law to be different is not a great strategy. We will continue to enforce federal law, that's what we're paid to do, until the federal law changes. The only exception to that is discretion and department guidance" (*Talk Left* 2010). As such, the last part of Sweetin's comments suggested—at least to critics—that the Denver DEA was ignoring Holder's previous memorandum distributed down from the DOJ.

At first, Bartkowicz's arrest reportedly sent "shock waves" across the country among legalization proponents, particularly since he was confirmed to be "a licensed medical marijuana caregiver" in the state of Colorado (*Huffington Post* 2011). In the aftermath of the raid, however, the DEA reportedly put forth "reasonable evidence" that Bartkowicz had not, in fact, been in "clear and unambiguous" compliance with Colorado state laws. In August 2010, Bartkowicz was tried in federal court, where it was ruled that he "could not use state law as a defense" (*Huffington Post* 2011). Two months later, Bartkowicz pleaded guilty and was sentenced to five years in prison for having "miserably failed" to abide by federal as well as state laws (*Huffington Post* 2011).

Similar raids have been reported in other states such as California, Montana, and Oregon, though the intent—as well as the source—behind the raids has not always been clear (e.g., see Phan 2011; *Bozeman Daily Chronicle* 2011; *San Francisco Chronicle* 2012). In some cases, it appears the DEA is, under the direction of the Obama administration and the DOJ, seeking to bust dispensaries that are abusing state laws in an attempt to sell and distribute medicinal marijuana to people intent on using it for recreational purposes (Saunders 2011; Hecht 2011). At other times, it appears that branches of the DEA may be acting on their own to enforce federal law despite the calls from Holder and Obama to pull back enforcement when it comes to the decriminalization of medicinal marijuana under state laws (*Talk Left* 2010; *Huffington Post* 2011). Still others, such as George Mull, president of the California Cannabis Association, have speculated that it may be that some local governments are requesting DEA raids, given, as he puts it, "some frustration on the part of local governments that they can't stop the proliferation of marijuana dispensaries" (see Phan 2011). Whatever the case, it seems apparent that a certain amount of fragmentation between the White House and a number of key executive branch agencies and departments has led to conflicting actions and mixed interpretations of the law across different states. As such, as long as discrepancies abound between state and federal drug laws, it may be difficult for the Obama administration (and future administrations) to be consistent in efforts to enforce drug laws.

Conclusion

From the time that Richard Nixon declared a war on drugs, Republicans have consistently pushed for strict enforcement of federal drug laws as a means to protect society and moral values from the proliferation of drugs. Democrats, on the other hand, have moved toward policies that support the decriminalization of medicinal marijuana and the implementation of treatment and rehabilitation programs. Although it is no surprise that Democrats have taken a more liberal position on the issue and Republicans a more conservative one, what has been somewhat unusual is the extent to which Democrats have adopted a states' rights approach, while Republicans have shunned states' rights in the process. In this chapter, I have discussed this historical irony and explored how recent policy shifts stand to impact policy concerning medicinal marijuana and, more generally, U.S. drug policy moving forward. In light of the major historical precedents, it seems safe to assume that Federalist philosophies will continue to have far less influence over presidential drug policies than will social values and political gamesmanship, thus further entrenching both parties in the same bitter debate over drug policy, at least for the foreseeable future. What is less clear, and merits further investigation, is the extent to which institutional fragmentation is negatively affecting the ability of the executive branch to cope with discrepancies in drug laws between the national and state levels of government.

Notes

1. But see Pickerill and Chen (2007).

2. One exception to the general partisan divide is the recent legislative bill introduced by Ron Paul (R-TX) and Barney Frank (D-MA) in June 2011 that would remove the federal government's prohibition of marijuana, leaving it to the states to decide whether and how to legalize it (see Peralta 2011). In this case, support for such legislation comes easy for Congressman Paul, given his libertarian views promoting smaller government and liberal social policies, while Congressman Frank's support reflects his willingness to eschew his general reputation as an ardent Federalist Democrat in favor of more lenient social policies. In fact, Frank was quoted as saying he was not necessarily advocating marijuana use, but that he does believe that "criminal prosecution is a waste of [federal] resources and an intrusion on personal freedom" (Peralta 2011).

3. Arizona's Senate Bill 1070, otherwise known as the Support Our Law Enforcement and Safe Neighborhoods Act, was signed into law by Jan Brewer, Arizona governor, on April 23, 2010. The bill includes provisions making it a misdemeanor crime for people to be in Arizona without documentation proving their U.S. citizenship or legal status, pushes state and local officials and agencies to enforce federal immigration laws, and sets restrictions against the sheltering, hiring, or even transportation of undocumented aliens (Arizona State Legislature 2010).

4. The Brownlow Committee (also known as the Brownlow Commission or the President's Committee on Administrative Management) was formed in 1937 and included three members: Louis Brownlow, Charles Merriam, and Luther Gulick. Together the three members forged key recommendations that largely shaped the modern executive branch as we know it today, including the creation of key staff to aid the president with administrative tasks for managing the executive branch, expanding presidential control over administrative departments, and incorporating the Bureau of the Budget, Civil Service Administration, and National Resources Board into the newly established Executive Office of the President.

5. Eighteen years later, Barack Obama would succeed with federal government expansion of health care where Clinton could not, signing the Patient Protection and Affordable Care Act into law on March 23, 2010. Nevertheless, Obama's victory came at a great cost in having to surrender the public option section of the bill and in seeing public support diminish across a year's worth of heavy negotiations that ended with a majority of the country opposing the bill upon passage, all in part due to discomfort surrounding the idea of expanded federal involvement in health care.

Bibliography

Anburajan, Aswini. 2007. "Obama Open to Limited Legalization." MSNBC. http://firstread.msnbc.msn.com/_news/2007/11/25/4423993-obama-open-to-limited-legalization. Accessed November 25, 2007.

Archibold, Randal C. 2009. "Arizona Enacts Stringent Law on Immigration." *New York Times.* http://www.nytimes.com/2010/04/24/us/politics/24immig.html. Accessed April 23, 2010.

Arizona State Legislature. 2010. "Senate Bill 1070." http://www.azleg.gov/legtext/49leg/2r/bills/sb1070s.pdf. Accessed April 23, 2010.

Beck, Glenn. 2009. "Obama Stimulus Package Really Socialism?" *Fox News.* http://www.foxnews.com/story/0,2933,483345,00.html. Accessed February 5, 2009.

Boaz, David. 2010. "Obama's 'New' Drug Strategy." *Cato at Liberty.* http://www.cato-at-liberty.org/2010/05/12/obamas-new-drug-strategy/. Accessed May 12, 2010.

Boyum, David, and Peter Reuter. 2005. *An Analytic Assessment of U.S. Drug Policy.* Washington, DC: AEI Press.

Bozeman Daily Chronicle. 2011. "Feds Raid Montana Medicinal Marijuana Businesses." http://www.bozemandailychronicle.com/news/article_96adb40a-4e72-11e0-b6b6-001cc4c002e0.html. Accessed October 10, 2011.

Burke, John P. 2000. *The Institutional Presidency: Organizing and Managing the White House from FDR to Clinton.* Baltimore, MD: Johns Hopkins University Press.

Cohen, Sidney. 1976. *The Drug Dilemma.* New York: McGraw-Hill.

Curtis, John M. 2010. "Arizona's Immigration Law Slapped by Feds." *LA City Buzz Examiner.* http://www.cxaminer.com/x-45268-LA-City-Buzz-Examiner~y2010m7d31-Arizonas-Immigration-Bill-Slapped-by-Feds. Accessed July 31, 2010.

Dickinson, Matthew J. 1996. *Bitter Harvest: FDR, Presidential Power and the Growth of the Presidential Branch.* Cambridge: Cambridge University Press.

Drug Policy Alliance. 2006. "The Right Response to the War on Drugs." http://www.drugpolicy.org/news/08_17_04gop.cfm. Accessed February 9, 2006.

Ferraiolo, Kathleen. 2007. "From Killer Weed to Popular Medicine: The Evolution of American Drug Control Policy, 1937–2000." *Journal of Policy History* 19, no. 2: 147–79.

Gray, Madison. 2009. "New York's Rockefeller Drug Laws." *TIME.* http://www.time.com/time/nation/article/0,8599,1888864,00.html. Accessed April 2, 2009.

Greenwald, Glenn. 2009. "Obama's Commendable Change in Federal Drug Enforcement." http://www.salon.com/news/opinion/glenn_greenwald/2009/10/19/drugs. Accessed October 19, 2009.

Hananel, Sam. 2010. "Obama Drug Policy Focuses on Prevention, Treatment." *Huffington Post*. http://www.huffingtonpost.com/2010/05/10/obama-drug-policy-focuses_n_571087.html. Accessed May 10, 2010.

Hart, John. 1995. *The Presidential Branch: From Washington to Clinton*. Chatham, NJ: Chatham House.

Hecht, Peter. 2011. "Federal Crackdown Leaves California Medical Marijuana Industry Weighing Risks." *Oakland Tribune*. http://www.insidebayarea.com/oaklandtribune/localnews/ci_19115697. Accessed October 14, 2011.

Huffington Post. 2011. "Chris Bartkowicz Sentenced to 5 Years in Prison." http://www.huffingtonpost.com/2011/01/28/chris-bartkowicz-sentenc_n_815528.html. Accessed October 10, 2011.

Inciardi, James A. 1999. *The Drug Legalization Debate*. 2nd ed. Thousand Oaks, CA: Sage Publications.

Khan, Huma. 2009. "In First 100 Days, Obama Flips Bush Admin's Policies." *ABC News*. http://abcnews.go.com/Politics/Obama100days/story?id=7042171&page=1. Accessed April 29, 2009.

Kincaid, Cliff. 2008. "Bush Embraces Obama's Socialism." *Accuracy in Media*. http://www.aim.org/aim-column/bush-embraces-obamas-socialism/. Accessed October 26, 2008.

Klein, Joe. 2009. "Why Legalizing Marijuana Makes Sense." *TIME*. http://www.time.com/time/nation/article/0,8599,1889021,00.html. Accessed April 2, 2009.

Limbaugh, Rush. 2009. "Barack Obama's Cruel Socialism." http://www.rushlimbaugh.com/home/daily/site_022709/content/01125113.guest.html. Accessed February 27, 2009.

Lusane, Clarence, with Dennis Desmond. 1991. *Pipe Dream Blues: Racism and the War on Drugs*. Boston: South End Press.

Mears, Bill. 2011. "Parts of Alabama Immigration Law Blocked by Federal Appeals Court." *CNN*. http://www.cnn.com/2011/10/14/us/alabama-immigration-law/. Accessed October 14, 2011.

Mick, Jason. 2010. "California Bay Area to be Silicon Valley of Pot, with Nation's First "Industrial" Farms." *DailyTech*. http://www.dailytech.com/California+Bay+Area+to+be+Silicon+Valley+of+Pot+With+Nations+First+Industrial+Farms/article19114.htm. Accessed July 22, 2010.

Morgan, Iwan W., and Philip J. Davies. 2008. *The Federal Nation: Perspectives on American Federalism*. New York: Palgrave Macmillan.

NORML. 2011a. "Active State Medical Marijuana Programs." NORML. http://norml.org/index.cfm?Group_ID=3391. Accessed October 10, 2011.

———. 2011b. "State by State Laws." NORML. http://norml.org/index.cfm?Group_ID=4516. Accessed October 10, 2011.

———. 2011c. "States That Have Decriminalized." NORML. http://norml.org/index.cfm?Group_ID=6331. Accessed October 10, 2011.

NPR. 2007. "Timeline: America's War on Drugs." http://www.npr.org/templates/story/story.php?storyId=9252490. Accessed April 2, 2007.

Nunn, Kenneth B. 2002. "Race, Crime and the Pool of Surplus Criminality: Or Why the 'War on Drugs' Was a 'War on Blacks.'" *Journal of Gender, Race & Justice* 6: 381–87.

O'Brien, Michael. 2010. "Obama Drug Plan 'Firmly Opposes' Legalization as California Vote Looms." *The Hill*. http://thehill.com/blogs/blog-briefing-room/news

/97101-obama-drug-plan-firmly-opposes-legalization-as-california-vote-looms. Accessed May 11, 2010.

Office of National Drug Control Policy. 2010. "National Drug Control Strategy." http://www.whitehouse.gov/sites/default/files/ondcp/policy-and-research/ndcs2010 _0.pdf. Accessed May 11, 2010.

———. 2011. "National Drug Control Strategy." http://www.whitehouse.gov/sites/de fault/files/ondcp/ndcs2011.pdf. Accessed June 12, 2011.

———. 2012. "National Drug Control Strategy." http://www.whitehouse.gov/sites/de fault/files/ondcp/2012_ndcs.pdf. Accessed April 17, 2012.

Paul, Rand. 2011. *The Tea Party Goes to Washington.* New York: Center Street.

Peralta, Eyder. 2011. "Ron Paul, Barney Frank Introduce Bill That Would End Pot Prohibition." National Public Radio. http://www.npr.org/blogs/thetwo-way/2011 /06/23/137372951/ron-paul-barney-frank-to-introduce-bill-that-would-end-pot -prohibition. Accessed June 12, 2011.

Phan, Suzanne. 2011. "Critical Time for Pot Dispensaries as Feds Shut Down Shops." *News 10 ABC.* http://www.news10.net/news/article/159332/2/Critical-time-for-pot -dispensaries-as-Feds-shutdown-shops. Accessed October 19, 2011.

Pickerill, J. Mitchell, and Paul Chen. 2007. "Medicinal Marijuana Policy and the Virtues of Federalism." *Journal of Federalism* 38, no. 1: 22–55.

Rasmussen. 2009. "56 Percent Oppose Any More Government Help for Banks." *Rasmussen Reports.* http://www.rasmussenreports.com/public_content/business/federal _bailout/february_2009/56_oppose_any_more_government_help_for_banks. Accessed February 11, 2009.

Reeves, Jay. 2011. "Immigration Law in Alabama to be Enforced, Toughest in US." *Christian Science Monitor.* http://www.csmonitor.com/USA/Latest-News-Wires /2011/0929/Immigration-law-in-Alabama-to-be-enforced-toughest-in-US. Accessed September 29, 2011.

Sánchez, Ray. 2010. "California's Proposition 19 Rejected by Voters." *ABC News.* http://abcnews.go.com/Politics/proposition-19-results-california-votes-reject -marijuana-measure/story?id=12037727. Accessed November 3, 2010.

San Francisco Chronicle. 2012. "Police Raid Oregon Medical Pot Outfit, Arrest Owner." http://www.sfgate.com/news/article/Police-raid-Ore-medical-pot-outfit-arrest-owner -3842692.php. Accessed September 5, 2012.

Saunders, Debra J. 2011. "Barack Obama, Drug Warrior." *San Francisco Chronicle.* http://www.sfgate.com/cgi-bin/article.cgi?f=/c/a/2011/10/14/IN621LH11D.DTL. Accessed October 16, 2011.

Schaler, Jeffrey A. 1998. *Drugs: Should We Legalize, Decriminalize or Deregulate?* Amherst, NY: Prometheus Books.

Schor, Elana. 2010. "With Focus on Demand Rather Than Supply, Barack Obama Gives Hope to Critics of U.S. 'War on Drugs.'" *Daily Caller.* http://dailycaller.com /2010/01/10/with-focus-on-demand-rather-than-supply-barack-obama-gives-hope -to-critics-of-u-s-war-on-drugs/. Accessed January 10, 2010.

Stein, Sam. 2009. "Obama Takes Pot Legalization Question during Townhall (Video)." *Huffington Post.* http://www.huffingtonpost.com/2009/03/26/obama-takes-pot -legalizat_n_179563.html. Accessed March 26, 2009.

Stimmel, Barry. 1996. *Drug Abuse and Social Policy in America: The War That Must Be Won.* New York: Haworth Medical Press.

Street, Paul, and Anthony DiMaggio. 2011. *Crashing the Tea Party: Mass Media and the Campaign to Remake American Politics.* Boulder, CO: Paradigm.

Talk Left. 2010. "DEA Disregards Obama and Holder on Medical Marijuana." *Talk Left.* http://www.talkleft.com/story/2010/2/13/22556/3411. Accessed October 10, 2011.

Trebach, Arnold S., and James A. Inciardi. 1993. *Legalize It? Debating American Drug Policy.* Washington, DC: American University Press.

Walker, David B. 1999. *The Rebirth of Federalism: Slouching toward Washington.* 2nd ed. New York: Chatham House Publishers.

Zimmerman, Joseph F. 1992. *Contemporary American Federalism: The Growth of National Power.* Westport, CT: Praeger.

CHAPTER SEVEN

Caught in the Middle

Undocumented Migrants' Experiences with Drug Violence

Jeremy Slack and Scott Whiteford

Introduction

The Arizona–Sonora section of the U.S.–Mexican border continues to be the most active sector for unauthorized border crossings and marijuana seizures.[1] These two activities have historically coexisted peacefully without much overlap. The economic interests involved in human smuggling and drug trafficking were quite distinct for a long time, both maintaining separate trails through the desert as well as the different needs for smuggling human beings that need to eat, sleep, and breathe as opposed to a commodity such as a package of drugs (Spener 2009). However, during the Calderón administration (2006–2012), an unspoken tacit agreement between law enforcement officials and drug cartels was broken along the U.S.–Mexican border. As a result, drug-related violence skyrocketed in almost every major border city. A crackdown by Mexican officials with support from the United States in the form of funding, intelligence, and equipment created a chaotic scenario as different groups vied for power and control of the profitable drug routes that supply the unquenchable demand for narcotics north of the border. This violent competition, which often reduced profits from drugs, created the need for more income streams such as extortion, kidnapping, and migration (Stratfor 2008; Gibler 2011) and also led to accusations that the Mexican government actively supported some cartels over others (Osorno 2010; Gibler 2011). Even so, the debate surrounding the connection between drugs and migration has failed to produce any major insights because the question itself has numerous pitfalls, such as the differing definitions of involvement. Are we talking about motive? Are we talking about willing versus coerced cooperation? Or are we talking simply about some monolithic entity called a drug *and* migration cartel? In order to avoid this trap, we analyze the contact between people engaged in clandestine border crossing with drug trafficking and organized crime as a way to better understand the impact of recent violence in Mexico's and the United States' simultaneous wars on drugs and migration. We must address all these questions in order to discern the connections between drugs and migration.

This chapter focuses on the new impacts of transnational criminal organizations (TCOs) that formerly limited their activities to drugs but now focus on undocumented immigration from and through Mexico to the United States. Our work with people who have recently crossed through the Sonoran desert and have been apprehended by the Border Patrol and returned to Mexico[2] produced surprising stories that show the impact of drugs on migration histories. These stories include instances of migrants being used as unwitting bait for the authorities in order for drug shipments to evade detection, kidnapping in drop houses used for the transport of drugs, and even personal experiences of smuggling drugs through the desert after unsuccessful migration attempts.

The debate over the connection between drugs and migration reached a new height on June 25, 2010, when Arizona governor Jan Brewer made the accusation that the majority of migrants are involved with drug trafficking.[3] While the vast majority of undocumented border crossers are not trafficking drugs, it is important to address why and how drugs and migration overlap, as well as the impacts of one phenomenon over the other. The new characteristics of clandestine border crossing put undocumented migrants in the middle of the larger geopolitical landscape of the wars on drugs, terrorism, and immigration along the border (Payan 2006).

As they navigate their journey northward, economic migrants, defined as those who choose to move in search of a better economic life for themselves and their families, increasingly contend with increased violence and exposure to criminal actors, actively attempting not only to exploit their money but their labor as well. They must be wary of kidnappings and extortion, cartels searching to pressure desperate individuals into their employ, and diverse threats from freelance thugs often masquerading as guides and unaffiliated coyotes[4] who are punished (along with those around them) for attempting to circumvent the monopolized control of the border.

Tony Payan (2006) documents how U.S. border enforcement has conflated the "three border wars" against drugs, immigration, and terrorism. He meticulously outlines how border enforcement has come to deal with these three different phenomena with the same tactics. What is not discussed is the reaction of the clandestine border industry (human smuggling and drug trafficking, among other things) to this one-shot enforcement strategy. We argue that taking an all-inclusive approach to border enforcement has caused immigration and drugs to overlap both geographically and substantively, creating significant hazards for undocumented migrants.

This transformation raises questions about the nature of violence on the border. The spaces of clandestine activity (in the case of our research this is mainly the paths through the Arizona–Sonora desert) have created complicated networks of victims and victimizers that are constantly changing. In order to better understand this hidden geography of violence, we must look not only at the institutional-level connections between drugs and migration (human smuggling mafias and drug cartels) but also examine individual participation in the drug trade. By highlighting the voices of the people who have recently experienced a clandestine border crossing, as well as those who have decided to take an active role in the drug trade, we hope to shed light not only on the plight of economic migrants caught in a dangerous situation but also on the individual agency that is involved in the constrained set of choices available on the border. Understanding how people make decisions to negotiate the complexity of the international and increasingly violent border region is critical to our understanding of the forces that draw people into the tentacles of the drug trade.

In this chapter we detail the different ways that drug trafficking and undocumented migration have become intertwined in response to border enforcement. By providing an overview of the development of immigration enforcement in the U.S. Southwest, we trace the changing routes and tactics for crossing the border into Arizona and how this has resulted in a newly profitable and important drug corridor.

We proceed by outlining the different challenges facing people attempting to cross the international border. The flow of people across the border is both influencing and being influenced by the larger geopolitical reality of the bloody drug violence in the region, a violence for migrants that has many different forms and consequences. To disentangle the interactions and impacts, we examine the different forms of violence that are woven into the crossing experience and the consequences of people simply trying to survive their journey to join family members or find work.

Unpredictable Crossings

Crossing the border without documents has been highly organized for many years (Conover 1987), but the actual experience of anyone trying to cross is complicated and confusing (Spener 2009). The physical challenges of hunger, pain, and thirst haunt migrants crossing the Arizona desert. People are shuffled from one guide to another, sent with different coyotes, or *polleros*, sold by *enganchadores* (people trying to attract clients in public places), and often held in safe houses and extorted for more money. When attempting to cross without the aid of a local guide, or when getting separated from a group, people often see more evidence of the connection between drugs and migration. The following story represents one example of this phenomenon.

Ramón's Story

After an attempt to cross through Altar/Sasabe had failed miserably, Ramón and his companions decided to head back and regroup. They had just been robbed at gunpoint, forced to strip down to their underwear, and relieved of all their food, money, and supplies by a group of *bajadores* (robbers). With no food or water left, they turned around and headed toward Mexico, but after another night in the desert with no food or water, they ran into a group of narcos (drug traffickers). They were carrying AR-15s, which they pointed at Ramón and his group, instructing them that they had to keep walking into the United States or die. Ramón said that they were using the migrants as a shield, so that the *burreros* (drug smugglers on foot) could cross their marijuana. "¡Si regresas, te mato!" (If you go back, I'll kill you), said one narco. They were forced to walk for another two nights. They had no food or water, and the only thing they found to drink was a puddle of green liquid that made them vomit. They found a backpack with some food in it, but they didn't know how long it had been there or if it was any good anymore. They were forced to walk from 6 a.m. until 8 p.m. without stopping. Finally, they saw the *Migra* (Border Patrol) and were able to turn themselves in. There were originally twenty people in the group but only eleven remained by the time they turned themselves in. Ramón said that this was the first time anything like this had happened to him, and he had been coming since 1993; he had crossed successfully eleven times before (personal communication, February 4, 2010).

This story represents the type of breakdown in the informal system that illustrates the unpredictable and quickly changing world that migrants have to negotiate at the border. While people share personal histories, rumors, and accounts of previous experiences, there are no sure paths across the desert to security and employment. The fluid nature of border crossing and the emergence of people working for the drug cartels have qualitatively changed the crossing experience. The social networks that inform people of the dangers are often fractured by the experiences such as incarceration in prisons, many of which do not allow calls to Mexico, as well as the general distance and lack of communication with friends and family at home. This limits knowledge of what to expect, especially for people who get information from relatives who have not crossed in recent years.

Our research is focused on people's experiences crossing the Arizona–Sonora border, which has different topography, history, and binational social networks than other sectors of the U.S.–Mexican border region. In order to better understand the development of a crossing experience where drugs now play a significant role, we must first look at the history of clandestine migration from Mexico to the United States and how Arizona–Sonora has become the principal geographic setting.

Undocumented Migration: Security Policy, Guides, Drugs, and the Arizona Legislature

Since the 1990s the United States has enacted several policies (i.e., Operation Gatekeeper, Operation Hold-the-Line, Operation Safeguard, Operation Río Grande, the Arizona Border Control Initiative, and the 1996 Illegal Immigration Reform and Immigrant Responsibility Act) to enforce the border in urban zones and move the flow of people into the most dangerous and inhospitable areas of the U.S. Southwest in an attempt to deter potential migrants (Nevins 2002; Andreas 2000). This resulted in thousands of deaths in the Sonoran Desert and the hope that it would deter people has proven false as the flow of unauthorized entrants continued unabated until the recession of the late 2000s (Comisión Nacional de Derechos Humanos 2007; Rubio-Goldsmith, McCormick, Martínez, and Duarte 2006). And even if Mexican migration has collapsed, Central American migration through Mexico and through the U.S.–Mexican border continues to escalate.

Data showed that July 2010 was the second deadliest month on record for migrant deaths in the desert. The yearly total for 2010 eventually rose to 252, the highest total of known migrant deaths in Pima County. Between 2001 and 2010, 1,650 migrant bodies were discovered in this area.

According to the Pima County Medical Examiner, most died from hyperthermia or heat exposure (McCombs 2010a; personal communication, August 2, 2010). While the number of human remains found in 2011 dropped from 252 to 183, considering a sizeable drop in the number of Border Patrol apprehensions, the Coalición de Derechos Humanos (Human Rights Coalition) estimated that the death rate actually doubled in 2009 (Rodríguez 2012). Although the Mexican government has a campaign to inform migrants about the dangers of crossing, many have no other option than to cross in the most remote areas, as soon as possible, regardless of the summer heat.

The rise in deaths is a result of the longer walks and harsher conditions associated with the post gatekeeper era (Nevins and Aizeki 2008). Wayne Cornelius (2001) analyzed migrant deaths before and after Operation Gatekeeper by looking at both the number of reported deaths and the causes of death. The number of reported deaths in 1995 and 1996 was 61 and 59, respectively, with the vast majority resulting from car accidents rather than exposure to extreme heat or hyperthermia (Cornelius 2005; Nevins and Aizeki 2008). Interestingly, there is still reason to believe that car crashes are overrepresented as a cause of death among migrants, because one can assume that almost all victims are reported, whereas deaths in the desert are harder to find. In fact, many bodies are never found. From 2000 to 2004, the average rose to 410 reported deaths per year (Cornelius 2005, 783). The cause of death shifted as well, with the majority of people now dying from hyperthermia rather than drowning or car accidents (Cornelius 2001, 2005; Nevins and Aizeki 2008; Hagan 2008). FY 2005 was the most deadly thus far, with 516 reported deaths border-wide.[5]

These deaths were the direct result of the plan outlined in the "Border Patrol Strategic Document: 1994 and Beyond," which was the first step in adopting a national security and immigration policy that would attempt to stop immigration by "prevention from deterrence" (United States Border Patrol 1994, 6). The strategy also outlines how controlling the main corridors for unauthorized entry will create alternative routes, shifting the flow of migrants to other areas that may become "hot spots" (7). This is exactly what happened in Arizona. Explicitly stated in the document is, "Violence will increase as effects of the strategy are felt" (4). The measures of success indicate a desire for a decrease in the rate of deaths or injury and criminal activity, but as of yet this has not been realized. This documented the intentional strategy to knowingly increase violence along the U.S. southern border. Doris Meissner, the former commissioner for the Immigration and Naturalization Service, signed the last page of the document on August 8, 1994.

With the adoption of this plan and the so-called post–gatekeeper era came a much more difficult, costly, and dangerous process of entering the United States. However, the clandestine flow of people north has largely continued unabated. The militarization of the border has succeeded in creating a more sophisticated and profitable human smuggling industry. Prior to these significant changes in policy, the process of crossing into the United States without documents was marked by harsh conditions but did not entail the same level of danger or risk of death, nor did it necessitate the same level of reliance on coyotes or guides (Samora 1971; Conover 1987). Massey, Durand, and Malone (2002) suggest that the people-smuggling trade arose following the termination of the bracero program, with the percentage of migrants using a coyote increasing from 40 percent to above 70 percent between 1965 and 1975. Between 1990 and 1998 the average price for "smuggling services" in the Tijuana area grew from $215 to $359, while outside of the Tijuana area the average cost rose from $150 to approximately $550, an increase of 250 percent (Massey, Durand, and Malone 2002). Compare this to the average price of over $1,600 today (Comisión Nacional de Derechos Humanos 2007), and it is clear that there have been drastic changes in the level of profitability and organization of clandestine border crossings. Moreover, in the past, scholars such as Gustavo López Castro (1998) have asserted that there was no connection between drug trafficking and human smuggling. While we cannot state, nor do we care to research, what and how organizational connections work, in our research we have found numerous firsthand evidence that migrants are frequently being used as a distraction for authorities, resulting in greater success rates smuggling the more valuable cargo, suggesting that regardless of how people cooperate, drug trafficking has an impact on migrants' lives.

David Spener's seminal book on coyotes meticulously outlines the different types of *coyotaje*, the different methods used to cross the border, but his focus is largely on South Texas and particularly how movement within the United States is facilitated by loose networks of freelance helpers (Spener 2009, 121–61). An FBI agent interviewed by Spener dubiously asserts that in the United States networks of guides are loose and nonhierarchical, but "across the border there definitely are kingpins that coordinate movement" (147). Spener's section on *narco-coyotaje* also poses some interesting contradictions to our experiences in Sonora–Arizona. In accordance with other scholars, he suggests that involvement with drugs is an aberrant form of *coyotaje* and not commonplace (López Castro 1998; Izcara 2012). He concedes that in 2007 the Gulf Cartel was meddling in Texas human smuggling but suggests that this was likely more of a protection fee, making sure coyotes pay in order to operate rather than direct control (Spener 2009, 159–60). Our contrasting data most likely stem from the difference in his geographical focus and the dramatic shifts as a result of the drug war in recent years. This topic appears more frequently in our interviews during the end of 2009 and 2010.

However, there is an important distinction regarding the question being asked. The way in which researchers have defined the overlap between drugs and migration has contributed to the finding that these are separate enterprises. The burden of proof becomes quite high when people are looking for evidence of a master manipulator or a coherent group of people making backroom plots to control both migration and drug trafficking. Howard Campbell (2009) has noted that the definition of a cartel is itself highly problematic, not only in the traditional monopolistic definition but also in the sense that it is a coherent group that always works together and to the same end. They are far looser organizations, with complicated and shifting practices and alliances. Some could point to coyotes who have participated in drug trafficking as well as human smuggling, which has been noted by some scholars, although rejected as evidence of overlap (Izcara 2012).

For example, in one interview, a nineteen-year-old migrant named Gerardo stated that he met another man in Mazatlán, Sinaloa, who was going north "*a la burreada*" (to take drugs on foot), but upon the conversations with Gerardo and two other friends he agreed to act as a simple guide and cross to work (personal communication, October 28, 2011). These identities and occupations are highly fluid, and trying to pigeonhole any actor as a coyote (human smuggler), guide, *enganchador* (recruiter or undocumented migrant "seller"), *burrero* (drug smuggler on foot), *bajador* (robber), *sicario* (paid assassin), or *ratero* (petty thief) is both temporally and spatially contingent upon the current options available to them. One thing is certain: the variety of options and the severity of the consequences have risen dramatically in recent years. While stories like this do not indicate a formalized relationship, they certainly do not denote two separate spheres, especially in a climate where killings based on even the slightest allegiance have become the norm.

The debate about what connotes involvement is never ending and nebulous. We would like to take a different approach to drugs and migration by examining the commonplace and often strikingly violent interactions people have with drugs while trying to cross into the United States. We feel that this change allows for a more fruitful discussion of not only the changing dynamics of undocumented migration but also a more nuanced understanding of the ways the so-called drug war is impacting different spheres of social life on the border and in Mexico.

This is not to say that people don't frequently claim all-out collusion and overlap between drugs and migration. During several interviews with municipal police officers in Nogales, Sonora, they wholeheartedly agreed that there had been some sort of consolidation. Migrants also frequently began to complain about the mixed agendas of their coyotes. One woman described her recent experience crossing where she suspected that the guides were really only concerned with trafficking drugs. "They were a group of forty-four in all. Suddenly the guides shouted that the *perrera*, a Border Patrol truck named after its resemblance to a dogcatcher, was coming. Everyone bolted and the guides disappeared, but there was actually no border patrol in sight. She asked, 'Why would they just leave us there if they didn't have something else more valuable?'" (personal communication, March 2, 2010).

Perhaps this experience is more in line with Spener's false *coyotaje*, whereupon individuals never intend to actually smuggle migrants into the United States, another aberrant form (Spener 2009, 155). However, our data suggest that these experiences may be much more common in the Arizona–Sonora area than the Texas border. More research is needed in other areas along the border to determine both the differences in the experience of being smuggled into the United States as well as how the processes of clandestine migration function border-wide.

A complicated interplay exists between enforcement and the efforts to circumvent these measures (Andreas 2000). As enforcement shifts and changes, so too do the ways people try to counteract the new measures aimed at stopping their activities. The only constant in this ever-changing dynamic is an increase in profitability as the enforcement increases. However, as drug smuggling and people smuggling have increased in profitability concurrently, they have also come into competition with each other in a number of ways. First and foremost, these large and increasingly organized cartels are forced to operate in the limited amount of space on the border. They share trails and pickup points along the highways and compete for the best routes. Second, the strategy of undocumented migration can help or hinder drug trafficking, and vice versa. Since it is much less costly (for the moment) for a group of migrants to get apprehended than for a shipment of drugs to get intercepted, there is greater incentive to prioritize the shipment of drugs. Conversely, the increased presence of migrants on these trails makes them more obvious to

Border Patrol agents, and therefore they attract more surveillance. For instance, in the past, migrants were not walking high into the mountains, but this has changed in an attempt to avoid the increased Border Patrol presence.

Payan (2006) notes that the vast majority of drugs are smuggled into the United States mixed in with cargo through legal ports of entry (POEs), and that smuggling through the desert is most likely unorganized individuals engaging in small-time drug trafficking. Spener (2009) also notes that the method for smuggling a commodity is much different for a human being, and that only a small amount of drugs actually comes into the United States on the backs of people. However, the fact that the United States Border Patrol seized 1.05 million pounds of drugs between the POEs (largely in Arizona), and based on our firsthand accounts, suggests that this may have changed (Department of Homeland Security 2010; Esquivel 2010).

The most common manifestation of this is coordinating groups of border crossers by dividing them into groups of fifteen to twenty people and sending them in staggered formation, one leaving thirty to sixty minutes before the next. This is usually done without the knowledge of the would-be migrants, and only when things fall apart, as with the case of Ramón, does the situation become clear. After five or six of these groups have been sent out, a group of ten individuals carrying backpacks filled with marijuana is sent behind them. Those with more valuable drug cargo are now able to keep tabs on the movement of the Border Patrol in response to the undocumented migrants and therefore increase their rate of success.[6]

Extremely large groups of people apprehended in the desert have become a common sign of this manipulation. On April 30, 2010, a group of 105 migrants was arrested outside the Baboquivari Mountains in southern Arizona (McCombs 2010b). We have been told about groups of up to one hundred people crossing. Groups of this size are easily detected. The chances for a successful crossing are slim; however, a lot of attention is required from the authorities to apprehend, transport, and process all of these individuals. Since the one thing that clandestine organizations have on their U.S. adversaries is a nearly unlimited supply of people, it makes sense that organizing a group of this size is a way of limiting the capacity of the Border Patrol and increasing success rates for more valuable cargo. Because more and more people fear the consequences of not using an established guide, this strategy has become more effective. The use of a nonaffiliated guide sheds some light on this situation as well.

Juanito's Story

Juanito was originally from Guerrero but had lived in California for over ten years. He explained how he got his own group of people together to cross after being deported for a DUI (driving under the influence). He may or may not have been their guide, but he said that he knew the way well and had never been caught by the *Migra*, only by the police. During the trip he did not see any other migrants but two groups of twenty-five *burreros*, all with backpacks filled with marijuana and some carrying guns. He complained that they got picked up by a vehicle earlier than the migrant pickup points, and consequently his group had to walk farther (personal communication, April 13, 2009).

The fact that he saw more drug smugglers than migrants is indicative of not using an established guide. This is similar to Ramón's story, whereupon leaving the group he was confronted with drug trafficking operating alongside clandestine migration. He might not have witnessed this phenomena if he had crossed with a local guide.

The flood of people through the desert, the economic recession in the United States, and the often sensationalized reporting of border crimes have led to a slew of anti-immigrant legislation. These bills include successful propositions to ban undocumented migrants from using public services, no in-state tuition for nonlegal residents, English-only legislation, and proposed bills to remove citizenship for children born to undocumented migrants in the United States. However, all of these legal maneuvers pale in comparison to May 2010's SB 1070 and Alabama's HB 56. With this legislation comes the potential to incarcerate thousands of legal residents, as well as unauthorized residents.

If similar bills spread to other states, it will pose a serious issue to an already marginalized and fearful group, which could in turn lead more people to participate in the drug trade. One individual named Alberto, who had lived and worked in Tucson for fifteen years and had two U.S.–citizen children, relayed his experience of being falsely accused of money laundering and deported to Mexico without a trial. His determination to see his family again ended with a six-month sentence in federal jail for reentry. He had no previous arrest records but was given a formal deportation through Operation Streamline[7] after a failed attempt to cross. Alberto stated his frustration over the long jail sentence, noting that many of the people arrested for trafficking drugs were released much sooner because evidence was "lost." He asked, "It makes me want to just go with drugs next time. If they get five days when they have drugs and I get sixty days for nothing, why shouldn't I?" (personal communication, December 9, 2009).

This is only one example of how "tough" immigration policies could lead to more participation in the drug industry—and perhaps the fact that it can be more profitable is an added incentive as well. The symbolic act of incarcerating people because of immigration offenses—which until recently had been treated as civil administrative violations—has also had the effect of increasing contact between economic migrants and career criminals. This in turn also increases the likelihood that people who can be considered economic migrants will engage in the drug trade, as they are recruited by drug smugglers in the jails where they serve their sentences. Otherwise law-abiding individuals are now facing extreme hardships due to lack of funds, extended periods of incarceration, and separation from their families. The tempting offer of $1,300–$1,800[8] for carrying a backpack through the desert, as opposed to paying $1,500–$3,000 for safe passage, becomes more plausible after multiple deportations and stays in jail. The next section here provides an individual account of the compounded effects of border militarization and a high-profile drug war started by former president Calderón's use of the military to interrupt drug trafficking in Mexico between 2006 and 2012, with a cost of over sixty thousand lives and perhaps even as many as one hundred thousand, as others contend (Flores 2012). José tells us the story of how he became involved in the drug trade.

José's Story

José is a short man with baggy clothes and a shaved head, who was originally from Veracruz but had been living in Ciudad Júarez, the epicenter of the drug violence in recent years. Despite having originally crossed as a migrant to work in Los Angeles ten years ago, he had crossed the border several times with backpacks filled with marijuana. His first trip was through Magdalena, Sonora, a town about forty miles south of the border. José and some friends drove a truck to a ranch outside of town. Due to the weight of the fifty pounds of marijuana and the supplies for the journey, they could only walk for short stretches. José explained that there were ten people carrying the drugs, as well as a guide and the *"encargado,"* or boss; both were armed. José informed me that the *encargado* knew top cartel members personally and that only his word would save people if they lost a shipment of drugs. The *encargado* told them that it was the *Migra* (Border Patrol) or soldiers or *bajadores* who took the drugs to ensure that no one ran off with the drugs. They walked for three days and nights, hiding and sleeping during the day and walking at night. They diverged from the traditional migrant paths after the first day and went really high up in the "sierra" where the *Migra* rarely goes. Soon they arrived at a series of ranches where people helped them transport the drugs by signaling when the coast was clear and providing shelter. Upon arrival in Tucson, Arizona, they were driven to the Tufesa bus station and sent back to Mexico. He said that they were supposed to pay him $1,300 there, but that they didn't. José said he was going to go back to see them in Mexico and collect his money. He shrugged and said "*No me pagaron. Esta vez, no me pagaron*" (They didn't pay me. This time, they didn't pay me) (personal communication, September, 4, 2009).

In all likelihood, José will be tasked with another journey through the desert in order to collect his pay. This starts a cycle that frequently ends in death or jail. People have been exposed to a form of violence and a criminal lifestyle as a direct result of the vulnerability and marginalization created by U.S. policies. We see this participation as an act of violence in and of itself, in that people are exposing themselves to a likely death or imprisonment as a response to their economic needs. Because there is individual agency involved in the decision to participate in the drug industry, it is important to acknowledge that this violence has a social and economic utility. In David Riches's discussion of violence, he talks about the need for perpetrators to legitimize violence; the most acceptable way to do this is to establish it as a form of tactical "preemption" (1986, 5). In drug trafficking or engaging in human smuggling, migrants are preempting their vulnerable state after failing to enter the United States.

The Organizations: Cartels and Coyotes

When Miguel Ángel Félix Gallardo, Mexico's ruling drug lord in the 1980s, ordered his successors to divide the border into different territories after his arrest in 1989, there was a tentative peace between the different cartels (Payan 2006, 865). This arrangement worked fairly smoothly until President Felipe Calderón made cracking down on the drug cartels one of his presidency's primary goals after a hotly divisive election in 2006. This bloody war has stirred up old rivalries and favored some cartels over others, creating opportunities for increased power and profit.

Conflicts are major financial burdens for clandestine organizations. The loss of manpower through incarceration or death and the need to purchase weapons, transport, and orchestrate armed confrontations with both authorities and other cartels are extremely expensive. Maintaining economic solvency and cash flow is imperative for a cartel leader's survival. This need is largely driven by the political economy of narco-corruption (Andreas 1998). Andreas writes:

> At its core drug corruption is a cost of doing business. While corruption in the form of bribes and payoffs has long been a part of the relationship between business and the state, it plays a more vital role in the case of drug smuggling because of the illicit nature of the activity. (1998, 160)

The very act of bribery takes the place of taxation on drug smuggling industry; however, failure to pay this tax carries a more serious penalty than failing to pay the IRS or Hacienda (Gianluca and Florentini 1995, in Andreas 1998). The corruption tax also differs in that it is a bracket that not only mirrors the amount of enforcement levels (Gianluca and Florentini 1995, in Andreas 1998), which are currently at their highest level, but it is also on a relative scale. The group that pays the most gets the most security, and those that pay the least are the most likely to have pictures of their bloody corpses on the covers of newspapers nationwide. The need to pay billions of dollars in bribes and kickbacks to officials is one of the principal motivators for the cartels to expand their economic-generating activities.

In order to fulfill the need to replace workers in the era of high turnover due to worker mortality, the thousands who flock to the border every day provide excellent recruiting grounds. They are broken down, tired, destitute, and generally frustrated over their powerlessness. The desire to become a hammer rather than a nail can be easily exploited. The TCOs have placed significant resources and effort into seducing people to join their organizations. The easiest targets are the people who have been deported, since their relative vulnerability and their need to recuperate lost resources lead them to take more chances. These organizations have also been changing and overlapping with drug smuggling over recent years. However, this involvement is not only with drug trafficking organizations but also with those involved in human smuggling as well. The way in which TCOs have been able to take advantage of the flow of undocumented migrants is yet another example of the flexibility and adaptability institutionalized by the cartels in response to U.S. and Mexican drug enforcement efforts (Payan 2006, 869).

The many shifts in the treatment of immigration have been accompanied by changes in our treatment of drugs. From steady increases in prison sentences for drug offenses to increasingly costly approaches to combat international drug cartels (Plan Colombia, Plan Mérida, Afghanistan), the militarized escalation of the war on drugs has been particularly pronounced at the U.S.–Mexican border (Andreas 2000; Nevins and Aizeki 2008; Payan 2006). This crackdown has led to more violence in Mexico for control of the border and therefore more pressure to increase or maintain profits. In order to do this, many groups have expanded their activities to the realm of migration.

However, it is important to note that the fight for the border works on many levels, and one of the most important is the geopolitical landscape of the cartels in Sonora. The conflict, largely between the Beltrán Leyva Cartel and "El Chapo" Guzmán's Sinaloa Federation, has increased exponentially over the last four years, until calming down in 2011, when "El Chapo" claimed a total victory.

Stories of rivalries, murders, tortures, and power have become the norm across the border. Different actors control different border regions, and the relationships between them have become increasingly murky, fueled by rumor, speculation, and more than a few mistaken identities. One can hardly keep abreast of the soap opera of new alliances, betrayals, and newcomers in the world of the cartels. However, what is clear is that their economic activity is no longer limited solely to drugs but has expanded to other realms.

One example is the prevalence of kidnappings. People frequently describe the so-called safe houses where they are held for days with little food or water, being filled with guns, drugs, and money. One man told us his story of being held at a safe house in Phoenix after successfully entering the United States.

Diego's Story

After walking for three days in the desert, Diego, age fifty-four, arrived in Phoenix to find that the price of his crossing had risen. The coyote wanted an extra 2,000 USD on top of the agreed-upon price. Some of the rooms were filled with people and the rest with drugs, weapons, and money. While he did not know how many people were there, he said that six Peruvians arrived in one group. Of the ten to twelve people in his room, two were women, and the guards raped them. Diego told me that you could hear crying constantly in the safe house. Luckily, Immigrations and Customs Enforcement broke in and busted up the safe house. Diego was only there for twelve hours (personal communication, September 24, 2009).

For migrants, the prevalence of kidnappings associated with unscrupulous human smugglers has devastating consequences. It is difficult to tell if kidnappings are the norm or if they are extreme events. However, kidnappings associated with safe houses that contain drugs often curtail more pronounced acts of violence, as in the case of the women being raped. Further, we have also documented instances where the captors attempt to negotiate deals that involve working as *sicarios*, or assassins, in order to obtain freedom. One article in the *Washington Post* was an interview with a man who was working as a guard for a safe house in order to pay off a debt (White and Salas 2009).

The expansion of activities related to drugs and other criminal organizations leads us to question how people negotiate, rationalize, or are trapped by the violent world of drug trafficking. While our research suggests that it is rare to coerce migrants to traffic drugs, trickery and compulsion are more common; the only constant is that people must have lived, worked, or made friends with someone involved with drugs who trusts them with the valuable cargo and physically demanding trek through the desert.

Conclusions

Addressing the connections between different criminal organizations always involves some level of conjecture. For instance, it is difficult to discern the frequency of events, what constitutes normal, and what is being done on purpose versus what is an accidental consequence of operation. Is it really the case that migrants are being used as covers to smuggle drugs? If so, why? Are coyotes working for drug cartels? Are they simply following the law of the land, or is it a coincidence? While our data suggest that this is a well-thought-out plan, we cannot rule out the possibility that a limited number of enterprising coyotes are acting independently to smuggle drugs. That is why we want to problematize the question most frequently posed by researchers: Are coyotes and drug cartels the same? We propose another question: How does the trafficking of drugs, as well as the violence being generated by it, impact the lives of people who are close to it? What we can do is use the voices of the migrants—their stories and fears and hopes—to explain what has been happening and how the force of the U.S. labor market and the $65 billion market for illegal drugs in the United States are destroying people's lives. There is a move to legalize marijuana in several states. This would have an enormous impact on reducing the exposure of economic migrants to armed drug traffickers. Although cartels smuggle other drugs such as methamphetamine, as well as marijuana, here in Sonora, and especially through the desert, marijuana is the most common (Esquivel 2010). Even more effective would be any type of comprehensive migration reform that would allow people a legal means of coming and going between their home countries and the United States. Not only would there be a better record of who enters the country, but it would also allow border security to focus solely on drugs and security. The thousands of people crossing through the desert each day create a needless distraction, and only by providing legal entry will we be able to obtain border security.

Despite all of the unconscionable half-truths and blatant lies about the border, one of the most offensive things being proposed is the now-ubiquitous slogan, "Secure the border then do immigration reform." This has no chance of working. Pouring billions into the Border Patrol and the Department of Homeland Security will only provide more profit incentives to continue to find a way around security measures. The border is too large, too porous, and too costly to seal completely, not to mention that the incentives for corruption increase exponentially with newer measures. There will never be a 100 percent secure border as long as Mexico and the United States maintain the economic, familial, and spatial ties that have shaped the region. Not only has it become almost a rite of passage for many rural Mexican youths to come to the United States to work, but this long history has cemented family ties in the United States. Many have almost completely lost ties to Mexico and will continue to return to the United States no matter what the consequences.

Moreover, the vast profits associated with border crossing make it impossible to seal. Corruption is common among border officials, and as enforcement increases, so does the price of the criminalized commodity, whether people or drugs. This leads to an increase in the size of bribes. The corruptibility of humanity, as well as the lack of transparency of the Department of Homeland Security, makes it hard for researchers to determine how this will play out over the long term.

It is imperative for the United States as a nation to address the results of its consumption of cheap labor and strong drugs. Approaches such as Plan Mérida, which gives billions in military aid to Mexico, only feed the fires and create an entrenched, constant battle that is costing thousands of civilian lives and is not only unwinnable without profound changes in the demand for drugs in the United States but serves to keep government contracts rolling in and defense budgets growing. We must first separate the objectives and then address each separately, or there is no hope of stemming the ever-expanding death toll of our paradoxical border.

Notes

1. http://www.cbp.gov/linkhandler/cgov/newsroom/publications/admin/perform
_account_rpt_2013.ctt/perform_account_rpt_2013.pdf.

2. We draw on a variety of periodical sources to document some of the more high-profile events that show the recent overlap between drugs and migration. These secondary sources will be used to complement eighty-nine semistructured interviews with recent border crossers focusing particularly on those individuals who had contact with the drug trade. These interviews were conducted with randomly selected individuals staying at a shelter for recently deported/repatriated migrants in Nogales, Sonora. They focused on violence for border crossers, which frequently led to discussions about the connections between the guides, known as *coyotes* or *polleros*, the bandits (*bajadores*), and drug trafficking by *burreros* (drug mules).

3. "Well, we all know that the majority of the people that are coming to Arizona and trespassing are now becoming drug mules. They're coming across our borders in huge numbers. The drug cartels have taken control of the immigration. So they are criminals. They're breaking the law when they are trespassing and they're criminals when they pack the marijuana and the drugs on their backs." When challenged, she continued to maintain that she was correct: "The simple truth is that the majority of human smuggling in our state is under the direction of the drug cartels, which are by definition smuggling drugs," she said in a statement. "It is common knowledge that Mexican drug cartels have merged human smuggling with drug trafficking." (*Tampa Bay Times* 2010).

4. Guides that are not part of the organized mafias that control migration; they work independently and can be persecuted by others to maintain monopolistic control.

5. No More Deaths, a non-profit, pro-immigrant organization, cites 238 migrant deaths in the Arizona desert, while the Secretaría de Relaciones Exteriores (Mexican Foreign Ministry) reports 516. See http://www.jornada.unam.mx/2007/04/26/index.php?section=politica&article=007n1pol. Accessed September 30, 2012.

6. This information is from multiple interviews where people have become aware of the fact that they are being used as covers for drug shipments.

7. Operation Streamline is a federal program to provide a daily criminal trial en masse (seventy to eighty defendants simultaneously) for unlawful entry into the United States. Currently the program exists in the Tucson, Yuma, Marfa, and Del Rio sectors.

8. This estimate is drawn from five interviews with people who related their experiences of carrying marijuana through the desert. We did not make it a habit to ask about these experiences within any structured or semistructured interviews.

Bibliography

Andreas, Peter. 1998. "The Political Economy of Narco-Corruption in Mexico." *Current History* 97, no. 618: 160.
———. 2000. *Border Games: Policing the U.S.–Mexico Divide.* Ithaca, NY: Cornell University Press.

Campbell, Howard. 2009. *Drug War Zone: Frontline Dispatches from the Streets of El Paso and Juárez.* Austin: University of Texas Press.

Comisión Nacional de Derechos Humanos. 2007. *Todos saben, nadie sabe: Trece años de muerte de migrantes: Reporte sobre impunidad y muerte en la frontera sur de Estados Unidos.*

———. 2009. *Informe Especial de la Comisión Nacional De Los Derechos Humanos sobre los Casos de Secuestro en contra de Migrantes.* June. http://www.cndh.org.mx /INFORMES/Especiales/infEspSecMigra.pdf. Accessed September 30, 2012.

Conover, Ted. 1987. *Coyotes: A Journey through the Secret World of America's Illegal Aliens.* New York: Vintage Books.

Cornelius, Wayne A. 2001. "Death at the Border: Efficacy and Unintended Consequences of U.S. Immigration Control Policy." *Population and Development Review* 27, no. 4: 661.

———. 2005. "Controlling 'Unwanted' Immigration: Lessons from the United States, 1993–2004." *Journal of Ethnic and Migration Studies* 31, no. 4: 775–94.

Department of Homeland Security. 2010. *Performance and Accountability Report 2009.* http://www.dhs.gov. Accessed on September 30, 2012.

Durand, Jorge, and Douglas S. Massey, eds. 2004. *Crossing the Border: Research from the Mexican Immigration Project.* New York: Russell Sage Foundation.

Esquivel, Jesus. 2010. "Arizona, puerta abierta para la mariguana del 'Chapo.'" *Proceso,* March 9. http://www.proceso.com.mx/rv/hemeroteca/detalleHemeroteca/151184. Accessed September 30, 2012.

Fiorentini, Gianaluca, and Sam Peltzman. 1995. *The Economics of Organized Crime.* Cambridge, MA: Cambridge University Press.

Flores, Raul. 2012. "ONG da cifre de muertos en el sexenio de Calderón: Suman mas de 100 mil." *Excelsior,* November 27. http://www.excelsior.com.mx/2012/11/27 /nacional/871927. Accessed April 17, 2013.

Gibler, John. 2011. *To Die in Mexico: Dispatches from Inside the Drug War.* San Francisco: City Lights Books.

Hagan, Jacqueline Maria. 2008. *Migration Miracle: Faith, Hope, and Meaning on the Undocumented Journey.* Cambridge, MA: Harvard University Press.

INEGI. *Conteo de Población y Vivienda.* http://www.inegi.gob.mx. Accessed September 30, 2012.

Instituto Nacional de Migración. 2012. *Boletín de estadísticas migratorias.* http://www .inami.gob.mx/index.php?page/sintesis_grafica-2005. Accesssed May 15, 2012.

Izcara, Simón Pedro. 2012. "Opinión de los polleros tamaulipecos sobre la política migratoria estadounidense." Migraciones Internacionales 6, no. 3: 32.

López Castro, Gustavo. 1998. "Factors That Influence Coyotes and Alien Smuggling." http://www.utexas.edu/lbj/uscir/binpapers/v3a-6lopez.pdf. Accessed September 30, 2012.

Marizco, Michel. 2007. "The Corridor of Killing: A Rash of Bloody Crimes Is Taking Lives on Both Sides of the Border." *Tucson Weekly,* April 19. http://www.tucsonweekly .com/tucson/the-corridor-of-killing/Content?oid=1087398. Accessed September 30, 2012.

———. 2009. "God's Gonna Cut you Down." June 11. http://borderreporter.com/2009 /06/gods-gonna-cut-you-down/. Accessed September 30, 2012.

———. 2010. "Cartel Polishes Image as Calderón Takes Hear." *Nogales International*, March 16. http://www.nogalesinternational.com/articles/2010/03/18/opinion/guest _opinion/doc4b9fa9b487d10265425349.txt. Accessed September 30, 2012.

Massey, Douglas S., Jorge Durand, and Nolan J. Malone. 2002. *Beyond Smoke and Mirrors: Mexican Immigration in an Era of Free Trade.* New York: Russell Sage Foundation.

McCombs, Brady. 2010a. "105 Migrants Arrested in Baboquivari Mountains." *Arizona Daily Star*, April 10. http://azstarnet.com/news/local/crime/article_8efef517 -56f0-5c5b-a314-b0a069133484.html. Accessed September 30, 2012.

———. 2010b. "Medical Examiner Turns to Trailer Unit for Storage of Bodies: July Proved Deadly Month for Migrants." *Arizona Daily Star*, August 3. http://azstarnet .com/news/local/border/article_e2da2bc8-9e08-55a5-bce6-bd16db7f3599.html. Accessed August 3, 2012.

Nevins, Joseph. 2002. *Operation Gatekeeper: The Rise of the "Illegal Alien" and the Making of the U.S.–Mexico Boundary.* New York: Routledge.

Nevins, Joseph, and Mizue Aizeki. 2008. *Dying to Live: A Story of U.S. Immigration in an Age of Global Apartheid.* San Francisco: City Lights Publishers.

Osorno, Diego Enrique. 2010. *El Cartel de Sinaloa: Una historia del uso político del narco.* Mexico City: Grijalbo.

Payan, Tony. 2006a. "The Drug War and the U.S.–Mexico Border: The State of Affairs." *South Atlantic Quarterly* 105, no. 4: 863–80.

———. 2006b. *The Three U.S.–Mexico Border Wars: Drugs, Immigration, and Homeland Security.* Westport, CT: Praeger Security International.

Ramos García, José Maria. 2005. "Seguridad ciudadana y la seguridad nacional en México: Hacia un marco conceptual." *Revista Mexicana de Ciencias Políticas y Sociales* 47, no. 194 (May–August): 33–54.

Riches, David, ed. 1986. *The Anthropology of Violence.* Oxford: Basil Blackwell.

Rodríguez, Kat. 2012. "Migrant Death Rate on Arizona Border More Than Double in Two Years While DHS Plans Expansion of Deadly Criminalization Policies." Press release. January 24. Prepared by the Coalición de Derechos Humanos. http:// www.nnirr.org/drupal/node/298. Accessed August 24, 2012.

Rubio-Goldsmith, Raquel, M. McCormick, D. Martínez, and I. M. Duarte. 2006. "The Funnel Effect and Recovered Bodies of Unauthorized Migrants." Paper for the Pima County Board of Supervisors.

Samora, Julián. 1971. *Los mojados: The Wetback Story.* Notre Dame, IN: University of Notre Dame Press.

SEGOB, CONAPO, INAMI, SRE, STPS, COLEF. 2006. *Encuesta sobre Migración en la Frontera Norte de Mexico, 2004.* Mexico City: Secretaría de Gobernación.

Spener, David. 2009. *Clandestine Crossings: Migrants and Coyotes on the Texas-Mexico Border.* Ithaca, NY: Cornell University Press.

SRE (Secretaría de Relaciones Exteriores). 2006. *Evaluaciones del Programa de Repatriaciones al Interior México-Estados Unidos.* Mexico City: SRE. http://www.sre .gob.mx/servicos/documentos/eva_finalo5.dos. Accessed September 30, 2012.

Stratfor. 2008. *Mexican Drug Cartels: Government Progress and Growing Violence.* http://www.offnews.info/downloads/MEXICAN-Cartels2008.pdf. Accessed May 15, 2012.

Tampa Bay Times. 2010. "The majority of the people that are coming to Arizona and trespassing are now becoming drug mules." *Politifact.* June 25. http://www.politifact .com/truth-o-meter/statements/2010/jun/30/jan-brewer/arizona-gov-brewer-says -majority-illegals-are-drug/. Accessed September 30, 2012.

United States Border Patrol. 1994. "Border Patrol Strategic Plan: 1994 and Beyond." Report prepared by the U.S. Border Patrol. July.

United States Joint Forces Command. 2008. *Joint Operating Environment 2008.* http://www.jfcom.mil/newslink/storyarchive/2008/JOE2008.pdf. Accessed September 30, 2012.

U.S. Department of State, Bureau of Public Affairs. 2008. *The Mérida Initiative.* April 8.

White, Josh, and Dagney Salas. 2009. "Better to Be Deported Alive Than to Be Dead." *Washington Post,* August 23.

PART THREE

Ending the War
Alternative Strategies

CHAPTER EIGHT

Challenging Foreign Policy from the Border

The Forty-Year War on Drugs

Kathleen Staudt and Beto O'Rourke

Introduction

With Operation Intercept, President Richard Nixon declared a war on drugs in 1969 (Grayson 2010, 28), and forty years after adopting this drug policy, U.S consumption remains as high as ever and violence in Mexico is worse than ever. Ironically, the primary successes in the war involve the growth of multibillion-dollar bureaucracies, a prison-industrial complex, and consequent economic stakes in protecting the bureaucratic status quo of ineffective, expensive policy strategies. By drug policy, we do not refer to alcohol, tobacco, or the many prescription drugs that are used and abused in the United States with six-digit early-death figures. Rather, we refer to those substances declared illegal in the twentieth century, such as the so-called soft drug, marijuana (aka cannabis), and the so-called hard drugs such as cocaine, heroin, and methamphetamine, among others. Our focus is on the prohibition policies that make cannabis illegal and that sustain drug cartels, which earn at least half or more of the estimated $25 billion from U.S. marijuana consumers in their brutal competition over space in gateway regions to the United States (Mendoza 2010; Fainaru and Booth 2009, who provide profit estimates from White House figures; Booth 2010; Castañeda, in Evans 2010).

In this chapter we analyze the challenge to the forty-year U.S. war on drugs, focusing on what heretofore has been neglected—the role of new and expanded border voices in a policy arena that is historically top-down, agency-centered, and based in Washington, D.C. We argue that border people challenged the typical foreign policy paradigm to open serious policy debates about the forty-year war on drugs and engage in high-visibility events, actions, and follow-up so that the debate both affected major dialogues about the drug war and infused a binational, Mexican–U.S. focus into policy change advocacy. In no other city in the United States does one find the shortcomings of drug-war policy so obvious, and in no other city did city council call for a debate about the war on drugs. In U.S. politics, such action has long been considered political suicide. The uniqueness of this El Paso case carves potential new pathways in U.S. politics, modeling meaningful activity for other regions of the country over the next decade. In this chapter, we draw on participant observation, ethnographic detail, documents, and the vantage points of diverse border people.

The prohibition of marijuana has local, state, national, and foreign policy significance, given the high-cost, high-failure border interdiction strategies at the U.S.–Mexican border and the heavy federal, state, and local law enforcement infrastructure in large border cities such as El Paso. Marijuana represents not only a lucrative business for organized crime, accounting for over half their profits, as noted earlier, but also their secure and stable vertically integrated economy. Cartels control the means of production and distribution (O'Rourke and Byrd 2011). When *Forbes* magazine featured the world's richest men, it included Sinaloa cartel leader, Joaquín "El Chapo" Guzmán, and it listed his business as "shipping" and ignored the tax-free control over production and distribution as well. As *Wall Street* journalist David Luhnow (2009) explained:

> Marijuana is also less risky to a drug gang's balance sheet. If a cocaine shipment is seized, the Mexican gang has to write off the expected profits from the shipment and the cost of paying Colombian suppliers, meaning they lose twice. But because gangs here grow their own marijuana, it's easier to absorb the losses from a seizure. Cartels also own the land where the marijuana is grown, meaning they can cheaply grow more supply rather than have to fork over more money to the Colombians for the next shipment of cocaine.

To develop our argument, its conceptual frame, and its empirical base, we divide this chapter into three parts. First we conceptualize the capital-city, agency-centered, and "agency-captured" (Payan 2006) foreign policy-making process amid assumed tenets of American pluralist democracy that posit a role for nongovernmental organizations (NGOs) and individual voices in determining policy. We then examine border people's stakes in the drug war policy and their meaning for economically interdependent border regions. Finally, we analyze the challenge that new and expanding border people's voices mounted on drug war policy, resulting in greater breadth in the arguments against the drug war and the discourse of media and other NGOs that deal with the war. In the closing section, we note the resistance that challengers make in pressing change in long-unquestioned policies such as the drug war.

Conceptualizing Foreign Policy Change

Typically, foreign policy is driven from capital cities with a top-down and state-centric approach among a relatively small network of political actors. Political scientist Hugh Heclo (1978) has written about "issue networks," often concentrated around Washington, D.C., and presumably among the more privileged dominant voices in U.S. politics rather than competing ethnic minorities or people at a spatial distance, such as the border. Political scientist Rodney Hero (1992) has conceptualized what he calls "two-tiered pluralism" rather than the idealized single-tiered system of American pluralism, which puts Latinos (including Mexican Americans) at a structural disadvantage in a second tier, less powerful than first-tier plural competition.

Foreign Policy Decisions as Usual: Top-Down Bureaucratic Politics

In the realistic political science classic on foreign policy making, *Essence of Decision: Explaining the Cuban Missile Crisis*, Graham Allison and Philip Zelnik (1999) proposed three models for analyzing foreign policy decisions: the Rational Actor model, the Organizational Behavior model, and the Governmental Politics model (also see Allison 1971). NGOs hardly figure into the decision-making process. Using the well-documented Cuban Missile Crisis, Allison and Zelnik take readers through the assumptions, concepts, and propositions of each explanatory framework to argue that the second and third models provide essential insights into understanding decisions in their full complexity. Halperin (1974), too, emphasizes the Governmental Politics model, titling his book *Bureaucratic Politics and Foreign Policy* and comparing decisions across three presidential administrations. With a focus on small-group dynamics, Irving Janis, in *Victims of Groupthink* (1982), began a research tradition that addressed motivations "to maintain group consensus," which can "cause deterioration of decision-making quality" (Hudson 2010, 2393). Even critics of the bureaucratic politics model (Goldgeier 2010) acknowledge the dominance of top-level leaders in bureaucracies, moved only with massive complex or popular mobilizations to question, challenge, and change foreign policy decisions. The sum total of these political scientists underscores, what Heclo (1978) maintained about the relatively small "networks" of those involved in policy reform.

We call attention to Allison and Zelnik's (1999) virtually exclusive focus on *in*-state actors in the decision-making process. Our approach focuses on outsiders—those people who challenge in-state actors for change, not only outside of Washington, D.C., but also at and from the border periphery—both from its citizens and its local council representatives—who live and work far from the centers of power.

Spatial distance is relevant here. While drug policy decisions are made in Washington, D.C., border people experience the consequences of decisions, whatever the quality of the policies. As O'Rourke has commented publicly, at the border, "the Emperor has no clothes." Historically drug policy decisions have been made about border people and border space rather than with border people, including their expertise, economic stakes in binational interdependence, and everyday knowledge about the region. Many elected politicians are wary of public discussion about sacrosanct policies, such as the war on drugs, or they have stakes in policy continuity, given their campaign contributions. Drawing on Janis's (1982) notion of "groupthink," we believe that politicians' political-risk avoidance has resulted in a mired consensus about continuing drug war policies, without an evaluation of their costs and ineffectiveness.

Framing Issues and Questions in Policy Debates

If massive mobilization is necessary to move the in-state, top-level bureaucratic apparatus, then yet another way to think about foreign policy change is to examine the construction and framing of messages, the mass media, and the communication of "allies and adversaries in international relations" (Roselle 2010, 2427). In communication analysis, people examine "*who* communicates *what* to *whom* via what *channels* for what *purpose*" (Roselle 2010, 2427). Policy analysis is often broken down into its multiple stages, including setting (or resetting) new agendas, formulating alternative approaches, adopting choices, and then implementing and evaluating them. Forty years of incrementally altered drug policies span most of those stages. We wonder whether drug-war messages, especially electronic, enter issue and policy networks, with the potential to compress the time and space that have historically muted border voices.

Over a forty-year period, drug policy has become a patchwork that typically results in greater expenditures for criminalization approaches: staff, interdiction, and prisons, given the "tough on crime" line that policy makers use to strengthen their budgetary hand (see Wallace-Wells 2007 for a drug czar-to-drug czar comparative analysis over presidential administrations). The war on drugs policy goes unexamined, absent evaluation of its effectiveness and costs, estimated to be a $50 billion annual price tag when including international to national, state, and local interdiction, court, and incarceration costs (American Civil Liberties Union 2009, 1). The U.S. Government Accountability Office (GAO), which generally issues multiple reports about major policy issues, completed only one report on drug control in 2009, after an eight-year hiatus, with a narrowly defined research question about whether adequate coordination exists between agencies within two cabinet departments (Justice and Homeland Security) to address the "nexus between drug trafficking and terrorism" (U.S. GAO 2009, 53). Indeed, the liberal use of the word "terrorism" loses focus when linked to immigrants and drug suppliers or consumers.

Inside the United States, various states and cities have nudged at marijuana prohibition policies that make possession or use a crime for adults. Seventeen states and Washington, D.C., now authorize the sale of medical marijuana, and in some state and local areas, officials have decriminalized possession as a civil or low-priority offense rather than criminal offense (though see Martin on record-setting 2007 arrest figures of 872,721, 90 percent of which were for marijuana possession [2009, 226]). In the cacophony of voices critical of prohibition, some consensus seems to be emerging in favor of a medical model, prevention and treatment, and/or "harm reduction" approaches (an approach for prevention and treatment outside of prisons that is associated with lower drug use incidence and addiction [International Drug Policy Consortium (IDPC) 2010]).

The Articulation of Critical Positions: Media and National and International NGOs

NGOs, the media, and think tanks of various ideological bents have criticized U.S. drug policy from outside Washington, D.C., and its policy networks. For those who are serious about limited government in market economies, drug war critiques have been plentiful. Libertarians (in the Cato Institute) and journalists in major business media, such as the *Wall Street Journal* and the *Economist*, have written numerous editorials in criticism of U.S. "supply-side" (interdiction) approaches in favor of "demand reduction" among U.S. consumers (see, for example, Carpenter 2009; www.cato.org). Former law enforcement officials in Law Enforcement Against Prohibition (LEAP) advocate an end to prohibition policies in favor of regulation, control, and taxation (www.leap.cc).

Some international relations scholars and special commissions have also disseminated high-profile books and reports that criticize the war on drugs. Peter Andreas and Ethan Nadelman (2006), in *Policing the Globe*, call our attention to the way U.S. criminalization approaches have been internationalized. United Nations drug policy enforcement machinery, such as the 1988 Convention against Trafficking in Illicit Narcotics and Dangerous Drugs, resulted in prohibition policies in many countries (Andreas 2000, 54), extended to 140 by 2009 (*The Economist* 2009). Such conventions tie the hands of many nations, some of which, in the interests of protecting nascent democracies from the spectacular cartel-linked corruption money, seek to move toward regulation rather than prohibition approaches, for example: the Latin American Commission on Drugs and Democracy (LACDD) (2009), with coauthors who include ex-presidents Zedillo (Mexico) and Cardoso (Brazil); the Report of the Global Commission on Drug Policy, with commissioners who include U.S. partisans on the right, such as George Schultz and Paul Volcker, and distinguished international leaders such as ten-year secretary-general of the United Nations, Kofi Annan (2011); and the Sixth Summit of the Americas, April 2012, with a communique raising questions about drug policy, but no mandate for change (www.summit-americas.org), given U.S. opposition but only a willingness to listen to policy debates. Despite these obstacles, various countries have moved toward legalization and/or decriminalization, such as Netherlands or, more recently, Portugal, Mexico, Argentina, and other countries in the Americas (on the continuing discretion available to nations, see IDPC 2010, 18–25).

The Drug Policy Alliance (DPA), begun in 2000, convenes biennial international conferences with multiple and diverse constituencies (www .drugpolicy.org). While Mexico and border issues entered DPA's biennial program agenda in 2009 and 2011, many other U.S. organizations that advocate legalizing, regulating, and taxing marijuana remain hardly aware of the border situation or connect violence in Mexico to the prohibition policies.

In the section that follows, we move to analyzing the border challenge to the war on drugs. At the U.S.–Mexican border, the social consequences of the drug war are direct, personal, and visible to the sizeable number of people who live in the border zone on both sides of the nearly two thousand-mile territorial line (14 million people) or in border states, four in the United States and six in Mexico (figures from 2000 censuses, in Staudt and Coronado 2002, chap. 1). Border voices, by no means monolithic, have moved toward approaches that would reduce U.S. demand for drugs trafficked through and in Mexico.

Border People's Stakes in the War on Drugs

Border people have special stakes and vantage points in turning around a prolonged, unsuccessful forty-year-old war. At the center point of the nearly two thousand-mile border, the Paso del Norte metropolitan region consists of two cities—El Paso, Texas, and Ciudad Juárez, Chihuahua—and a total population of approximately 2 million mostly bilingual, Mexican-heritage people. These cities coexist immediately adjacent to each other, with downtowns of both cities running into each other (see figure 8.1). In historian Oscar Martínez's (1994) typology from his book *Border People*, this border region is "interdependent," with relatives, friends, and coworkers who share common interests and, until recently, cross the border regularly to visit, work, and shop.

Consider the economic interdependence of the two cities: Juarenses spend $1.7–$1.8 billion in the El Paso economy annually, and there are nearly sixty thousand jobs in El Paso (including an export-processing factory [*maquiladora*] supplier) dependent on economic activity in Ciudad Juárez. In the retail sector alone, the Federal Reserve Bank estimates that 10–15 percent of El Paso's retail activity can be attributed to Mexican shoppers, accounting for $950 million of El Paso gross sales supporting 13,600 jobs.[1] Since the tragedy of September 11, 2001, U.S. border control policies, including drug policy and the border fence/wall built through approximately eight hundred miles of the nearly two thousand-mile border, have begun to turn an "interdependent" border into an "alienated" one, another of Martínez's categories.

Rising murder rates in Ciudad Juárez prompted border people to act on failed policies rather than remain spectators to such policies. Recently, but specifically since 2007, Ciudad Juárez exhibited outlier murder rates, with approximately 1,600 drug-related murders in 2008, 2,600 murders in

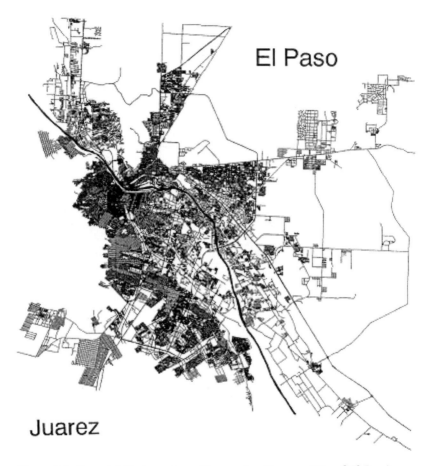

El Paso

Juarez

Figure 8.1. Paso del Norte metropolitan region (Source: City of El Paso)

2009, 3,200 murders in 2010, and well over 2,000 in 2011. Ciudad Juárez alone has seen more than 10,000 drug-related murders since 2007. Using weapons smuggled from outside Mexico, mostly in southwestern U.S. states, with their limited gun control laws and access to assault weapons and guns, *sicarios* (paid killers) engage in ruthless, terrorizing murders, complete with grisly mutilations (Monárrez Fragoso 2010). Until recent civil society activism emerged, an atmosphere of fear and intimidation shrouded the city as competing drug cartels and gangs, in the context of police impunity and impotence, fought to control space in the region, the major land gateway for drug trafficking. To this cauldron one must add the Mexican Federal Police, military personnel, and alleged death squads. Campbell (2009) calls the binational border region a "drug war zone," "a cultural matrix with logics, practices, patterns, symbols, and worldviews that criss-cross and transcend international boundaries, moral categories, social classes, and ethnic groups" (8). Paradoxically, El Paso, with its professional police and sheriff departments, prides itself as the first- or second-safest big city in the United States in its category, as measured by felony crime in annual Congressional Quarterly Press city rankings, based on FBI crime statistics (www.cqpress.com). San Diego, also near the border, is counted among the top-ten safest cities in the United States as well. These rankings offer a contrast to the broad-based macabre journalistic stories about the border as a whole, including the U.S. side, narrating chaos and violence. They also contradict the spillover violence rhetoric among some U.S. politicians and make clear that the price of the war on drugs is paid in gruesome violence, primarily on one side of the border.

Experts estimate that most illegal drugs enter the United States through official ports of entry—the busy, congested gateways for pedestrians and vehicles, including cars and trucks. The United States and Mexico—not at war with each other—are major trading partners, facilitated through the North American Free Trade Agreement; hundreds of foreign-owned export-processing factories (*maquiladoras*) in Ciudad Juárez, 75 percent of them U.S. owned, pay slightly more than the legal minimum wage of approximately 30–40 USD weekly to assembly-line workers, once a female majority but now a gender-balanced workforce of nearly two hundred thousand. These low-level earnings do not constitute living wages, perhaps driving people into the drug trade. Yet despite this characterization, the National Institute of Drug Abuse reports no more and no less addiction rates in El Paso than in other cities in Texas: 2 percent for illicit drugs and 8 percent for alcohol (Washington Valdez 2010a). Like the mainstream population, many try or use illegal drugs and alcohol but do not suffer from addiction.

North-bound traffic, both pedestrian and vehicle, enters El Paso's ports of entry annually in this gateway region for legal commerce and interaction: nearly 40 million people, 16 million cars, and approximately 1 million trucks (2007–2008 figures from the U.S. Department of Homeland Security/Customs and Border Protection 2008), but down in 2011 (given the spike in local violence in Ciudad Juárez) to over 9 million cars and 720,000 trucks (U.S. Department of Homeland Security/Customs and Border Protection 2011). Despite technology and drug-sniffing dogs, various factors facilitate drug entry to consumers in the United States: long lines at the ports, corruption, and traffickers' clever subterfuge (Campbell 2009). Experts also estimate that only 10 percent of drugs are interdicted; the remaining drugs get through.

The 2008 and 2011 press releases from the U.S. Department of Homeland Security/Customs and Border Protection figures show that drug seizures in the El Paso sector (West Texas and New Mexico) overwhelmingly consist of marijuana, 99 percent and 98.6 percent, respectively, measured in pounds (2008, 2011):

	2007	2011
Marijuana	168,900	92,056
Cocaine	774	1,228
Heroin	3	7
Methamphetamine	5	10

Marijuana is the profitable, mainstay good that organized criminals supply to U.S. customers and, increasingly, customers in Mexico. Interdiction strategies catch soft drugs that, based on medical studies, such as found in the British journal *Lancet*, are believed to have less serious consequences than alcohol and tobacco (Global Commission on Drug Policy 2011).

U.S. drug prohibition policy is markedly different than alcohol policy, legalized and taxed after the U.S. Prohibition era ended in 1933, thereafter supported by powerful political and economic interests in production, distribution, and marketing. Once the Prohibition era began, by the mid-1920s organized criminals rose to produce and distribute alcohol, without quality control; police joined bootleggers in sharing profits from distribution. Massive disregard for Prohibition laws, plus a mobilization against Prohibition policies based mainly on cost rationales, led to the only repeal of a U.S. constitutional amendment (Okrent 2010). We see some parallels with the current era, but in a new context, where all the actors have deep material stakes: the growth of huge bureaucracies at the national, state, and local levels; the militarization of the border region; and the private industry contractors connected to the Border Security Industrial Complex and the prison-industrial complex (Payan 2006; Staudt, Payan, and Dunn 2009). These entrenched interests make it more difficult to achieve a broader consensus to resolve the problems caused by the war on drugs.

Drug Policies: High-Cost Militarization Strategies

The U.S.–Mexican border has been militarized as a low-intensity war zone for two decades (Dunn 1996), peaking with the 1993 Border Blockades under former Border Patrol Sector Chief Silvestre Reyes (Dunn 2009) and the Bush administration's construction of an additional approximately seven hundred miles of wall, fence, or *muro de odio* (wall of hate), with labels dependent on which side one is on in ideological or national terms. Mexico's corrupt and complicit local and state police forces have long operated with impunity, and its 2009 decriminalization policy enforcement strategies (up to three warnings) provide problematic police forces with yet more extortion opportunities (see concluding chapter, this volume). In 2008 President Felipe Calderón sent in the Federal Police and the military to reestablish government control in Ciudad Juárez, with limited success, given the rise in murder rates mentioned previously.

A major architect of the Border Security Industrial Complex and immigration strategies had been eight-term El Paso congressman and previous U.S. House Intelligence Committee chair Silvestre Reyes, a well-placed "border voice." For eight years, Reyes hosted an annual Border Security conference at the University of Texas at El Paso (UTEP), where defense contractors, surveillance companies, Washington, D.C., bureaucrats, and political appointees articulated policies *at* the border and *to* border people, but not *with* border people. Approximately eight hundred people attended the conference in 2009, with high-profile speakers from drug czar Gil Kerlikowske and border czar Alan Bersin to U.S. Department of Homeland Security Secretary Janet Napolitano. As El Paso County Sheriff Richard Wiles stated, "The only reason we've got national attention is because it's on the backs of dead people in Juárez" (reporting on a local media panel at which we both spoke).

The annual Border Security conference, held at the UTEP campus, conceived in narrow, national security–state terms, exhibited the long-standing "Iron Triangle" of complicity between politicians, bureaucratic agencies, and corporate contractors around continuing the status quo through the distribution of tax dollars (a classic term in political science, succeeded by issue networks, cited earlier [Heclo 1978]). Not surprisingly, major sources of Reyes's campaign contributions come from such industries in which some of his extended family members are employed (Barry 2009; Citizens for Responsible Ethics in Congress 2012).

As noted earlier, Mexico also militarized its northern border, with thousands of military personnel patrolling the city and then, after they failed to reduce the level of violence, replaced by thousands of Federal Police. Yet murder rates continued to rise, possibly committed by military forces themselves, reminiscent of the "dirty wars" in Mexico, Argentina, Uruguay, and Chile in the 1970s. Noted Mexican drug policy scholar Luis Astorga has written about the way drug trafficking has been threaded within various layers of corrupt government at the federal, state, and municipal levels over many decades (Global Public Policy Forum on the U.S. War on Drugs, 2009). With military abuses "cleansing" the city of supposed thugs, over two hundred complaints were filed with the State of Chihuahua Human Rights Commission. Human rights advocates and journalists have been threatened, and several of them have been assassinated.

The Border Region: Wherefore Federalism?

In the United States well-developed Federalism and the history of states' rights would seem to offer space, if not for altering national policies to deal with locally defined solutions then at least for tempering policy enforcement. Occasionally, border leaders and activists have used their political muscle to challenge national policies. For example, in 2006, locally elected officials and community-based organizations in El Paso challenged immigration enforcement policies and the use of county sheriff deputies to identify undocumented residents for deportation through engagement with the sheriff and electoral candidate forums for his replacement after the deportation of eight hundred people in a three-month period (Staudt 2008). In another (albeit unsuccessful) example, former El Paso county attorney, now state senator, José Rodríguez filed a lawsuit in 2008 alleging constitutional violation of separation-of-powers principles after a Bush appointee, Secretary of Homeland Security Michael Chertoff, with congressional waiver authorization, ignored environmental laws to build the border fence/ wall.

More typically, federal law enforcement agencies blanket the region with their rules, diminishing democracy and Federalism at the border. In remarkable public comments, speakers make this control all too obvious. In a speech at the 2007 annual Border Security conference, Michael Chertoff, the Department of Homeland Security secretary, made a public statement, reminiscent of Vietnam War discourse, about the changing character of the border region under the national law enforcement umbrella: "We don't want to destroy the border in order to save it" (Staudt 2009, 6). At the same conference, a former military officer opened his speech in broken Spanish, mixing up the pronouns in a well-known phrase. He said "*Su casa es mi casa*" (Your house is my house) rather than the hospitable "*Mi casa es su casa*" (My house is your house). Snickers and murmurs rolled through the audience of hundreds at this seemingly subconscious slip (Staudt observation). Regarding Secretary Chertoff, the border fence/wall, and an impending summit in Senator Hutchison's D.C. office, the El Paso mayor, John Cook, said, "You can't have some guy from Kansas telling you how to handle your international border when I have 10 million people a year traveling back and forth across my border. If you've got money to build the walls, give it to me and I'll build bridges" (Mittelstadt 2007). The construction of the wall has come to a halt today, not because bureaucrats and private contractors would not want to build it but because it has become too costly to build and maintain at a time of scarce resources.

The Paso del Norte region, once part of northern Mexico—along with most of the now-southwestern United States—until the 1848 Treaty of Guadalupe Hidalgo, was a frontier settlement, railroad transportation hub, and site for Fort Bliss, a large Army base established in 1849. As settlers arrived, the Spanish-speaking Mexican-heritage majority's voice was contained with cultural assimilation through education, poll taxes, and at-large local elections until the civil rights movement and structural reforms moved to district-based local electoral systems (Romo 2005; Staudt 2009).

By the late 1970s, voters elected more diverse representatives, but voter turnout rates have long been depressed at approximately 10 to 40 percent (depending on the election) for El Paso's current 378,000 registered voters in a county of approximately 800,000. Historically, few organizations engage in the political process, except for economic chambers, teachers' associations, and community-based organizations affiliated with the Texas Industrial Areas Foundation and human rights networks. Civic capacity, defined as the ability to influence and change policies through voting and organized power, has been weak but is nevertheless growing. Tony Payan analyzes what he calls the "democratic deficit" at the border: "local border residents have lesser levels of autonomy in decision making around their own policy issues" (2010, 224), while law enforcement actors are "central players in what can and cannot be done by local residents along the border" (223). El Paso's history and its border location make for unique challenges compared to other parts of the United States. As noted earlier in this chapter, we identify one of these challenges as *spatial*, given El Paso's location on the border, distant from Washington, D.C. (and nearly six hundred miles from Austin, the state's capital city).

Border People Challenge the War on Drugs: Cacophonous Voices

El Paso, once home to a lively political climate at the turn of the twentieth century and the early years of the Mexican Revolution (Romo 2005), underwent assimilation, racism in the guise of public health, language policies, and impoverishment. Over the last thirty years, civic capacity has grown, including cross-border activism (Staudt and Coronado 2002), despite the existence of two sovereign governments. Yet El Paso's per capita income rests at 60 percent of the national per capita income. Now, in the early twenty-first century, El Paso faces a fork in the road between two competing, potentially contradictory economic development strategies: one, border trade, based on manufacturing in the gateway trade region of the Americas, and the other, border control, based on the militarized federal law enforcement.

A Pioneering City Council Acts

In January 2009 the El Paso City Council considered a resolution from the City Border Relations Committee to express solidarity with Juarenses, given the violence, outlier murder rates, and transformation of long-standing border cooperation to the security–state atmosphere. Then representative Beto O'Rourke, with representative Steve Ortega, offered a short amendment that inspired backlash and economic threats from other elected representatives. The short amendment called for "supporting an honest open national debate on ending the prohibition on narcotics." After some discussion and public testimony, the eight-member council passed the amendment unanimously. Initially, Mayor John Cook did nothing, but the campaign would soon begin for his reelection, which was only four months away. He vetoed the resolution and then called a press conference to criticize "potheads" for making El Paso the "laughingstock of the country." Once again, El Paso was the only city in the entire country calling for debate on the drug war. But the political and media attacks show the risks political leaders face when questioning sacrosanct policies.

Later, council members revealed that Congressman Reyes called them individually with vague threats that federal "stimulus" money would not be forthcoming to El Paso with a resolution like this. El Paso's state-level politicians in the Texas House of Representatives also contacted them with nearly identical language. Raging media figures, from the local to the national, including CNN's Lou Dobbs, misinterpreted the call for debate. A week after the council's vote, the item was once again on its agenda in an effort to override the mayor's veto. Four council representatives changed their minds and voted against the resolution. However, the veto was enough to spark national media coverage and a hunger for in-depth debate and discussion over the long-unquestioned drug policy. The drama illustrated limitations and possibilities in U.S. pluralist democracy, that is, people's freedom to question and analyze policies, yet the threats, stigma, and risks that posed limits to that freedom. As O'Rourke later stated at the DPA's large International Drug Policy Reform Conference in November, normally local councils "do not weigh in on national public policies, but the border is disproportionately burdened with policies on the War on Drugs, immigration, and the border wall" (Staudt personal observation 2009).

Campus–Community Conference to Debate the Drug War

After the political explosions at the El Paso City Council, border leaders from the binational community of the El Paso–Ciudad Juárez business, nonprofit, and campus communities, including the University of Texas at El Paso Students for Sensible Drug Policy chapter, formed a planning committee to hold a policy conference on the war on drugs (on which we both served). For seven months thereafter, committee members raised money and invited a balanced group of experts from the academic, government, advocacy, and media sectors to a large, no-cost, two-day conference on September 21–22 entitled the "Global Public Policy Forum on the U.S. War on Drugs." The first day the conference was held at UTEP, and the second day was held in El Paso's downtown, with university officials estimating an attendance of eight hundred the first day and full-house capacity of two hundred on the second day. Given the binational composition of the planning committee, the conference also included an evening event in Ciudad Juárez that brought Sergio Fajardo, the ex-mayor of Medellín Colombia, to speak to an audience of fifteen hundred. (A four-page summary of the conference and information about the balanced group of academic, advocate, and official speakers is available at http://waron drugsconference.utep.edu.) While no formal vote was taken, the consensus sentiment at the close of the conference was that policies ought to reduce U.S. drug demand, prevent drug use, treat addiction, and either decriminalize or legalize marijuana. National and binational regional media gave the conference considerable visibility, from the local print and televised press to the *Economist, Houston Chronicle, Dallas Morning News, San Antonio Express News,* and *San Diego Union Tribune.*

Continuing Mobilization Expands

Meanwhile, representatives O'Rourke, Susie Byrd, and Steve Ortega from the El Paso City Council decided to move beyond debate into action through introducing a comprehensive resolution in February 2010 about drug policies and their havoc on El Paso's neighbor city. Since 2009, El Paso border constituency contacts through e-mails and phone calls had been running about 70 percent in favor of debate and action. The 2010 resolution called on both the presidents of Mexico and the United States to meet at the border and to make the violence a priority concern. Furthermore, it called for more policy support for drug prevention and treatment for drug addiction. The most controversial call in the resolution was for policy change that would legalize, regulate, and tax marijuana—an end to the prohibition policy—as one major means to reduce the violence in Mexico. Of course, such resolutions at the local level have symbolic, rather than real import for laws made at the state and national levels.

A crowd had gathered to provide public comments at the February 10 council meeting, filling up the two hundred-seat theatre-style room, with video streaming and an online view at the city's website, www.elpasotexas .gov. Before comments began, other council representatives positioned themselves publicly before the vote and public statements. While advocating concern for the tragedies in El Paso's neighbor city, several council representatives hinted that they would support the resolution if the controversial measure was removed. Representative O'Rourke evoked the words of a former president when he reported FDR's response to people who came to him about civil rights: "I know you're right. Now make me do something about it."

After council introductions, a lengthy list of people spoke up to five minutes each about their positions. Border people did not speak with one voice, but at least they spoke about a heretofore muted topic, an untouchable policy. A slight majority spoke in favor of the resolution, including high-visibility community leaders, but several critics made remarks that served as reminders of the xenophobia and hate—reminiscent of the racism and nativism against immigrants, including German "beer drinkers," which Okrent (2010) analyzed in the years leading up to the Eighteenth Amendment (Prohibition) in 1918. We note the hostile voice of Armando Cardoza: "You're supposed to be Americans. . . . It's not your job to go against the law. Quit calling it OUR sister city. No one wants a diseased prostitute as a sister." The virulent nature of his comments about Mexico and Mexicans startled many in the audience, with audible reaction (Staudt personal observation).

When the matter came up for a vote, council members were divided 4–4, so the mayor cast his vote against the resolution, thereby defeating it. Then council members who voted against the measure proposed that the controversial marijuana measure be removed, passing it 6–2, but two voted no, including O'Rourke.

Once debate opened, more voices joined in to grow the action and multiply the numbers of those involved. In 2010 the noted University of Arizona professor and border historian Oscar Martínez convened a binational group that met to discuss possible strategies, including legal action. There was full consensus regarding the major strategic propositions, including the legalization of marijuana. The group also discussed the possibility of stiffening gun regulation, given the leaky, north–south smuggling of guns and assault weapons through gun-control loopholes, such as sales at gun shows. However, the city attorney expressed concern about prospects for a costly defense associated with possible litigation, thus reducing the viability of this strategy. The group also considered whether the city could initiate closure of the international bridges that link the two cities but decided against it based on the likelihood that the action would be blocked at the council level.

As Presidents Obama and Calderón prepared to meet in Washington, D.C., in mid-May. 2010, the El Pasoans in the group decided to write a declaration on their position, asked border residents in the United States to sign the document, raised money for a full-page newspaper ad with a press conference, and communicated the event and resolution to major foreign policy actors, the media, and the foreign policy bureaucracy in Washington, D.C., in order to open the presidents' dialogue to include drug policy reform. Over one hundred high-visibility people signed the document, and the action was covered with both negative and positive spins, plus an op-ed piece (Martínez, Staudt, Byrd, O'Rourke, and Ortega 2010). In front-page coverage, the local *El Paso Times* headlined the story with a phrase about "legalizing pot," thereby marginalizing and diminishing the complexity of the issue (Washington Valdez 2010b).

Just before both presidents met in Washington, D.C., several visible and less visible events had occurred. First, Arizona passed its anti-immigrant law, which had a clear impact on President Calderón's critical remarks in his address to the U.S. Congress. Second, an eighty-page "National Drug Control Strategy" document was released from the Office of National Drug Control Policy in the White House, which called for a greater emphasis on drug prevention and treatment, without using the word *war* on drugs. However, drug interdiction and criminalization approaches would continue (Office of National Drug Control Policy 2010).

Moreover, the next Congressman Reyes Border Security conference in August 2010 took on a different tone, as businesspeople and academics in the community called for a new narrative about border cooperation and trade with less emphasis on control yet secure and legal trade. Multiple new border voices on panels spoke to these concerns, with representative Reyes beginning to articulate publicly the need to talk about trade. His remarks may have come too late, as border constituencies hungered for a different paradigm—one based on trade and cooperation rather than on control and militarization. He lost the primary election in 2012, a sign that he may have strayed too far from the needs of the border community and too close to the national culture of security that borderlanders have paid for so highly. After the conference, several border people spoke at other conferences to take the border theme to national and international conferences, including the International Drug Policy Reform Conference (November 2009, Albuquerque), the national Students for Sensible Drug Policy conference (March 2010, San Francisco), and the International Drug Policy conference (November 2011, Los Angeles). Border voices grew and spread their discourses, albeit to a behemoth drug war establishment.

Reflections on Border Voices in Drug Policy Reform

Border people played a new and expanded role in moving the national debate on the U.S. war on drugs. Their voices thereby strengthened civic capacity in the Paso del Norte region and spread new insight to other organizations pressing for change. However, the forty-year-old drug war apparatus is strong and entrenched. Border people, a majority "minority" population at the border, live at considerable spatial distance from the centers of power but are engulfed within the central apparatus law enforcement machinery that, ironically, diminishes local authority under Federalism. However, border leaders, by courageously insisting on public debate about a failed policy, nudged at the monolithic, hardly questioned drug policy complex. U.S. drug consumption and the unintended consequences of the prohibition policy fuel the violence in Mexico that is tearing the country apart, generating fear among residents and undermining border communities and economies. Militarization and control strategies have created monsters: brutal cartels that network with organized crime in the United States to distribute profitable products in high demand. In El Paso-Ciudad Juárez, after open and honest debate with academic, advocacy, and government experts expressing multiple points of view, growing numbers of new border voices launched the case for drug policy reform from the border region with a nuance on drug policy reform strategies: Mexico and its violence. The saga will not end here, and time will tell whether the foreign policy bureaucracy and its uncritical "groupthink" mentality will perpetuate an ineffective "war."

We do not believe that better drug prevention and treatment, or an end to prohibition policies on marijuana, will absolutely end the brutal violence unleashed in northern Mexico. This violence has not diminished with militarization strategies, but the worst of the violence has shifted to northeastern Mexico and Tamaulipus specifically. However, we believe the violence could be cut in half and begin to diminish with professional, honest police institutions in Mexico. Imagine if marijuana—the leading drug confiscated in interdiction strategies—had not been outlawed nearly a century ago but, rather, regulated and taxed three, ten, twenty, or thirty years ago. Recall our earlier reference to White House estimates that over half of Mexican drug trafficking organizations' revenues came from the sale of marijuana to U.S. consumers. The temptation to corrupt government officials and police, and to fight over the control of space, would not be as overwhelming as it has become now.

If border people are to have peace and security restored, clearly U.S. drug demand must be reduced through one of several politically contentious policy alternative strategies. These strategies include decriminalization or legalization, particularly for high-demand, high-profit drugs like marijuana, with effects and consequences less dangerous than alcohol (a drug regulated after Prohibition ended in 1933). Another key strategy would be to shift budgetary priorities to drug prevention and drug addiction treatment programs. Decriminalization would maintain an interdiction approach at borders, thus sustaining the Border Security Industrial Complex, while legalization would offer opportunities to grow and sell in the United States under licenses and would be packaged for quality content control. Yet the U.S. political climate of fear, partisan polarization, and xenophobia—sustained by the drug warriors and their bureaucracies— make it risky for politicians to discuss options like these publicly, much less to develop sensible policy proposals. Border voices have joined and strengthened other voices to call for policy change, a change that is mindful of our neighbor and important trading partner, Mexico.

Note

1. Figures come from the City of El Paso Economic Development Department and the Institute for Policy and Economic Development, from sources that include data from REDCo, the U.S. Department of Commerce International Trade Division, and universities on both sides of the border that sponsor surveys that document retail sales.

Bibliography

Allison, Graham T. 1971. *The Essence of Decision: Explaining the Cuban Missile Crisis.* Glenview, IL: Scott, Foresman, and Co.

Allison, Graham T., and Philip Zelnik. 1999. *Essence of Decision: Explaining the Cuban Missile Crisis.* New York: Longman.

American Civil Liberties Union. 2009. "Caught in the Net: The Impact of Drug Policies on Women and Families." ACLU. http://www.fairlaws4families. Accessed October 23, 2012.

Andreas, Peter. 2000. *Border Games: Policing the U.S.–Mexico Divide.* Ithaca, NY: Cornell University Press.

Andreas, Peter, and Ethan Nadelman. 2006. *Policing the Globe.* Chicago: University of Chicago Press.

Barry, T. 2009. "National Security Business on the Border: Former Border Patrol Chief Silvestre Reyes Now a Major Player in New Military, Intelligence and Homeland Security Complex." Americas Policy Program. http://www.americaspolicy.org. Accessed September 1, 2012.

Booth, William. 2010. "Mexico's Deadly Drug Violence Claims Hundreds of Lives in Past 5 Days." *Washington Post,* June 16, A1. http://www.washingtonpost.com/wp-dyn/content/article/2009/10/06/AR2009100603847.html. Accessed June 17, 2010.

Campbell, Howard. 2009. *Drug War Zone: Frontline Dispatches from the Streets of El Paso and Juarez.* Austin: University of Texas Press.

Carpenter, Ted G. 2009. *Troubled Neighbor: Mexico's Drug Violence Poses a Threat to the United States.* February 2. Washington, DC: Cato Institute, #631.

Citizens for Responsible Ethics in Congress (CREW). 2012. "Report." http://www.crew.org. Accessed September 7, 2012.

Drug Policy Alliance (DPA). 2009. International Drug Policy Conference, Border Panel (on which both authors presented). November.

Dunn, Timothy F. 1996. *The Militarization of the U.S.–Mexico Border 1978–1992.* Austin: University of Texas Press.

———. 2009. *Blockading the Border and Human Rights: The El Paso Texas Operation That Remade U.S. Border Enforcement.* Austin: University of Texas Press.

Economist. 2009. "How to Stop the Drug Wars," March 7–13.

Evans, Tom. 2010. "Former Mexican Official Urges Legalizing Marijuana." CNN, February 2. http://www.cnn.com/2010/WORLD/americas/02/02/us.mexico.marijuana/index.html. Accessed June 17, 2010.

Fainaru, S., and W. Booth. 2009. "Cartels Face an Economic Battle." *Washington Post,* October 7. http://articles.washingtonpost.com/2009-10-07/world/36925085_1_mexican-drug-drug-cartels-marijuana-sales. Accessed June 17, 2010.

Global Commission on Drug Policy. 2011. *Report of the Global Commission on Drug Policy,* June. http://www.globalcommissionondrugs.org/reports/. Accessed July 1, 2011.

Global Public Policy Forum on the U.S. War on Drugs. 2009. University of Texas at El Paso, September 20–22. http://warondrugsconference.utep.edu. Co-designed by Staudt and thus accessed multiple times since June 1, 2009.

Goldgeier, James M. 2010. "Foreign Policy Decision Making." In *The International Studies Encyclopedia,* edited by R. A. Denemark, 2446–60. Oxford and West Sussex, UK: Wiley-Blackwell.

Grayson, George W. 2010. *Mexico: Narco-Violence and a Failed State?* New Brunswick, NJ: Transaction Publishers.

Halperin, Morton. 1974. *Bureaucratic Politics and Foreign Policy.* Washington, DC: Brookings Institution.

Heclo, Hugh. 1978. "Issue Networks and the Executive Establishment." In *The New American Political System*, edited by A. King, 87–124. Washington, DC: American Enterprise Institute.

Hero, Rodney. 1992. *Latinos and the U.S. Political System: Two-Tiered Pluralism.* Philadelphia, PA: Temple University Press.

Hudson, V. M. 2010. "Foreign Policy Analysis: Origins (1954–93) and Contestations." In *The International Studies Encyclopedia*, edited by R. A. Denemark, 2384–2409. Oxford and West Sussex, UK: Wiley-Blackwell.

International Drug Policy Consortium (IDPC). 2010. "Drug Policy Guide." http://www.druglawreform.info. Accessed July 22, 2010.

Janis, Irving L. 1982. *Victims of Groupthink.* Boston: Houghton-Mifflin.

Latin American Commission on Drugs and Democracy (LACDD). 2009. "Drugs and Democracy: A Paradigm Shift." http://drugsanddemocracy.org/files/2009/02/declaracao_ingles_site.pdf. Accessed October 24, 2012.

Luhnow, David. 2009. "Saving Mexico." *Wall Street Journal*, December 26. http://online.wsj.com/article/SB10001424052748704254604574614230731506644.html. Accessed April 8, 2013.

Martin, William C. 2009. "Texas High Ways." *Texas Monthly* (October): 150–51, 226, 342–48.

Martínez, Oscar. 1994. *Border People: Life and Society in the U.S.–Mexico Borderlands.* Tucson: University of Arizona Press.

Martínez, Oscar, Kathy Staudt, Susie Byrd, Beto O'Rourke, and Steve Ortega. 2010. "Quelling Drug Violence Means Policy Changes." *El Paso Times*, May 16, 11B.

Mendoza, Martha. 2010. "U.S. Drug War Has Met None of Its Goals." *El Paso Times*, May 16.

Mittelstadt, Michelle. 2007. "Border-City Mayors to Vent about Fence." *Houston Chronicle*, January 10. http://www.chron.com/disp/story.mpl/front/4459603.html. Accessed January 10, 2012.

Monárrez Fragoso, Julia. 2010. "Death in a Transnational Metropolitan Region." In *Cities and Citizenship at the U.S.–Mexico Border: The Paso del Norte Metropolitan Region*, edited by K. Staudt, C. Fuentes, and J. E. Monárrez Fragoso, 43–70. New York: Palgrave USA.

Office of National Drug Control Policy. 2010. Various documents. http://www.whitehousedrugpolicy.gov. Accessed March 1, 2010.

Okrent, Daniel. 2010. *Last Call: The Rise and Fall of Prohibition.* New York: Scribner.

O'Rourke, Beto, and Susie Byrd. 2011. *Dealing Death and Drugs: The Big Business of Dope in the U.S. and Mexico.* El Paso, TX: Cinco Puntos Press.

Payan, Tony. 2006. *Cops, Soldiers, and Diplomats: Explaining Agency Behavior in the War on Drugs.* Lanham, MD: Lexington Books.

———. 2010. "Crossborder Governance in a Tristate, Binational Region." In *Cities and Citizenship at the U.S.–Mexico Border: The Paso del Norte Metropolitan Region*, edited by K. Staudt, C. Fuentes, and J. E. Monárrez Fragoso, 217–44. New York: Palgrave USA.

Romo, David. 2005. *Ringside Seat to a Revolution: An Underground History of El Paso and Ciudad Juárez from 1893–1923.* El Paso, TX: Cinco Puntos Press.

Roselle, Laura. 2010. "Foreign Policy and Communication." In *The International Studies Encyclopedia,* edited by R. A. Denemark, 2427–45. Oxford and West Sussex, UK: Wiley-Blackwell.

Staudt, Kathleen. 2008. "Bordering the Other in the U.S. Southwest: El Pasoans Confront the Local Sheriff on Immigration Enforcement." In *Keeping Out the Other: Immigration Enforcement Today,* edited by P. Kretsedemas and D. Brotherton, 291–313. New York: Columbia University Press.

———. 2009. "Violence at the Border: Broadening the Discourse to Include Feminism, Human Security, and Deeper Democracy." In *Violence, Security and Human Rights at the U.S.–Mexico Border,* edited by K. Staudt, T. Payan, and Z. A. Kruszewski, 1–27. Tucson: University of Arizona Press.

Staudt, Kathleen, and Irasema Coronado. 2002. *Fronteras No Más: Toward Social Justice at the U.S.–Mexico Border.* New York: Palgrave USA.

Staudt, Kathleen, Tony Payan, and Timothy Dunn. 2009. "Closing Reflections: Bordering Human Rights, Social Democratic Feminism, and Broad-Based Security." In *Human Rights along the U.S.–Mexico Border,* edited by K. Staudt, T. Payan, and Z. A. Kruszewski, 185–202. Tucson: University of Arizona Press.

U.S. Department of Homeland Security/Customs and Border Protection. 2008, 2011. News releases. "Major Port Improvements and Significant Enforcement Activity Highlight Recently Completed Fiscal Year for U.S. Customs and Border Protection Officers Working at El Paso Area Ports of Entry." November 5.

U.S. Government Accountability Office (GAO). 2009. "Drug Control: Better Coordination with the Department of Homeland Security and an Updated Accountability Framework Can Further Enhance DEA's Efforts to Meet Post-9/11 Responsibilities." GAO-09-63. Washington, DC: GAO.

Wallace-Wells, Ben. 2007. "How America Lost the War on Drugs." *Rolling Stone,* December 13. http://www.rollingstone.com/politics/news/how-america-lost-the-war-on-drugs-20110324. Accessed April 1, 2007.

Washington Valdez, Diana. 2010a. "Drug Addiction Trends to Youth, More Violence." *El Paso Times,* January 6, A1, 7.

———. 2010b. "Legalizing Pot Could Help Juárez, Officials Say." *El Paso Times,* May 18, A1.

CHAPTER NINE

The Role of Citizens and Civil Society in Mexico's Security Crisis

Daniel M. Sabet

Introduction[1]

As has been noted throughout this volume, since at least 2005, Mexico has confronted an acute security crisis that has resulted in tens of thousands of organized crime-related killings. A central theme has been the inability of the Mexican state to stop the violence affecting the country in general and the border cities in particular. Massive military deployments, the dramatic growth of the Federal Police (Policía Federal), major increases to public security budgets, police reform efforts, and the almost complete attention of the Felipe Calderón Hinojosa administration have failed to bring the violence under control. This book has provided several potential explanations for the perpetuation of violence in Mexico. In this chapter I take a complementary but somewhat different approach and ask: What is the role of civil society in overcoming Mexico's security crisis?

Frequently overlooked in analyses of how to meet the threat of organized crime is the role of civil society and average citizens. Leoluca Orlando (2001), the former mayor of Palermo, Sicily, argues that it was precisely citizen mobilization that allowed Italian authorities to effectively respond to the Sicilian Mafia in the 1990s. He documents businessmen and women refusing to pay extortion money, massive protests against the Mafia, denunciations by the Catholic Church, efforts by newspapers to encourage discussion of the challenges facing Palermo, and campaigns emphasizing the city's non-Mafia cultural roots. Without a cultural, popular base, Sicilian organized crime became more vulnerable to the formal criminal justice system.

While there is an understandable tendency to focus on law enforcement solutions to crime problems (particularly serious crime problems), there is a risk in failing to recognize that law enforcement is highly dependent on the actions and responses of ordinary citizens. This chapter explores several important roles for citizens in improving the effectiveness of law enforcement efforts. Police need average citizens to comply with laws so that law enforcement can focus its efforts on more serious crime problems. Successful police investigations and prosecutions require citizens to report crime, provide information, and serve as witnesses. Police need financial and political support from citizens (typically through taxes) to ensure adequate salaries and economic resources, and (although many officers might disagree) they need oversight to ensure sufficient incentives to act in the public interest.

Unfortunately, this chapter will provide evidence to suggest that citizens are often not compliant with the law, frequently fail to report crime and "coproduce" public security, distrust the police more than they support them, and have limited opportunities for oversight. I argue that the relationship between citizens and their police is governed by vicious cycles. Citizens often fail to play these positive roles because of their distrust of the police, which is viewed as ineffective and corrupt. However rational citizen disengagement may be, it only ensures further police ineffectiveness and additional misconduct.

This chapter documents the existence of these vicious cycles, but—even more important—it explores efforts by Mexican civil society to break them. At the national level, anticrime crusaders such as Isabel Miranda de Wallace, María Elena Morera, Alejandro Marti, and Javier Sicilia (all of whom had family members victimized by organized crime) have galvanized public support and garnered national attention. This analysis focuses on the experience of civil society efforts in four northern Mexican cities: Mexicali, Tijuana, Chihuahua, and Hermosillo. In these localities, I find important efforts to promote legal compliance, "coproduction," and support for the police; however, there are fewer successful cases of civil society holding police accountable. This chapter is part of a larger research project on police professionalization in Mexico, and, as such, it benefits from extensive interviews with police, police leaders, journalists, and members of civil society in these four locations.

The Role of Citizens and Civil Society

The police exist to enforce the law; however, law enforcement is an insufficient tool to ensure legal compliance (Tyler 1990; Mastrokski, Snipes, and Supina 1996). Obviously "criminals" have little interest in following the law, but compliance is also a concern for the broader citizenry. Individuals may wish to avoid or evade a wide array of laws, such as registering vehicles, complying with traffic laws, paying taxes, obtaining proper licenses, complying with alcohol sales legislation, properly disposing of waste, or buying stolen and pirated goods, to name a few. The more law abiding a society is, the more the police can focus their attention on serious crime and dangerous criminals. More important, while individual violations of the aforementioned laws often have little public impact, widespread violations might foster serious public security concerns, encourage police corruption, and create an environment favorable to organized crime.

Second, numerous public goods cannot be purely "produced" by a public agency and "consumed" by clients; rather, it is desirable, and at times necessary, for citizens to play a role in the production process, or for the good to be "coproduced" (Davis and Ostrom 1991). Citizens can contribute to the public good of security in several ways, including reporting crime, providing information to the police, serving as witnesses, and taking preventive measures. Despite the common perception that most crimes are solved CSI style, sleuthing, television detectives, and, in fact, research clearly shows that the vast majority of cases are resolved because the victim, witnesses, or accomplices come forward with information (Chaiken, Greenwood, and Petersilia 1977; Cosgrove and Wycoff 1997; Bieck and Oettmeier 1998). Simply put, the police cannot be effective without the actions of citizens. Coproduction efforts can even become formalized in civil society through neighborhood watch organizations, after-school youth programs, drug rehabilitation groups, and prevention efforts.[2]

Third, in a related vein, the police also depend on citizens for political and economic capital. For example, citizens can actively support or tolerate tax increases that result in higher police salaries and more resources for the police department. Although Mexican municipalities depend heavily on federal transfers, they do have the legal faculties to raise funds through property taxes and various fees. The former mayor of Bogotá, Antanas Mockus, who oversaw a dramatic turnaround in Bogotá's security situation, attributed a large portion of his success to increasing the city's tax revenues (Mockus n.d.). Local resources can also be mobilized outside the formal tax system through philanthropic institutions, the business community, and civil society to supplement federal government transfers via resources, in-kind goods, and pro-bono services.

Fourth, citizens can use elections and other more direct means to help hold government officials and the police they lead accountable and to create incentives for professional policing. For citizens and civil society, this could mean submitting complaints to oversight agencies, contacting representatives and attending public meetings, reducing information asymmetries through watchdog activities, participating in formal oversight mechanisms, and—of course—voting. Internationally, there are several instances where police disciplinary cases are directly overseen by citizen review committees (Walker 2000). While not mutually exclusive, these actions often go beyond the traditional strategy of pressuring public officials to "do more" to combat insecurity.

Unfortunately, there are clear deficiencies in all of these areas. This is perhaps most evident in the area of legal compliance and particularly the topic of bribe payments. Transparencia Mexicana (Transparencia Mexicana 2010) has conducted a series of studies documenting the quantity and amount of bribe payments in Mexico. According to its 2010 report, surveyed individuals who tried to avoid a traffic ticket (of a total sample of 15,326 households) reported paying a bribe 68.0 percent of the time, an increase over four previous iterations of the study dating back to 2001. Figure 9.1 presents data from the AmericasBarometer survey, revealing that survey respondents in Mexico are more likely to believe that "given the way things are, bribe payments are justified" than in all but two of thirteen other countries examined.

To be sure, there are of course many cases where citizens are the *victims* of corruption. They might be extorted by the police, despite having violated no law, or officers might inflate the consequences of a small violation to pressure citizens into paying a bribe. Nonetheless, there are many cases where citizens *offer* bribes to the police to avoid sanctions when they have in fact violated the law. Police officers interviewed for my study consistently argued that—in most cases—citizens offer the bribe first. One police administrator critical of police corruption compellingly argued:

> There is one that receives, but there is also one that gives. There are 5 million government officials in this country and 100 million outside of the government. Did such a small percentage really corrupt the whole country? To dance the tango you need two; for corruption you need two. (Sabet 2012)

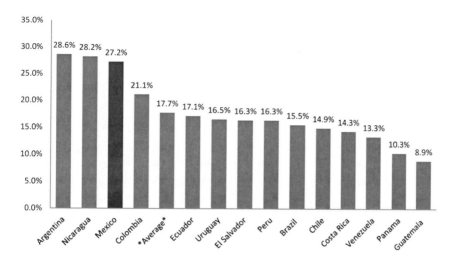

Figure 9.1. Percent of respondents who feel that, given the way things are, paying a bribe is justifiable across fourteen Latin American countries

In interviews, members of civil society also recognized the culpability of the community in police corruption; as one journalist commented, "Nobody has ever asked me for a bribe. Perhaps they want to, but they wait for you to offer. So who is to blame?" These statements do not in any way absolve police of responsibility for the problem of bribery, but they do suggest a vicious cycle of self-perpetuating corruption.

The lack of compliance can be seen in numerous other arenas as well. For example, the importation of used cars is severely limited in Mexico, but the restrictions are difficult to enforce given the large market of used cars just across the border in the United States. As a result, it is frequently estimated that there are around 2 million illegally imported vehicles circulating in Mexico.[3] These consumers are supported by organizations, which have emerged to contest the legitimacy of the import restrictions and to protect drivers from law enforcement actions. While the practice helps provide low-cost vehicles to lower-income residents, it also facilitates car theft, inhibits police investigations, and deprives officers of information in traffic stops (Sabet 2011). A review of newspaper archives reveals numerous instances where everyday criminals, organized crime assassins, and the victims were found to be driving unlicensed vehicles registered with various consumer groups. Similar incentives and crime problems are created by markets for stolen, counterfeit, and pirated goods. As a result, citizen noncompliance not only creates more work for police, but it creates conditions more favorable to serious criminal activity.

Coproduction also appears to be deficient. Through its victimization survey of over 45,000 individuals, the Instituto Ciudadano de Estudios sobre la Inseguridad (2010) estimates that only 22 percent of crimes in 2008 were reported to authorities, and it finds similar percentages for 2004 and 2007, 23 percent and 21 percent, respectively.[4] In contrast, similar surveys in Chile find that 42 percent of crimes are reported (Dammert 2005).[5] When asked why crimes were not reported, 9 percent said because the crime was of little importance, and 8 percent said because they did not have any evidence, but the other responses offer cause for concern: 39 percent felt that it would be a waste of time, 16 percent did not trust the authorities, and 10 percent saw the process as being too bureaucratic (Instituto Ciudadano de Estudios sobre la Inseguridad 2010).[6] There is, in fact, a widespread perception that citizens are not reporting crimes, fear coming forward with information, and do not serve as witnesses. Again, this behavior might be entirely understandable given reports of corrupt cops and reprisals against citizens who do come forward; nonetheless, it without question hinders the effectiveness of law enforcement.

The evidence also suggests that there is insufficient local, political, and financial support for the police. As shown in table 9.1, municipal budgets are dependent on federal transfers rather than local sources of funding. Nationwide, Mexico's municipalities draw almost 72 percent of their revenue from federal transfers. The research cities' budgets presented in the table fare better, but still they depended on federal funds for more than half of their budgets. Part of the problem at the municipal level is the lack of administrative capacity to levy and collect taxes, but, more importantly, there is a general unwillingness to enact needed tax increases. From the perspective of local governments, it is far easier to solicit additional transfers from the federal government than to tax local constituents. This is precisely what happened with the Municipal Public Security Subsidy initiated by the Calderón administration in 2008, which raised municipal police budgets by a substantial percentage. Prior to this new subsidy, there had been woefully insufficient economic resources to improve the quality of public security, raise salaries, purchase sufficient equipment, or properly maintain existing equipment. Even training had been affected, as police deployments had traditionally not provided sufficient flexibility to temporarily remove officers from service for ongoing training.[7]

Finally, largely as a result of a lack of political opportunity but perhaps also because of an inability of civil society organizations to expand existing opportunities, civilian oversight of the police has been minimal. The most important tool of accountability afforded citizens in a democracy is

Table 9.1. 2007 Municipal revenues with percent local sources versus federal and state (in Mexican 1,000s of pesos)

	Total	Local Revenues	Federal and State Revenues	Available from Previous Period Plus Financing*
Tijuana	2,945,319	1,267,855	1,677,464	0
		43.0%	57.0%	
Mexicali	2,064,886	844,082	1,083,545	137,259
		43.8%	56.2%	
Chihuahua	1,473,629	643,174	830,455	0
		43.6%	56.4%	
Hermosillo	1,573,863	826,887	746,976	0
		52.5%	47.5%	
Total municipalities	192,367,800	49,424,100	126,049,100	16,894,600
		28.2%	71.8%	

*Data are not provided by the Instituto Nacional de Estadística, Geografía e Informática for three of the research sites; however, they do appear for the total municipalities.

Note: Percentages are local revenues as a percent of the total and federal and state revenues as a percent of the total for Tijuana, Chihuahua, and Hermosillo. For Mexicali and total municipalities, the amount available from the previous period, plus financing, is subtracted from the total to ensure that the percentages are comparable.

Source: El Ingresos y Gasto Público en México 2009.

of course the vote. Unfortunately, citizens have a hard time punishing candidates for failing to address security concerns. Electoral rules dictate that municipal administrations are only three years and officials cannot be reelected. Without the option of reelection, citizens lose an important tool to reward good service and punish political failings. Instead, dependent on the party nomination process for the next political office, officials wishing to remain in public service have stronger incentives to satisfy party leaders than the citizens they serve (Guillén López 2006). Furthermore, citizens do not directly elect local council members, who instead run on the mayor's party ticket. As council members owe their jobs to the mayor and as the electoral rules almost guarantee the winning party a supermajority on the city council, there is very little horizontal accountability (Guillén López 2006). More generally, however, elections are regarded as a very blunt instrument, which require complementary accountability tools (Melena 2004).

There are several such complementary tools potentially available to citizens and civil society organizations. Police departments often have a citizen public security council that attracts the participation of prominent members of society. State human rights commissions and municipal oversight agencies have mechanisms to receive and investigate citizen complaints of police misconduct. In addition, municipal administrations provide annual reports to their citizens and are increasingly making public security data available on city websites. As will be discussed below, however, these mechanisms have not led to meaningful accountability.

Clearly there are deficient levels of compliance, coproduction, support, and oversight; however, altering this status quo confronts several vicious cycles. It is unlikely that citizens will come forward with information and volunteer to serve as witnesses if they do not view the police as trustworthy. And in fact, there is no shortage of evidence to suggest that many citizens do not trust the police. As figure 9.2 illustrates, Mexicans rate their police poorly and lower than most other countries in the Americas. Of course, an effective police force would probably garner greater trust, but herein lies the irony of the vicious cycle, as the police cannot be more effective without greater citizen compliance, coproduction and support. In other words, distrust results in police ineffectiveness, which furthers continued distrust and continued ineffectiveness.

In the following section I consider civil society efforts to convert these vicious cycles into virtuous ones across the four research sites. Civil society has the moral authority to promote compliance and coproduction and the human and financial resources to provide support to the police. Absent greater accountability, however, these efforts will be insufficient to engen-

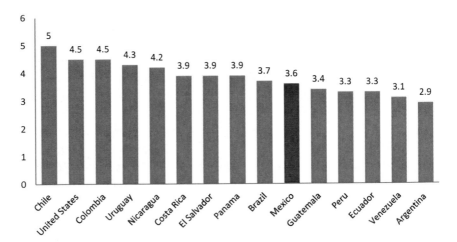

Figure 9.2. Confidence in the police in comparative perspective ranging from 0 (no confidence) to 6 (high confidence)

der trust in the police among the larger citizenry. Required is something of a pact between civil society and the police, whereby civil society leverages greater compliance, coproduction, and support for expanded tools to oversee and hold police accountable.

Attempts to Break the Cycles

There have been several interesting civil society efforts to boost legal compliance in Mexico. The previously uncommon term "culture of lawfulness" (*cultura de la legalidad*) can now be found in speeches, educational curriculum, newspapers, and public discourse. A large network of government and civil society groups has developed educational initiatives to promote such a culture in schools, the police, the media, and the business community.[8] In all four of the research sites, secondary students in the public education system attend "culture of lawfulness" courses, where they are invited to think critically about their role in a society governed by the rule of law. In particular, the state of Baja California has been a leader in this area. It started teaching a culture of lawfulness course in its secondary schools as early as 1989, demonstrated positive results, and became home to a national Culture of Lawfulness Center (Godson and Kenney 2002).

In addition to hosting culture of lawfulness educational programs in its schools, Chihuahua City is also home to Hábitos Buenos (Good Habits). The organization was not originally motivated by insecurity. Instead, its founders were business consultants promoting quality management. Because they frequently saw that bad habits returned shortly after their interventions, they began developing educational programs designed to help participants internalize good habits. Given the city's deteriorating public security situation, they were gradually drawn toward the policy arena and have since been trying to promote "good habits" in the police and in the community.

In nearby Ciudad Juárez, the organization Plan Estratégico de Juárez (Juárez Strategic Plan) has asked residents to sign a "Pact for Juárez," which calls for both civic engagement and respect for the law. It has encouraged, for example, legal registration of used vehicles imported from the United States. These local efforts complement a variety of nationwide campaigns. For example, the Mexico City-based nonprofit organization México Unido Contra la Delincuencia (Mexico United against Crime) hosts an annual poster competition to oppose crime and leads workshops promoting a culture of lawfulness.

A number of governmental and civil society programs have also targeted specific behaviors. For example, the DARE (Drug Abuse Resistance Education) program, developed in the United States to help build teen resistance to drugs, has spread throughout much of Mexico, and as of 2008 it was operating in fourteen states and ninety-seven cities, including all four of the research sites.[9] The DARE program is run through the police department; however, it is overseen and supported by a citizen board of directors. Other efforts have sought to raise awareness about domestic violence, and three of the research cities have special domestic violence units within their police forces.

The need for greater compliance parallels the need for greater citizen "coproduction" of public security. While this need is recognized by government officials, encouraging coproduction has been particularly problematic because of the low levels of trust in the police and public officials more generally. Several administrations have attempted to organize neighborhood groups to such an end; however, Mexico has a long history of governmental abuse of such organizations for partisan purposes (Padilla Delgado 2000; Cornelius, Craig, and Fox 1994). More recently, residents complain that such efforts are empty attempts to create an appearance of governmental concern for security in the neighborhood. One official responsible for organizing the community recognized the distrust among citizens: "We go to the community and the people there say, 'You don't do anything. All you do is come in and organize us.'"

Mexicali's Citizen Public Security Committee (Comité Ciudadano de Seguridad Pública) found a compelling way to overcome the distrust problem. Using the neighborhood watch model developed in the United States, Mexicali's committee replaced the government in promoting the formation of neighborhood groups. If a problem arises, the committee is then able to serve as a more autonomous interlocutor between citizen concerns and police authorities. For example, the committee has two lawyers on staff available to address citizens' concerns. In theory, if the neighborhood watch group calls the police and the police never arrive, the lawyers are able to review the dispatcher's records and determine why. The success of the program in Mexicali has led to attempts to expand the initiative throughout the state.

The business community has also tried to encourage coproduction. Traditionally, business leaders in Mexico's northern cities have been hesitant to recognize the gravity of the security problem for fear of discouraging tourism and business investment. However, as the situation worsened in the mid-2000s, the perception of insecurity could no longer be minimized, and the business community overcame its ambivalence to play a more active role in recognizing and addressing security concerns. In Tijuana, for example, the Chamber of Commerce (Cámara de Comercio—CANACO) initiated a program called "Ponle dedo al ratero" which roughly translates as "target the criminal." Through the program, CANACO worked with the police to publish something akin to a most-wanted list of burglars and rewards police involved in apprehensions. Many Tijuana business groups also played an active role in Alianza Civil (Civil Alliance), a coalition of fifty-five organizations active in public security issues and crime prevention.

Perhaps the most interesting civil society initiatives entail actions to support the police. In Mexicali, a supportive role for civil society began with the aforementioned DARE program. Beginning in 1998, Mexicali was one of the first Mexican municipalities to adopt the DARE program, and it would eventually become the national training center for preparing DARE police officers from throughout Mexico. The DARE model requires interested police departments to establish a citizen board that will oversee the program. Board members are asked to provide work, wisdom, and/or wealth. As such, Mexicali board members, through their own contributions and fund-raising, have paid for student books, a bonus for DARE police officers to top off their police salaries, computers, and DARE patrol cars. The board meets every two months, oversees the finances and program implementation, and leads fund-raising efforts in the community.

DARE's citizen board was used as a model for Mexicali's Business Alliance (Alianza Empresarial), which was created in 2005. The alliance is a grouping of civic and business leaders that not only raises money for the police but tries to counter the force's negative image. The alliance oversees an annual police raffle, has donated bullet-proof vests and police vehicles, has built a gymnasium for the police, and has facilitated housing loans for police officers.

Perhaps the most impressive example of civil society support for the police was found in Chihuahua. Chihuahua lacked a citizen committee until 2005, when the business association COPARMEX sold the idea to an incoming mayor. The committee hit the ground running and divided into a number of subcommittees with membership determined so as to best mobilize community resources in support of the police.

A subcommittee on certification made up of businessmen and women and university faculty familiar with ISO-9000 certification processes works closely with the department's newly created Center for Quality to help ensure that the department effectively negotiates the certification processes for ISO-9000 and the Commission on Accreditation of Law Enforcement Agencies.

The subcommittee on dignifying the police includes members of the restaurant business association and housing development association. The restaurants organized to provide discounts to police and their families, and the developers worked with the department to provide home loans to police, a market that they are not normally able to access. The subcommittee also oversees a police and firefighter of the month award.

Education officials on the professionalization subcommittee have provided the police access to the city's educational resources. This relationship has facilitated courses on computing, administration, and high school equivalency and has led to the development of technical, college, and master's degree programs for police.

The community policing committee purchased a vehicle for police patrolling the downtown and promoted the installation of surveillance cameras linked to the police department.

A committee focused on family issues helped the department improve its capacity to deal with domestic violence and improve its support of victims.

While these groups' contribution to the police is significant, they perhaps serve an even more important function: changing the relationship between police and citizens. When a member of the citizen council in Chihuahua was asked why he works with the police despite the force's negative image, he responded that he is "working to change that attitude—to work with the police and help them become better." Or as one interview respondent in Mexicali eloquently put it, he wants to ensure "that society sees the police officer as someone that takes care of me rather than someone that screws me."

Despite these positive efforts to promote legal compliance and foster support for the police, complementary opportunities for citizen oversight have been minimal. Citizen oversight and accountability have been constrained by at least four factors. First, while formal opportunities exist, they afford only limited authority. For example, the citizen public security councils represent an opportunity for potential oversight; however, they are better designed to mobilize community resources. In Chihuahua, for example, the otherwise successful committee had no legal oversight authority. One civil society organization in Hermosillo derisively referred to the citizen committee there as a "complacency committee" instead of the "citizen committee." By putting civic and business leaders in direct contact with public security officials, such committees do afford citizen councillors an opening to impact policy and hold officials accountable. Nonetheless, in interviews many committee participants complained that this typically amounted to pushing government officials "to do more" and officials promising to redouble their efforts.

Second, citizens and civil society organizations have had only limited access to information to effectively monitor public security. For example, a review of annual government reports across the four research municipalities reveals that, despite transparency laws, there are no standardized indicators or methods for data presentation that would allow citizens to track government progress over time. To illustrate, in its first annual report, the Rodolfo Valdez Gutiérrez administration in Mexicali presented select statistical indicators comparing 2007 and 2008, the last year of the previous administration and the first year of the Valdez administration (Valdez Gutiérrez 2008). Perhaps not surprisingly, all of the statistics showed dramatic improvements. The skeptical reader, however, had no way to know how the administration had performed on other indicators, or if the previous year had been an aberration from a general trend. Furthermore, both members of civil society and government officials confirm that the public security crisis has led to an increase in denied information requests at all levels of government.

In response, there has been a movement to establish citizen public security monitors (*observatorios ciudadanos*) to compile and track public security indicators, mechanisms that have been successful in other Latin American countries, particularly Colombia.[10] Nonetheless, as of this writing, there is no example of a successful monitor in Mexico. Also at the time of this writing, a *national*-level citizen monitor was still struggling to get off the ground, and—in the research sites—there was no local observatory in Sonora and only limited advances had been made in Baja California and Chihuahua.

In theory, journalists have a major role to play in analyzing and processing information to help citizens make informed decisions; however, media coverage of public security is severely constrained. A review of thousands of newspaper articles across the four research sites from *La Frontera* in Tijuana, *La Crónica* in Mexicali, *El Imparcial* in Hermosillo, and *El Diario* and *El Heraldo* in Chihuahua confirms the perception that newspapers and the journalists who write for them (many of whom earn less than police do) primarily present the daily facts of crime events and public security topics with little in the way of analysis. A given local paper might have only two reporters covering public security with little time for real investigations. Delving deeply is also risky for reporters. Interviewed journalists from these and other outlets reported that they do not publish much of what they know simply because it would be too dangerous. Journalist killings and kidnappings have unfortunately become all too common (Hervieu, Flores Martínez, and Julliard 2009). As a result, many newspapers have severely self-censored their reporting. Papers in three of the sites had a policy that they would not report any material that could not be attributed. Ostensibly this policy was designed to ensure that rumors were not presented as fact; however, it shifted responsibility for statements away from the paper itself. As a result, articles tended to be based on official government statements rather than on journalistic investigation.

Third, civil society organizations have had a hard time expanding existing political opportunities and creating new ones. A group of prominent civic leaders in Hermosillo, called Hermosillo 2025, developed a proposal for the establishment of a citizen board that would oversee the police procurement process and be responsible for approving equipment purchases. The group felt that municipal administrations, which only last three years and cannot be reelected, have little incentive to make long-term investments. Promoters argued that the citizen board would not only prevent corruption and ensure the efficient use of funds but provide a long-term vision to investment in public security. Unfortunately, they pitched the proposal to four administrations and failed to see it adopted. One member of civil society was forced to conclude in an interview, "Society doesn't have any weight. The authorities are not accustomed to listen to civil society. They see us as a threat—that they are going to lose their authority."

Fourth, successful citizen oversight is subject to the approval and support of the executive in office. As such, while there have been successful cases of citizen oversight during a given administration, they have not led to permanent advances. In Tijuana, for example, the local citizen council had been a powerful social actor. Its members had organized neighborhood committees in conjunction with the municipal government and helped lead a march around much of the state to draw attention to insecurity. Nonetheless, with a change of administration in 2007, and subsequent marginalization by the new mayor, the citizen council basically ceased to exist.

The challenges presented by all of these factors can be seen in the most promising experiment in citizen oversight, which occurred in Baja California during the administration of Eugenia Elorduy Walther (2001–2007). Baja California's state citizen council is made up of a majority of citizens drawn from the leadership of parallel municipal committees along with government officials. While the council's formal mandate is not radically different in Baja California than in other jurisdictions, Elorduy Walther did far more to empower the council. He ensured that the state's attorney general and secretariat of public security attended every meeting, gave the council access to conduct multiple public evaluations, allowed the councillors a central place in policy discussions, and provided the body with an operational budget.[11]

Citizen evaluations were one of the council's major successes. Indicators have always been made available to the public, but, as discussed earlier, traditionally government officials have determined what indicators to present and how to present them. The council, however, was not only afforded access to the government's raw data, but it was allowed to present the information as it saw fit. The result was a series of studies that brought to light many of the deficiencies of the criminal justice system in the state.[12] Members of the council contended in interviews that the evaluations had significant impacts on policy and funding for the criminal justice system. They also allowed the citizen council to place more targeted and effective pressure on public officials. For example, according to one council member, data revealing that only a small percentage of federal detainees were ever brought before a judge allowed the council to pressure federal authorities for more successful prosecutions. Unfortunately, the success of the council was not only due to the citizens who participated on it but the political opportunity created by the Elorduy Walther administration. After the successor administration took over, no such citizen evaluation was conducted.

While accountability has been an elusive goal, the success of citizen oversight in the DARE program suggests that civil society might leverage its resources to obtain greater accountability and governmental responsiveness. Most outreach programs in Mexican policing only last the three years of a given administration; however, the DARE program in Mexicali has outlasted four administrations. Given the operational pressures on the police, there are strong incentives for police leaders to transfer officers assigned to prevention programs to police patrols. In Mexicali, however, the citizen-run board ensured that DARE officers work full time on the program. To prevent higher-level operational officers from undermining the program, the board successfully advocated for the creation of a DARE commander at the equivalent rank of captain. To be sure, DARE is a popular program, but it would be hard to imagine local authorities fulfilling these commitments if they did not depend on the board financially. This suggests, interestingly enough, that opportunities for greater citizen oversight might be bolstered by greater citizen support.

Unfortunately, this strategy of exchanging support for greater oversight appears to be the exception rather than the norm. In Chihuahua, the impressive efforts of the citizen committee to encourage coproduction and provide support to the police had begun to open opportunities for greater oversight; however, a change in administration caused these opportunities to contract (Sabet 2012).

Conclusion

Unfortunately, discussions of public security in Mexico too often leave out "the public" and tend to focus exclusively on the formal criminal justice system. As shown here, however, ordinary citizens and civil society organizations have an important role to play in improving Mexico's security situation. When citizens fail to comply with the law and do not coproduce public security, they create an environment that facilitates criminality, corruption, and ineffective policing. Nonetheless, despite their shared culpability, blaming citizens is no more productive than blaming the police. Instead, a series of vicious cycles reinforces a noncompliant, low coproduction, ineffective, and corrupt equilibrium. The question, therefore, is this: How can the vicious cycles be broken?

Vicious cycles, by their nature, are difficult to interrupt. The police force requires citizen support to be effective, but citizens cannot be expected to trust and support an ineffective police force. Altering these cycles requires actions by both of these groups of actors, yet neither has the incentive to change its behavior without parallel changes made by the other. Fortunately, civil society organizations—as intermediaries between citizens and government—offer a potential means to resolve this collective action problem, and as this chapter shows numerous efforts have been made to encourage legal compliance, coproduction, and support. Unfortunately, however, without comparable opportunities for meaningful accountability, these civil society efforts will not be able to reverse the cycle. From an optimistic perspective, there appears to be a clear way out of this dilemma: civil society can leverage its financial and political support for the police to expand oversight opportunities. As evidenced by the DARE citizen board in Mexicali and as envisioned by the Juarez Strategic Plan Association, there is a need for a new "pact" between citizens and public security officials. On the other hand, however, such "pacts" are the exception rather than the norm, and it remains to be seen if civil society actors can expand the existing opportunities, overcome the resistance to meaningful oversight, and ensure the continuity of oversight efforts across administrations.

Notes

1. Some material from this chapter appears in Sabet 2012. I would like to thank Stanford University Press for allowing it to be used here. I would also like to thank the National Strategy Information Center, which has actively promoted some of the ideas contained here. I am also grateful to the many individuals who agreed to be interviewed for this research.

2. In its extreme, coproduction could lead to normatively undesirable vigilantism and paramilitary groups that supplant police forces and create new public security problems.

3. See, for example, Gavina 2011.

4. The "black statistic," or *cifra negra*, is actually higher than 79 percent, as it also includes an additional 6 percent of crime that was reported but did not result in the creation of a case file.

5. Mexico's "dark statistic," or unreported crime, is closer to Argentina, where the police generate a similar level of distrust, and reported bribe solicitation is also very high (Tudela and López 2006).

6. Other responses bring the total to 100 percent.

7. The Municipal Public Security Subsidy did require local governments to match 30 percent of the federal investment and dedicate this money to police remuneration, creating an important incentive to dedicate more local revenue to public security.

8. In the interest of full disclosure, the author formerly worked with the Culture of Lawfulness Project, an initiative of the National Strategy Information Center, which works with police, schools, government officials, and media in promoting a culture of lawfulness in Mexico.

9. Number provided by Mexicali officials. Mexicali is the Mexico coordinator and training center for DARE International.

10. See, for example, Instituto de Investigación y Desarrollo en Prevención de Violencia y Promoción de Convivencia Social 2008.

11. In addition to traditional public funding, the council is funded by an interesting mechanism to increase local financial support for the police. Businesses in the state agreed to an additional tax that goes into a trust for public security, education, and infrastructure investments.

12. See, for example, Consejo Ciudadano de Seguridad Pública 2005.

Bibliography

Bieck, William, and Tim Oettmeier. 1998. "The Houston Police Department: Integrating Investigative Operations through Neighborhood Oriented Policing." Washington, DC: Police Executive Research Forum.

Chaiken, J., P. Greenwood, and J. Petersilia. 1977. "The Criminal Investigation Process: A Summary Report." *Policy Analysis* 3: 187–217.

Consejo Ciudadano de Seguridad Pública (CCSP). 2005. *Evaluación de las Instituciones de Seguridad Pública*. Mexicali, BC: Consejo Ciudadano de Seguridad Pública.

Cornelius, Wayne, Ann L. Craig, and Jonathan Fox, eds. 1994. *Transforming State-Society Relations: The National Solidarity Strategy.* La Jolla, CA: Center for U.S.– Mexican Studies.

Cosgrove, Colleen, and Mary Ann Wycoff. 1997. "Investigations in the Community Context." Washington, DC: Police Executive Research Forum.

Dammert, Lucía. 2005. *Violencia criminal y seguridad ciudadana en Chile.* Santiago: Naciones Unidas.

Davis, Gina, and Elinor Ostrom. 1991. "A Public Economy Approach to Education: Choice and Coproduction." *International Political Science Review* 12, no. 4: 313–35.

El Ingresos y el Gasto Público en México. 2009. http://www.inegi.org.mx/prod_serv /contenidos/espanol/bvinegi/productos/integracion/sociodemografico/igpm/2009 /IGPM-2009.pdf. Accessed April 22, 2013.

Gavina, Dulce. 2011. "Incian pláticas para legalizer autos 'chocolate.' " *El Sol de Cuautla,* October 6.

Godson, Roy, and Dennis Jay Kenney. 2002. "Fostering a Culture of Lawfulness on the Mexico–U.S. Border: Evaluation of a Pilot School-Based Program." In *Transnational Crime and Public Security: Challenges to Mexico and the United States,* edited by John Bailey and Jorge Chabat. La Jolla, CA: Center for U.S–Mexican Studies.

Guillén López, Tonatiuh. 2006. "Democracia Representativa y Participativa en los Municipios de México: Procesos en Tensión." In *Democracia y Ciudadanía: Participación Ciudadana y Deliberación Pública en Gobiernos Locales Mexicanos,* edited by Andrew W. Selee and Leticia Santín del Río. Washington, DC: Woodrow Wilson International Center for Scholars.

Hervieu, Benôit, Balbina Flores Martínez, and Jean-François Julliard. 2009. *Mexico: Behind the Scenes of Impunity.* Paris: Reporters without Borders.

Instituto Ciudadano de Estudios sobre la Inseguridad (ICESI). 2010. *Análisis de la ENSI-6/2009: Victimización, Incidencia y Cifra Negra en México.* Mexico City: Instituto Ciudadano de Estudios sobre la Inseguridad.

Instituto de Investigación y Desarrollo en Prevención de Violencia y Promoción de Convivencia Social (CISALVA). 2008. *Guía Metodológica para la Replicación de Observatorios Municipales de Violencia.* Cali: Centro Editorial CATORSE SCS.

Instituto Nacional de Estadística, Geografía e Informática. 2009. *El ingreso y el gasto público en México: 2009.* Aguascalientes, México: Instituto Nacional de Estadística, Geografía e Informática.

Mastrokski, Stephen D., Jeffrey B. Snipes, and Anne E. Supina. 1996. "Compliance on Demand: The Public's Responses to Specific Police Requests." *Journal of Crime and Delinquency* 33: 269–305.

Melena, Carmen. 2004. "Social Accountability: An Introduction to the Concept and Emerging Practice." Social Development Papers No. 76. Washington, DC: World Bank.

Mockus, Antanas. n.d. Bogotá: "Acción y Pedogógica y Gobierno." Unpublished manuscript.

Orlando, Leoluca. 2001. *Fighting the Mafia and Renewing Sicilian Culture.* San Francisco: Encounter Books.

Padilla Delgado, Héctor Antonio. 2000. "Democracia y Gobernabilidad en una Experiencia Local: El Caso de Ciudad Juárez Visto desde la Perspectiva de la Clase

Política." In *Transición Democrática y Gobernabilidad: México y América Latina*, edited by Julio Labatista, Martín del Campo, Antonio Camou, and Noemí Lujan Ponce, 131–62. Mexico City: Plaza y Valdés.

Sabet, Daniel M. 2011. "Informality, Illegality, and Criminality in Mexico and Its Border Communities." Paper presented at the Workshop on the Social Impacts of Informality on Borderlands: Cross-Regional Perspectives. Johannesburg, South Africa, December 4.

———. 2012. *Police Reform in Mexico: Informal Politics and the Challenge of Institutional Change*. Palo Alto, CA: Stanford University Press.

Transparencia Mexicana (TM). 2010. *Índice Nacional de Corrupción y Buen Gobierno: Informe Ejecutivo*. Mexico City: Transparencia Mexicana.

Tudela, Patricio, and Beatriz López. 2006. *Informe: Políticas Públicas de Seguridad Ciudadana—Argentina*. Santiago: Banco Interamericano de Desarrollo.

Tyler, Tom R. 1990. *Why People Obey the Law*. New Haven, CT: Yale University Press.

Valdez Gutiérrez, Rodolfo. 2008. *Primer Informe de Gobierno: Un año a tu servicio*. Mexicali: BC: XXIX H. Ayuntamiento de Mexicali.

Walker, Samuel. 2000. *Police Accountability: The Role of Citizen Oversight*. East Windsor, CT: Wadsworth.

CHAPTER TEN

Regulating Drugs as a Crime

A Challenge for the Social Sciences[1]

Israel Alvarado Martínez and Germán Guillén López

Introduction

In this chapter we examine the problem of drug trafficking and drug use with an eye to decriminalization and legalization. We analyze the current legal and regulatory framework built around psychotropic substances and present some key challenges to the prohibitionist framework that has prevailed for the last forty years. We further explore what these challenges imply for the penal and criminological *sciences*. To accomplish this, we focus on four perspectives on the issue: (1) the criminological; (2) the political-criminal; (3) the penal-dogmatic; and (4) the prosecutorial.

The ultimate goal of this chapter is a fourfold examination of drug trafficking and drug use in order to identify the tipping points where the penal and criminological sciences can help on the road to a new framework on *illegal* drugs. In the process of analyzing these tipping points, we hope to show how the traditional penal and criminological approaches around drug trafficking and drug use, designed around the *individual* trafficker or user, are inadequate to address the phenomenon of *group* organized crime. Similarly, we draw attention to the way in which the modern state seems to react vis-à-vis the dual problem of prohibition and the decriminalization/legalization of the use of drugs by reinforcing a patently inadequate normative framework that regulates activities linked to so-called crimes against public health or drug trafficking/drug use criminal activities. We also deal with the discussion of whether public health is really the *public good* being affected by drug-related criminal activity, or whether the discourse that places *public health* at the center of the debate on drugs, something done heavily in Mexico, is merely a red herring to hide the inadequacies of the overall framework to deal with illegal drugs. Finally, we highlight the ineffectiveness of the traditional system of criminal investigations and prosecutions when it comes to drug offenses and the government's claim that it requires exceptional means to investigate and prosecute such crimes, including sometimes the violation of human and due process rights.

Crime or Public Health: A Definitional Perspective

From a strictly criminological point of view, drug trafficking is not first and foremost a *crime against public health* as it is often claimed by the government, the legal profession, and the media in Mexico. Instead, drug trafficking is simply an aberrant activity typified by the penal code as a crime because it profits from the exploitation of the chemical dependence of a group of individuals (García-Pablos 1986). It must be emphasized that it is classified as a criminal activity in part because it seeks to exploit this chemical dependence of a group of individuals for profit. In fact, a major point often made when analyzing drug trafficking is the fact that its economic profits have skyrocketed since the 1960s, although this is particularly because of an increase in the consumption of psychotropic substances in the developed countries, such as the United States, but increasingly in other less-developed nations as well (Herrero 2007). The profit motive is seen as particularly heinous. The combination of addiction and profit is not easy to deal with when it comes to drug consumption and drug trafficking. Disentangling these issues is not a trivial debate either, given that this link is the foundation of the current prohibitionist regime. For over four decades, governments all over the world, as well as legislators, jurists, hygienists, moralists, religious leaders, law enforcement agents, psychiatrists, and sociologists, among others, have insisted, depending on where they sit, that it is, among other things, a criminal problem, although others have also insisted that it is a public health issue. Each of these groups conceives the problem through its own lens, however, but most agree on a prohibitionist approach. The prohibitionist approach to drug dependence, with all the strategies and tactics that it generates, however, has failed to stop drug trafficking and drug use. In fact, nearly all of these groups agree that there has been a considerable increase in drug consumption even as they agree in maintaining the current antidrug framework. Each of these groups has made these paradoxical claims in conferences, reports, and legislation, even when they move to tweak regulations, create health institutions, and design programs to tackle the problem of illegal drugs. Paradoxically as well, most of these groups claim to be working toward a common purpose, ending the drug threat. Interestingly, however, the prohibitionist agreement among these groups turns to disagreement when it comes to whether to emphasize, primarily, punitive measures against traffickers and users or whether to deal with drug abuse as a public health issue. There is, however, an increasingly larger group that argues that the "war on drugs" has failed and that drugs should be decriminalized or even legalized.

While drug use is not a new phenomenon or even unique to our time—there is evidence that in all societies at all times, individuals and groups have engaged in the use of psychotropic substances—what *is* new and unique in our era is the massive dimensions to which this problem has grown and the ways in which it has begun to affect larger and larger groups of individuals, posing challenges to our social, economic, and political affairs. According to estimates by the United Nations Drug Control Program (UNDCP 2000), approximately 185 million people consume illicit substances worldwide. This number, according to the UNDCP's 2000 report, includes 147 million consumers of cannabis, 13 million consumers of cocaine, and another 13 million consumers of opiates, of which 9 million consume heroin. If we add to this the consumers of confection drugs, the dimensions of the problem are indeed staggering. If these data were not enough, the trend in North America and Europe has not registered decreases in the consumption of any psychotropic substance. If anything, drug consumption seems to have stabilized in some regions of the continent, with the consumption of methamphetamines, opiates, and Ecstasy remaining fairly stable, while in other parts of Europe there has been an increase in the consumption of cocaine, cannabis, and Ecstasy. Despite these relatively well-known stabilizing trends in drug consumption, it must be acknowledged that it is difficult to determine accurately the proportional increase in the consumption of drugs in contemporary society. We have to remember that this is inherently a hidden business. Any numbers are approximations, not only due to the fact that the business is by nature clandestine but also due to the fact that our comparisons to human groups that preceded us cannot be accurately calculated because we have no such equivalent numbers on drug consumption over a long period of time. Thus all figures are approximate and should be taken with a grain of salt.

But even if the numbers are hard to come by, particularly those in the past, it is relatively easier to speculate about the obvious dangers that drug use represents for the overall social welfare of our modern society. Today, the trafficking and consumption of illicit substances stand as a thorny health, economic, political, and social problem, which originates in the aftermath of what drug dependence entails both for the individual who consumes psychotropic substances as well as for his or her environment, including the family, workplace, and community at large. Indeed, it can be seen that a drug use habit generates serious repercussions not only in the physical and mental health of the individual but in society in general, all the way to the public health system, because addictive and uncontrolled drug use leads to the spread of diseases such as hepatitis, HIV/AIDS, mental pathologies, and even death. Moreover, and to the core of our argument here, the issue of drug use gets particularly challenging when it is linked to other areas of society, specifically criminology and the penal code.[2]

Organized Criminal Groups as Viewed by Criminologists

Thus leaving aside many of the consequences of drug trafficking and use in terms of public health, other aspects are also worrisome, including the economic impact of money laundering, the political corruption it generates, and the social dysfunction it produces. But nowhere does drug prohibition interact more perniciously with drug trafficking and use than in the legal and criminological arenas. In fact, one must consider that the illicit drug market in interaction with prohibition has led to the emergence of powerful and well-organized trafficking groups, with an economic might unparalleled in the history of crime, and that these organizations, at their medium and higher levels, have acquired an uncanny ability to evade criminal prosecution, leaving only a long trail of petty criminal and dealers and consumers in prison or dead in the streets of cities in many countries (Manifiesto 1989). Thus the criminological aspects of illegal drugs require special attention. In order to understand how this complex interaction between illegal drugs and prohibition works, we attempt to systematize the main characteristics of these criminal organizations.

Organized crime is an *activity by a group of individuals who cooperate on an activity defined by the system as outside the law.* That is, a fundamental component of organized crime is the association of two or more individuals who engage in an agreement to break the law itself by supplying a good that the law forbids and by profiting from doing so. This implies that the actor in this type of crime will always be a group or a collective. The *structure* of the group implies that its activities are carried out in an "organized" fashion, that is, the activities to be carried out are distributed among the associates of the group, where each member has specific functions, tasks, and responsibilities and generally responds to someone within the organization. The members are thus engaged in a division of criminal labor and possess a criminal specialization.[3] Regardless of who leads the organization, it has a *permanent and self-renewing character*. This implies that the criminal group has a presence in the illicit market for some period of time and is sufficiently able to keep carrying out its illegal activities even after the death or imprisonment of their top or mid-level leaders. Criminal succession is a key issue in this regard. The organization is also *vertical* in nature. This implies that the group is willing to concentrate great power in a single individual or a small core of individuals within the organization and subject itself to a chain of command that leads up to these heads or chiefs of the criminal clan. It also means that whoever wishes to remain a member of the organization must demonstrate at all times total obedience to the gang's leader or leaders, even in the face of death. This imposes discipline and lowers the risk of being detected and combated by law enforcement. Thus criminal organizations generally have a *code of discipline and use coercion* to ensure compliance. This aspect of organized crime implies that the members of the group must exhibit a high degree of discipline in following orders and executing their tasks. Those who break the group's rules both accept that they can be punished rigidly and the executioners accept to punish the rule-breaker harshly. Moreover, breaking certain pacts, for example, the "code of silence," entails the maximum and even ultimate punishment—death. This ultimate punishment, death, generally administered generously, is the mechanism by which internal solidarity is ensured and the survival of the organization is guaranteed against those who would betray it. In addition, an organization has at its disposal a *variety of instruments* to carry out its activities and ensure loyalty. In other words, criminal organizations resort to a variety of means, from bribes to death, in order to ensure the survival of the organization and ultimately its profitability. Still, there is a hierarchy of means. As much as possible, they try to take advantage of persuasion, through corruption of public officials and bureaucrats, but when this is no longer possible they disobey the law unscrupulously or even seize opportunities to exercise violence. Public executions, torture, and the disappearance of enemies, including governmental or other actors who take action against them, are not beneath them (Alvarado Martínez and Gullién López 2006).

In addition to these well-known characteristics or criminal organizations, the modus operandi of organized crime, as defined by the law, differs sharply from conventional crime. In organized crime there is clear *professionalization* and *distribution of activities* among its members. Criminal organizations dedicated to drug trafficking carry out their activities with relative success thanks to, among other things, criteria of rationality. Rational schemes make it easier for individuals belonging to these organizations to integrate and operate as a compact criminal structure because each carries out—in complementary ways—certain tasks for which they have been specifically trained or instructed. In addition to a division of labor, organized criminal groups have a *business-like structure.* Group crime, because of its organizational and functional structure, is increasingly similar to "multinational corporations." Such an assessment is made because these criminal groups use business management methods, market control schemes, and corporate techniques in their operations, with the primary purpose of increasing profits while strengthening their structure. It is no longer uncommon to speak of "divisions" within the organization, including the merchandise buyers, the transportation wing, the financial section, the operational component, and the enforcement group.

In addition, the criminal groups of interest here are no longer local. There has been a rapid and increasing *internationalization of activities.* When it comes to drug-related organized crime, we speak of genuine international criminal organizations, especially when chronicling certain criminal organizations whose operational network extends to several countries, such as the Sinaloa Cartel. That such a situation exists is due, among other things, to the fact that these organizations take advantage of scientific and technological advances, including developments in communications and transportation technologies and the increasingly freer transit of people, money, and goods across borders. Often the production, trafficking, and consumption of illicit drugs will span several countries, with production in one country, transit in another, and consumption in yet another. Criminal organizations today have also learned the art of networking. They have an increasingly complex set of *relations with other criminal organizations* both at home and abroad. While recognizing the autonomous nature of each criminal organization, it is increasingly common to find several organizations in relationships of support and coordination with other groups of organized criminals and even terrorist groups, insurgent movements, or guerrillas and, when necessary and possible, with governments of countries that are seeking their support in order to achieve certain political objectives. These cozy relationships that integrate criminal organizations into veritable keiretsu guarantee the elimination of competition and other complications to their illegal activities.

Criminal groups have also increased their capacity to move their substantial profits into the legal economy. These organizations take advantage of the financial infrastructure of several countries to protect, hide, and launder their profits. These efforts are collectively referred to as money laundering. Money laundering activities are carried out utilizing their own means and infrastructure as much as possible but increasingly through a rational distribution of tasks, with entire divisions dedicated to laundering the profits by inserting them into the formal economy of several countries. The number of financial institutions engaged, wittingly or unwittingly, in money laundering has been growing in the last years. At the same time, these organizations have become quite agile at identifying the weak points within governmental and law enforcement structures in order to weaken their resolve to fight them. This is done through the *constant use of corruption as a facilitative tool for illicit activities.* The strength achieved by large criminal organizations can hardly be conceived without assessing one of their biggest weapons, the use of economic resources to corrupt law enforcement, bureaucrats, and even politicians and private institutions in order to achieve their goals. Important sectors of society and government are corrupted to achieve their cooperation, or at least not to stand in the way of their activities. This helps with the execution of their activities with the fewest possible obstacles (Alvarado Martínez and Guillén López 2006). It is key to understand these characteristics of organized crime in order to see them for what they are, veritable business organizations, albeit outlaw organizations. If we understand this, we can understand how these groups operate and where their strengths and vulnerabilities are.

A Politico-Criminal Perspective on Illicit Drugs

For decades, the politico-criminal model when it comes to illegal drugs has focused on a "frontal combat" against trafficking and the activities that surround it. It claims to be at "war" with drug-related organized crime all along the chain, in the originating or producing countries, in the transit countries, and in the final destination or consuming countries. The politico-criminal model aims to stop the production, trafficking, and consumption of illegal drugs.[4] The politico-criminal scaffolding is supported by the conviction that the only way to stop harm done by the illicit drugs is repression, that is, relentless prosecution. There is talk of "ending the scourge," "stemming the flow," and "fighting crime," in addition to "defending our children," "preserving our communities," and "shielding our families." The resources thrown at the problem everywhere are enormous—more than likely higher than the profits of organized crime. Yet evidence is mounting that, despite the strong prohibition with all that it entails, repression and prosecution, illicit drugs continue to flourish all along the entire chain. Hardly anyone can claim that the "war" on drugs has succeeded in curbing the growth of the international market for illegal drugs, even if they claim, without being able to prove it, that if this "war" were not fought things would be worse than they are now.

Alternative Voices

Many are increasingly pondering the war on drug's failure. Hence, at the politico-criminal level, and due to the lack of success, voices for alternative solutions are emerging, and more citizens are now convinced that drug prohibition as public policy has failed. These are the groups that have proposed the decriminalization and even the legalization of illicit drugs. They claim that governments must now contemplate alternative solutions that may, finally, achieve a permanent solution. These harm-control advocates view decriminalization and legalization as the solution to reduce drug consumption through education and treatment and the way to achieve a reduction in the power of organized crime. Nevertheless, an influential group of experts still holds the opinion that prohibition continues to be the best political option against illicit drugs. The pro-prohibition group is propped up primarily by the political and law enforcement apparatus of the United States but firmly supported by many others, including high-level officials at the United Nations. An increasing and important number of political voices, however, are joining the chorus of the alternative solutions group, including former Latin American presidents, American governors, and even some current heads of state in the Americas. But the alternative group faces the power of the first group, which considers decriminalization and legalization a bad idea, one far from reality and even illogical, and that, if adopted, its benefits would be exceeded by the severe damages that it will wreak on communities across the globe. Their argument is well known—attrition, which claims that fighting drugs has actually minimized the problem and without relentless hammering it would be much worse.

In relation to those who are in favor of the decriminalization or legalization of drugs, it must be noted that this position focuses on a thorough criticism of the current view that national governments have taken vis-à-vis psychotropic substances and their effects. They believe that the prohibitionist stance does not assess—with objectivity—the true essence of the substances subject to ban. In other words, not all drugs are created equal, and many of them are legal and may even have a palliative and even a medicinal value. In addition, some add that the worst problem, at least in the United States, is legally available drugs, not controlled substances. To shore up their vision, the defenders of a liberal regime on illegal substances present the following arguments. First, they claim that there is research on toxic substances that demonstrates the presence and use of drugs for various purposes in all societies across time. In other words, psychotropic substances have existed and have been used by humans throughout history, in controlled ways, without posing a danger to society. This shows, they say, that the danger of drugs does not come from drugs per se but from the relationship and attitude that humans have toward and around them. Second, they claim that prohibition at the international level is based on an arrogant and patronizing culture of discrimination by dominant societies. This has to do with the imposition of the values of the strong over the weak. Thus substances that are not considered to be in the sphere of the acceptable to the strong, so to speak, are prohibited (e.g., hashish, marijuana, coca leaves, etc.), while other drugs that do fall within the parameters of the dominant cultural model are used and abused with lower or no penalties at all and enjoy a high degree of permissiveness (e.g., alcohol and tobacco). These *legal* drugs, they claim, pose an equal or a greater health hazard and social cost than those that are prohibited. Third, the excessive criminalization of some drugs has political purposes. This somewhat more obscure argument posits that the criminalization of behaviors surrounding drugs and drug trafficking is due to ulterior motives, such as maintaining a negative stereotype against which we must fight and thereby justifying the existence of a benevolent state, indispensable and necessary to combat this dangerous "public enemy." It makes the state and its apparatus legitimate before the eyes of society. The moral panic around drugs legitimizes and justifies a number of repressive actions by the state. Fourth, in this day and age, the ineffectiveness of the repressive strategy as a method for addressing the problem of drugs has been demonstrated by many scholars. This approach only generates, immediately or eventually, effects completely opposite to those intended. The markup premiums are so high that eventually there is an incentive for more entrants resulting in drugs being more readily available to anyone who wants to get them, there is a greater variety of them, and they may be of higher quality as dealers struggle to satisfy their clients with the best. Eventually even their price comes down as the supply increases because of the enormous profits that incentivize more individuals to enter the supply chain. Thus, to the contrary, the current policy converts toxic substances into a very expensive commodity, which leads to the emergence of powerful drug trafficking organizations and contributes to the consolidation of a very lucrative black market.

In addition, prohibitionist laws have failed as guarantors of freedom and security for people. Legal provisions around drugs, such as sentencing guidelines, are an attack on some of the central tenets of the rule of law and equal protection, because they have an uneven impact on different groups in the administration of justice. The legislative "evolution" of the regulatory apparatus around illegal drugs and the constant but ever-more punitive changes to the law, especially those that have been going on since 1988, have only managed to increase the arrests of consumers and those accused of drug trafficking and dealing, crowding our prisons and adding an enormous burden on already strained government budgets. This is untenable when compared to the permissive attitude toward alcohol and tobacco, substances that add more victims than all other drugs combined, to repress other substances that can be equally controlled and even reduced through harm reduction strategies. Similarly, it is questionable to ban certain substances while not clarifying what medical, political, economic, and social criteria were taken into consideration to determine which drugs are legal and which are illegal. This has never really been clarified as a matter of public policy. The implication is that with a more permissive but regulatory criminal policy instead of a repressive policy like the one we currently have, the international trafficking of drugs, money laundering, the corruption of financial institutions, and political corruption such as the bribing of law enforcement and bureaucrats, in addition to the violence produced, would no longer be a problem. Governments should regulate the traffic of these substances as a business, and drugs themselves should be treated as commodities, which should be regulated and taxed accordingly. If this were done, it would greatly reduce the enormous social and economic cost derived from the prohibitionist laws and their implementation. The system built around a well-regulated drug use and commercialization system would be confined to the realm of good health care policy concentrated on a limited number of consumers, many of whom are already within the most extreme parameters of addiction and require health care in any event. Similarly, a good counseling and drug-exit program would contribute to setting specific objectives for the improvement of their personal and social circumstances and would create greater certainty around the kind of social assistance that they would require. The kind of social control exercised around drugs may in fact have as many obviously unhealthy consequences as a different regulatory system around the use of drugs.

In financial and budgetary terms, the maintenance costs of prohibitionist legislation are enormous. They imply great public expenditures in the maintenance of various state institutions, such as law enforcement agencies, specialized police agencies, and court and prison systems, all created to combat illicit drugs. Current drug policy produces serious effects on the culture of bureaucracies, including arrogant, heavy-handed, and overbearing efforts aimed at punishing individuals. Alternatives are disdainfully dismissed and ridiculed as illusory. Consumers are demonized. Drug consumption is associated with rebellious or immoral behavior that, invariably, punishes the young, a group against which there is already a culture of criminalization.

But political opposition to prohibitionism is growing. In all, if instead of continuing to repress drugs, their consumption, and commercialization were decriminalized or legalized, we could focus on harm reduction strategies. It is even possible that deaths by consuming adulterated illicit drugs would decrease. Counterfactual and real experiments show that under a different regime we can reduce consumption and over time weaken organized crime. The greatest drug danger is, in fact, the lack of control over quality, profit, distribution, and health effects (Guillén López 2009).

Drug Regime Change and Their Advocates

After reviewing the arguments presented by those who would advocate a change in illegal drug regime, it can be said that those who want the decriminalization/legalization (D/L) of drugs are a potential coalition of several groups. First, there are those who think that D/L would over time end trafficking and the pernicious effects that accompany it. This group includes health care professionals, academics, and even some former law enforcement agents. Some politicians are beginning to join the debate in favor of regime change, as we said earlier. Another group defends the right of individuals to decide for themselves whether to consume drugs or not. These are mostly libertarian ideologues. A third group considers forbidden psychotropic substances not as harmful to health as governmental propaganda asserts. Many of these groups speak specifically to marijuana, although there is disagreement on the harm that other drugs may produce. Many argue that marijuana is a good drug to experiment with in order to produce an alternative drug regime as it appears to be somewhat similar to alcohol and tobacco in many ways and produces less of a crisis for emergency respondents and few, if any, deaths. A final group comprises those who have occasionally used prohibited drugs and have not experienced the negative consequences of their consumption. All of these groups, many of them consisting of casual users, are relatively invulnerable to addiction and claim that drug consumption can be controlled, reduced, and even abandoned over time. The problem with these different advocates of an alternate regime is that they are not as well organized and cohesive as prohibitionists and do not have the state on their side. Their work is truly an uphill battle.

When speaking of political coalitions, however, there is always another side. Thus it is important to consider those who are against D/L. Anti-D/L groups claim that the arguments for D/L are superficial and that the alleged outcomes of D/L are speculative. While many accept some of the explanations of the liberalization advocates, they argue that a new regime may contain aspects that are not well understood and have not been thought through carefully. They also claim that the empirical evidence, which shows that regime change would actually represent an expansion of liberties, savings in financial resources, and a reduction of harm, is flimsy at best, as few have seriously detailed what an alternate regime would look like. They call for greater scientific rigor in testing the hypotheses generated around a potential new, more permissive drug regime. Some of the criticisms they present against those who argue for regime change include the following. First, those who favor D/L seem to have deliberately forgotten the attrition benefits offered by the current policy in matters related to the control of the production and manufacture of illicit substances. In other words, it is possible that the problem might actually get worse if drugs were decriminalized or legalized. This means that liberalization advocates do not account for the benefits of the measures deployed for the protection of public health. With the liberalization of supply and the elimination of current barriers that impede the free circulation of prohibited substances, the only thing that would be achieved would be a decrease in the cost of such products. Drugs would become even more readily available and their access easier. This could in turn lead to at least an initial increase in consumption. And even with liberalization, drugs would continue to be a very profitable business, as the tobacco and alcohol business has become, and its handling would go from the hands of the traffickers to the hands of multinational and national legal oligopolies who could promote their use, further normalizing the consumption of psychotropic substances within the scheme of the free market, unless specifically regulated to curb advertising and marketing. They would have an incentive to increase consumption in order to generate more profit, and thereby they could increase the consumption of drugs. In addition, opponents of an alternate drug regime argue that the D/L of certain drugs, such as marijuana, would carry with it a new wave of politico-criminal problems both in the adult and juvenile population, as behavior under the influence would have to be regulated and enforced. What they fail to indicate, however, is whether the cost of enforcing human behavior under the influence is about the same or less than the cost of enforcing drug production and trafficking. It is also erroneous, according to some, to think that the facilitation of access to drugs would eliminate their attractiveness for certain groups because their prohibition is per se attractive to some. They find fault with this logic. In countries that have legislatively authorized consumption, for example, including some places in the United States, and Holland, Sweden, Switzerland, and other countries, it was demonstrated that the only thing that easier access to drugs accomplished was to increase the number of consumers. This has, of course, not been demonstrated. But anti-D/L groups argue that when drugs are accessed more easily through medical prescriptions, there is a risk of creating a second market for these drugs, where prescriptions can be traded. This creates secondary markets that would in effect constitute yet another problem. The Dutch experience with drugs, they point out, clearly shows that their approval does not diminish the number of consumers, since, despite the permissiveness and the legal tolerance in relation to the consumption and sale of small quantities of soft drugs, especially cannabis, established since 1970, the percentage of addicts has remained fairly stable. Of course, the costs of enforcement have decreased.

Furthermore, they argue, the idea that D/L would stop the development of organized crime currently operating is also wrong. It is misguided to assert, as it is commonly done, that prohibitionism contributes to organized crime and that under a D/L regime organized crime would simply disappear. These arguments do not seem to take into account the reconversion capacity of organized crime structures and the ease with which they can expel from the market other illegal organizations tolerated by them. It is also possible, they claim, that opening the drug market would make them turn to expanding their illegal activities to other groups, such as minors and individuals mentally unfit to make decisions on drug consumption. Such groups would remain protected against drugs in any event, and they would continue to be a niche for organized crime to move into. Of course, anti-D/L advocates ignore the fact that the alcohol and tobacco regime has worked, even vis-à-vis those protected groups and the resources currently used to prevent competent adults from engaging in drug consumption, and related activities could be used to protect these groups as well. Finally, as proof that D/L is not a feasible option to solve the drug problem, or at least not a socially accepted option, anti-D/L groups argue, there is a growing backlash against more permissive policies in countries and regions where these policies have already been adopted, such as in Switzerland, whose society rejected D/L through the referendum of November 29, 1998. This backlash extends to the United States, where it is evident that liberalizing policies have also found some resistance or been defeated in some states. This is, however, a flawed argument, given that this backlash in no way considers whether it originates in a failure of policy or simply a political triumph of antiliberalization groups. Still, recently and faced with failure, Mexico, Colombia, and Guatemala proposed to reconsider prohibitionism within the framework of the United Nations—a first-ever proposal at such a high level.

In summary, there are numerous arguments on both sides and lots of hypotheses to test. While there are merits to D/L, those who oppose it insist that D/L could potentially exacerbate a number of problems, including: (1) an increase in violence and criminal acts; (2) an increase in harm to individual and collective health; (3) an increase in social costs; (4) a decrease in labor productivity; (5) decreased family and social cohesion; (6) continued narco-trafficking; and (7) a degree of harm to the right of others to health and security. These are all, however, hypotheses rather than proven statements. As with those who advocate D/L, some arguments are theoretically stronger than others, but none are empirically or scientifically backed by serious studies. In some sense, anti-D/L advocates suffer from many of the same flaws that pro-D/L advocates do.

Crime Theory and the Construction of Drug Offenses

Theoretically, criminal prosecution in and of itself, and as it relates to human and due process rights, is a phenomenon that seeks to heighten the effect of law on society, presumably to increase public safety. Criminal prosecution also assumes that there is a set of rational criteria designed to balance the actions of the state and the punishment of the individual who breaks the law. Thus criminal prosecution puts limits on the state in its relationship with the law breaker through due process. In this sense, criminal prosecution is a balancing feature of democracy, at least in principle, even though it varies in detail from country to country. The equilibrium between the power of the state and the protection of the prosecuted has had an influence on the practice of justice administration by the fact that the types of "offenses" that are defined as crimes are constructed through specific characteristics and according to certain parameters established by the law in advance. In cases where preestablished principles and rules are not followed, limiting the state in the exercise of power, the offender and the offense, and their relationship to the rest of the criminal code, are deeply affected. In the case of illegal drugs, an analysis of the criminal laws that regulate drug trafficking and drug use shows that the legal framework has ambiguous features that rely heavily on subjective judgments to construct the offense, to deal with the offender, and to generate exceptions to the general guidelines to detect, investigate, and punish criminal activities. Let us break down this analysis term by term.

The Material Object

A number of issues related to the material object of the law should be considered when it comes to our understanding of the term *drug*. Some of these issues are contradictory, depending on the features of the *crime* at hand and the *actors* examined. At one level we have substances that, independent of their chemical qualities, are socially accepted and desirable (medication) or frowned upon but allowed (alcoholic beverages, tobacco, coffee). These are drugs but are not commonly referred to as drugs. Their production, commercialization, and use are sanctioned by the law and taxed by governments, even though they are psychotropic substances. The words *drug* and *illegal* rarely, if ever, appear together when it comes to these substances. Moreover, these drugs are often considered part of what we know as *progress* (medical, economic, technological, etc.). This is thought-provoking when we contrast them with the kinds of drugs that are considered illegal. That some *psychotropic* substances are "good" and "progressive" while others are "harmful" and "noxious" reveals a degree of axiological arbitrariness surrounding the term *drug* itself and its use in official discourse. Thus the legal implications around the material object itself (a pill, a drink, a cigarette, a toke, etc.) depend on the cultural construction around the use and understanding of the word *drug*. This construction, of course, spills over into the so-called drug-related crimes. Depending on the cultural classification of the object, the substance is placed on the list of drugs allowed in national and international legislation and administrative laws or not allowed on the same list. This problem is further highlighted by the fact that there are always new drugs being generated and regulation is always behind. Thus the list of authorized and unauthorized "drugs" is never up to date, giving the state a degree of arbitrariness and placing anyone in danger of being labeled a criminal. The individual is in effect left in a state of helplessness in regard to the changing nature and construction of the word *drug*. What is placed on the schedule of illegal drugs is often not politically negotiable at all between society and the state but arbitrarily decided by politicians and bureaucrats. So in keeping with the principle of legal certainty, interesting hypotheses arise. How can an individual who is dealing drugs that are not yet prohibited because they have not made it to the list be prosecuted?[5]

At another level are those who argue that given the permissive attitude toward alcohol and tobacco, the prohibition of certain drugs, for example, marijuana, on the grounds that it protects public health, is at the very least implausible and hardly credible. Marijuana has not proven to be worse than tobacco or alcohol, at many levels. Equally, the prohibition of certain substances is debatable, since it has not yet been determined, among other things, which medical criteria were considered to decree, which drugs are useful and therefore legal, and the circumstances under which certain substances are simply harmful and therefore should be illegal, period. In general, the debate is apolitical, as it is often done by the state under the excuse that it is protecting the public from something harmful as judged by the state itself. In addition, the validity bestowed on the illegibility of a substance only needs a presumed danger, a subjective judgment that someone has to make, usually a bureaucrat, in order to be declared illegal. This declaration occurs through an authoritarian process, often without proof that it causes harm. It is sufficient that the *drug* is deemed "harmful" or "dangerous" to be declared legal or illegal.[6]

The Behavior

In addition to an examination of the object—drugs—it is necessary to look at the behavior that surrounds it. It is complex for a legislator in any country to comply with the obligations assumed by her or his country internationally and domestically when it comes to drugs previously labeled "dangerous"—

production, trafficking, pushing, or use. Each link in the chain must be criminalized separately, and each involves several discreet behaviors, all of which have to be considered for coverage under the law. In the process of legislating, it is easy for the state to overreach. In this regard, the individual behaviors listed in international agreements, that is, those that make up the so-called crime chain or *iter criminis*, are many, and some are quite subjective. Some make it to the legislation, while others do not. Besides, for each, legislators must consider a punishment too. And, ideally, the punishment schedule should be based on an optimal formula to deter crime or effectiveness criteria. Yet who is to say what effectiveness is? Moreover, the kind and rigor of the penalty on any one behavior that contributes to the illicit drug chain, no matter how tenuous the link may be, must be considered. And it is often impossible to calibrate behavior and penalty and rigor at the finest level, given the complexity of the illegal drug chain. How should a *halcón* or watchman, for example, or someone who crosses an international port of entry carrying drugs but without her or his knowledge or consent be punished? Are there different kinds of dealers, traffickers, and users? The obligation being nuanced in legislating all this can be seen as unfortunate if we consider how difficult it is to accommodate the principles of security, harmfulness, proportionality, equality, and presumption of innocence in dealing with such complex issues in any one event.[7] In the meantime, jails and prisons get filled up because the state, naturally, falls on the side of punishment instead of rehabilitation, education, or treatment, even when the legal criteria are unclear or ambiguous.

Subjectivity

In addition to the object and individual's behavior, the judgments made surrounding drugs—moral, legal, and so on—deserve analysis. The subjective judgment made, whether by politicians, religious leaders, judges, law enforcers, or moralists, on any behavior associated with drugs, is not an easy task. Drug-related criminal offenses are classified as crimes of commission but also crimes of intent. The criminal is thought to have an objective and to have actively and consciously chosen to participate, even when the objective is not achieved and regardless of the circumstances that surround his or her "choice." Structural constraints are dismissed in favor of absolute individual responsibility. These judgments are made by someone who assigns in his or her view the depth and breadth of intent. But intent is a notoriously difficult thing to measure. In some cases it is even complicated to differentiate intent from an unwitting act, and much guesswork is ultimately done by those who make the judgment. Quantity, for example, is one such guesswork parameter. Did the individual intend to consume that amount or is he or she a distributor? Someone had to set a limit, and a minute amount can mean the difference in the kind of penalty or the rigor of it. The ideological bent of the judge is itself a factor seldom accounted for. Similarly, it may be difficult in forensic practice to discover the mental motive in those cases where the consumer is a small-time dealer who engages in this behavior in order to get the drug dose that he or she needs or someone who does it because there simply is no other employment available.[8] This is not to justify any one behavior but to point out how subjectivity operates on a drug crime.

Thus drug-related crimes are crimes that require an abstract judgment as to their danger, which cannot always be objectively measured. This is relevant because illegal drug-related behaviors are dogmatically framed within the so-called dangerous crimes (ultimately pivoting on an assessment of risk). The level of danger or real risk is not up to the judge. Judges do not need to ascertain if there is an objective threat, because this has already been defined by the law with absolute presumption of culpability. Sometimes the law does not allow proof to the contrary. Witness, for example, laws on mandatory sentencing that have contributed so much to the current chaotic social costs of drug laws on individuals and society as a whole. Based on this, it can be stated that since the behavior is considered a priori dangerous, in most cases, the judgment is not even up to the judge. The entire historical and cultural context of drugs and their use is not up for discussion. It is an authoritarian imposition of a punitive nature, even when alternatives are available. The crime presupposes an activity that has a beginning and an end, and the entire chain is culpable and not up for negotiation, even political negotiation. This is increasingly questionable in the sciences of law. The doctrine and jurisprudence majority do not accept imperfect forms of execution, with only rare exceptions.[9]

Authorship and Participation

Because of the way in which criminal drug offenses are defined, the anti-drug system pivots on a unitary, individualized concept of authorship and participation. This is problematic, however, because the proposition that authorship and participation are individual acts that must be punished is one thing, but *organized crime* implies more than individual authorship or participation. What is being punished in *organized* crime is a phenomenon also subject to interpretation, one that is too broad. In other words, are the authorship and participation of a crime punishable, with collusion adding to that punishment, or is collusion punishable onto itself, separate from individual authorship or participation? This makes it impossible, in accordance with the principles of proportionality and equality, to practice a just valuation of the various contributions by individuals in drug-related crimes. Undoubtedly, from this perspective, any contribution made during an illegal act, minimal as it may be, would be considered within the sphere of authorship or participation, adding to the punishment and reinforcing the entire punitive system already in place. Fortunately, there are—both in Latin American doctrine and in the Anglo-Saxon tradition of jurisprudence—groups that, although not the majority, are increasingly calling for an interpretation of the law that will consider more restrictive theories of authorship and participation. Not all crimes, though they may appear in a crime schedule, can be attributed to *organized* crime. Authorship and participation in crime, therefore, must be debated, and important and nuanced differentiations as to the contribution of each criminal act have to be made in regard to all actors involved.[10]

Extraordinary Means in Investigating and Prosecuting Drug Offenses: Due Process

As we saw, an analysis of several elements in the chain of drug crimes shows how easy it is for the state to exceed its authority. In this section we consider the ways in which the state oversteps its hypothetical boundaries in the administration of justice, particularly in regard to human and due process rights. Drug laws have had a deep impact on the justice administration system of both countries, Mexico and the United States, particularly as bureaucrats expand their discretionary powers and extend the means to "punish" certain activities, sometimes rewriting or reinterpreting the law itself. For some time, international legislation, as well as comparative law and jurisprudence, has stressed the difficulties faced by the traditional instruments of criminal prosecution when it comes to investigating drug production, trafficking, and use activities. Among these, drug trafficking carried out by organized crime groups has drawn a lot of international attention. The legislative bodies of many different countries have included in their legal and justice systems new features that expand the state's discretion, strategies and tactics for addressing the activities of organized criminals and the constant growth of drug consumption and drug trafficking. In the process, more of our rights are simply tramped upon. This expansion of the state's police powers includes some of the following tactics.

Surveillance

Applied to drug-related crimes, surveillance activities consist of allowing illicit or suspicious shipments of narcotics, psychotropic substances, precursor chemicals, and other such materials to circulate in one or more countries or to pass through them. The purpose is to track the chain of illegal activities. But in the process, the state is permitting illegal activities to proceed, with the authorization of law enforcement agencies and judges and other authorities. Surveillance presupposes the commission of a criminal act—often trafficking. Few have questioned this tactic because the authorities have knowledge that an illegal act is being committed. Instead of interrupting the criminal act, the movement of prohibited merchandise— under their surveillance and control—is allowed, presumably to identify, detect, and arrest those individuals who, in concert with those responsible for the shipment, are in charge of receiving it and subsequently placing the drugs in the illegal market. Through surveillance, it is known that an illicit act is being committed, but it is not stopped. The law is broken to protect the law in the name of obtaining evidence of the participation in this crime of certain members of a criminal organization. This is what happened not only with U.S. law enforcement agencies allowing drugs to flow through Mexico and into the United States but also with guns and assault weapons, and as it has become more evident, with the authorization of laundering activities—all presumably to track the whole chain of crime but often losing control of drugs, funds, and weapons.

Undercover Agents

Undercover agents represent another extraordinary means of investigation that facilitates infiltration of an organized crime group by the state, through a police agent, who hides his or her true identity, with the purpose of obtaining information on its members, structure, activities, and fields of operation. The information obtained can be used in a criminal trial and thus plays a role in the eventual sentencing of the criminals for the illicit acts they perpetrated. While the undercover agent often participates in criminal activities, he or she is immune and becomes exempt from punishment.

An undercover agent is only one of many infiltration techniques, such as the anonymous person who reports a crime, the police informant, the repentant criminal, the secret agent, or the agent provocateur. Even when there are distinctive and even criminal characteristics of each of these individuals, these are often favored with lesser punishment by the state, thus introducing sometimes questionable and uneven standards of punishment.[11] Hardly anyone has questioned this or measured its impact on the system of justice or its integrity.

Wiretapping

This activity, in terms of drug trafficking acts committed by a criminal organization, can be carried out, de facto, by police or ministerial officials who have the appropriate judicial authorization, although it seems that wiretapping without judicial permission is becoming more common and acceptable, clearly undermining our administration of the justice system and allowing the state greater leeway to bend our rights. Wiretapping is done to obtain information that will aid the prosecuting authorities in capturing and prosecuting organized crime members who participate in the trafficking of illegal substances. However, this means of investigation, as with the others previously mentioned, implies relaxation of the fundamental rights and guarantees of the investigated. It threatens the right to privacy in communications, among other things. This is particularly true when agencies go rogue and refuse to either show sufficient evidence to a judge, do not follow the judicial restrictions imposed, or simply skip getting wiretapping authorization altogether. Often this permission is easier to skip when operating in a foreign country. Worse, the rights of foreign citizens are often discounted quickly and dismissed by roguish law enforcement agencies. This in turn can create serious resentment and even international conflict.

Agent Provocateur

This tactic does not seek or generate the commission of the crime but instead aims to elicit bad behavior from a third party in order to be able to charge them with a crime. No proof of an illicit act already perpetrated is required. It is sufficient to set up a trap and cause the perpetration of an act for which there are only suspicions or some indications. That is, agent provocateurs seek the commission of a crime, which results in entrapment. Such provocations, as charges in court, are handled by the judicial system less and less as a violation of due process rights but as legitimate crimes, without regard to the entrapment that they represent. That is why we should differentiate the criminal act from the act generated by the action of an agent provocateur. While in the first the police action aims at the discovery of evidence about a previous crime or one that is already committed, the provoked crime impacts people who did not intend to commit a crime, that is, cases in which the individual would not have acted in that way had it not been for the effective provocation of the agent.

These are just some of the central concerns that arise when the state becomes obsessed with a policy issue and begins to define and redefine the crime and arbitrarily and apolitically expand the means to fight it at will. Human and due process rights often fall by the wayside, and the constitutional order is upset. Slowly the state can encroach on one's right to privacy, one's right to competent defense, one's right to not testify against oneself, one's right to protection against coerced confessions, and so on. Mexico is a classic example of this, but the United States has slowly moved in that direction as the rhetoric of war is increasingly used in regard to drugs.

Nevertheless, the complex reality of organized crime and its operations requires extraordinary efforts to gather evidence and to allow for the discovery and capture of criminals. With traditional methods, it is hard to achieve success against criminal drug trafficking organizations. But we should not capitulate on our rights in order to fight organized crime. In other words, organized crime, in addition to supplying the market with drugs, may be provoking the state into undermining the very principles under which our administration of justice systems are presumably founded, however different they may be in practice. Thus we should insist that all rights be protected, even in the middle of this "war." In the implementation of any investigation, the state should have the burden of proof, and it should justify every one of its actions. The authorization of certain tactics should be valid only in the case of a criminal investigation undertaken against an organized criminal group but always mindful of the protection of the rights of every individual involved. The judicial system should have full control of the means and the continuation of any investigation, and evidence gathered illegally should be excluded. Finally, some provisions should be added to protect the testimony and the personal integrity of the person providing it. In other words, the protection of *witnesses*, *legal experts*, and *victims* should be primordial. The constitutional protection of witnesses, victims, and even perpetrators is paramount, because violations of the process will undermine our entire system of justice. The burden should be on the government at all times and never on the accused. No relaxation of these rules should be allowed in any degree, and protections should encompass all procedural rights. Although in some countries, such as the United States, this is widely understood, even if sometimes not fully respected, in others, such as Mexico, these protections are still the exception rather than the norm.[12]

Conclusions

Drug production and trafficking is not a crime against public health, as the Mexican government has argued, partly to legitimize its actions. It is a well-typified crime, and it is covered by penal law. Second, during the last four decades, there has been an increase in the consumption of drugs, which is now a thorny issue. The problem should be considered from all angles and not simply from a criminal perspective. We should resist the temptation to allow organized crime around illegal drugs to chip away at more and more of our rights and upset our constitutional order. Third, the illicit drug market has led to the emergence of powerful organizations with unparalleled power in the history of crime. We should consider the impact of the law on organized crime and of organized crime on the law to ensure that we protect our judicial systems. If we do not understand this, we will end up compromising the entire system of the administration of justice and make almost no distinction between one type of crime and another. Fourth, the politico-criminal model that has regulated drugs for decades has evolved into a "war," with increasingly militarized strategies and tactics, something that may compromise our judicial systems as well. This approach may be one-dimensional when we consider that the trafficking of substances considered illicit has become internationalized, spanning from producing countries to consuming countries, and that trying to put a stop to it with militarized instruments to end the production, trafficking, dealing, and consumption of drugs may result in a criminological mess. Fifth, due to the lack of success, criminal doctrine scholars and many others today insist on reconsidering drug prohibition to create alternative regimes, including decriminalization and legalization. If the alternative fails to achieve the yearned-for solution that has been sought for the problem, prohibition can always be restored. However, D/L should be the result of careful study and extensive debates, given that groups of credible experts still hold the opinion that prohibition continues to be the best politico-criminal option against drugs. Sixth, criminal prosecution must keep all constitutional safeguards intact, and we should prevent the arbitrary and even abusive intervention of the state under the pretext of a criminal investigation. Seventh, criminological theories have had an influence on how crime is dealt with and viewed today. Criminal offenses should consider the cultural and political construction of crime as well as the scientific discoveries that might aid in resolving it. Eighth, criminal norms that regulate drugs contain ambiguous features that affect the ways in which we view the offense and the offender and suggest that we are increasingly willing to compromise our own rights to stop this "scourge." Finally, for some time, international treaties, as well as comparative law and jurisprudence, have stressed the difficulties faced by the traditional instruments of criminal prosecution when it comes to investigating drug crime activities effectively. Such contradictions must be considered carefully as well when fighting organized crime groups. If we do not view the problem of drug trafficking as much more complicated than simply a "war," we will lose much more than we will gain—namely, our rights—and at the end we may not even come close to ending a business as ancient as humankind itself.

Notes

1. Translated by Rafael Núñez and Tony Payan.

2. Illicit drug trafficking has a special relationship with a wide variety of offenses, hence we have to understand the entire crime chain or cycle in order to grasp this complex issue.

3. Despite this, there is another type in which they are recognized. There are at least three models that do not show vertical and pyramidal structures: hierarchical clustering, the core group, and the criminal network. Overall, these are the types of groups: (1) standard hierarchy: a leader, defined activities, very rigid internal discipline, and known by name, ethnic, or cultural identity; induce violence to the interior; (2) regional hierarchy: a leader, central command, regional autonomy, regional population distribution, multiple activities, and ethnic or cultural identity; violence is essential to maintain order; (3) aggregate hierarchy: association of criminal groups, decisions taken by council, the main group has identity, and there is autonomy of all groups; its conformation responds to the social context; (4) central group: flexible network, limited membership, horizontal structure, and internal discipline; no identity of its members and rarely has a name; and, (5) criminal network: developed activities by key individuals, differences in contact tasks or activities, loyalty or ties more important than the identity, and low public profile.

4. See United Nations Single Convention on Narcotic Drugs (1961); Protocol of March 25, 1972; Vienna Convention on Psychotropic Substances (1971); and Convention against Illicit Traffic in Narcotic Drugs and Psychotropic Substances of Vienna (1988).

5. The material object, within the notion of the elements that make up an offense, has a particular meaning, since it is one that turns on the person and upon

which rests the typical action, that is, it is the object around which the disapproved human behavior is developed.

6. Legal goods are the material objects that, according to the criminal legislator, a person needs for her full development. In addition, there are immaterial goods, the norms required by a society to live in harmony. The former are referred to as individual *legal interests*, the latter *collective legal interests*.

7. Punitive action focuses on objectively identifiable behaviors, those that undermine the law and are worthy of prohibition and criminal penalty.

8. This presupposes that there is a subjective type that includes fraud, and in some cases additional judgments are made. In this sense, fraud equals intention, and drug trafficking is presumably a willful act. It is also necessary to remember that the intent is thought to exist because our will governs our actions, that is, the author's knowledge of the action and circumstances and his or her consent to perform the behavior result in culpability.

9. *Iter criminis* refers to the route that the author of a crime takes from the moment he or she conceives the idea to the consummation of the crime. This process is partly immaterial and partly material. It consists of the stages that describe the different conditions of criminal evolution: preparatory acts, attempts, and completion. Understanding and discovering this route are crucial in any prosecutorial work.

10. The prosecution must show that a criminal act is not always the product of a single person, but in many cases it is the product of several individuals. This presents significant challenges when parceling out to each of the participants criminal responsibility for an act. Each individual's part of the crime has to be sorted out. For some time, this issue has been debated, considering the importance and significance of the contribution made by each person in relation to the offense. To do this, the cooperation of some of the implicated is often necessary. The result is that some individuals involved in criminal acts receive a full sentence for their decisive role in the crime and others, in making contributions to the investigation, receive a lesser sentence.

11. Unlike the undercover agent, the unnamed complainant, the police informer or collaborator, and the remorseful criminal do not hold the status of officials. Their contribution is not always clearly regulated by the law because they lack official status and are often incidental to a particular event. The agent provocateur may or may not be an official. But his or her work is always controversial. The agent provocateur primarily performs a quick task, less comprehensive and thorough than the undercover agent. His or her job is to cause others to violate the law. Thus the admissibility of the agent provocateur's work in court can be disputed by the defense. Regarding the secret agent, his or her labor is rather different from the undercover agent's within the administrative organization, and his or her work is designed to protect others' interests (e.g., national security), whereas the undercover agent obeys the logic of an investigation already in progress.

12. Historically, such formulas have tended to protect the evidence.

Bibliography

Alvarado Martínez, Israel, and Germán Gullién López. 2006. "Consideraciones político-criminológicas en el ámbito de la delincuencia organizada. Un reto legislativo." *Revista Mexicana de Justicia*. No. 16. Mexico City: Sexta Época. 107–8.

———. 2009. "La protección a víctimas, testigos y menores: Un compromiso de la reforma constitucional." *Iter Criminis: Revista de Ciencias Penales*, no. 7. Cuarta Época; 75–88.

Baratta, Alessandro. 1993. "Fundamentos ideológicos de la actual política criminal sobre drogas." In *La actual política criminal en materia de drogas: Una perspectiva comparada*, edited by José Luis Díez Ripollés and Patricia Laurenzo Copello, 1–17. Valencia, Spain: Librería Tirant lo Blanch.

Díez-Ripollés, José Luis. 1989. *Los delitos relativos a drogas tóxicas, estupefacientes y sustancias psicotrópicas. Estudio de las modificaciones introducidas por la Ley Orgánica 1/1988 de 24 de marzo.* Madrid: Tecnos.

García-Pablos, Antonio. 1986. *Bases para una política criminal de la droga, la problemática de la droga en España. Análisis y propuestas político-criminales.* Madrid: Edersa.

Grupo de Estudios de Política Criminal. 1989. *Manifiesto por una nueva política sobre la droga.* Málaga, Spain: Departamento de Derecho Público. http://perso.unifr.ch/derechopenal/assets/files/anuario/an_1989_07.pdf. Accessed April 24, 2013.

Guillén López, Germán. 2007. *Discusión Autoría y participación en el tráfico de drogas (Art. 368 del Código Penal Español).* Universitas Vitæ. Salamanca, Spain: University of Salamanca Editions.

———. 2009. *Discusión político-criminal entorno al tráfico de drogas. Revista Estudios en Derecho y Gobierno.* Bogotá: Universidad Católica de Colombia.

Herrero, César. 2001. *Criminología. Parte General y Especial.* 2nd ed. Madrid: Dykinson S.L.

———. 2007. *Criminología. Parte General y Especial.* 3rd ed. Madrid: Dykinson S.L.

Kreuzer, Arthur. 1982. "Las drogas en la República Federal de Alemania. Problemática y aspectos político criminales." In *La reforma penal. Cuatro cuestiones fundamentales.* Madrid: Instituto Alemán.

Lafont Nicuesa, Luis. 2003. "Comentario sobre la legalización del tráfico de drogas y algunos problemas sobre los tipos penales vigentes en el derecho español." *Revista del Ministerio Fiscal*, no. 11: 9–40.

Manifiesto. 1989. *Una nueva alternativa a la actual Política Criminal en Materia de Drogas.* Presented by the Group of Political Criminals. Málaga, Spain.

Muñoz Conde, Francisco Jose and Bella Aunion Acosta. 1993. "Drogas y Derecho penal." In *La actual política criminal en materia de drogas: Una perspectiva comparada*, edited by José Luis Díez Ripollés and Patricia Laurenzo Copello, 567–82. Valencia, Spain: Librería Tirant lo Blanch.

Nadelmann, Ethan. 1994. "Pensando seriamente sobre alternativas a la Prohibición de drogas." In *Drogas y control penal en los Andes: Deseos, utopías y efectos perversos.* Lima, Peru: Comisión Andina de Juristas.

Neuman, Elías. 2004. "El modelo neoliberal y la legalización de las drogas." In *SERTA: In memoriam Alexandri Baratta*, edited by Fernando Pérez Álvarez, 1349–62. Salamanca, Spain: CISE/Universidad de Salamanca.

Sequeros Sazatornil, Fernando. 2000. *El tráfico de drogas ante el ordenamiento jurídico: Evolución normativa, doctrinal y jurisprudencial.* Madrid: La Ley, 351–54.

United Nations. 1961. "United Nations Single Convention on Narcotic Drugs." http://www.unodc.org/pdf/convention_1961_en.pdf.

———. 1971. "Protocol of March 25, 1972; Vienna Convention on Psychotropic Substances." http://treaties.un.org/pages/ViewDetails.aspx?src=TREATY&mtdsg_no=VI-17&chapter=6&lang=en.

———. 1988. "Convention against Illicit Traffic in Narcotic Drugs and Psychotropic Substances of Vienna." http://www.unodc.org/pdf/convention_1988_en.pdf.

United Nations Office for Drug Control and Prevention. 2000. "World Drug Report 2000." Oxford, UK: United Nations. http://www.unodc.org/pdf/world_drug_report_2000/report_2001-01-22_1.pdf. Accessed April 24, 2013.

Van Dijk, Jan, et al. 2003. "Manual against Transnational Organized Crime." Report prepared by the United Nations Office on Drugs and Crime. February.

CHAPTER ELEVEN

The U.S. Causes but Cannot (or Will Not) Solve Mexico's Drug Problems

Jonathan P. Caulkins and Eric L. Sevigny

Introduction

Most of the world's illegal drugs are exported across international boundaries. It is common to ask how interventions in source and/or transit countries affect drug use and drug-related problems downstream, but one can also ask how drug policies in final market countries affect problems upstream in source and transit countries. Here we investigate whether changes in U.S. policies—notably their heavy reliance on incarceration—might strengthen Mexico's ability to deal with drug problems.

Mexican Americans imprisoned in the United States for drug violations in 2004 look very much like their fellow citizens of other ancestries. Foreign nationals in U.S. prisons, in contrast, were typically involved with much greater quantities of drugs, although they were not more likely to report being in large organizations or having weapons involvement. Since they represent less than 10 percent of all drug law violators in prison, it would be possible to change incarceration rates for foreign nationals without making a dramatic change in overall U.S. incarceration policy.

However, that would not alter the fundamentals. The United States and Mexico are and would remain linked through international drug trafficking, with U.S. demand supporting large-scale trafficking through Mexico. The only U.S. policy reform that would rapidly ameliorate trafficking-related problems in Mexico is legalization (not just decriminalization) of all drugs (not just marijuana). That is a political nonstarter in the United States, and not only because U.S. leaders are obdurate; from the U.S.

perspective, across-the-board legalization is at best risky and likely contrary to its interests. U.S. and Mexican interests in this regard are not aligned. Since any politically viable change in U.S. policy would not make a decisive difference for Mexican drug problems in the short term—or even medium term, Mexico must deal with its present crisis primarily through domestic actions; it should not wait for a solution in the form of changes in U.S. policy.

Mexico's Role in U.S. Drug Market Supply

Much of the U.S. demand for illegal drugs is supplied through Mexico. Cocaine (including crack) is by far the most important drug market in the United States. It accounts for about 60 percent of both black market revenues and drug-related social costs (Caulkins, Pacula, Paddock, and Chiesa 2002; Office of National Drug Control Policy 2004). Mexico has nothing directly to do with cocaine production, which occurs almost entirely in South America (United Nations Office on Drugs and Crime 2009). However, for the last twenty years, Mexico has been the primary transit country. Heroin, methamphetamine, and marijuana represent the second tier of illegal drug markets in the United States. All have black markets of roughly comparable value. Each individually is only about one-sixth as important in the United States as cocaine/crack, but all three are much more important than whatever substance is ranked fifth. Indeed, all other illegal drugs combined are of almost no consequence when analyzing U.S.–Mexican drug market connections.[1] These are broad generalizations. Marijuana differs importantly from heroin and methamphetamine by being relatively inexpensive. Not coincidentally, it is also the most widely used and is not importantly linked to nondrug crime or violence in the United States. Nevertheless, in very round terms one can think of U.S. drug markets as being two-thirds cocaine (including crack) and one-third heroin, methamphetamine, and marijuana combined.

From Mexico's perspective, heroin, methamphetamine, and marijuana collectively are more than one-third of the problem because they are all produced in Mexico, whereas Mexico is only a transit country for cocaine. And marijuana looms relatively larger because its prices are marked up less within the United States. Hence, a larger proportion of users' spending on marijuana makes it back to producers than is the case with the other drugs. How much more problematic is unclear, because we lack good data describing how the revenues of Mexican drug trafficking organizations (DTOs) are distributed across drug markets[2] (Office of National Drug Control Policy 2001, 2003; Drug Availability Steering Committee 2002).

Kilmer, Caulkins, Liccardo Pacula, MacCoun, and Reuter (2010) attempted to pull together the incomplete and not always entirely reliable data pertinent to this question. Their best estimate of Mexican DTOs' gross revenue from exporting marijuana to border wholesale markets was $1.5 billion (with a range from $1.1 to $2.0 billion).[3] They also provided exploratory estimates for the other drugs, whose point estimates were: cocaine, $3.4 billion; methamphetamine, $0.6 billion; and heroin, $1.1 billion, including both heroin produced in Mexico and Colombian heroin transshipped through Mexico. All of these estimates are small compared to the total U.S. retail drug market of roughly $65 billion (Office of National Drug Control Policy 2001) because Mexican exporters do not sell directly to U.S. users, and prices are marked up by a factor of six to ten within the United States (Babor, Caulkins, Edwards, Foxcroft, Humphreys, Medina Mora, Obot, Rehm, Reuter, Room, Rossow, and Strang 2010). Despite the uncertainties, it is clear that all four substances generate substantial revenues for Mexican traffickers. The consequences for Mexico of these large black markets include very high rates of drug-related violence and corruption, as well as readily available drugs at lower prices.

We assume later in this chapter that reducing the volume of drugs moving from Mexico to the United States and/or the flow of drug dollars from the United States to Mexico would benefit Mexico. This is not an innocuous assumption. Reuter (2009) observes that shrinking a drug market could increase violence if it exacerbated interorganizational competition. More generally, most drug markets are not highly violent, even though a few—including Mexican high-level drug trafficking—can be spectacularly violent (Beittel 2009; Reuter 2009). So market size is not all that matters, but all other things being equal, it is a relevant metric.

Drug Regime Change Could Help, but Only in Theory: Decriminalization Would Exacerbate Mexico's Problems

The most consequential choice in drug policy is whether the substance in question can be legally produced and distributed for unsupervised consumption by a substantial segment of the population (Kleiman 1992). We refer to that choice as legalization versus prohibition. Any form of drug legalization in the United States would all but eliminate the corresponding black market in Mexico. Prohibition can greatly reduce consumption relative to a legalization regime. However, a frustrating reality is that alternative drug control policies and programs within a prohibition framework can have a fairly limited ability to produce further dramatic reductions in the scale of drug use and drug markets (Babor et al. 2010). Hence, almost any form of prohibition will generate a black market that is very roughly as large as the current market and so create problems in Mexico that are roughly comparable to those of today.

Often drug policy is described as a trinary choice, with decriminalization listed as a third option. That makes sense when focusing on consequences for the final market country but not from the perspective of source and transit countries.

Decriminalization means substantially reducing or eliminating sanctions for drug users while continuing to prohibit production and distribution. Thus supply continues to be in the hands of criminal enterprises. Furthermore, demand will tend to increase because decriminalization eliminates important risks for buyers (MacCoun and Reuter 2001). The evidence to date from marijuana decriminalization suggests that the increase may be modest (Room, Fischer, Hall, Lenton, and Reuter 2010). Nevertheless, the black markets remain, and if anything they are even larger. Hence, from the perspective of source and transit countries, decriminalization in final market countries is a pure loss. (Decriminalization in the source and transit countries may or may not be beneficial to those countries; that is a completely separate question.)

The implications of this are terribly important and often misunderstood (Kleiman, Caulkins, and Hawken 2011). Sloppy reasoning would argue that since legalization would solve the problem of black markets in source and transit countries, and since decriminalization is in some sense halfway to legalization, then decriminalization would benefit source and transit countries half as much as legalization. Such reasoning is simply wrongheaded. Relative to prohibition, decriminalization is more likely to exacerbate rather than ameliorate the black markets in source and transit countries.[4]

A Caution Concerning Legalization

Legalization might solve two salient aspects of Mexico's drug problem—the violence and corruption associated with black markets. However, legalization in the United States could also adversely affect price and availability for Mexican users. If Mexico also legalized those drugs, prices would fall and availability would increase. If Mexico retained its prohibition, it would no longer be a producer or transit country. However, the Mexican–U.S. border is porous in both directions, so if prices were much higher in Mexico than in the United States, that might induce smuggling from north to south.

Simply put, prices matter. Extensive empirical literature shows that drug use varies inversely with price; lower prices induce greater use and greater use-related harms such as emergency room visits (for reviews, see Grossman 2005; Babor et al. 2010).

There is some debate as to how much lower legal prices would be, but the most likely scenario is that untaxed prices would fall precipitously, and excise taxes could not make up for all of the drop, even for marijuana (Caulkins et al. 2012). For example, Kilmer et al. (2010) estimated that if California Proposition 19 had passed, high-grade marijuana could be legally produced in California for $38 per ounce versus current prices of $300 to $450 per ounce, even if the risk of federal enforcement limited production to grow houses (as opposed to large-scale greenhouses or farm-based production).

Proposition 19 did not specify a tax rate, but the Ammiano marijuana legalization bill would have imposed a tax of $50 per ounce. That rate is far less than what is needed to restore prices to prelegalization levels, and yet it is far greater on a per unit weight basis than other excise taxes: $50 per ounce for tobacco would correspond to $35 per pack, and even taxes of $3 to $4 per pack have engendered considerable gray market tax evasion (Merriman 2010). Indeed, Canada's cigarette tax of roughly $3 per pack ($0.15 per gram) provoked a rapid expansion in black market sales and so had to be repealed (Galbraith and Kaiserman 1997). Some suggest that enforcement can be used to force compliance (Becker et al. 2006), but with a $50 per ounce excise tax, the financial reward of evading taxes on a pound of marijuana would be greater than the current rewards of smuggling a pound of Mexican commercial-grade marijuana into the United States—something that even a very considerable enforcement threat has failed to deter (see Kilmer et al. 2010 and Caulkins et al. 2012 for details).

The situation for cocaine and heroin is even more extreme. Both are available in source countries in ready-to-use form at roughly 1 percent of their current retail price in the United States, and transportation costs are negligible. A kilogram of cocaine that would sell for over $100,000 at retail in the United States can be purchased in Colombia for $1,500 and—if legal—could be delivered by express mail for less than $50.

Some commentators note that there are substantial markups for some legal agricultural products between farm-gate and retail shelves (Miron 2003). However, for no legal product does simple distribution (as opposed to processing, such as turning grain into breakfast cereal) increase the value per unit weight by anything close to what now occurs for illegal drugs. The cocaine and heroin that sell for so little in source countries are already in finished form, and shipping costs of $50 per kilogram are negligible compared to a price of $1,500 per kilogram. Hence, untaxed legal cocaine and heroin would cost at most a few dollars per gram, which is but a few percent of the current retail price in the United States. Even if $50 per ounce excise taxes could be collected, that is still less than $2 per gram.

Drug Policy Choices within a Prohibition Regime

We have examined elsewhere what the effectiveness of various drug options are for controlling drug problems in the United States (Babor et al. 2010; Caulkins 2009; Caulkins and Kleiman 2011; Caulkins and Reuter 2010). Those assessments carry judgments about the effectiveness of the interventions themselves with an analytic framework for translating those direct effects into overall implications for market equilibrium and associated outcomes. Here we retain the same judgments about effectiveness but shift outcomes, asking how these programs would affect outcomes in Mexico. In the interest of space, we merely state capsule summaries rather than repeat the reviews of the relevant primary literature cited earlier.

Reducing Demand

Any intervention that reduces demand for illegal drugs in the United States will help Mexico. Shrinking demand will tend to reduce the quantity that Mexico produces and transships. To the extent that such interventions erode prices, the reduction in trafficking revenues would be even greater, in percentage terms, than the reduction in quantities supplied. So, just as the United States has an incentive to subsidize supply reduction programs in Mexico, Mexico has an incentive to subsidize demand reduction programs in the United States.

The bad news, from Mexico's perspective, is that conventional demand control programs are not highly effective. Primary prevention in particular achieves nothing close to the preventive effect of vaccination for childhood diseases. Even the best primary prevention programs will probably reduce participants' lifetime consumption by single-digit percentages (Miller and Hendrie 2009). Furthermore, over the next decade, the vast majority of U.S. drug demand will come from people who are already older than thirteen or fourteen. Hence, even if traditional prevention programs magically became 100 percent effective, the impact on drug demand would be minimal for the next five or even ten years (Caulkins et al. 2002).

Treatment does not suffer from such delays, but the "treatment works" mantra hides the fact that treatment works well only with respect to certain criteria. Many studies find that treatment's social benefits exceed its costs (Cartwright 2000; Harwood, Malhrota, Villarivera, Liu, Chong, and Gilani 2002; Belenko, Patapsis, and French 2005), but that is not because treatment succeeds at reducing drug use by a large percentage.

Rydell and Everingham (1994) offer one of the most-cited analyses of treatment's cost-effectiveness. However, one of their equally important but less-cited conclusions was that even if every dependent cocaine user enrolled in treatment every year, it would still take fifteen years for cocaine use to fall by 50 percent, and that conclusion was based on treatment effectiveness estimates that have been criticized as too optimistic (Manski, Pepper, and Thomas 1999).

The resolution of this apparent paradox is simple. Treatment is a good investment because dependent users generate spectacularly high social costs per year of active use, not because treatment has high effectiveness in any absolute sense (McLellan, McKay, Forman, Cacciola, and Kemp 2005; Pollack, Reuter, and Sevigny 2011). The most common outcome of drug treatment is relapse. The situation is notably better with regard to opiates, where there are pharmacotherapies that can effectively substitute for the illegal drugs (Amato, Davoli, Perucci, Ferri, Faggiano, and Mattick 2005). However, stimulants are the larger problem in the United States, and even after a generation of concerted effort, there is no such thing as an effective pharmacotherapy for cocaine, crack, methamphetamine, or any other stimulant.

Reducing Supply

The United States devotes the greatest share of its drug control resources to law enforcement. U.S. incarceration rates exploded from the period

1975–2000, far surpassing those in other Western countries (Kuhn 2001), and drug-related incarceration has been a major driver of these rates (Blumstein and Beck 1999; Mauer 2001). Most imprisoned drug law violators were involved in supplying drugs, albeit sometimes in minor roles; users who had no involvement in drug distribution or any other nondrug crime make up a very small proportion of the prison population (Sevigny and Caulkins 2004).

This enforcement accounts for an important share of the large markup in prices between the U.S. border and retail (Caulkins and Reuter 1998, 2010). Higher retail prices suppress consumption (Grossman 2005) and, in turn, U.S. demand on international drug markets. Hence, Mexico benefits from the United States' energetic pursuit of domestic drug dealers.[5]

However, the extent to which this helps Mexico is limited by the fact that incarcerating drug dealers is not terribly effective at suppressing drug use. Kuziemko and Levitt (2004) estimate that the 1985–1996 increase in the number of drug law violators behind bars drove cocaine prices by only 5 to 15 percent above what they otherwise would have been.

A crucial point is that the effect of supply control is highly nonlinear. Shifting from legalization to prohibition with enough enforcement to achieve the structural consequences of product illegality has enormous effects, driving prices far above the legal price and so greatly reducing use. However, expanding incarceration further, beyond that baseline, has much more modest incremental effects (Caulkins and Reuter 2010). So, the United States could cut incarceration of drug law violators by 50 percent without causing large increases in drug use and attendant adverse effects on Mexico, even though eliminating the second 50 percent could have dramatic consequences (Caulkins and Reuter 2006).

That is, to the extent that punishing suppliers affects drug markets at all, it affects markets in ways that Mexico should like. However, expanding incarceration will have negligible effects on drug use.

There are exceptions to this general rule. First, if aggressive enforcement pushes production of marijuana and methamphetamine out of the United States and into Mexico, that is clearly a loss for Mexico.[6] So, to be more precise, Mexico should be pleased with the United States' tough domestic enforcement against cocaine and heroin suppliers but wish that the United States would go easy on marijuana cultivation and domestic methamphetamine production.

Second, seizing drugs in the United States is bad for Mexico because it increases demand for drugs produced in or shipped through Mexico.

Seized drugs are not replaced one for one. Seizing drugs increases the cost to suppliers of successfully providing a gram for purchase at retail, and the suppliers pass along those increased costs to users in the form of higher prices. Those higher prices suppress use. The amount by which use goes down per kilogram seized depends on many particulars, including the elasticity of demand and the replacement cost of drugs at the point seized (for details, see Caulkins and Kleiman 2011; Caulkins and Reuter 2010). However, it is likely that, on average, drug seizures in the United States increase demand for drugs produced in or shipped through Mexico.

Third, incarcerating suppliers might create violent competition over managerial succession and/or interorganizationally over opportunities to supply the incarcerated person's customers (Reuter 2009). If the person incarcerated in the United States operated in Mexico, that collateral violence could exacerbate drug-related violence in Mexico.

A fourth potential exception is the possibility that intense border enforcement gives a competitive advantage to larger and more sophisticated organizations (Caulkins and Padman 1993), which may be more damaging to Mexico than would be a larger number of smaller organizations moving the same quantity of drugs and sharing the same profits.

Interventions in Colombia and Afghanistan

The United States also pursues counterdrug activities in source countries, notably Colombia and Afghanistan. By and large, these interventions have no direct effect on Mexico. The primary reason is simply that interventions in source countries have little effect on retail prices or consumption in final market countries (Babor et al. 2010), and any drugs seized or destroyed upstream of Mexico do not increase the volume that is shipped through Mexico the way that drugs seized in the United States do.

For Afghanistan there is the additional fact that opiates markets are currently more hemispheric than global. Most of what is consumed in the Western Hemisphere is produced in Colombia and Mexico, not Afghanistan.[7]

In theory there could be exceptions to this rule. If law enforcement efforts in Colombia somehow made it very hard for Colombians to ship cocaine to Mexico, while making it very easy to ship directly to the United States or through some other channel, that might shift smuggling routes away from Mexico. By some cold calculus, it might be in the United

States' interest to play favorites, condemning some less important country to being a narco-state in order to siphon trafficking away from Mexico, but such realpolitik has rarely entered the drug policy discourse.

Coerced or Mandated Abstinence

The previous discussion suggests that none of the conventional U.S. drug policy pillars is likely to offer much help to Mexico. The better chance of achieving a larger, more immediate effect comes from so-called coerced or mandated abstinence programs that apply the stick of enforcement to users, not suppliers, but they do so in an intelligent way (Kleiman 2009).

These programs combine frequent drug testing with immediate and certain but modest sanctions for failed tests (e.g., one or two days in jail, starting immediately after the failed test). Incremental enhancements to conventional sanctions do not produce powerful deterrent effects (Durlauf and Nagin 2010), but the more modern approach tries to "Get Deterrence Right" (Kennedy 2008) by designing environments grounded in realistic models of human decision making. Notably, they stress certainty and celerity (swiftness) over severity.

A famous example is Hawaii's Opportunity Probation with Enforcement (HOPE) program, which cut the number of failed or missed drug tests by 80 percent relative to regular probation and cut by more than half both new arrests and days of incarceration (Hawken and Kleiman 2007). South Dakota's 24/7 Sobriety Program is another example (Caulkins and DuPont 2010). Originally intended for repeat drunk driving offenders, the program achieved a better than 99 percent rate of testing clean and led South Dakota to expand it to illegal drugs and to most forms of community release, including pretrial release, probation and parole, and suspended sentences.

Not every dependent user can achieve abstinence through these interventions, but the programs provide a form of "behavioral triage" (Hawken 2010) that allows scarce treatment resources to focus on the subset of dependent individuals with the greatest need. What makes coerced abstinence important from Mexico's perspective is that most cocaine, heroin, and methamphetamine consumed in the United States is used by people who are nominally under criminal justice supervision (e.g., on probation or parole), so they are subject to frequent testing with consequences for failed tests.

Imprisonment of Drug-Law Violators in the United States and Effects on Mexico

Choices with regard to drug enforcement include not only "how much?" but also "what kind?" and "against whom?" Presumably, the effects on Mexico of the United States imposing a five-year prison term are different in each of the following scenarios: (1) a European American selling Colombian heroin at retail in Boston; (2) a Mexican national drug courier transporting methamphetamine across the border; and (3) a Mexican American cocaine kingpin whose smuggling organization spans the Mexican–U.S. border. Hence, in this section we present original empirical work investigating just whom the United States imprisons for drug law violations. We begin by examining the distribution of federal and state prison populations by offense type and ethnic/national identity. Then, to assess the relative cross-border use of imprisonment, we compare U.S. and Mexican imprisonment rates. Last, we examine the combined offense-related profiles of federal and state drug law violators.[8] Our analysis makes use of data from the 2004 Survey of Inmates in State and Federal Correctional Facilities (SISFCF), a nationally representative survey of imprisoned individuals administered every five to seven years (Bureau of Justice Statistics 2007).

Data and Methods

The 2004 SISFCF is the most recent in a series that extends back to 1974.[9] The survey employed a two-stage sampling design, completing interviews with 14,499 inmates from 287 state facilities and 3,686 inmates from 39 federal institutions. The total response rates were 89 percent and 85 percent, respectively (Bureau of Justice Statistics 2007). Our analyses and point estimates are weighted to account for this nonresponse and other sampling design elements. These estimates have estimable confidence intervals, but for ease of presentation we do not report them here. Also, the data are self-reported, which introduces a degree of nonsampling error that cannot be estimated.

Our results generalize to the adult imprisoned population of federal ($N = 129,299$) and state ($N = 1,226,171$) inmates as of January 2004. Thus our analysis excludes inmates held in local jails (generally pretrial detainees and offenders sentenced to less than one year), who account for about one-third of all inmates incarcerated in the United States on any given day. Hence, we stress that this chapter assesses the effects of U.S.

imprisonment rather than total U.S. *incarceration* as a whole (i.e., also including jails).

We define our sample of drug offenders as the $n = 4,572$ respondents with a primary drug offense plus an additional $n = 135$ "nondrug" cases (e.g., conspiracy, racketeering, weapons) that were clearly drug related according to additional incident characteristic information. For certain analyses, we use a subsample of drug offenders ($n = 4,211$), because $n = 496$ respondents with a controlling drug offense were erroneously never asked the survey's drug offense incident characteristic questions (which collect information on drug type and quantity, role in the offense, and organizational involvement).

Ethnic/National Identity and Imprisonment for Drug Crimes

In total, we estimate that there were 335,550 drug offenders imprisoned in the United States in 2004, representing one-quarter (24.8 percent) of the 1.36 million federal and state inmates. Proportionately, more federal (57.3 percent) than state (21.3 percent) inmates were incarcerated for a drug crime, but in absolute terms the great majority of drug offenders were held in state (78 percent) versus federal (22 percent) prisons.

We distinguish ethnic/national identity as follows: (1) U.S. citizens with no Mexican ancestry (i.e., "non-Mexican Americans"); (2) U.S.-born or naturalized citizens of Mexican ancestry (i.e., "Mexican Americans"); (3) citizens of Mexico who are not also U.S. citizens (i.e., "Mexican Nationals"); and (4) others who are citizens of neither Mexico nor the United States (i.e., "Other Foreign Nationals").

According to this categorization, the majority in prison were non-Mexican Americans (84.7 percent), followed by Mexican Americans (9.0 percent), Mexican Nationals (3.2 percent), and Other Foreign Nationals (3.1 percent). Note that these groups are not monolithic; non-Mexican American, for example, includes blacks, whites, and other non-Mexican Hispanics, among others.

Both the proportion of inmates convicted of a drug offense and the seriousness of the conviction offense differ by ethnic/national identity. As shown in table 11.1, the proportion of federal inmates incarcerated for a drug law violation ranges from half for Mexican Nationals to nearly seven in ten for Mexican Americans. Among drug offenders, U.S. citizens were relatively more likely to be convicted of drug trafficking/sales, whereas Mexican Nationals and Other Foreign Nationals were more likely to be

Table 11.1. Conviction offense by ethnic/national identity, federal inmates, 2004

Conviction offense	Non-Mexican Americans	Mexican Americans	Mexican Nationals	Other Foreign Nationals	Total
Drug offense	55.5	68.9	50.0	68.4	57.3
Trafficking/Sales	77.6	79.1	70.8	68.8	76.3
Possession w/intent	13.8	11.9	14.0	12.8	13.5
Simple possession	3.6	4.2	12.4	8.9	4.8
Other/Unknown	5.0	4.9	2.8	9.4	5.3
Nondrug offense	44.5	31.1	50.0	31.6	42.7
N	99,682	8,705	8,831	12,081	129,999

Source: Bureau of Justice Statistics. http://bjs.gov/index.cfm?ty=tp&tid=13.

convicted of, respectively, simple possession and other drug offenses (mainly conspiracy and racketeering).

The state-level data reveal a different distribution. As table 11.2 shows, the proportion of inmates incarcerated for a drug offense ranged from about one-fifth of Mexican Americans to one-quarter of Mexican Nationals. In contrast to federal inmates, Mexican Americans in state prisons had the least serious drug conviction profile, with about one-half sentenced for trafficking/sales and one-third for simple possession. Other Foreign Nationals, on the other hand, had the most serious drug conviction profile with the greatest percentage convicted of trafficking/sales and the smallest percentage convicted of simple possession.

Mexican prisons are notoriously porous (e.g., Stevenson 2010), so imprisoning Mexican traffickers in U.S. rather than Mexican prisons ought to be good for Mexico. The question of how many Mexican Nationals are imprisoned in the United States versus Mexico has not been answered before. Our estimates, presented in table 11.3, suggest that almost one-fifth (18.4 percent) of the Mexican Nationals who were in prison for any crime in 2004 were incarcerated in the United States.[10] For drug offenses, the share is larger, about one-quarter (25.9 percent), which would grow even larger were jail inmates included in the analysis. Even so, it is striking that one out of every four Mexicans imprisoned for a drug offense is serving that time in a U.S. facility.

Still, Mexican Nationals account for only 4 percent of all people imprisoned in the United States for drug law violations. That is rather surprising in light of Mexico's role in supplying U.S. drug markets, which suggests that Mexican drug organizations do not vertically integrate very far down into domestic U.S. drug distribution networks.

Table 11.2. Conviction offense by ethnic/national identity, state inmates, 2004

Conviction offense	Non-Mexican Americans	Mexican Americans	Mexican Nationals	Other Foreign Nationals	Total
Drug offense	21.4	19.9	24.3	21.8	21.3
Trafficking/Sales	57.5	51.7	58.1	71.3	57.3
Possession w/intent	12.7	10.5	13.8	9.3	12.4
Simple possession	26.4	33.4	27.0	19.4	26.8
Other/Unknown	2.5	4.4	1.1	0.0	3.4
Nondrug offense	78.6	80.1	75.7	78.2	78.7
N	1,048,703	112,929	34,144	30,395	1,226,171

Source: Bureau of Justice Statistics. http://bjs.gov/index.cfm?ty=tp&tid=13.

Table 11.3. Estimating the proportion of incarcerated Mexican nationals held in U.S. versus Mexican prisons, 2004

	Number of Mexican Nationals in Prison for All Crimes	Percentage of Mexican Nationals in Prison for a Drug Crime	Number of Mexican Nationals in Prison for a Drug Crime
United States			
Federal	8,831	50.0	4,418
State	34,144	24.3	8,309
Total	42,975	29.6	12,727
Mexico			
Federal	49,442	51.0	25,215
State	140,721	8.0	11,258
Total	190,163	19.2	36,473
Total U.S. share	18.4%	—	25.9%

Source: See Caulkins and Sevigny (2010) for the derivation of these figures.

However, those imprisoned for drug law violations in the United States are a heterogeneous group, and most are not kingpins (Sevigny and Caulkins 2004). So, it could still be that Mexican Nationals and/or Mexican Americans play a disproportionate role in the highest-level, most organized, and/or most violent aspects of drug distribution in the United States, even if their aggregate numbers in prison are not overwhelming. We explore these possibilities in the next sections.

Market Indicators: Drug Type, Quantity, and Purity

We first examine ethnic/national differences in drug market characteristics, focusing on the type and quantity of drugs involved for the five major drugs of abuse (i.e., heroin, methamphetamine, powder cocaine, crack cocaine, and marijuana). In addition, we examine data on purity for heroin and powder cocaine (the SISFCF does not ask about purity for other drugs). These data are presented in table 11.4.

Overall, nearly two-thirds of the drug inmates were involved with cocaine, whether powder (32 percent) or crack (33 percent). Methamphetamine offenders accounted for almost one-fifth (19 percent), with marijuana (13 percent) and heroin (10 percent) rounding out the bottom half.[11] Although all groups were to some extent involved with each of these drugs, our findings confirm some well-recognized links between ethnic/national identity and trafficking in particular drugs: non-Mexican Americans with crack cocaine, Mexican Americans with methamphetamine and marijuana, Mexican Nationals with methamphetamine and powder cocaine, and Other Foreign Nationals with heroin and powder cocaine.

In terms of quantity and purity, foreign nationals sit atop the distribution hierarchy, followed in turn by Mexican Americans and non-Mexican Americans. Indeed, with certain predictable exceptions, Foreign Nationals tended to traffic in pounds and kilograms of product that was (for heroin and cocaine) upward of 80 percent pure. Conversely, U.S. citizens tended to deal in grams and ounces with purities less than 80 percent.

Role in the Offense

The inmate survey asks respondents a series of questions about their individual role in the offense at the time of arrest. From these questions, we constructed a single measure of the most serious role reported based on a generally accepted hierarchy of culpability (Sevigny and Caulkins 2004; United States Sentencing Commission 2007). Results are presented in table 11.5.

Although enforcement pressure and prison risk vary by level of involvement in the drug trade, the role in the offense follows a classic pyramidal

Table 11.4. Select drug market indicators by ethnic/national identity, federal and state drug inmates, 2004

Drug market indicator[a]	Non-Mexican Americans	Mexican Americans	Mexican Nationals	Other Foreign Nationals	Total
Heroin offender (Col. %)	9.6	13.5	13.4	17.2	10.4
Heroin quantity (median)	3.5	3.0	2.0	207.0	3.5
Heroin purity (median)	60.0	50.0	50.0	98.0	60.0
Methamphetamine offender (Col. %)	17.5	31.5	30.3	3.8	18.6
Methamphetamine quantity (median)	10.0	28.4	453.6	32.0	15.6
Powder cocaine offender (Col. %)	29.2	34.9	42.7	60.1	31.6
Powder cocaine quantity (median)	29.9	28.4	498.0	1,000.0	56.0
Powder cocaine purity (median)	67.0	79.0	80.0	85.0	70.0
Crack cocaine offender (Col. %)	37.8	9.9	8.5	13.4	33.3
Crack cocaine quantity (median)	4.0	14.0	907.2	90.0	5.0
Marijuana offender (Col. %)	12.5	18.4	10.5	10.2	12.8
Marijuana quantity (median)	28.9	2,722	90,718	153,000	99.0
N	250,601	25,454	10,718	13,140	299,913

[a] Percentages for drug type may total greater than 100 percent because multiple drugs could be reported. Drug quantities are expressed in grams. All calculations are based on non-missing data, the amount of which varies by indicator.

distribution: relatively few high-level traffickers (10.4 percent being importers, producers, or financiers), more mid-level distributors (13 percent being wholesalers), and far greater numbers of low-level sellers/handlers (35 percent being retailers, couriers, mules, etc.). The exception to this is that possessors were not incarcerated in numbers sufficient to support the distributional hierarchy (especially since a nontrivial number report "possessing" very large quantities that belie this low-level status). Last, quite a

Table 11.5. Role in the offense at time of arrest by ethnic/national identity, federal and state drug inmates, 2004

Highest Role in the Offense	Non-Mexican Americans	Mexican Americans	Mexican Nationals	Other Foreign Nationals	Total
Importer	1.7	5.6	4.0	9.9	2.5
Producer	7.8	2.2	2.8	0.2	6.8
Money launderer	1.1	1.1	0.1	0.8	1.1
Wholesaler	13.1	11.0	14.9	13.3	13.0
Retailer	32.3	18.2	19.2	12.2	29.8
Courier/Mule/ Loader	4.1	8.0	12.9	15.2	5.2
Possessor	24.2	38.1	20.3	14.5	24.8
Unspecified role	15.6	15.8	25.9	34.0	16.8
N	250,601	25,454	10,718	13,140	299,913

Source: Bureau of Justice Statistics. http://bjs.gov/index.cfm?ty=tp&tid=13.

few offenders failed to identify a specific role, which is a function of poor questionnaire design.

Not surprisingly, the role in the offense varies by ethnic/national identity. Several points from table 11.5 are worth mentioning. First, non-Mexican Americans are much less likely than the other ethnic/national groups to be directly involved with importing drugs into the United States, whereas the opposite is true regarding the production or manufacturing of illegal drugs. In other words, these data show that relatively few non-Mexican Americans directly facilitate the cross-border movement of drugs into the United States; conversely, relatively few Foreign Nationals (and Mexican Americans, for that matter) set up illegal growing, cooking, or manufacturing operations in the United States. Second, U.S. citizens are more likely than Foreign Nationals to be money launderers. Third, all groups are involved in U.S. wholesale distribution to an important degree. While hardly noteworthy for U.S. citizens, the sizable share of Mexican and Other Foreign National wholesalers suggests that they maintain some amount of command and control over large-quantity drug transactions within U.S. borders. Fourth, although non-Mexican Americans dominate retail drug distribution, both in relative and absolute numbers, the fact that one out of five of the imprisoned Mexican National drug offenders and one out of eight other Foreign Nationals were involved in retail drug selling indicates some penetration into U.S. retail markets, even if together they account for just 4 percent of all retailers. Fifth, one out of four Other

Foreign Nationals were directly involved with transporting drugs into the United States either as a high-level importers or low-level movers/handlers, but Mexican Nationals and Mexican Americans also played substantial roles in the cross-border transit of drugs (17 percent and 14 percent, respectively). However, Mexican Nationals were more typically employed as low-level couriers/mules/loaders. Sixth, Mexican Americans were much more likely than other groups to report being simple possessors of drugs.

Organizational Involvement

Table 11.6 shows that no more than one out of ten drug offenders viewed herself or himself as being part of a DTO in the year prior to her or his arrest. What is more, Mexican Nationals were about half as likely to report an association with a DTO as were the other ethnic/national groups—an unexpected finding given their prominent role both as couriers/mules/loaders and large-quantity traffickers. This also is at odds with media and government reports of violent and large-scale DTOs controlling the Mexican drug trade. It is more consistent with the idea that drug trafficking is conducted by many individual entrepreneurs and small groups of traffickers networking and cooperating as needed (Eck and Gersh 2000). An alternative story is that DTOs, particularly Mexican DTOs, are adept at

Table 11.6. DTO involvement in the year prior to arrest by ethnic/national identity, federal and state drug inmates, 2004

Organizational involvement	Non-Mexican Americans	Mexican Americans	Mexican Nationals	Other Foreign Nationals	Total
Drug group member	8.1	9.4	4.8	10.5	8.2
Leader/Organizer	27.0	19.5	34.9	16.1	25.8
Middleman	21.0	16.8	21.5	12.1	20.1
Seller	29.9	15.6	18.8	13.4	27.4
Underling	12.4	28.5	3.2	51.3	16.0
Other role	9.7	19.7	21.6	7.2	10.8
No drug group involvement	91.0	90.2	94.0	88.6	90.0
Missing data	0.9	0.4	1.1	1.0	0.9
N	250,601	25,454	10,718	13,140	299,913

Source: Bureau of Justice Statistics, http://bjs.gov/index.cfm?ty=tp&tid=13.

avoiding law enforcement which, given the extent of corruption in Mexico, is not implausible.

Weapons Involvement

Media accounts and government reports have emphasized the recent spate of drug-related violence in Mexico (Beittel 2009). Fueling this violence is a flow of guns and money heading south, just as illegal immigrants and drugs flow north. Recent data reveal that 87–90 percent of guns seized in Mexico and submitted for tracing to the ATF originate in the United States (Chu and Krouse 2009; Government Accountability Office 2009). Although the 2004 SISFCF predates both the recent trends in violence and the stepped-up enforcement of gun trafficking along the southwest border, the data might provide an early or a baseline assessment of the U.S.–Mexican drug–gun connection. We examined several indicators of weapon involvement by ethnic/national identity for both drug and nondrug offenders.

Overall, Mexican National drug offenders were no more likely than both non-Mexican and Mexican American drug offenders to be involved with firearms (13 percent versus 14–16 percent). Furthermore, Mexican Nationals convicted of other (nondrug) crimes were actually less likely overall than the other groups to be weapon involved (22 percent versus 27–34 percent). Inasmuch as Mexican Nationals were rarely convicted of crimes indicative of gun trafficking (i.e., nondrug offenders with a current weapon conviction), it appears that weapon involvement among Mexican Nationals, like the other groups, is more a product of general criminality than of any major involvement with gun trafficking.

Conclusions

Mexico plays a prominent role in producing and transshipping drugs that are consumed in the United States, a role that generates considerable harm in Mexico. Legalizing all drugs in the United States would solve most of Mexico's problems with drug trafficking, but U.S. public opinion remains sharply opposed to legalizing cocaine and other "hard" drugs. Furthermore, from the U.S. perspective, legalizing all drugs would be at best a risky gamble (Caulkins and Lee 2012), so U.S. and Mexican interests diverge with respect to legalization.

The idea of legalizing just marijuana is gathering increasing support in the United States, with public opinion now roughly evenly divided on the question, but legalizing only marijuana would not decisively change conditions in Mexico.

Decriminalization, which some might informally think of as being "halfway" between prohibition and legalization, would not solve half of Mexico's drug problems that derive from U.S. demand; indeed, it would likely make matters worse. Furthermore, while Mexico has a vested interest in seeing the United States expand its demand control efforts, conventional demand control can only chip away at the market over time, not cut it down fast enough to solve Mexico's immediate crisis. Paradoxically, although the U.S. prohibition causes most of Mexico's drug problems, Mexico would not necessarily benefit from the United States scaling back on its aggressive domestic supply control efforts.

Incarceration is a particularly pronounced component of U.S. drug policy, and both Mexican Americans and Mexican Nationals living in the United States are exposed to that heightened risk of imprisonment. Indeed, both groups are somewhat overrepresented in American prisons for drug law violations, but that overrepresentation is very modest compared to the overrepresentation of African Americans. Over 90 percent of the burden of imprisonment for violating U.S. drug laws falls on U.S. citizens, and the share falling on Mexican Americans (8.5 percent) is not highly inconsistent with the Mexican American share of the U.S. population (6.1 percent).

We compared various characteristics of drug inmates across four ethnic/national groups: non-Mexican Americans, Mexican Americans, Mexican Nationals, and Other Foreign Nationals. Predictably, non-Mexican Americans were overrepresented among those who grew or manufactured drugs within the United States, whereas the other groups were overrepresented among importers. However, in most other respects, Mexican American drug inmates looked much like their fellow citizens who were not of Mexican ancestry. In contrast, noncitizens, whether nationals of Mexico or another country, were much more likely than American citizens to be involved with larger quantities and higher purities of drugs.

Large-scale drug importation is often associated with large and violent drug trafficking organizations. However, the noncitizen inmates—both Mexican Nationals and others—did not report rates of organizational membership or weapons involvement that stood out from those of U.S. citizens. That is, only a small minority (roughly 10 percent) reported being part of an organization, and a comparably small proportion was weapon involved. One interpretation of this would be that some of the worst behaviors of

Mexican drug trafficking organizations stay primarily on the Mexican side of the U.S.–Mexican border, but it could also reflect the age of the data (collected in 2004), unwillingness to report, or success of the largest and most violent organizations at avoiding incarceration.

From a Mexican perspective, this analysis dashes hopes that the actions of the United States will greatly ameliorate the problems that U.S. drug demand causes for Mexico. The one thing that would make a substantial difference (legalization of the expensive illegal drugs—cocaine/crack, heroin, and methamphetamine) is not politically plausible. Scaling back on the extreme levels of imprisonment for drug law violations may be plausible; after all, letting 90 percent of drug law violators out of prison would still leave imprisonment rates at the levels of the first Reagan administration. However, it is not clear whether reducing incarceration would help Mexico, and, at any rate, most of the inmates are American citizens, so American policy makers could be excused for thinking of drug sentencing as primarily a domestic issue to be determined by domestic imperatives.

Nevertheless, precisely because such a relatively modest proportion of U.S. drug inmates are foreign nationals and/or were directly involved in importation, a substantial change in sentencing policies toward those groups could be accomplished without altering the basic stance of American drug policy. Hence, if policy makers believed that such a policy change would materially benefit Mexico (as well as the United States), it might be possible to implement such reform in the absence of a major shift in U.S. policy.[12]

Notes

1. The other major drug category is diverted pharmaceuticals, which account for a startling share of overdoses (Substance Abuse and Mental Health Services Administration 2008), but they are not importantly implicated in Mexican drug trafficking.

2. Speculation abounds and figures are produced, but they are methodologically suspect. Agnosticism is probably the most scientifically defensible position at this point.

3. Note that various indicators suggest that since Kilmer et al.'s (2010) analysis, the U.S. domestic production share of the U.S. marijuana market has been increasing, perhaps rapidly, so marijuana's importance for DTOs' revenues may have declined relative to what the figures cited earlier would suggest.

4. Marijuana, as usual, is a special case, in this instance because it is produced in final market countries. If marijuana decriminalization extended to legalizing production for personal use, the net effects of increased use and increased domestic production on demand for imported marijuana are ambiguous. There is no practical analog for cocaine, heroin, or methamphetamine.

5. Indeed, Mexico should be happy that the United States is so aggressive about incarcerating nondrug offenders as well, since many are drug users, and incarcerating them incapacitates some portion of U.S. demand.

6. Short of legalization, no plausible easing of enforcement against cocaine or heroin would make its production practical in the United States. Methamphetamine is manufactured, not derived from plants, and marijuana can profitably be grown indoors because it can generate over $1,000 in retail value per square foot of growing area versus more like $5 per square foot for coca bushes and poppy plants as conventionally cultivated.

7. This traditional view has been challenged (Paoli, Greenfield, and Reuter 2009). The argument is that estimated U.S. consumption (twenty-two tons) greatly exceeds estimated South and Central American production (perhaps ten tons). However, given the frailty of both consumption and production estimates, we remain persuaded by the fact that heroin seized in the United States rarely displays the chemical "signature" of Southwest or Southeast Asian production.

8. We examine federal and state drug inmates together out of concern for both space limitations and data sparseness.

9. Even though the 2004 Survey of Inmates in State and Federal Correctional Facilities (SISFCF) is the most recent available, one caveat is that the data are already eight years old. The Mexican drug trade has become particularly violent in recent years; most of this increase has occurred in just the last five years (Trans-Border Institute 2010). It will therefore be useful to replicate these analyses when data from the 2012 administration of the SISFCF become available to researchers.

10. The comparable figure for Canadian Nationals is 1.8 percent.

11. Because 11.2 percent of respondents reported involvement with multiple drugs, these data are not mutually exclusive, and reported figures do not total 100 percent.

12. This chapter is an abbreviated and updated version of Caulkins and Sevigny (2010). We acknowledge and thank Sidney Weintraub and the Center for Strategic and International Studies for support of the original version.

Bibliography

Amato, Laura, Marina Davoli, Carlo A. Perucci, Marica Ferri, Fabrizio Faggiano, and Richard P. Mattick. 2005. "An Overview of Systematic Reviews of the Effectiveness of Opiate Maintenance Therapies: Available Evidence to Inform Clinical Practice and Research." *Journal of Substance Abuse Treatment* 28: 321–30.

Babor, Thomas, Jonathan Caulkins, Griffith Edwards, David Foxcroft, Keith Humphreys, Maria Medina Mora, Isidore Obot, Jurgen Rehm, Peter Reuter, Robin Room, Ingeborg Rossow, and John Strang. 2010. *Drug Policy and the Public Good.* New York: Oxford University Press.

Becker, Gary S., Kevin M. Murphy, and Michael Grossman. 2006. "The Market for Illegal Goods: The Case of Drugs." *Journal of Political Economy* 114, no.1: 36–60.

Beittel, June. 2009. *Mexico's Drug-Related Violence.* Washington, DC: Congressional Research Service.

Belenko, Steven, Nicholas Patapsis, and Michael T. French, eds. 2005. *Economic Benefits of Drug Treatment: A Critical Review of the Evidence for Policy Makers.*

Philadelphia: Treatment Research Institute at the University of Pennsylvania. http://www.tresearch.org/resources/specials/2005Feb_EconomicBenefits.pdf. Accessed November 9, 2009.

Blumstein, Alfred, and Alan J. Beck. 1999. "Population Growth in U.S. Prisons, 1980–1996." In *Crime and Justice*, edited by Michael Tonry and Joan Petersilia, 17–61. Chicago: University of Chicago Press.

Brouwer, Kimberly C., Patricia Case, Rebeca Ramos, Carlos Magis-Rodríguez, Jesús Bucardo, Thomas L. Patterson, and Steffanie A. Strathdee. 2006. "Trends in Production, Trafficking, and Consumption of Methamphetamine and Cocaine in Mexico." *Substance Use and Misuse* 41: 707–27.

Bureau of Justice Statistics. 2007. "Survey of Inmates in State and Federal Correctional Facilities, 2004 [Computer file]." ICPSR04572-v1. Ann Arbor, MI: Interuniversity Consortium for Political and Social Research.

Cartwright, William S. 2000. "Cost-Benefit Analysis of Drug Treatment Services: A Review of the Literature." *Journal of Mental Health Policy Economics* 3: 11–26.

Caulkins, Jonathan P. 2009. "Illicit Substance Abuse and Addiction." In *Investing in the Disadvantaged: Assessing the Benefits and Costs of Social Policies*, edited by David L. Weimer and Aidan R. Vining, 83–102. Washington, DC: Georgetown University Press.

Caulkins, Jonathan P., and Robert L. DuPont. 2010. "Is 24/7 Sobriety a Good Goal for Repeat DUI Offenders?" *Addiction* 105: 575–77.

Caulkins, Jonathan P., Angela Hawken, Beau Kilmer, and Mark A. R. Kleiman. 2012. *Marijuana Legalization: What Everyone Needs to Know*. New York: Oxford University Press.

Caulkins, Jonathan P., and Mark A. R. Kleiman. 2011. "Drugs and Crime." In *Oxford Handbook of Crime and Criminal Justice*, edited by Michael Tonry, 275–320. New York: Oxford University Press.

Caulkins, Jonathan P., and Michael A. C. Lee. 2012. "The Drug-Policy Roulette." *National Affairs* 12: 35–51.

Caulkins, Jonathan P., Rosalie Pacula, Susan Paddock, and James Chiesa. 2002. *School-Based Drug Prevention: What Kind of Drug Use Does It Prevent?* Santa Monica, CA: Rand Corporation.

Caulkins, Jonathan P., and Rema Padman. 1993. "Interdiction's Impact on the Structure and Behavior of the Export-Import Sector for Illicit Drugs." *Zeitschrift fur Operations Research* 37: 207–24.

Caulkins, Jonathan P., and Peter Reuter. 1998. "What Price Data Tell Us About Drug Markets." *Journal of Drug Issues* 28: 593–612.

——. 2006. "Reorienting U.S. Drug Policy." *Issues in Science and Technology* 23, no. 1: 79–85.

——. 2010. "How Drug Enforcement Affects Drug Prices." In *Crime and Justice—A Review of Research*, vol. 39, edited by Michael Tonry, 213–72. Chicago: University of Chicago Press.

Caulkins, Jonathan P., and Eric Sevigny. 2010. "The Effects of Drug Enforcement and Imprisonment on Source Countries: The Case of the U.S. and Mexico." Appendix C in *Cooperative Mexico–U.S. Antinarcotics Efforts*, edited by Sidney Weintraub and Duncan Wood, 99–127. Washington, DC: Center for Strategic and International Studies.

Chu, Vivian, and William Krouse. 2009. *Gun Trafficking and the Southwest Border.* Washington, DC: Congressional Research Service.

Drug Availability Steering Committee. 2002. *Drug Availability Estimates in the United States.* Washington, DC: U.S. Government Printing Office.

Durlauf, Steven N., and Daniel Nagin. 2010. "The Deterrent Effect of Imprisonment." In *Controlling Crime: Strategies and Tradeoffs,* edited by Philip J. Cook, Jens Ludwig, and Justin McCrary, 43–94. Chicago: University of Chicago Press.

Eck, John, and Jeffrey Gersh. 2000. "Drug Trafficking as a Cottage Industry." In *Illegal Drug Markets: From Research to Prevention Policy,* edited by Mangai Natarajan and Mike Hough, 241–71. Monsey, NY: Criminal Justice Press.

Economist. 2012. "Narconomics: From HR to CSR: Management Lessons from Mexico's Drug Lords," July 28.

Fries, Arthur, Robert W. Anthony, Andrew Cseko Jr., Carl C. Gaither, and Eric Schulman. 2008. *The Price and Purity of Illicit Drugs: 1981–2007.* Alexandria, VA: Institute for Defense Analysis.

Galbraith, John W., and Murray Kaiserman. 1997. "Taxation, Smuggling, and Demand for Cigarettes in Canada: Evidence from Time-Series Data." *Journal of Health Economics* 16: 287–301.

Government Accountability Office. 2009. *Firearms Trafficking: U.S. Efforts to Combat Arms Trafficking to Mexico Face Planning and Coordination Challenges.* Washington, DC: United States Government Accountability Office. http://www.gao.gov /assets/130/122818.pdf. Accessed November 9, 2009.

Grossman, Michael. 2005. "Individual Behaviours and Substance Use: The Role of Price." In *Substance Use: Individual Behaviour, Social Interactions, Markets, and Politics, Advances in Health Economics and Health Services Research,* vol. 16, edited by B. Lindgren and M. Grossman, 407–39. Amsterdam: Elsevier.

Harwood, Henrick J., Deepti Malhrota, Christel Villarivera, Connie Liu, Umi Chong, and Jawaria Gilani. 2002. *Cost Effectiveness and Cost Benefit Analysis of Substance Abuse Treatment: A Literature Review.* Washington, DC: U.S. Department of Health and Human Services, SAMHSA.

Hawken Angela. 2010. "A Behavioral Triage Model for Identifying and Treating Substance-Abusing Offenders." *Journal of Drug Policy Analysis* 3, no. 1: 1.

Hawken, Angela, and Mark Kleiman. 2007. "H.O.P.E. for Reform: What a Novel Probation Program in Hawaii Might Teach Other States." *American Prospect* Online, April 10. http://www.prospect.org/cs/articles?article=hope_for_reform. Accessed November 12, 2009.

Kennedy, David M. 2008. *Deterrence and Crime Prevention: Reconsidering the Prospect of Sanction.* Abingdon, UK, and New York: Routledge.

Kilmer, Beau, Jonathan P. Caulkins, Rosalie Liccardo Pacula, Robert MacCoun, and Peter Reuter. 2010. *Altered State? Assessing How Marijuana Legalization in California Could Influence Marijuana Consumption and Public Budgets.* Santa Monica, CA: Rand Corporation.

Kleiman, Mark A. R. 1992. *Against Excess: Drug Policy for Results.* New York: Basic Books.

———. 2009. *When Brute Force Fails: Strategy for Crime Control.* Princeton, NJ: Princeton University Press.

Kleiman, Mark A. R., Jonathan P. Caulkins, and Angela Hawken. 2011. *Drugs and Drug Policy: What Everyone Needs to Know.* New York: Oxford University Press.

Kuhn, André. 2001. "Incarcerations Rates across the World." In *Penal Reform in Overcrowded Times,* edited by Michael Tonry, 101–14. New York: Oxford University Press.

Kuziemko, Ilyana, and Steven D. Levitt. 2004. "An Empirical Analysis of Imprisoning Drug Offenders." *Journal of Public Economics* 88: 2043–66.

MacCoun, Robert, and Peter Reuter. 2001. *Drug War Heresies.* New York: Cambridge University Press.

Manski, Charles F., John V. Pepper, and Yonette F. Thomas, eds. 1999. *Assessment of Two Cost-Effectiveness Studies on Cocaine Control Policy.* Washington, DC: National Academy Press.

Mauer, Marc. 2001. "The Causes and Consequences of Prison Growth in the United States." *Punishment and Society* 3: 9–20.

McLellan, A. Thomas, James R. McKay, Robert Forman, John Cacciola, and Jack Kemp. 2005. "Reconsidering the Evaluation of Addiction Treatment: From Retrospective Follow-up to Concurrent Recovery Monitoring." *Addiction* 100: 447–58.

Merriman, David. 2010. "The Micro-Geography of Tax Avoidance: Evidence from Littered Cigarette Packs in Chicago." *American Economic Journal: Economic Policy* 2: 61–84.

Miller, T., and D. Hendrie. 2009. *Substance Abuse Prevention Dollars and Cents: A Cost-Benefit Analysis.* Rockville, MD: Center for Substance Abuse Prevention, Substance Abuse and Mental Health Services Administration.

Miron, Jeffrey A. 2003. "The Effect of Drug Prohibition on Drug Prices: Evidence from the Markets for Cocaine and Heroin." *Review of Economics and Statistics* 85, no. 3: 522–30.

Office of National Drug Control Policy (ONDCP). 2001. *What America's Users Spend on Illegal Drugs.* Washington, DC: The White House.

———. 2003. *Drug Data Summary.* Washington, DC: The White House.

———. 2004. *The Economic Costs of Drug Abuse in the United States, 1992–2002.* Washington, DC: The White House.

Paoli, Letizia, Victoria Greenfield, and Peter Reuter. 2009. *The World Heroin Market: Can Supply Be Cut?* New York: Oxford University Press.

Pollack, Harold, Peter Reuter, and Eric Sevigny. 2011. "If Drug Treatment Works So Well, Why Are So Many Drug Users in Prison?" In *Controlling Crime: Strategies and Tradeoffs,* edited by Philip J. Cook, Jens Ludwig, and Justin McCrary, 125–60. Chicago: University of Chicago Press.

Reuter, Peter. 2009. "Systemic Violence in Drug Markets." *Crime, Law, and Social Change* 52, no. 3: 275–84.

Room, Robin, Benedikt Fischer, Wayne Hall, Simon Lenton, and Peter Reuter. 2010. *Cannabis: Moving Beyond the Stalemate.* New York: Oxford University Press.

Rydell, C. Peter, and Susan S. Everingham. 1994. *Controlling Cocaine. Supply versus Demand Programs.* Santa Monica, CA: Rand Corporation.

Sevigny, Eric, and Jonathan P. Caulkins. 2004. "Kingpins or Mules? An Analysis of Drug Offenders Incarcerated in Federal and State Prisons." *Criminology and Public Policy* 3, no. 3: 401–34.

Stevenson, Mark. 2010. "Mexico: Prison Guards Let Killers Out, Lent Guns." *Washington Post*, July 25.

Substance Abuse and Mental Health Services Administration (SAMHSA). 2008. *Drug Abuse Warning Network, 2006: National Estimates of Drug-Related Emergency Department Visits*. Rockville, MD: Author.

Trans-Border Institute. 2010. *Drug Violence in Mexico: Data and Analysis from 2001–2009*. San Diego, CA: Justice in Mexico Project, University of San Diego.

United Nations Office on Drugs and Crime (UNODC). 2008, 2009. *World Drug Report*. New York: Oxford University Press.

United States Sentencing Commission (USSC). 2007. *Special Report to Congress: Cocaine and Federal Sentencing Policy*. Washington, DC: Author.

A War That Can't Be Won?

Tony Payan and Kathleen Staudt

Introduction

In this volume a group of both Mexican and U.S. scholars analyzed the war on drugs and presented nuanced evidence from both sides of the border about the complexity of "fighting" clean wars on drugs. The chapters written by these scholars bring a special vantage point to the study of drug wars that heretofore has not existed, that is, a binational U.S.–Mexican perspective, emphasizing the "consequences" of an increasingly militarized conflict. We wanted to do so because we know that the war on drugs knows no borders and it has to be understood as a transnational phenomenon in its causes and consequences. Through this binational and borderlands perspective, the overall lesson of this volume is that the drug war wreaks special consequences on the borderlands of northern Mexico and the southwestern United States. In effect, the death toll has been staggering, reaching nearly one hundred thousand deaths in Mexico alone, by some accounts. It is also clear that most do not know how to "end" the war on drugs. There appears to be no clear "exit" strategy in sight, and there is no clear measure of "success."

Consequently, most chapters stopped short of advocating a position on the drug war itself or on changing policy toward illegal drugs, whether that change involved decriminalization or outright legalization with a regulatory and taxation system behind it. Here we aim to sort through some of the key implications that contributing analysts have sketched in this volume for shaping new ways of thinking about drug wars and drug policies in Mexico and the United States and at the national, state, and local/municipal levels in both countries.

We begin with an assessment of where we are now, a forty-plus-year drug war, overwhelmingly dominated by U.S. priorities, strategies, and tactics, and with a far-reaching agenda that radiates in both bilateral and multilateral directions, including to the United Nations. Our intention is to analyze various gradual steps to "de-Americanize" the war on drugs, something suggested by Bollinger in 1994. The "war on drugs" is considered so cliché that even the White House in 2009 sought a name change to remove the war terminology (*Wall Street Journal* 2009; *Drug Reporter* 2012), and President Obama is seeking alternatives to de-escalate it without "expecting miracles," as he put it in his customary restrained approach (*Daily Beast* 2012). In the second section we examine the role that bureaucracies play in creating and maintaining the war on drugs. Many government agencies have become materially and ideologically vested in the status quo and appear prepared to lobby hard to maintain the prohibitionist regime and preclude any alternative approaches, believing that they stand to lose much under a new drug regime. In a third section, we examine the emerging resistance to U.S. drug policy in Latin America. As it has become clear, several important Latin American nations are beginning to resist this fundamentally American prohibitionist policy. Several Latin American presidents and former presidents have in fact called for alternative options. Fourth, we draw important conclusions about the costs of the militarization of the U.S.–Mexican border, largely driven by the war on drugs. Finally, we deal with alternatives to the war on drugs. These alternatives are not easy by any means, and some are quite controversial. Moreover, depending on the alternative offered, the implications for law enforcement, regulation, taxation, and opportunities for crime are important and deserve to be thoroughly debated.

The War on Drugs at Age Forty-Plus

In September 2009 a conference on the war on drugs took place in El Paso, Texas (see http://warondrugsconference.utep.edu). Policy makers, health professionals, academics, journalists, and the general public were invited. During the two-day conference and numerous presentations, the attendees debated the record of the drug war at age forty-plus. The old adage "where you stand depends on where you sit" was in full display. Government officials, such as Drug Enforcement Administration (DEA) administrator Anthony Placido, argued—amid PowerPoint slides with multicolor photos of supposed marijuana-induced brain damage—that alternatives to the war on drugs were not likely to resolve this thorny policy problem and that policy continuity, with greater vigor, was what the country needed. Any failures of the war on drugs, he implied, could potentially be attributed to the fact that the government had not been tough enough. What he proposed amounted to an escalation of the war on drugs. This approach continues to prevail today, although public opinion is divided (Caulkins, Hawken, Kilmer, and Kleiman 2012). Health officials, such as Dr. Westley Clark, argued that drug addiction should be decriminalized and treated as a public health issue. And this position has an increasing number of advocates (Cohen 2004). Some activists, including many associated with the group Law Enforcement Against Prohibition (http://www .leap.cc), such as former Judge James P. Gray (2001) and Terry Nelson, a former law enforcement official, argued that the current policy had failed and that it was time to try new approaches, including legalization. Journalists Angela Kocherga and Alfredo Corchado put on display the heavy costs of the war on drugs, counted in executions and bodies, both in Mexico and on the U.S.–Mexican border. The numbers were staggering—some calculate nearly one hundred thousand violent deaths in Mexico alone. Academics offered comparative and historical analyses, such as Craig Reinarman's, showing lower incidence rates in the Netherlands than in California's Bay Area, and David Courtwright, illustrating the global shifts in policy approaches over centuries. The general lesson drawn from that war on drugs conference in 2009 was a surprising consensus that drug policy is failing to do what the U.S. government had promised it would do and that the costs were reaching an unsustainable state. It was also agreed that alternative policies were needed, but few such alternatives emerged from the conference and few have been put forth after that, except for the occasional call for legalization (O'Rourke and Byrd 2011), a term increasingly being displaced by the words "regulation and taxation." An important conclusion is that the war on drugs has reached a stalemate but is also at a loss over where to go next. A curious twist in this debate is the recent idea that the cartels themselves fear the legalization of drugs, given the massive loss of income that they would suffer if marijuana were legalized in the United States (Washington-Valdez 2012).

In the meantime, Mexico has decriminalized the possession of small amounts of drugs. Even if this decriminalization strategy was directed at preventing corrupt law enforcement officials from extorting money from illegal drug consumers—more effectively targeting corruption by decreasing opportunity for it—the move was interpreted as one toward the decriminalization and possible legalization of drugs, particularly because it comes on the heels of an increasing Latin American disposition toward alternatives to the war on drugs. Even so, Mexico's 2009 decriminalization of the small-time possession of drugs—five grams for marijuana, half a gram for cocaine, 50 milligrams for heroin, 40 milligrams for methamphetamine, and .015 milligrams for LSD—leaves much of the drug business untouched, including production, trafficking, and larger-scale dealing. There is no study yet on whether this has had the intended effect of taking away discretion—and decreasing corruption—among the street-level law enforcement bureaucrats, as Lipsky (2010) would call them. We do not know if taking away the discretion from the street-level cop in Mexico has also taken away his or her ability to negotiate, penalize, and overlook (for a price) the possession of drugs. In addition, former president Calderón, along with other Latin American presidents, argued for real alternatives at the United Nations General Assembly in September 2012 (Winter 2012).

The general conclusion is that the war on drugs looks at best to be a questionable proposition and at worst a failed strategy as we pass its fortieth anniversary. The alternative voices, however, are still many, evenly divided, and swimming against a tide of the U.S. government's determination to continue and even escalate the war on drugs. Change is not proximate, but its wheels are turning. As an IDEAS conference, "The Global Drug Wars," at the London School of Economics puts it, the war on drugs—or the system of drug control—has proven quite durable, even in the face of failure for over one hundred years, but there is now hope for reform (IDEAS 2012).

Bureaucratic Games

The literature on bureaucratic politics is quite extensive. Multiple publications since the 1960s have documented the imperial tendencies of bureaucrats (Holden 1966; Allison and Zelikow 1999) and their willingness to defend governmental programs, even when these have ceased to be effective. This tendency to create vested interests in wars and stand by them even when all indicators show that the policy has failed has been applied to the war on drugs (Payan 2006). Law enforcement agencies have a particularly tough time changing course once they have set out on a path, even when all evidence demonstrates that the return on investment is practically zero. A recent report by the United Nations Office on Drugs and

Crime shows—again—that the production of cocaine has no relationship to the increasing expenditures on drug enforcement, and that, since 2011, coca cultivation in South America has actually increased. The White House Office on National Drug Control Policy, not surprisingly, rather than accept this as something to be explained, released a memo contradicting the United Nations and arguing that there was a "significant" drop in cocaine production (ONDCP 2012). Yet the United States prides itself on government with scientifically based evaluation studies, focused on outcomes. What the numbers really are is hard to tell, as bureaucracies may use various formulas to justify the desired rather than the real results. This is all done without regard for scientific evidence. The DEA has insisted, for example, that all drugs are equally harmful, and it has taken a highly moralistic stand against all of them, even when government-sponsored studies have destroyed its position regarding marijuana as "medically useless" (Grant, Atkinson, Gouax, and Wilsey 2012). The DEA has insisted on expanding the drug schedule and treating drugs as all the same, adding penalties that have put well over one million people in prison for nonviolent drug offenses, further burdening the public budget and dismissing important evidence that harm-reduction strategies might work better, including drug addiction treatment, supervised injection facilities, syringe access, drug replacement therapy, and aggressive education (Nodine 2006).

Holding bureaucrats accountable both for effective results and for the way in which they deal with the public is a much-needed turn in drug policy today. Subjecting drug policy bureaucrats to scrutiny would constitute another good policy shift in the direction of a different drug policy regime. The process of holding them accountable, however, must be democratic, and the mechanisms must be carefully chosen (Gormley and Balla 2007). Citizen panels, for example, should not be out of the question. Drug policy in the United States is beginning to show that it has reached a state where accountability is sorely needed. Besides the uncertainty with which bureaucrats handle the information they provide the public, there are two egregious examples of this that have emerged recently.

The first is Operation Fast and Furious. As the United States has become more effective on "Americanizing" the war on drugs and internationalizing its approach, the bureaucracies claim that a certain jurisdiction over drug policy has also become more international and has expanded their presence throughout Latin America and, to some extent, in Europe and other continents. Latin America, however, has been the playground for drug policy bureaucrats since the 1980s. For several years, as early as 2006, and certainly since 2009, the Bureau of Alcohol, Tobacco, Firearms, and Explosives (ATF) (http://www.atf.gov) allowed thousands of weapons, including highly sophisticated assault weapons, to enter Mexico in order to track them over time dismantle the weapons smuggling rings. The result was not what the ATF intended, many of the weapons ended up in the hands of the cartels, and at least three were confirmed to have been used to kill two U.S. agents, a Border Patrol agent gunned down in Arizona with an AK-47 who was allowed to "walk" by the ATF during the operation, and the assassination of Jaime Zapata, a DEA agent, in San Luis Potosí in Mexico. Many more were used in numerous crimes throughout western and northern Mexico. The discovery of this botched operation brought renewed tension to U.S.–Mexican relations, and only the willingness of the Mexican government to continue to collaborate with the U.S. government prevented binational cooperation from becoming unraveled.

Bureaucracies gone rogue are not a new phenomenon, however. Recent allegations have surfaced that U.S. government bureaucrats, particularly DEA agents, allowed major drug traffickers to both smuggle enormous amounts of drugs from South America to Mexico to the United States and even to Europe and then permitted the laundering of millions of dollars in order to "track" the operations and routes of drug dealers and traffickers. Unfortunately, U.S. agents also lost track of that money, effectively providing Mexican cartels with millions in cash to run their operations and allowing drugs to flow into the American and European market (ABC News 2012).

These incidents are a sign that the war on drugs has become a bureaucratic phenomenon and is increasingly escaping the control of both the American government and most certainly the American public. This is further reinforced both by the constant opposition of drug war bureaucrats to experimenting with alternative policies (Drug Enforcement Administration 2012) and the increasing militarization with which bureaucrats are "fighting" this "war." In effect, since 1989, the U.S. government has pushed drug policy in the direction of increased militarization, first by involving the Department of Defense (DoD) in the drug war and then, when the DoD resisted extensive participation, by enabling drug war bureaucrats to militarize their law enforcement capabilities, providing them with resources, training, and hardware almost exclusively reserved for the armed forces (Payan 2006).

Finally, it has become clear that as antidrug American bureaucracies have grown to take on the war on drugs, the transnational organizations dedicated to drug trafficking have become even better, staying a step ahead of the game. They are quick to adapt, using multiple methods for smuggling drugs, including sophisticated tunnels, low-flying aircraft, and makeshift submarines, and moving production to the United States. They change routes easily in response to law enforcement operations, moving from the Caribbean to Mexico in the late 1980s and from Mexico to Central America more recently, and now there is evidence that they are moving from Mexico back to the Caribbean (Rossi 2012). They shift from land to sea to underground tunnels with a great degree of ease. They have also corrupted growing numbers of law enforcement agents, principally in Mexico, but also in the United States. Their organizations have shown a high degree of flexibility and adaptability and an ever-growing willingness to use extreme force against both government agents and rivals. "El Chapo" Guzmán, the leader of the Sinaloa Cartel, now enjoys a quasi-celebrity status, and the *Economist* set him up as an example to legitimate businesses in the craft of management (*Economist* 2012). His empire now extends to Europe as well (EFE 2012). In fact, a recent report by the Woodrow Wilson Center in 2012, analyzing the major trends in drug trafficking and organized crime in the Americas, shows that, if anything, drug trafficking organizations are better than ever at what they do, and all indicators point to a generalized failure in containing their expansion, globalization, and capacity to counter national and international strategies to stop them (Bagley 2012). This surely adds to the urgency of holding bureaucrats accountable for the $1 trillion they have spent over forty-plus years in stemming the flow of drugs, with almost nothing to show for it.

Exporting the Drug War and Latin American Growing Resistance

The birth of the nation-state and the professionalization of armies brought about a new way of fighting wars. Nations, predicted a statesman, will fight wars, and people in the cities will not know that a war is going on. No nation has been more able and willing to export its battles to foreign soil than the United States. The war on drugs is no exception. Once drug policy was declared a "war" by President Richard Nixon, the imperative was to minimize the inconvenience to the American public and export its costs as much as possible. This became a reality in the 1980s, when Colombia became the first foreign territory to adopt and enact a quintessentially American policy and transform it into a war. The Colombian government was willing to pay in blood and treasure for what was essentially an American domestic policy choice, prohibitionism. By the 1990s, the war on drugs extended to other countries, including Peru, Ecuador, and Bolivia, and in the last few years, it has been raging on in Mexico. The increasing involvement of the United States in determining drug policy in countries such as Mexico has become evident, as cables have been leaked revealing the extent of this involvement (Petrich Moreno 2012). This involvement has not been without tensions, and it is quite possible that Ambassador Carlos Pascual's departure from Mexico may have involved fundamental disagreements on the American aggressiveness regarding the objectives and methods of the drug war on Mexican soil (Petrich Moreno 2012).

The U.S. government found in President Felipe Calderón (2006–2012) its strongest ally yet in the war on drugs. Calderón implemented fully militarized strategies against drug cartels and involved the Mexican military in the war on drugs in ways that previous Mexican presidents had been reluctant to do. Much like Colombia in the 1990s, Mexico adopted the American war on drugs full throttle, but Calderón would pay a heavy price, as the Mexican public began to have serious doubts about whether the war on drugs could be won at all. This price reached too high of a level, and by 2011 the Mexican government stopped reporting the number of deaths, fueling the controversy over the real number of casualties caused by the war on drugs (Prado and Herrera 2012). To highlight the binational nature of the conflict, Mexican poet Javier Sicilia traveled throughout Mexico and then the United States, drawing attention to the costs of the war on drugs. Although the caravan was not given wide coverage in the United States, some blogs did cover it extensively (http://www.theragblog .blogspot.ca), and it did stir important criticisms of the war on drugs in Mexico. In the United States, influential opinion sources such as the *Huffington Post* began to insist on the failure of the war on drugs (*Huffington Post* 2012). Over time, media reports on gruesome public executions throughout Mexico began to sow doubts both on the war on drugs and on the prohibitionist regime. This was the case not only in Mexico but also in the United States, where the initiatives to pass medical marijuana laws and then to outright legalize it in Colorado and Washington State accelerated.

Important signs of resistance are also coming from Latin America. Uruguay's president called for the "regulated and controlled legalization of marijuana" (Cave 2012). By the end of his administration, even President Calderón, a staunch advocate of the war on drugs, had expressed doubts, declaring in his last appearance before the United Nations that it was time to transform the international thinking on drug policy. Presidents Pérez Molina of Guatemala and Santos of Colombia said much the same thing (Al Jazeera 2012). Finally, in Mexico, there was puzzlement in regard to the war on drugs because the November 2012 vote in the United States brought important initiatives on legalizing marijuana (approved in Washington and Colorado) and pushed the medical marijuana initiatives approved to nearly twenty states. Given Mexican support for the war on drugs under the Calderón administration, the Peña administration wondered if it was worth continuing to support the war on drugs, even if Mexico continued its administration of justice reform efforts (Booth 2012). This is significant, given that these are the countries that have paid the heaviest price regarding the drug war. But the United States, with its bloated drug war bureaucratic apparatus, is likely to continue to push. The combination of resistance from Latin America and internal resistance from local constituencies within the United States increasingly pushing for reform in drug public policy may yet amount to policy change in the future. But what does that alternative drug control system look like? What should it be? Before we answer this question, it is worth drawing attention to the heavy price paid for the drug war by the U.S.–Mexican border and all borderlanders.

The Militarization of the Drug War and the U.S.–Mexican Border

It is worth pointing out that nowhere has the war on drugs been felt more strongly than on the U.S.–Mexican border. Some of the highest death tallies are plot scattered in border towns and cities. Ciudad Juárez alone saw over eleven thousand people killed during the Calderón administration. The state of Tamaulipas continues to be quite a violent state, and the Los Zetas group, though under fire by the government, does not seem to be weakening. The border states in Mexico, once the darlings of progressiveness, openness, and market liberalization, have been done in by the war on drugs and have lost their importance within the Mexican economy and political landscape. Even cities such as Monterrey are now under siege and likely to suffer long-term consequences due to the violence.

In addition, the U.S.–Mexican border is closing, making it harder for borderlanders to make use of cross-border resources to procure better lives for themselves and their families. Any sense of cross-border intimacy is being lost, and bureaucracies are now in nearly full discretionary control along the border. There is no measure of success against the war on drugs from a border perspective, as long as the American drug consumer markets remain insatiable and the incentives for entry into the supply chain so high.

Alternatives to the Drug War

There are perhaps no clear-cut, black-and-white alternatives to the war on drugs. After all, psychotropic substances do cause a lot of damage to an individual's health and wealth, although not all to the same degree. Thus we must ask: Which drugs are we discussing? Marijuana? Heroin? Cocaine? Methamphetamine? Or all of these and more? Moreover, people who are seeking pain relief and prone to addiction may abuse legal prescription drugs, such as oxycodone, or leave these drugs in medicine cabinets for thrill-seeking teen relatives to share at pill-popping parties. The National Institute on Drug Abuse now reports that, after cannabis, prescription drugs are the most abused drugs in the United States (National Institute on Drug Abuse 2011). And we would be remiss if we excluded the very serious benefits that medicinal marijuana would provide to those suffering from a whole host of treatments for ailments such as cancer. Finally, serious damage to health and wealth occurs with the punitive approach to jailing people, even for nonviolent drug offenses. According to the website Drug Sense (http://www.drugsense.org), well over one million people are arrested each year for drug offenses, many for possession of small amounts of marijuana. This approach burdens people of color especially, jailing them and undermining their futures, including disenfranchising many for the rest of their lives. On wealth considerations, we also cannot forget taxpayers, who fund expensive criminalization strategies that do little to alleviate addiction or the circumstances that cultivate addiction but more often than not aggravate those circumstances. Drug Sense also reports that each year the government, at the federal, state, and local levels, spends between $50 and $60 billion in enforcing the war on drugs. To spend billions at the state and local levels during high-deficit times seems to be the ultimate folly (Miron and Waldock 2010).

In the sections that follow, we offer a number of reasonable approaches to the current drug war, with the understanding that the solution is not easy at all (*Drug Reporter* 2012).

From Criminalization to Prevention through Education and Treatment

There is an emerging consensus that some important policy shifts within the current approach could be employed to bring to an end the bloody onslaught that Colombia and Mexico have experienced in the last two decades and that Central America appears poised to suffer and the more silent, but no less punishing, results of the U.S. domestic war on drugs. Such potential policy shifts change budget priorities from law enforcement to research, treatment, and prevention through education. Collectively, research, treatment, and prevention and a solid curriculum in the education system are known as harm-reduction strategies. Those who point to this budgetary policy shift in the direction of prevention in the form of treatment and education often cite the successful and sustained antitobacco campaign that the U.S. government and society have waged over the last half-century, effectively reducing smoking to its lowest level since the 1930s to 20.6 percent in 2010 (Centers for Disease Control and Prevention 2012). Medical research has shown that tobacco is more harmful to people's health than marijuana; the same is true for alcohol (Kim 2012). Yet neither tobacco nor the alcohol distribution system operates under prohibitionist regimes (except for some "dry counties" in the United States, where borders with "wet counties" offer lively spaces for commercial sales). Rather, regulation and taxation regimes govern these unhealthy products. This, however, is not an endorsement of marijuana but a case for tackling it with a strategy more akin to our approach against tobacco and alcohol use. With a strategy focused on prevention and education, analysts would have to consider the factors that contribute to developing drug addiction or drug consumption habits, something that requires further research. Many authors argue that drug addiction, for example, is related to poverty and unemployment, poor mental health, sexual or physical abuse or neglect, and the lack of education and medical treatment, including treatment for mental illness (as people "self-medicate" with drugs or alcohol). These factors have been explored comparatively, yielding partial but solid evidence that there are certain sociocultural correlatives to drug abuse (Greberman and Wada 1994; Kaestner 1998). A budgetary shift would have to focus on researching, understanding, and altering those factors. Public policy would then have to be designed to address these issues among the most vulnerable populations.

If we know the social, economic, and health correlatives of drug use, it is possible to design a drug policy that effectively addresses drug use correlates to ease the forces that simmer under drug addiction. The implication of going to the sociocultural, health, and even economic roots of drug addiction habits would be both to create a system of on-demand treatment programs for drug abuse and to tailor such programs to specific communities, sometimes to include job training, psychological and psychiatric treatment, counseling, teaching social and parenting skills, expanding access to health care, offering disease-screening programs, and providing longer-term treatment for those already abusing drugs. Harm reduction programs would also fall into this category, particularly because the evidence, though somewhat mixed, shows that they appear to be somewhat effective (Jarlais 2000; see also the National Harm Reduction Conference that occurs annually at http://www.harmreduction.org). Harm reduction programs, however, are quite controversial in the United States, a value-laden conflict that cannot be resolved with data but with political constituencies that press for a firm political will that will eventually manufacture a general consensus.

Decriminalization

Two other important features of an alternative drug policy regime constituting relatively minor but important changes in drug policy are a modification in mandatory sentencing laws and the acknowledgment of what is already a widespread practice among local law enforcement agents—the removal of penalties for the possession of small amounts of drugs. The first led to overpopulation in the prison system, something that, according to the Pew Center on the States (Pew Center on the States 2009) cost American taxpayers an estimated $68 billion, an increasing cost that American taxpayers never fully acknowledged but that may best be used to fund a different approach to drug use, particularly given that these prison costs may have far exceeded the costs of a potential budgetary shift toward education and treatment. The effects of this shift are already evident two years after small but substantial reforms to mandatory sentencing laws were made in regard to crack cocaine—a reform that continues sentencing disparities between drugs perceived to be used by whites and people of color.

The second feature is an unacknowledged reality; many police officers across the country will not arrest individuals found in possession of small amounts of drugs, particularly if no other crime is involved (Stop the Drug Wars 2011). However, more research is needed and should be funded in order to measure the effects of these changes on the overall drug policy. Part of modifying the overall approach to drug policy is revising forfeiture laws. It is probably fair to seize property used in committing a crime, but forfeiture should be effective upon conviction, and it should not affect the families of those convicted or their future eligibility for government benefits. The same can be said of voting. The refusal to reinstate the right to vote after conviction is effectively disenfranchising a huge number of individuals in the country and making democracy less effective and representative.

Defederalization

One of the most controversial yet thought-provoking alternative proposals that have emerged in the last few years is a bipartisan proposal put forth by Ron Paul (R-TX) and Barney Frank (D-MA), both now retired, which recommends the defederalization of marijuana laws (*Huffington Post* 2011; also see the Villalobos chapter in this volume). This proposal is theoretically supported by several studies that look at the evolution of public policy in the United States. From education to health care to gun control to welfare to, more recently, illegal drugs and immigration, U.S. state and local governments have shown both a high degree of willingness and an ability to create public policy experiments from which a general federal policy can emerge. Defederalizing marijuana laws, and allowing the states to become the social laboratories of different policies in order to see if local governments can best deal with drug policy or fashion out the best policies, is potentially a fruitful idea.

Defederalization has begun to occur with the seventeen states and the District of Columbia that have legalized "medical marijuana." Yet the federal government provides mixed messages on whether it respects state authority to pass and implement such laws. The Obama administration has cracked down on many marijuana dispensaries, particularly in California, where the cannabis industry is flourishing and experimenting with new modes of production, distribution, and regulation. Even so, many other states are beginning to push the frontiers of drug laws by moving to legalize marijuana beyond its medicinal uses, as we saw in the November 2012 ballots in Washington, Oregon, and Colorado. The marijuana law, which many experts believe is the ideal law to experiment with in terms of public policy changes, is beginning to look like a patchwork of ideas and regulations. Some states strictly enforce licensed medical providers, while other states seem to offer license for people to claim medical issues for leisurely drug use instead. Even so, the states are the ideal laboratories for public policy—true laboratories of democracy, as Chief Justice Brandeis called them (Greve 2001). It is the equivalent of having fifty social labs to test different laws and regulations and then gather the final best practices to refederalize marijuana laws under a reasonable national policy.

California voters wondered, in 2010, whether to pass Proposition 19, which was meant to regulate, control, and tax cannabis. Around that issue at that time the Rand Corporation, a think tank based in Los Angeles, produced several studies. One study looked at the amount of revenue that Proposition 19 advocates predicted its passage would generate to local governments, approximately $1.4 billion (Kilmer, Caulkins, Bond, and Reuter 2010). Another looked at the effects of Proposition 19's passage on drugs trafficked from countries to the south, including Mexico (Kilmer, Caulkins, Bond, and Reuter 2010). At the University of San Diego Trans-Border Institute Conference on Proposition 19 and its effect on violence in Mexico, a Rand economist spoke about the studies, citing several intriguing consequences. First, California could be a net exporter of marijuana to other U.S. states, thereby requiring—if federal law did not change—"border enforcement" strategies around California borders and in airports. Second, this economist predicted a 2 to 20 percent drop in murderous violence in Mexico, given the partial dependency of organized crime on marijuana (besides other drugs and crime), which is a vertically controlled business of production, processing, and shipment. As one professor in the audience commented publicly, such a reduction would probably be a more effective strategy than any yet pursued in the United States or Mexico to reduce murder rates (Staudt personal observation 2010). Among unknown factors would be consumer demand for high-quality cannabis versus what some call imported "slag" that may or may not be mixed with other elements.

The International Drug War

The United States remains a nation with an enormous gravitational pull on other nations, particularly in Latin America. American drug policy is one more example of this. Prohibition is quintessentially an American policy, whose ideology and many of its costs have been transferred to Latin America, including Mexico. The war on drugs, like other American wars, has a beginning in the legislative hallways of the United States, but its most brutal consequences are in foreign lands. The war on drugs in Colombia or Mexico cannot be understood without an understanding of the way we do policy in the United States and the way the U.S. government can transfer many of the costs to foreign soil. In that sense, Mexico saw its murder rate rise from five out of one hundred thousand in the 1990s to eighteen out of one hundred thousand in 2012 (but far higher in several states) because of the war on drugs. In addition, the Mexican government has paid billions of dollars supporting a war, when those resources could have gone into strengthening public investment in Mexico's development. The argument has to be made, of course, that Mexico needs to bring about the rule of law within its own country, but it has begun to do so even under enormous pressure by the United States to use strategies and tactics—such as deploying the military into the streets of Mexican cities—that would not be acceptable to the American public within the United States. The Mérida Initiative, touted as crucial aid from the United States to Mexico, has in the end been a tepid display of resources, many of which end up in the pockets of American consulting firms that obtain the juicy contracts for the provision of goods and services to maintain the American drug war. Few of those dollars have resulted in actual development aid to Mexico in order to wrest away youth from the claws of cartels and gangs.

The role of American weapons in feeding the killing frenzy in Latin America has also not gone unnoticed. After the Assault Weapons Ban was allowed to expire in 2006, powerful guns began to show up in Mexican streets, adding to the firepower and the ferocity of the cartels and street gangs. The presence of American weapons on the side of the cartels, along with a deeper analysis of the pull of the American black market for drugs, gave rise to protests not only from Mexico but from other Latin American countries. This has in turn created a major push to seek global alternatives to the drug war, a call that has an increasing number of important figures, from former to current presidents and a new and growing movement within the United States itself.

But the drug war has its advocates within the political class and the bureaucrats who have, for decades, built jobs and careers based on drug prohibition. The law enforcement industrial complex built around the war on drugs is phenomenal and supported by billions of dollars and the solid belief that America should stay the course. And the bureaucrats know how to play this game better than anyone else.

Concluding Thoughts

The authors of this volume know and understand that crafting an exit strategy to the drug war is not easy. Not calling it a drug war is a first step; allowing local communities to experiment with different drug control systems is an important second step, already being implemented in the various marijuana laws and ordinances passed in the United States; and considering holistic solutions that include a major push on harm reduction strategies is a key third step. This does not exonerate the authorities from ensuring that drugs that create much harm are carefully regulated, nor does it let Mexico off the hook in fighting corruption and reforming its justice system. But the current war on drugs, as it stands, must be declared a failure because only this acknowledgment will enable us to see beyond, dealing with drugs as a public health problem and not a criminal issue, something we are convinced will wrest away the power of cartels to corrupt our law enforcement agencies and our courts, to profit from public health issues, and to acquire ever-growing firepower to make the lives of border-landers and vulnerable citizens a true living hell. The chaos experienced by Mexico in the Calderón administration is sufficient proof that the war on drugs as it has stood for forty-plus years is not sustainable, and even if the solution is not easy, we must push forward and seek new concepts to reimagine drug public policy and more effective and just solutions.

Bibliography

ABC News. 2012. "U.S. Agents Helped Launder Millions in Drug Proceeds." January 9. http://abcnews.go.com/International/wireStory/13-bodies-found-gas-station-western-mexico-15321347. Accessed January 12, 2012.

Al Jazeera. 2012. "Time for a Tactical Shift in the Drug War." September 28. http://www.aljazeera.com/programmes/insidestoryamericas/2012/09/201292893813797388.html. Accessed November 20, 2012.

Allison, Graham T., and Philip Zelikow. 1999. *Essence of Decision: Explaining the Cuban Missile Crisis.* New York: Pearson.

Bagley, Bruce. 2012. *Drug Trafficking and Organized Crime in the Americas: Major Trends in the Twenty-First Century.* Washington, DC: Woodrow Wilson Center.

Bollinger, Lorenz. 1994. *De-Americanizing Drug Policy: The Search for Alternatives for Failed Repression.* Pieterlen, Switzerland: P. Lang.

Booth, William. 2012. "Mexico Says Marijuana Legalization in U.S. Could Change Anti-Drug Strategies." *Washington Post,* November 8. http://www.washingtonpost.com/world/the_americas/mexico-says-marijuana-legalization-in-us-could-change-anti-drug-strategies/2012/11/08/7e6d45ba-29ca-11e2-aaa5-ac786110c486_story.html. Accessed November 25, 2012.

Caulkins, Jonathan P., Angela Hawken, Beau Kilmer, and Mark A. R. Kleiman. 2012. *Marijuana Legalization: What Everyone Needs to Know.* New York: Oxford University Press.

Cave, Damien. 2012. "South America Sees Drug Path to Legalization." *New York Times,* July 29. http://www.nytimes.com/2012/07/30/world/americas/uruguay-considers-legalizing-marijuana-to-stop-traffickers.html?pagewanted=all. Accessed November 20, 2012.

Centers for Disease Control and Prevention (CDC). 2012. "Smoking and Tobacco Use." http://www.cdc.gov/tobacco/index.htm. Accessed November 1, 2012.

Cohen, Peter J. 2004. *Drugs, Addiction, and the Law: Policy, Politics, and Public Health.* Durham, NC: Carolina Academic Press.

Daily Beast. 2012. "Obama Deescalating the War on Drugs," July 5. http://readersup portednews.org/opinion2/277-75/12262-focus-obama-deescalating-the-war-on -drugs. Accessed November 21, 2012.

Drug Enforcement Administration. 2012. "A Message from the Drug Enforcement Administration." http://www.justice.gov/dea/demand/speakout/director.htm. Accessed January 9, 2012.

Drug Reporter. 2012. "The Golden Mean of Drug Policy?" September 25. *Drug Reporter* electronic document and speech. http://drogriporter.hu/en/goldenmean. Accessed November 25, 2012.

Economist. 2012. "From HR to CSR: Management Lessons from Mexico's Drug Lords," July 28.

EFE. 2012. "Detectan del Cártel de Sinaloa en Europa." October 3. http://latinocali fornia.com/home/2012/10/detectan-actividades-del-cartel-de-sinaloa-en-europa/. Accessed November 25, 2012.

Gormley, William T., and Steven J. Balla. 2007. *Bureaucracy and Democracy: Accountability and Performance.* Washington, DC: CQ Press.

Grant, Igor, J. Hampton Atkinson, Ben Gouax, and Barth Wilsey. 2012. "Medical Marijuana: Clearing Away the Smoke." *Open Neurology Journal* 6: 18–25.

Gray, James P. 2001. *Why Our Drug Laws Have Failed and What We Can Do About It: A Judicial Indictment of the War on Drugs.* Philadelphia, PA: Temple University Press.

Greberman, Sharyn Bowman, and Kiyoshi Wada. 1994. "Social and Legal Factors Related to Drug Abuse in the United States and Japan." *Public Health Reports* 109, no. 6: 731–37.

Greve, Michael S. 2001. "Laboratories of Democracy: Anatomy of a Metaphor." *AEI Online.* March 31. http://www.aei.org/article/politics-and-public-opinion/elec tions/laboratories-of-democracy/. Accessed November 5, 2012.

Holden, Matthew Jr. 1966. "'Imperialism' in Bureaucracy." *American Political Science Review* 60, no. 4: 943–51.

Huffington Post. 2010. "Well Done Congress, Make Fair Sentencing Retroactive." August 4. http://www.huffingtonpost.com/julie-stewart/well-done-congress-now-ma _b_671008.html. Accessed December 4, 2011.

——. 2011. "Marijuana Bill in Congress: Barney Frank, Ron Paul Legislation Would End Federal Ban on Pot." June 22. http://www.huffingtonpost.com/2011/06/22 /marijuana-bill-barney-frank-ron-paul_n_882707.html. Accessed December 5, 2011.

——. 2012. "Politicians Ignore Failed 'War on Drugs' at Their (and Our) Peril," August 28. http://www.huffingtonpost.com/leonard-frieling/politicians-ignore-failed -war-on-drugs_b_1832723.html. Accessed November 21, 2012.

IDEAS. 2012. "Governing the Global Drug Wars." October. London: London School of Economics. http://www2.lse.ac.uk/IDEAS/publications/reports/SR014.aspx. Accessed November 25, 2012.

Jarlais, Des. 2000. "Research, Politics and Needle Exchange." *American Journal of Public Health* 90, no. 9: 1385–87.

Kaestner, Robert. 1998. "Does Drug Use Cause Poverty?" National Bureau of Economic Research—NBER Working Paper No. 6406. February. http://www.nber.org /papers/w6406. Accessed November 1, 2012.

Kilmer, Beau, Jonathan P. Caulkins, Brittany M. Bond, and Peter H. Reuter. 2010. *Reducing Drug Trafficking and Revenues in Mexico: Would Legalizing Marijuana in California Help?* Santa Monica, CA: Rand Corporation.

Kilmer, Beau, Jonathan P. Caulkins, Rosalie Liccardo Pacula, Robert J. McCoun, and Peter H. Reuter. 2010. *Altered States? Assessing How Marijuana Legalization in California Could Influence Marijuana Consumption and Public Budgets.* Santa Monica, CA: Rand Corporation.

Kim, Leland. 2012. "Marijuana Shown to Be Less Damaging to Lungs than Tobacco." January 10. http://www.ucsf.edu/news/2012/01/11282/marijuana-shown-be-less-damaging-lungs-tobacco. Accessed November 1, 2012.

Lipsky, Michael. 2010. *Street-Level Bureaucracy: Dilemmas of the Individual in Public Service.* New York: Russell Sage Foundation.

Miron, Jeffrey A., and Katherine Waldock. 2010. *The Budgetary Impact of Ending Drug Prohibition.* Washington, DC: Cato Institute.

National Harm Reduction Conference. http://www.hardreduction.org (Staudt attended and presented in 2010). Accessed April 5, 2013.

National Institute on Drug Abuse. 2011. "Topics in Brief: Prescription Drugs." http://www.drugabuse.gov/publications/topics-in-brief/prescription-drug-abuse. Accessed November 1, 2012.

Nodine, Elizabeth. 2006. "Harm Reduction: Policies in Public Health." April 25. http://www.cwru.edu/med/epidbio/mphp439/Harm_Reduction_Policies.htm. Accessed November 21, 2012.

Office of National Drug Control Policy. 2011. *Update: New Data Shows Cocaine Market Remains Under Stress.* June 16 Press Release. http://www.whitehouse.gov/ondcp/news-releases-remarks/update-new-data-show-cocaine-market-remains-under-stress. Accessed November 21, 2012.

———. 2012. "Survey Shows Significant Drop in Cocaine Production in Colombia." July 30. Washington, DC: White House ONDCP. http://www.whitehouse.gov/ondcp/news-releases-remarks/survey-shows-significant-drop-in-cocaine-production-in-colombia. Accessed November 21, 2012.

O'Rourke, Beto, and Susie Byrd. 2011. *Death and Drugs: The Big Business of Dope in the U.S. and Mexico.* El Paso, Texas: Cinco Puntos Press.

Payan, Tony. 2006. *Cops, Soldiers and Diplomats: Explaining Agency Behavior in the War on Drugs.* Lanham, MD: Lexington Books.

Petrich Moreno, Blanche. 2012. "WikiLeaks and the War on Drugs." *Nation,* July 25. http://www.thenation.com/article/169076/wikileaks-and-war-drugs. Accessed November 20, 2012.

Pew Center on the States. 2009. "1 in 31 U.S. Adults Are Behind Bars, on Parole or Probation." March 2. http://www.pewcenteronthestates.org/news_room_detail.aspx?id=49398. Accessed November 29, 2011.

Prado, H., and Rolando Herrera. 2012. "Esconde Federación la Cifra de Ejecutados." *Reforma,* August 15. http://diario.mx/Nacional/2012-08-15_6174d544/. Accessed November 20, 2012.

Reuter, Peter. 1992. "Hawks Ascendant: The Punitive Trend of American Drug Policy." *Daedalus* 121, no. 3: 15–52.

Rossi, Victoria. 2012. "US Observes Uptick in Drug Trafficking Through Caribbean." *InSight Crime,* September 10. http://www.insightcrime.org/news-briefs/united-states-drug-trafficking-caribbean. Accessed November 20, 2012.

Stop the Drug Wars. 2011. http://stopthedrugwar.org/chronicle-old/395/westernpa
.shtml. Accessed December 15, 2011.

United Nations Office on Drugs and Crime. 2012. "Colombia Coca Cultivation Survey 2011." June. Vienna, Austria: UNODC.

Wall Street Journal. 2009. "Q&A with the Drug Czar." May 14. http://online.wsj.com/
article/SB124233331735120871.html. Accessed October 31, 2012.

Washington-Valdez, Diana. 2012. "Colorado, Washington and Oregon Votes on Legalizing Marijuana May Affect Mexico Drug Trade." *El Paso Times*, November 1.
http://www.elpasotimes.com/news/ci_21900716/colorado-washington-and-oregon
-vote-legalizing-marijuana?source=most_viewed. Accessed November 1, 2012.

Winter, Brian. 2012. "U.S.-Led 'War on Drugs' Questioned at U.N." *Reuters*, September 26. http://www.reuters.com/article/2012/09/26/us-un-assembly-mexico-drugs
-idUSBRE88P1Q520120926. Accessed November 1, 2012.

Contributors

Israel Alvarado Martínez is the Director of the Federal Judicial District and a professor and researcher for the National Institute of Criminal Sciences in Mexico City. He is also a researcher for the National Research System of the National Council of Science and Technology. He has lectured at several conferences and taught courses at the Universidad Nacional Autónoma de Mexico and the Universidad Panamericana. He is an author, coauthor, and coordinator of more than ten books and has published more than thirty articles in numerous journals. His area of expertise focuses on criminal science, criminal law, and justice. He previously served as advocate general of the advisory coordinator for the President of the Commission of Government of the Federal District Legislative Assembly, and last, as an environmental consultant in criminal matters for the Commission for Environmental Cooperation of North America.

Raúl Benítez Manaut is a professor and researcher in the political and social sciences department of the National Autonomous University of Mexico City. He is currently president of the Association for Analysis of Security with Democracy. He specializes in security issues in North America. He has lectured in numerous universities around the world on matters of Mexican security. He is the author of various articles and books, including *Military Theory and the War in El Salvador*, *Mexico and the New Challenges to Hemispheric Security* and *Crisis and Militarization in Central America*.

Jonathan P. Caulkins is a professor of operations research and public policy at Carnegie Mellon University's Qatar Campus and Heinz College of Public Policy and Information Systems Management. He specializes in systems analysis of problems pertaining to drugs, crime, terror, violence, and prevention. Other interests include reputation and brand management, software quality, optimal control, black markets, airline operations, and personnel performance evaluation. He has taught quantitative decision making on four continents to students from fifty countries. He has over one hundred refereed articles in journals and has authored or coauthored nine books, including *Drugs and Drug Policy: What Everyone Needs to Know*, *Drug Policy and the Public Good*, and *Optimal Control of Nonlinear Processes: With Applications in Drugs, Corruption, and Terror*. His latest book is on marijuana legalization, voted on in three U.S. states in the fall of 2012. He is a past codirector of Rand's Drug

Policy Research Center (1994–1996) and founding director of Rand's Pittsburgh office (1999–2001) and continues to work through Rand on a variety of government projects.

Guadalupe Correa-Cabrera holds a PhD in political science from the New School for Social Research. She is associate professor and chair of the government department at the University of Texas at Brownsville. Her areas of expertise are comparative politics, Mexican politics, U.S.–Mexican relations, and border studies. Her teaching fields include public policies in the U.S.–Mexican border region, U.S.–Mexican relations, American Hispanic politics, and Latin American politics. She is currently developing a project on the explanations of violence and organized crime in the eastern U.S.–Mexican border region. Her most recent book is titled *Democracy in "Two Mexicos": Political Institutions in Oaxaca and Nuevo León*.

Carlos Antonio Flores Pérez was born in 1972 in Mexico City. He graduated from the National Autonomous University of Mexico, where he received in 2005 his PhD in political science. He is the author of *El Estado en crisis: Crimen organizado y política. Desafíos para la consolidación democrática* and *Historias de polvo y sangre. Génesis y evolución del tráfico de drogas en el Estado de Tamaulipas* (forthcoming) and the coauthor of six other books. He has given many lectures on Mexican organized crime and drug trafficking in different universities, government agencies, and private institutions in the United States, Norway, Netherlands, Mexico, Colombia, Brazil, and Peru. He has been a visiting professor at the University of Oslo, Norway, and the University of Connecticut. He is a research affiliate for the University of Connecticut's Human Rights Institute and is currently associate professor at the Center for Research and Higher Studies in Social Anthropology in Mexico City.

Germán Guillén López is a professor and researcher at the Universidad de Sonora and is a member of the National Research System of the National Council of Science and Technology. He currently serves as the external counsel of the Special Unit for Implementation of the Constitutional Reforms in Criminal Matters in the Superior Court of the Federal District and as a litigator and legal advisor. His areas of research are on law and criminal science with a concentration in criminology. He was also a researcher at the Belisario Domínguez Research Institute of the Senate of the Republic of Mexico and the Justice Studies Center of the Americas in Chile. He is an author and coauthor of published articles in several journals and has lectured around the world on issues related to public safety and criminal sciences. In addition to his research and writing, he has participated as a member in diverse academic organizations in Mexico and Colombia. He previously served as the manager of the crime prevention department at the National Public Safety System.

Z. Anthony Kruszewski is a professor of political science at the University of Texas at El Paso. Tony Kruszewski obtained his PhD in political science from the University of Chicago. He arrived in El Paso in 1972 and has since been dedicated to the advancement of border studies. He was one of the original founders of the Association for Borderlands Studies (ABS). Tony has published extensively on the U.S.–Mexican border and minorities as well as on the Cold War. He has also taught in Europe and has delivered lectures all over the world. In 2006, he was codirector and co-organizer of the *Lineae Terrarum: International Borders Conference*, along with Tony Payan. More recently, Tony published a coedited volume with Kathy Staudt and Tony Payan on human rights along the U.S.–Mexican border.

William C. Martin is the Harry and Hazel Chavanne Senior Fellow and director of the drug policy program at Rice University's Baker Institute. He received his PhD from Harvard in 1969 and taught in Rice's sociology department for thirty-eight years. He has written seven books, including *With God on Our Side: The Rise of the Religious Right in America*, the companion volume to the PBS miniseries of the same title. His writings have appeared in *Texas Monthly*, the *Atlantic, Harper's,* and *Esquire,* in addition to professional journals.

Marcos Pablo Moloeznik is a full professor and researcher at the University of Guadalajara in Mexico. He is a member of the National Researcher System, Level II. His expertise is in the area of security, with a particular emphasis on the Mexican armed forces and the militarization of public safety and security in Mexico and Latin America. His most recent publications address the war on drugs and the role that the Mexican navy has played in the Latin American context. He is also a member of the International Red Cross.

José Nava has an MA in interdisciplinary studies from the University of Texas at Brownsville (UTB). He is currently a student in the master's program for public administration and management at UTB and a graduate research assistant. He has participated in projects related to organized crime in the state of Tamaulipas and its northern border. Although born in Brownsville, Texas, he was raised in the city of Matamoros, Tamaulipas. After completing his bachelor's degree in criminal justice, he enlisted in the U.S. Marine Corps, where he served as a rifleman in an infantry unit, deploying in support of combat operations in both the Afghanistan and Iraq theaters of operations. His interest in drug-related violence in Mexico has been borne out of his experiences in the Middle East, as well as from his personal experience living on both sides of the border.

Beto O'Rourke is a lifelong El Pasoan, a graduate of Columbia University, and was, for six years, a member of the El Paso City Council. It was there that he first raised the prospect of changing U.S. drug control policy in response to the horrific violence in neighboring Ciudad Juárez. He is the coauthor, along with Susie Byrd, of *Dealing Death and Drugs,* which looks at the drug war from the perspective of the U.S.–Mexican border. In the fall of 2012, O'Rourke was elected to represent the Sixteenth Congressional District, representing West Texas and the border in the U.S. Congress, 2013–2015.

Tony Payan is the director of the Mexico Center and a Fellow at the Baker institute of Rice University. He is an associate professor of political science at the University of Texas at El Paso. He also collaborates with the doctoral graduate faculty at the Universidad Autónoma de Ciudad Juárez. Payan earned his BA in philosophy and classical languages (Greek and Latin) from the University of Dallas and his MBA from the University of Dallas Graduate School of Management. He received in 2001 his doctorate degree in international relations from Georgetown University. Payan's research focuses on the applicability of international relations theory to the U.S.–Mexican border and other border environments. His work theorizes various topics regarding international borders, including border governability, foreign policy attitudes on the border, and the manifestation of U.S. foreign policy at its borders. Payan's publications include the two books *Cops, Soldiers and Diplomats: Understanding Agency Behavior in the War on Drugs* and *The Three U.S.–Mexico Border Wars: Drugs, Immigration and Homeland Security*. He has coedited three other volumes: *Gobernabilidad e Ingobernabilidad en la Región Paso del Norte, Human Rights along the U.S.–Mexico Border: Gendered Violence and Insecurity*, and *De Soldaderas a Activistas: La mujer chihuahuense en los albores del Siglo XXI*. He also has authored book chapters and academic articles.

Daniel M. Sabet is director of the Center for Enterprise and Society at the University of Liberal Arts Bangladesh and affiliated researcher at Georgetown University's Edmund A. Walsh School of Foreign Service. He is author of the book *Police Reform in Mexico: Informal Politics and the Challenge of Institutional Change*, which examines the policy design, implementation, and institutionalization problems confronting Mexico's police reformers. This research agenda emerged out of Sabet's work coordinating rule of law educational programs for police throughout Latin America as part of the Culture of Lawfulness Project. Sabet's previous book, *Nonprofits and Their Networks: Cleaning the Waters along Mexico's Northern Border*, explores the emergence of an autonomous civil society in Mexico. Sabet earned his PhD in political science from Indiana University.

Eric L. Sevigny is an assistant professor at the University of South Carolina in the Department of Criminology and Criminal Justice. He holds a BA in psychology from Middlebury College and a PhD in public and international affairs from the University of Pittsburgh. His primary research interests are in the areas of drug policy, sentencing and incarceration, and measurement for monitoring and performance assessment. His recent work focuses on the impact of drug courts on prison and jail populations, the effects of state medical marijuana laws on crime and public health outcomes, trends in marijuana potency, and the development of composite indicators to measure trends and interstate variations in drug-related consequences.

Jeremy Slack is a doctoral candidate at the School of Geography and Development of the University of Arizona. His doctoral project is titled *Migration, Violence and Security on the U.S.–Mexico Border: Critical Policy Issues*. He is currently the principal investigator of a major grant by the Ford Foundation to look into migration issues, including their intersection with drug trafficking. His publications include *Migration and the Production of (In)Security on the U.S.–Mexico Border* with D. Martínez, *Viajes Violentos: La Transformación de la Migración Clandestina hacia Sonora y Arizona* with Scott Whiteford, *Migration and Violence on the Arizona-Sonora Border* with Scott Whiteford, and *Methods of Violence: Researcher Safety and Adaptability in Times of Conflict* with D. Martínez and P. Vandervoet.

Kathleen (Kathy) Staudt received her PhD from the University of Wisconsin in 1976. She is a professor of political science at the University of Texas at El Paso (UTEP) and teaches courses on public policy, democracy, borders, and women and politics. She founded and directed UTEP's Center for Civic Engagement for ten years. She has published seventeen books, the last seven of which focus on the U.S.–Mexican border, including *Violence and Activism at the Border: Gender, Fear, and Everyday Life in Ciudad Juárez* and the edited volumes *Human Rights along the U.S.–Mexico Border: Gendered Violence and Insecurity* and *Cities and Citizenship . . . The Paso del Norte Metropolitan Region*, with colleagues César Fuentes and Julia Monárrez at COLEF/ Cd. Juárez. She coauthored a forthcoming book with Zulma Méndez on the courage and resilience of border activists in high-risk environments. In 2009 she coordinated the campus–community Global Public Policy Forum on the War on Drugs (http:// warondrugsconference.utep.edu).

José D. Villalobos is an assistant professor at the University of Texas at El Paso (UTEP). He received his BA from the University of Texas at San Antonio and his PhD from Texas A&M University. His dissertation work was nationally recognized in 2009 by the American Political Science Association as the best dissertation on the U.S. presidency. Since joining UTEP, he has produced over two dozen publications, including articles in *Political Research Quarterly, Presidential Studies Quarterly, Administration & Society, Race, Gender & Class*, the *International Journal of Public Opinion Research*, the *International Journal of Public Administration*, the *International Journal of Conflict Management*, and *Review of Policy Research*. He currently serves as a board member of the Presidents & Executive Politics section of the American Political Science Association and served from 2008 to 2011 as president of the Midwest Latino/a Caucus of the Midwest Political Science Association.

Scott Whiteford is a professor at the Center for Latin American Studies of the University of Arizona. He has led a five-country project funded by the Hewlett Foundation on globalization, borders, and environmental security in Latin America. His research examines a range of policy issues, including the World Bank's recent water management reforms and decentralization. On a more theoretical level, his work examines issues of power, environmental justice and health, and how global processes play out at the local level. His recent coedited books include *Seguridad, Agua y Desarrollo: El Futuro de La Frontera México-Estados-Unidos; Globalization, Water and Health: Resource Management in Times of Scarcity; Managing a Sacred Gift: Changing Water Management Strategies in Mexico*; and eight other volumes published in Spanish and English.

Index